hañobook
of
Life

VOL. 1

JASON PLOTNER

TATE PUBLISHING
AND ENTERPRISES, LLC

Handbook Of Life: Vol. 1
Copyright © 2014 by Jason Plotner. All rights reserved.

Published by Tate Publishing & Enterprises, LLC
127 E. Trade Center Terrace | Mustang, Oklahoma 73064 USA
1.888.361.9473 | www.tatepublishing.com

Tate Publishing is committed to excellence in the publishing industry. The company reflects the philosophy established by the founders, based on Psalm 68:11,
"The Lord gave the word and great was the company of those who published it."

Book design copyright © 2014 by Tate Publishing, LLC. All rights reserved.
Cover design by Carlo Nino Suico
Interior design by Mary Jean Archival

Published in the United States of America
ISBN: 978-1-63185-350-0
Self-Help / General
14.06.30

To my grandfather Herbert Van Zile (1921–2010)

My grandfather had a very strong spiritual foundation, and he promoted the good within humanity. I thoroughly enjoyed all of our philosophical conversations that we had whenever we shared time together. I was fortunate to be able to spend time with him before he passed away. His memory forever lives in my home and with my family.

acknowledgments

I would like to express my sincere personal gratitude to my lifelong friend Brad Havertape, who made it possible for me to begin working with my publisher. Brad chose to assist me in my path to become a writer, and I will always remember his extension of support.

CONTENTS

Preface 11

Introduction 29

The Life Path 45

Communication 155

Cognition and Abstract Thought 171

Behavior 253

Genetics 317

The Central Nervous System 335

The Development Stages 391

PREFACE

Everyone in life at some point seeks the answers regarding their own personal existence and about the meaning of life. This natural human phenomenon involves a core inner drive which has existed from the beginning of time. The life path can take people in many different directions due to a variety of factors that can include genetics, intrinsic personal factors, family, friends, the starting life environment, other environments experienced, societal elements, spirituality, and higher powers. People must fully explore their core inner feelings in order to become aligned with their life's design.

The unexamined life is not worth living.

—Plato

For some people, these core explorative life thoughts may surface at a very young age and their efforts to search for the answers will start very early within their life path. While in other people, the impulse to find life's answers may manifest much later. Regardless of when the innate impulse manifest, there is also an intense core inner drive that burns deep within the unconscious of all people. This core inner drive which is an enigma will continue to push people forward in their life and regardless of all the lower level knowledge that is acquired this higher level core inner drive will not yield.

Ultimately people will not consciously find the answers surrounding this core inner drive, but rather the answers will meet with them at some point during their life. People however must actively continue to move toward their life answers as the apex of life cannot be reached with a *passive effort*. When the apex of truths and spirituality are reached within the life path, the supernatural insights will flood through a person like a tidal wave as they will have reached their social and spiritual nirvana. If a person does not navigate toward the higher answers in life, if they deny or delay, or if they procrastinate and wait too long, they can experience devastating social and spiritual repercussions. The repercussions can be detected when people finally realize and accept that they have passed on the wealth of social opportunities and spirituality that they have been offered during their life course and this experience can be a very suffocating feeling which is the sands of time running out on them. To avoid this social affliction and life causality, people must not ignore and/or avoid the impalpable and bodiless life cues that they come across within their life path. In Corinthians within the New Testament, it's explained that people looking at life temporally is barrier to faith: "While we look not at the things which are seen, but at the things which are not seen, for the things which are seen are temporal, but the things which are not seen are eternal" (2 Corinthians 4:18, KJV). People must make the leap and not delay as further explained in Corinthians: "For we walk by faith not by sight" (2 Corinthians 5:7, KJV). The powerful force of attraction exerted by the lusts of temporal things on earth must not be a barrier to the pure path of spirituality and life.

In life, the acquisition of crystallized knowledge and facts can generate personal power for people and this power can guide people toward a clearer social reality. But the people that go throughout life without seeking the elusive higher knowledge, truths, or the pursuit of a greater life meaning, will remain intellectually and spiritually deprived and the thirst of their core inner drive will never be fully quenched. This is why some people will never feel fully satisfied in life and it's due to their pursuit and their insatiable desire of only the temporal things in life. A nihilist will never fully experience all of life's fruits, this expedient lifestyle can also deprive people of their own personal growth, and it can also have an impact on the collective level of humanity. Individual people and the collective humanity cannot fully evolve without the ethereal element of spirituality. Along the life path, there are many social obstacles that can interfere with a spiritual direction. People must remain resilient and not let others impede their life course. In the New Testament, Ephesians explains how the shield of faith can protect people versus the negative element: "Above all, taking shield of faith wherewith ye shall be able to quench all fiery darts of the wicked" (Ephesians 6:16, KJV). With a strong foundation and the acquisition of spiritual knowledge, people can defend themselves versus the forces of iniquity.

It's common that people who deny truths and knowledge in life will also choose to cast their shallow, narrow, and uninformed glib opinions upon others and this social action sets forth a very negative form of energy within their life paths. These people are negative social codependents which keep humanity from evolving. When making a choice, one has to consider which outcome is more likely and must determine where the ambiguity lies. Presumptions and their corresponding contentions are vulnerable to criticism without justification.

Ignorance is the root and stem of all evil.

—Plato (BC)

Even the small microcosm amounts of negative energy from each individual, which may not seem significant when measured on an individual level, can be concentrated and channeled into a collective and socially toxic negative force which can devastate the positive forward evolution of humanity. In the environment, the keystone or indicator species reflects the health of the system, and as a parallel, the good within humanity is measured in order to measure the health of society. The dreadful societal contagion of opinion is fully capable of leading to the eradication within the use of logos in humanity and has the potential to allow the negative forces within humanity to capitalize on the vile infection that this contagion is capable of rendering.

Science is the father of knowledge, but opinion breeds ignorance.

—Homer (BC)

Some people look at the world as a purely temporal place and they devote their energy toward discovering as much as they can about the earth and everything around it, while others will also incorporate a spiritual belief system for their life guidance. Because life's truths are not transparent in nature, which is the design for humanity, people will choose different life paths. Even though there are those in life who have reached an apex and this can be clearly seen by others, this reality will often be ignored by many because ultimately each person must find their life path on their own, which is also part of life's design. Although the pursuit of life's truths and meanings is an individual path, there are mystical signs, symbols, signals, and also people along the life path that can, on occasion, be imponderable life guides. The key is for people to follow and stay close to their core and over time these cues will become more transparent. In the New Testament, John communicates that those who follow in faith can be conduits, but that those who do not walk the path of faith will not receive any messages: "He that is of God heareth God's words, ye therefore hear them not, ye are not of God" (John 8:47, KJV). Spiritual messages are not delivered on demand and they are rarely given unto those who do not follow the pure path of faith.

Sometimes, people will not be able to clearly see, find, or understand these life guides, signals, or messages, and this can create obscurity within their life path. Also when people are trying to decide on which influences and social guides to follow and use within their life paths, they need to turn to the use of their core instinct, logic, and reasoning when deciding versus only going with the *opinions* of others. Those in life who cast opinions without true knowledge behind their oration are not the correct life guides. Because the true ultimate goal of each individual is to reach their individual life apex, each life experience, which may seem small on the surface level, is in a collective sense a much larger matter on the whole within the life field. Those who only cast opinions are ultimately negatively impacting everyone within humanity on the collective level.

> *A fool finds no pleasure in understanding but delights in airing their own opinions.*

> —Plato

It's common that the people who do not evolve on an abstract, cognitive, and/or spiritual level will firmly *believe* that they are helping the greater good with their opinions, but if they really open up their eyes to the entire social picture and view things through different social perspectives, they could see the error in their ways. So many valuable opportunities in life are left behind by the social errors, which transpire as a result of the casting of *opinions*. Opinions can be devastating to both individuals and to humanity when they are rendered upon the malleable within society.

> *Anyone who doesn't take truth seriously in small matters cannot be trusted in larger ones either.*

> —Einstein

There are countless people in the world doing things so many different ways that the world is like a giant social switchboard and people have to carefully choose which social connections to make in order to reach their life beacons. People are plugged into the social switchboard within the process of socialization and they go through life making connections. Depending on which types of connections people make, their paths can be very diverse. Some people's investigative approach in life is a sluggish path, and to them, this course seems like a *safer* way to search for life's answers. While other people surge quickly forward looking for their answers and feel finding the answers *quickly* is the proper path. There are also those people that do not seek the answers to life and existence at all or they wait until they are much older to explore. Although finding the answers late in one's life can still yield some rewards, so many people opportunities and numerous life opportunities are left behind for the self and for others, when people consciously wait until the end to find the true answers. In the New Testament, Matthew explains that some people close themselves off to the path of faith: "People's heart is waxed gross, their ears are dull of hearing, and their eyes they have closed" (Matthew 13:15, KJV). When people close themselves off from pure spirituality and faith, they open their doors to the iniquities of the world and evil.

Unfortunately the reason some people wait until the end of their lives to seek the higher answers is for their own personal comfort. Life was not designed to be purely comfortable, because higher planed personal growth and spirituality does not lie in the pure comfort of temporal possessions. This connective social variance between people can cause very different life paths to occur amongst the people and it can also potentially create incredibly strong harmonic energy imbalances to transpire on multiple levels in the social rings that exist within humanity. There are people who live for temporal possessions, wealth, and pleasures, and they consciously wait until they are advanced in age and years to take on pure faith. The Lord knows all and this does not please him. In Timothy within the New Testament, this concept is discussed:

"Lovers of pleasures more than lovers of God" (2 Timothy 3:4, KJV). The Lord is well aware of those who suffer for him and he is also aware of those who chose to create comfort in their lives ahead of seeking him. When people choose this life path, they reproach faith and this is discussed in the New Testament within Romans: "What fruit had ye then in those things whereof ye are now ashamed, for the end of those things is death" (Romans 6:21, KJV). The Lord does not favor people consciously choosing this path and denying pure faith. Often these people will stand before others when they are well aged and proclaim their admission of error. But the Lord being aware of all was privy to their design and they chose to have their treasure on earth.

When people in life are channeled into a social group that has the same or a similar life frequency and/or undercurrent in their life's homing beacon system, they will more often be able to choose the right connections within the social switchboard and they will generally freely stream along toward their life beacon. But when people are mixed in with others that have either not activated their life homing systems yet, or that have their homing systems set to different frequencies, their life paths can be altered much more significantly because choosing which connections to follow and use is much more convoluted. In Ephesians within the New Testament, it's explained that people should walk along their own path of faith versus following others who walk the path of vanity: "Henceforth walk not as other gentiles walk, in the vanity of their mind" (Ephesians 4:17, KJV).

Also when people contrast their own life paths as compared to others this can often create a staggering confusion and sometimes even a paralyzing tension. But within the design of life each person has their own path and their own social challenges to face. When people encounter others with varying life course frequencies this can do a number of things to their own life course circuitry and the interference can potentially create energy shortages and overloads within their life path. In the New Testament James outlines the evil that extends from envy and strife. "For where envying and strife is, there is confusion and every evil work" (James 3:16, KJV). People must not compare their life paths to others or this can create a tremendous amount of friction within their life path. Every soul is born unto different circumstances and every person defines their life choices setting the stage for the meaning of their existence. People need to let their inner core drive them toward their path and they need to avoid being distracted by the paths of others. One poor choice based on envy can create a ripple in the path which may alter the life course.

There are also some people in life who will block other people's frequencies, others who will continually try and cut in front of people's signal, still more who will try and change the frequency that other people are on, and even some people who will try and eliminate the connections that people can choose from. Competing energy forces and social conflict are part of the social balance system that exists within the life path. When these types of things happen, people can realize shortages in their systems, but these people must have the strength and fortitude to continue and press on as each individual has a great amount of value in their own life and on the collective level of humanity. It takes an indomitable will to navigate within the life course. People simply must not let the negative social forces stand in their way along their pure life path.

> Great spirits have always encountered violent opposition from mediocre minds.
>
> —Einstein

What people need to realize is that the life frequency that they choose on their life homing system is what will ultimately help them choose the right connections to reach their life beacon. Within the design of life, people will almost always come across some poor connections in their paths, some people even more than others, and this logic can be found within probability. When people begin to wonder why everything is happening to them, they are basing this on comparisons to those that are in their immediate and general social system comparison group. In other areas and in other social rings outside of their own immediate social boundaries, there are many other people in life who are also asking the same questions. People must recognize that they are not alone in their social plight and find their strength within the unity of a positive vision. Although it may seem that some people are much more fortuitous within their life journeys, not everyone in life can have equal amounts of everything and this social reality exists across all life spectrums. There is never a perfect balance within any life element along the continuum, there is only a constant sum. In the New Testament Corinthians, details how weakness can be transformed into strength: "For my strength is made perfect in my weakness" (Corinthians 12:9, KJV). The ability for people to endure and become resilient within the pure life path gives people a strength that cannot be realized by those who have suffered no affliction. People must be strong and endure along their paths. In the environment, convergent evolution is when species that are not closely related can acquire similar characteristics in varying environments. The parallel would be different people from all around the world rising up and persevering in similar difficult circumstances and evolving on a human level despite their afflictions.

In life, some people will know that they are moving in the right direction and that they have chosen the right connections and others will remain very uncertain and they will feel in the dark on how to interpret the various signs and signals along their life path. However, when people are not fickle and they choose the correct life beacon and they do not let others disturb their routing, they can normally maintain a much steadier life course. Regardless of which type of people that enter into a person's life path, people can still choose their own positive existence and they must be admonished to endure. The perception and interpretation of what a positive life existence is belongs to each individual, and that is also part of life's design. People should have no qualms about choosing a pure life path. Corinthians within the New Testament outlines the reward for faith and purity: "For our light affliction, which is but for a moment, worketh for us for a far more exceeding and eternal weight of glory" (2 Corinthians 4:12, KJV). The negative element in society is hedging their big bet on the wrong market. Those who follow the pure path of faith will receive their treasure which far exceeds any treasure that can be accumulated on earth. The negative element will have had their reward and they will receive no more.

Sometimes the obstacles within leading a positive existence can seem unbearable and often this is by comparison to the life paths of others. When people see others around them that seem to have so much, this can create frustration, but people must remember that each person has a different life path, and, in addition, other people may be choosing *different* life courses which can include the life courses of *iniquity*. There are some people in life who separate from faith to orchestrate their accumulation and those who have a pure faith must not follow them in their lustful and evil path. In the New Testament, Corinthians provides guidance within this area: "Wherefore come out from among them, and be ye separate, saith the Lord, and touch no unclean thing, and I will receive you" (2 Corinthians 6:17, KJV). The same social scenarios that plague humanity now have been around throughout all time. Galatians in the New Testament provides the answers surrounding the quelling of the temptation of lusts: "Walk in the spirit, and ye shall not fulfill the lust of the flesh" (Galatians 5:16, KJV). A strong spiritual foundation can help people to avoid the lusts of the flesh.

Some people in life have the philosophy of "It does not matter how you get there, it's getting there that matters." This is the flawed philosophy that the negative element in society wishes people to believe. If this life philosophy were actually true, everyone would have adopted and followed it from the beginning of time and through to the present, there is simply much more to life than this distorted and elementary assertion. People should be very leery of those who operate under these shallow and evil social principles. The people in society operating under those deceptive principles are part of the negative social resistance. And the reason that all people have not followed that social assertion over time is because of the signs, symbols, and the people that have come before us and that will come again.

Dignity does not consist in honors, but in deserving them.

—Aristotle

In order for people to be part of the collective good of humanity and to reach their individual life plateaus and apexes, people must endure. People must never forlorn their hope regardless of how interminable the obstacles within their life course can appear.

You must be the change you wish to see in the world.

—Gandhi

When people are making the correct type of life connections and if they are on the right frequency, they will actually begin feel in tune with the harmonic flow of positive energy. If people are making connections and they are not on the right frequency for their life beacon, they will often feel life *static* and *interference* within their life course. This life path static and interference can bog down people's systems. When people are not convinced that their life frequency and/or their beacon is the right one, this can cause people to create their own energy shortages and it can also allow other people to create further negative energy surges upon them, which can heavily impact their life course. People must not allow any negative social codependents to deprecate and destroy their positive life energy force. In the New Testament, Luke discusses the variance between people: "He that is faithful in that which is least is faithful also in much, and he that is unjust in the least is unjust also in much" (Luke 16:10, KJV). People should not allow those who waver in their life choices and in their faith to infect them with their contagious life and spiritual wavering. A strong spiritual foundation and a strong support network are the keys to overcoming negative energy surges.

Everyone in life has their own life circuitry design within their system, some of these designs are more complex, some designs are built stronger, and some of these designs will require frequent servicing during the life path. Depending on the type of wiring and circuitry that a person has within, their interaction with certain other people or certain connections may cause energy surges and imbalances to occur within their system. If these imbalances occur sometimes, people must seek out positive network support connections which can help them to restore their power, but if these connections are not sought, people's systems can potentially reach *burnout* if the imbalances are prolonged. To avoid a system burnout, people must seek to escape their plight and their poignant suffering by seeking the help of trusted sources. If people do not have the right support network in place and/or if the people in their support network ignore their plight, they should turn to their faith to ask for answers. Often through this turn to faith, others are mystically prompted and compelled to take action. Anyone who is aware of the plight of others and that is capable of assisting them should provide them with assistance. Those in life who are blessed with strength are commanded to help those who are weak. In Romans within the New Testament, this topic is covered: "We then that are strong ought to bear the infirmities of the weak, and not to please ourselves" (Romans 15:1, KJV). Those who have ample and do not give back will impact their own path.

There are many symbolic influences throughout life that can impact the decisions that people have to make. These signs, signals, and the corresponding life choices can have a profound impact on people's chosen frequency, connections choices, and on their chosen life beacon. The myriad of life signal inputs that are being received continually on the life path can become very difficult for people to process. With all the signal inputs that people are exposed to in life, they are also required in many cases to process the proper output signals. Because life's social switchboard system can be so dynamic sometimes, people's signals will get crossed, especially if the others in their network are sending mixed signals. The life path is full of vicissitudes and people can run through a gamut of emotions when trying to navigate the course. When people are interacting with those of little faith and/or those who operate under the façade of duplicity, they can be exposed to the noxious poisons of earthly lusts within those interactions. In the New Testament, Luke speaks of being aware of those who don't share the same life values: "Take heed and beware of covetousness, for a man's life consisteth not in the abundance of the things which he posesseth" (Luke 12:15, kjv). If people build up their spiritual foundation and acquire knowledge over time, they will be able to navigate around those who are walking on a different path. The design of life includes the interaction with those that will block people's life paths and/or that will try to destroy people in full and this can done overtly or covertly.

> *In the practice of tolerance, ones enemy is the best teacher.*
>
> —Dalai Lama (1935–)

Every single encounter in life, each life experience, and all the connections that are made in life can all teach people something noble. Many times people forget about the incredible amounts of knowledge that can be obtained through each life experience. In order for people to fully *harvest* the available knowledge in life, people must remain positive in order to remain open and have room in their mental stores to carry forward their acquired knowledge. Negative energy and negative social forces can fill people's mental stores and they can block the harvesting process.

People need to navigate away from the negative social forces in order to ensure that their knowledge can be fully harvested. Timothy within the New Testament discusses the deception that can come between people and their path of faith: "But evil men and seducers shall wax worse and worse, deceiving and being deceived" (2 Timothy 3:4, KJV). Evil continues to survive and it must be marked in order to try and help others to avoid it.

What many people unfortunately fail to realize or understand is that their difficult life path and the lessons that lie within can become powerful insights, tools, and instruments which can be reinforced within themselves and can be taught to others. The interaction with evil, which is unfortunate on the surface level, can in fact educate people on how to instruct others on how to go about navigating around it. This process via the power of social diffusion can provide humanity will an even greater amount of collective good. If a person realizes that their sequential life efforts are building them up toward a higher plane of knowledge and that they are helping others either directly or indirectly in the process, they can realize a tremendous surge of positive energy back into their life paths. Although people's resources may become meager within their social exposures to the negative social forces and evil, they must persist on their pure and positive life path. In the New Testament, Matthew outlines the reward for those who are persecuted for good: "Blessed are those who are persecuted for righteousness sake, for theirs is the kingdom of heaven" (Matthew 5:10, KJV). People must be compelled to do everything they can to be a success in life without sacrificing their path of purity. Trading one's soul for earthly gain is a sacrifice that no one should make.

Unfortunately, although being part of life's grand design, part of life for most people is dealing with other people who are unsure about their own life beacon and/or who wait until they are very old to consider a life beacon. These stray people can heavily influence and impact others who know what their life beacons are and then people are forced to make difficult decisions because they are within the same *connective social network* as the others who are not plugged in. In order to navigate within and around life's negative forces and social experiences, people need to become more adept at *reading the signs and symbols*. The negative social forces wish to create a veil of social obscurity for the positive element, so the positive element must educate itself in order to avoid the social pitfalls that have been set for them.

> *You have to learn the rules of the game and then you have to play better than anyone else.*

> —Einstein

Learning the rules of the game doesn't mean that the positive element has to play the game of life the same way that the negative element does, but rather it allows the positive element to track and mark the evildoers within the game by their methods and works via their acquired knowledge and understanding.

Life and the process of socialization are much more difficult for those who are unable to begin picking up on the signs and symbols that are present. The people who know the life rules (social dominators) will take full advantage of those who are *social novices* and they will exploit them continually. People must learn from their life experiences and then they must watch for the signs and symbols as they go forward in life. The people who maintain a positive life course and that seek growth within their spirituality can also receive messages that the negative elements in society cannot receive. It's also important for people to recognize that these messages are not supplied on demand, but instead they manifest by the way of a supernatural life enigma. In the New Testament, Peter communicates that the will of men does not dictate the receipt of messages, but rather that messages are received by manifestation onto the just: "For the prophecy came not in old time by the will of man, but holy men of God spake as they were moved by the Holy Ghost" (2 Peter 1, KJV).

There have been many people over the course of all time that have demanded signs and messages, and these people have either refused to believe that others have received them or they choose to mock and ignore those who receive these gifts.

The only way to keep the positive energy balance that exists within humanity in place is for individuals to realize that they each have the power to contribute to the *collective pool* of the positive life force. People must learn that this social conflict process is a universal and continual *perpetual cycle* and that the energy continuum always has the potential to turn negative. The negative social forces in society are working diligently to persuade others to take their evil path which is easier, but their social path has a cost to the individuals who are partaking and also a cost to the collective within humanity. People must understand what they are trading because the negative social forces will not explain the social and spiritual toll. If people are looking for higher meanings in life, contributing to the maintenance of the positive energy force of humanity on the collective level is an integral part of life's higher meanings.

Only a life that is lived for others is a life worthwhile.

—Einstein

As there are no absolutions in life and life's meaning is not transparent, a person must follow their own chosen path and try to connect into the social networks that promote their positive energy flow and most closely align with their core beliefs and values which move them toward their life beacon. The best way to maintain the right direction and energy in life is through finding the right life support networks. If a person denies that there is interference in their life and/or ignores the static being caused by others, this can impede their opportunity to reach their life beacon. People must always reach out to their positive support networks within their life course. But if people's support networks *fail* them, this can make their life paths much more isolating and difficult.

> *In the end we will not remember the words of our enemies, but the silence of our friends.*

—Dalai Lama

Everyone in life has a very unique opportunity to find the meaning in their lives. The way people choose to live their lives has both an individual impact and a collective impact. Each person has colossal amount of positive energy that they can potentially contribute, and if *even more* people chose the positive life path, the negative social forces within humanity would be *suffocated* and they would wither away.

> *What you leave behind is not what is engraved in stone monuments, but is woven into the lives of others.*

—Pericles (495–429) BC

People must never forget how important they are to everyone and to humanity. People must be strong and resist the negative social forces whose goal is to take people down their path of iniquity. Matthew in the New Testament outlines the importance of people preserving their path of purity: "Fear not them which kill the body, but are not able to kill the soul, but rather fear him which is able to destroy both the soul and the body in hell" (Matthew 10:28, KJV). People must choose the pure path and gather together to create a better world and to evolve humanity. There are social and spiritual solutions available, but people must be willing to accept the truths and realities that lead to these solutions and also be open to accept the sources of these solutions. There is no perfect panacea on earth, but there is an eternal panacea for those that seek it with faith.

INTRODUCTION

There was a seed of inspiration, which was growing deep within me throughout my life, and once the roots from the seed had fully encompassed my inner core, I was inspired to create this work. The seed was present long before I realized it was there, and as the seed continued to grow, its force continued to manifest within me and it began to have a greater presence over time. Due to the positive fusion between my core nature and the force of the emerging seed, I began to become a highly reflective and analytical person very early in my life. Although I always understood that I thought about things differently from most others, I didn't realize what the reason was behind that difference for a very long time. I have been described by some people over the course of time as seeming to be *aloof*, but this social *mis*perception is due only to my thinking nature.

Although a very strong inner drive was present inside of me from a very young age, the reason for this core drive did not emerge until much later in my life. There was much difficulty in trying to explain a feeling to others, when, in fact, the basis of the feeling was still not known to me. From a very young age, I could sense through my early social experiences that a social paradigm shift was required in people and within humanity, and I have always been resolute in my core position, but in my younger years, I had not yet acquired the crystallized knowledge and social tools necessary to convey such a complex message. In order to define and construct this complex message, I would have to go through a series of life experiences and social trials, as well as having to acquire the knowledge and tools necessary in order to convey the complete message to others.

As time went by in my early years, I was eventually funneled into some areas in which I could begin to express my abstract and fluid cognitive and instinctual abilities. In school I was placed into various classes, which allowed me to begin to openly express my ability to elicit the complex analysis of existing material (film and literature), but I was never really challenged with any major social platforms until I was involved in a series of debates during my last year of high school. These social debates provided me with a very strong sense of the power that can be generated within the evaluation of complex social dynamics that exist within humanity. But ultimately the forward momentum and the surge of energy that was affected upon me from those school debates were stalled as I did not get involved within any other life forums concerning complex social issues or dynamics thereafter. But the delay was part of the ultimate design.

While in school, the only people who were aware of my intellectual abilities and my powerful social insights were my teachers and some of these teachers had a very difficult time understanding how such a young person could formulate such strong associations and concise insights. I was never intrinsically compelled to share the intellectual aspect of my life with anyone, and I believe this was due to a greater design. In life and within the process of socialization, if a person is frequently and sequentially recognized for their intellectual ability over time then it is comprehensible for others to accept those abilities, but if a person is not known for their ability then it is part of human nature for people to cast doubt and to diminish anything that is produced by an unknown plebeian. The world has no extrinsic ethos (knowledge of me), but the goal is to create positive motion within the intrinsic ethos (the impression created), as true pathos (emotion) and ethos (character) comes from one's words and language and not just appearances.

Within the grand design, it was necessary for me to be an unknown and to realize through my own life social experiences and the acquisition of knowledge that there have been and that there will continue to be others that have gifts, abilities, and ideas which are shunned not due to their strength and value, but due to their derivation and their origin. In order to create the correct caliber of a social message to deliver, I too had to have and to share these types of life experiences. This type of negative and repressive social phenomenon has been happening since the beginning of time and it was my personal calling to further expose it. The work is very pointed to elicit the pathos, that the ire from the message will turn to calm and calculated positive social mobility and evolution.

When one is fecund and/or is blessed with spiritual gifts and is adept at predicting the course of social outcomes and events with foresight, which are often imperceptible to others, people tend to become conflicted in their opinions toward one. As it's in the core nature of people via their egos to perceive and identify life elements on their own and to make their own life choices, having contention with the gifted fecund is a natural ego defense mechanism for many people. So in essence not only is the momentum of positive social and spiritual change within humanity inhibited by the forces of the negative resistance, but it's also impeded by people's egos and/or their vain jealously in society when they decide that they want to *choose* who can come up with the visions, ideas, and solutions that can create social inertia within innovation and the evolution of humanity. In the New Testament, John wrote about an example of what challenges that those who are chosen face: "I have chosen you out of the world, therefore the world hateth you" (John 15:20, KJV). This passage was regarding Jesus choosing his apostles, but it can also apply to anyone else who the Lord has looked upon throughout all time from the past to the present. It's unfortunately part of human nature for some people to scoff at others who have received messages and/or gifts.

People do not *choose* the vanguards of social and spiritual innovation and those who receive messages and gifts, but rather they are born and selected. This inhibitory social phenomenon is an element of societal dysfunction, which the negative social forces will gladly continue to nourish. When people live to only choose who they want to recognize within humanity, this causes them to overlook the other people in life who can actually supply them with the social and/or spiritual solutions. And those who are supporting the negative elements and foundations in society know this. The negative social forces are often well aware of what the correct social, spiritual, and life solutions are and they move quickly to dispel the legitimacy of the people producing the answers. This social process is normally quite easy and effortless for them because their efforts are reinforced by the others in society, who continually overlook the people who have the social and/or spiritual solutions in favor of choosing their own personal and *choice* selections. The reason that the negative social forces also know some of the answers is because there are some fecund and gifted people within their societal groups as well, but they use their powers for selfish and/or evil means instead of for the good of humanity. In the New Testament within Matthew, this issue was discussed: "Many prophets and righteous men have desired to see those things which ye see and have not seen them, and to hear those things which ye hear and have not heard them" (Matthew 13:17, KJV). Throughout all time, there have always been people who believe that they should be the ones to receive gifts and messages. But this is not how the design of life works and everyone needs to base their life path on faith, patience, and understanding versus focusing on why only certain people are the recipients of gifts and/or messages. The blessing is that they are being received at all.

Because each of us on earth has such a limited time to make a social impact due to the brevity of our mortal existence, it's paramount that we utilize our time and energy to try and grow ourselves on a personal level, and also to take part in the positive social and spiritual growth of humanity. For those who have received gifts and/or messages, they need to bestow them upon humanity. In Luke, the New Testament discusses the obligation of those who receive special gifts and messages to expound their nature and meaning unto humanity: "For unto whomsoever much is given, of him shall much be required" (Luke 12:48, KJV). One should not fear exposing their gifts rather they should be implored to share them. In the New Testament, Matthew wrote about the message of Jesus in this critical area within humanity: "Let your light shine before men, that they see your good works and glorify your father which is in heaven" (Matthew 5:16, KJV).

The derivation of my personal motivation to create an inspired collective message occurred during the culmination of several of my own life elements whereby I had an epiphany and began to render this work in the incipient stage of its development. As many of the events that have occurred in my life are central and are highly germane to some of the social and spiritual plights that exist in the process of socialization and within humanity, this book is the personification of my personal will to elicit positive social and spiritual change. In James within the New Testament, the trials of men are discussed: "Who is a wise man and endued with knowledge among you, let him show out a good conversation his works with meekness of wisdom" (James 3:13, KJV). A man who has learned through his own ignorant mistakes and who has been a fool and then moves toward purity attains social and spiritual wisdom. This area is further covered in the New Testament within

Corinthians: "Let no man deceive himself, if any man among you seemeth to be wise in this world, let him become fool, that he may be wise" (Corinthians 3:18, KJV). Wisdom typically comes with age and this acquired wisdom should promote personal and spiritual growth. In Titus within the New Testament, some key elements of wisdom are outlined: "That aged men be sober, grave, temperate, sound in faith, in charity, in patience" (Titus 2:2, KJV). During the course of my life, I have heard various people state, "that no one likes a know-it-all." This emotionally charged type of thought lacks logic, reasoning, spiritual knowledge, and foresight. Unfortunately there are some people within the life path who refuse to accept life's truths and realities.

I have always believed in my core that the epitome within humanity should be those who serve the collective good and that seek to serve a higher purpose and it has been my lifelong personal quest to promote this ideology. People must understand that humans are fallible and that people can make mistakes, but it's their core values, core nature, and their corresponding social and spiritual actions that build up and manifest over time that will ultimately define them. People must also understand that there are social and spiritual continuums within humanity that extends from those in society who are almost angelic to those that are heinous and malevolent in their nature. When people teach their young that all of the people in the world are inherently good, they are actually providing the negative social element that exists within society with additional social fuel and energy for their devious work as this social and spiritual outlook breeds social and spiritual ignorance and perpetuates social malformation. In the New Testament, the life path is discussed in Matthew: "Because straight is the gate, and narrow is the way, which leadeth unto life, and few there be that find it" (Matthew 7:14, KJV). People must not be deceived by the wolves and their evil extensions of lusts. In Luke within the New Testament, the straight gate is discussed further: "Strive to enter at the straight gate, for many, I say unto you will seek to enter in, and shall not be able" (Luke 13:24, KJV).

Unfortunately in life, many people believe that they are restricted in their actions and that they are unable to exude their pure core nature and their spirituality within the process of socialization because of the negative social elements which exist within society which seek to prohibit the expression and maintain the level of paucity that exists within the positive social dynamic. The negative social forces within societies will seek to quell any oracles that can resonate a positive message and vision that could expose their negative design, but this prohibitive action must not stop people from promoting the necessary positive social and spiritual changes that are needed within humanity. In the New Testament, Mark discusses the commandment to not be ashamed of glorifying the Lord and/or his words: "Whosoever therefore shall be ashamed of me and my words, in this adulterous and sinful generation, of him also shall the son of man be ashamed of, when he cometh in the glory of his father with the holy angels" (Mark 8:38, KJV). People should not let others dictate their life path and in order to create a more comfortable social environment for those who are positive, pure people need to seek each other out, gather, and protest any social environment in which their personal and/or spiritual freedom is being restricted. As a parallel, in the environment, ecological succession involves facilitation, which is when a species modifies an environment to meet the needs of other species and inhibition is when a species makes an environment unsuitable for other species. Humanity should be much further along within this area, but in many cases, the evolution of intelligence is used for the segregation of human growth versus the propagation.

The ultimate purpose of my efforts is to disseminate the social and spiritual truths and realities that the negative social forces seek to keep hidden and in obscurity from the populous and to edify them in a lucid manner versus using an ornate metaphysical view. This work initially manifested within the conflation of ideas which then propelled me to continue my search for social, spiritual, and life truths and meanings in order to convey a unifying message to people and with the purpose to shatter the existing societal polarization that exist across many social dynamics. In life, when a person discovers their personal mission, this can create animosity and confusion amongst the other people found within their network. In the New Testament, Luke explains some of the things that can occur as a result of one partaking within their life calling: "And ye shall betrayed both by parents, and brethren, and kinsfolk, and friends" (Luke 21:16, KJV). It can be very difficult for the people who haven't received their life calling yet, to conceive the sacrifices that must be made by those who have received their message and are working to fulfill their mission in life. The ultimate commandment is to build a spiritual path and in some cases relations can suffer and must be forsaken in order for people to move toward their spiritual apex.

While compiling the information for this work over the years, I have frequently ruminated over the content as my goal was to avoid having a nondescript message and to instead formulate an unprecedented approach in order to create a certain level of novelty in the expression. When a person or people are of a thinking nature and they are out to protest the state of the present system of social and spiritual dynamics, this thinking effort can be a very arduous task. Generally most people are not receptive to change and the resistance to change is amplified capaciously when the negative resistance within humanity is impacted. Within the New Testament, Galatians speaks of revealing the truth and the social consequences: "Am I therefore your enemy, because I tell you the truth?" (Galatians 4:16, KJV). Many people within humanity resist the truth because it doesn't fit within their chosen life plan or model. The fierce and menacing resistance that is felt by those who seek to share the truths and realities in life is a force that has been shared by many throughout all time. The passage of truth is often a treacherous one.

The path of defining and seeking social and spiritual change within socialization can be very barren as many people within the process of socialization will challenge those who seek a positive social change and they will attempt to ostracize and eliminate them. People must be strong and realize that a true positive life effort will never be futile and that positive social and spiritual change within humanity is a plausible reality. In Romans within the New Testament, knowledge is extended in the area of the good fight: "Be not overcome of evil, but overcome evil with good" (Romans 12:21, KJV). The soldiers of good must overcome the soldiers of evil.

In my personal life efforts to exude truth, it had become compulsory that I find the necessary conduit to express my ideas on a larger scale, which had been limited in the past to miniscule and obscure social forums. This work is the nexus between my ideas and a larger forum which can extract the concepts that are of a seminal nature and then people can begin to further level the social playing field between the positive social forces and the negative resistance. I have applied some very *fervent* commentary within this work in order to truly reach people and galvanize their efforts toward a positive social and spiritual metamorphosis. My mission has been purely to help people and to glorify the Lord. There are far too many people within humanity that choose instead to promote themselves. "He that speaketh of himself seeketh his own glory, but he that seeketh his glory that sent him the same is true, and no unrighteousness is in him" (John 7:18, KJV). Jesus condemns people seeking personal glory, so my intent lies within an effort to promote his work for the people.

I firmly believe that this work will lend further credence to the visualization that the negative forces that exist within humanity can be overtaken by imparting further knowledge and truths upon people, which can empower them with positive energy that can be harvested to defeat the existing negative social forces. My hope is that my efforts within explaining how each person in life is an important microcosm within the whole of humanity will be laudable. Each individual that builds up a strong and positive foundation within their life and in their spiritual path will have built up a strong defense *versus* the negative social forces and evil. In Matthew within the New Testament, building a strong foundation is discussed: "I will liken him unto a wise-man, which built his house upon a rock" (Matthew 7:24, KJV). If even *more* people create a strong foundation of purity, evil will not be able to sweep them away and instead, evil will be vanquished.

One of the reasons why societal and spiritual issues remain perpetual and cyclical in their nature is due to the fact that many people acquiesce to the current social dynamics which does nothing to change them. When people are unwitting as to the course of the existing social dynamics, this is no excuse and this oblivious social approach only further perpetuates the growth and the strengthening of the roots of the negative social foundations and evil. When people ignore the social reality, they themselves are becoming negative social codependents that are enabling the negative resistance to flourish and gain more social leverage. When people ignore the existing social reality, it allows the evil of the wolves to come unto the flock. In the New Testament, John spoke of the way that the wolves operate: "He that entereth not by the door into the sheepfold, but climbeth up some other way, the same is a thief and a robber" (John 10:1, KJV). Jesus spoke regarding the deceitful and cunning ways of the wolves. People must not ignore the social reality, they must instead mark those who do evil and track their movements. In Romans within the New Testament, it discusses marking the wicked, but reserving the retribution for the Lord: "Avenge not yourselves, for it is written, vengeance is mine, I will repay, saith the Lord" (Romans 12:19, KJV). But if people are not vigilant in this area, the flock will become overrun by ravenous wolves and their evil.

People must instead be indignant toward those who are not concerned about being forthright about their personal social position, their spirituality, and/or about the collective good of humanity. Some people can also seem blasé to the social dynamics, which exist because the elements are so engrained into society, but they do not realize the ramifications of their casual social and spiritual approach. Many times in life, people are more worried about being cast out and forsaken from amongst the negative element in society to which they are socially bound than they are regarding their duty to the positive element within humanity. This harmful social action impedes the growth and evolution of humanity. In Luke within the New Testament, the need for separation is discussed: "Blessed are ye when men shall hate you, and when they separate you from their company, and shall reproach you, and cast your name as evil, for the son of man's sake" (Luke 6:22, KJV). When the positive element within humanity extracts itself away from and isn't subjugated by the negative social forces, they are severing the bonds of iniquity that the negative social element of evil relies on for their foothold of existence.

The people who are backing the negative social dynamics and elements within society want the pure people within humanity to become listless in their efforts for social and spiritual change in order for them to be able to maintain their own uninterrupted social course. Many people within their life paths become socially detached and unaware of the ominous and evil forebodings that express what is coming in the future. The subtle differences within the societal perspective must be examined carefully as important social and spiritual cues and elements can be lost within the social nuances. Unfortunately there are many people within humanity who are requiring and seeking a distinguishable sign to appear before them in order for them to be propelled. But the design in life is for the signs to be amorphous and bodiless. In Matthew within the New Testament, the revelation of signs is discussed:

"A wicked and adulterous generation seeketh after a sign and there shall no sign be given unto it" (Matthew 16:4, KJV). Only the people truly following the straight path will normally receive signs and the design of the straight path includes people being vigilant in their efforts versus listless in promoting the positive within humanity.

There are still others in society that do protest the present state of social and spiritual dynamics, but they act with an arbitrary style, which is highly unobtrusive and yields no social gain. Positive social momentum is accrued through actions stemming from words and not through words alone. Society is at a social impasse on many of its critical social and spiritual dynamics due many covariant factors and elements, and when people are only mulling over these social and spiritual elements versus taking action, there is no traction and forward momentum being attained. People must become more circumspect in considering their individual power and ability to help change social dynamics and further develop human nature. People must also be dauntless and courageous in their efforts to affect positive social change. Within this effort, people need to withdraw themselves from iniquity and mark those who promote it. In the New Testament, this withdrawal is discussed within Thessalonians: "Now me commandeth you, brethren, in the name of our Lord Jesus Christ, that ye withdraw yourselves from every brother that worketh disorderly, and not after the tradition which he received of us" (2 Thessalonians 3:14, KJV). People must understand and recognize that over time with the persistence and effort of the positive social element that the negative element will ultimately have nowhere to hide, and they will be found gathered amongst themselves ashamed of their acts. In Thessalonians within the New Testament, this is detailed. "Have no company with him, that he may be ashamed" (2 Thessalonians 3:14). The positive element must simply counteract the efforts of evil to achieve this.

Society must be very persistent in attempting to dissuade people from pursuing a life course that will contribute to the existing negative social stratification, which is stalling the forward evolution of humanity. Other social forces such as the media, through its nefarious designs, often propagate the negative social stratifications that are already in place and people are much more labile to these socially appealing forces. People must not solely rely on luminaries for their social inspiration and they must also recognize that no one is obsolete in the design of life. The youth in particular within humanity is heavily impacted by the media and this is all by design because the media recognizes that the youth has not yet obtained the wisdom which is required to recognize their evil design. This is why their design of evil must be offset by the positive elements within humanity. The media tells people to eat, drink, and be merry and to live for today, because there may not be a tomorrow. Unfortunately what the media is purveying is the design of evil. The design of life is for people to prepare in purity for the end and not within the lusts of sin. In the New Testament, Ephesians entails the path that lies ahead for those that follow the media's design: "For this ye know that no whoremonger, nor unclean person, nor covetous man, who is an idolater, hath any inheritance in the kingdom of Christ and God" (Ephesians 5:5, KJV). The media does not care about people's souls, it only cares about sales. Many people within humanity are purely and centrally focused on their free will, which is actually part of the design of life, but free will doesn't involve being encompassed within the infectious clutches of the media. When people conform to what the media is telling them to do then true free will is being extinguished. True free will within the design of life entails the understanding of human fallibility within life choices, but it does not exist when people are brainwashed and influenced to perform the acts of lusts which lie within the design of evil.

The goal of all of my efforts has and will continue to be geared toward augmenting the forces of positive social energy that can be harvested to contend with the negative resistance that exist within many concrete negative social dynamics. The people in societies that stand by the negative and limited social dynamics, which are holding back the progression of humanity, are not conciliatory in their beliefs and their social positions and unfortunately many of these people evolve into power positions within the process of socialization. These negatively driven people in social power positions are also supported by others in society and this menacing social union forms a socially bonded element that also does not seek positive social change. The negative social forces are also always looking to convert people over to their side of the social continuum. In addition, the negative social element has an intricate social guidance and tracking system to monitor this social paradigm shifting. The positive social forces within humanity must be vigilant within their own social efforts to offset the clever and treacherous social maneuvers which are rendered by the negative elements within society. In Ephesians within the New Testament, the vain works of the wicked are discussed: "Let no man deceive you with vain works, for because of these things cometh the wrath of God upon the children of disobedience" (Ephesians 5:6, KJV). People must work vigilantly to save their own souls and the souls of others in the fight versus evil.

Many of the people within society that are reveling in their own worth and that are in a fixated state of stupor will continue their dissolute habits which have caused them to turn a blind eye to the needs of the collective good and humanity. The *ego-syntonic* behavior (considered appropriate to the individual) of these people is one of the critical negative social root systems that are entangled within the growth of the collective and the social action is confounding and suffocating the positive evolution of humanity. The hope and the direction of this work is that the forces of positive energy which in part are lying dormant, can be garnered together to penetrate and destroy the negative social forces which are inhibiting the growth of humanity. And that those who stand against the promotion of human growth will one day bemoan their decisions and the social positions in which they lived by. People must understand that *regret* is only an intellectual response and that *remorse* is a true and sincere emotional response. The people in society without true *character* are immune to remorse and they only regret when they are caught in their devious social acts. This contrived ideology for social retribution is a necessary means to an end as the attempt to enhance the nature, evolution, and longevity of humanity can never be labeled as a superfluous effort. In Luke within the New Testament, the fate of the wicked is outlined: "Woe unto you that laugh now, for ye shall mourn and weep" (Luke 6:25, KJV). Those who *mock* and *cast out* the good and pure will answer for their earthly iniquities. The good and pure have always been made to suffer at the hands of the wicked. The light was sent to fight the darkness so the positive element in society must be certain that the light remains.

In social and spiritual problem solving, people must identify and then review the issues, and then break down the issues into their smallest components in order to reach the roots of the issues. I created this work in order to enable people to better find and define the roots of social and spiritual issues. This work begins with a social and spiritual overview and then later it breaks down the life course into smaller social components. Writing this book was one large step for me, but it can potentially be one enormous step for humanity. In the same fashion, a child develops and grows over time to become an adult humanity must change its collective schema to evolve. In this work, I have combined and interlaced some commonly understood and accepted terminology to go along with my own social perspectives, which in almost all cases matches and aligns with the perspectives of the eminent social innovators, philosophers, and spiritual figures that have come before me. The negative social forces that exist within society have always combated these social and spiritual perspectives because they realize that their social life lines would be severed if humanity progressed and evolved to the next level. Human evolution is the light and the negative resistance is the dark, people are the hope and evil is the doom. The goal of this work is to try and provide everyone with an equal opportunity to identify, visualize, and interpret the vast myriad of social and spiritual elements that can impact their life course, and to also help level the social playing field in order to realize a new social and spiritual dawn. I will fully reveal the remaining elements within my personal inspiration for this work within it. People must understand that humanity cannot evolve without their personal acceptance of the social and spiritual truths and realities that exist and the corresponding social actions that are required to affect positive social change. The negative forces seek to divide people and confuse them in a blinding cloud of ambiguity and this is what allows them to exist. People must focus with purity and pierce through the veil of the cloud to form a vision.

> *In order to carry out a positive action we must develop a positive vision.*
>
> —Dalai Lama

tbε Lιϝε ϸατb

Sociology, Philosophy, Spirituality, and Socialization

Sociology may be loosely described as science as it is able to identify causal relationships over complex social phenomena.

—Max Weber

S ociology is the study of social action using critical analysis. *Philosophy* involves the use of logical reasoning versus the focus on empirical analysis, and the use of reason versus a focus on collecting data to interpret. The sciences of sociology and philosophy can be converged creatively to reach even higher levels of social understanding and social innovation.

Being that humanities issues keep repeating themselves over the course of time, the experts must align in order to eliminate the mistakes of humanity that will ultimately one day, when paired with technology, perpetuate a future chaos, which will lead to a social bedlam that cannot be controlled and/or diminished.

We cannot solve our problems with the same thinking we used when we created them.

—Einstein

To obviate the prevalence of the cyclical social issues in societies, people must solve the complex issues within humanity by first looking at the issues from the whole perspective and then break them down into smaller units. One of the major issues within society and humanity is that the *same types* of leaders are continually cycled into the leadership roles and this is why the errors of humanity are cyclical in nature. The same types of personalities and characters that run nations now could be planted into other periods within history and vice versa, and with few exceptions, the general results would be the same.

If world leaders and the societies, which fall under them on a collective level, continue to become overly arrogant over time, reality could slip away within the hubris, and this *tragic flaw* could bring down humanity. Ambition, arrogance, and other actions can lead toward the demise of all humanity. In order to avoid the same mistakes that have been made before, people must apply a highly creative approach to social analysis, be able to see across many spectrums, and at the same time, the arrogance of those in power must not block or impede social innovation. It is unconscionable for leaders and those in eminent social roles to become complacent in their social positions as society is always in flux and humanity must not falter in the effort to evolve. In the New Testament, Matthew outlined the course of this direction: "Every kingdom divided against itself is brought to desolation and every city or house divided shall not stand" (Matthew 12:25, KJV). The people of the world which is humanity are at the mercy of those in power. When those in power bicker over personal and political agendas, there is no social progress. When leaders are divided, they become a barrier to innovation versus an instrument for social evolution. It's an embarrassment for people to stand and watch those with so much power act as children in their understanding. Those in power over the masses must not forsake those who they represent. Colossians in the New Testament discusses the duty of those that serve over people to be just within their calling: "Masters give unto your servants that which is just and equal, knowing that ye also have a master in heaven" (Colossians 4:1, KJV). There is much more riding on leading nations than political agendas. The health and the evolution of humanity are also at stake.

By people applying ideas from other sciences and fields, a greater level of social creativity and innovation can be realized. *Weber's psychophysics law* can also be applied to sociology and it states that "the change needed is proportional to the intensity of the original stimulus" (the more intense that a stimuli is, the more intense the change needs to be to notice any difference). This law can be applied to both people, their environment, and on a larger scale to *humanity*. The law can apply to the personalities of individual people, to the personalities of societies, and it can measure changes in the normal polarity ranges that people and societies present over time. The impacts of the changes in individuals and in societies over time can create a myriad of social phenomenon. When the time comes that humanity is unable to distinguish a critical change within the societal milieu, this will create an iretractable social chaos, and it will be too late to change its course.

The human *social drive* is the innate tension which is pre-wired into people and it is only relieved by people who are moving toward a need or goal. Human drive can vary widely across individuals, but it fuels everything that occurs within the human socialization process. The process of human socialization is an intense process and many people have studied socialization over time. Some people have also posed theories which try and explain how the socialization process works, but defining the process is not an exact science.

However, there are some very identifiable elements and measures within socialization which have manifested over time and that can have a major impact on both individuals and society. Because of the impacts of certain elements within socialization, the social sciences were developed in order to measure those critical elements and to help protect humanity from the extreme effects that certain social elements can have.

> *At his best man is the noblest of all animals, separated from the law and justice he is the worst.*

> —Aristotle (BC)

Because of the fact that conflict is pre-wired into humanity and that there are both positive and negative human drives, humanity must work to maintain the positive balance of energy within the social continuum. In the New Testament within Corinthians, there is stress placed on gaining an understanding of the elements and refraining from malice: "Brethren, be not children in understanding, howbeit in malice be ye children, but in understanding me men" (Corinthians 14:20, KJV). If an understanding is not realized then humanity stands to suffer.

The social sciences are an extremely important field in life that evolved over time and they were designed to apply logic, reasoning, and vision within the appraisal of the human condition and to the process of ascertaining the degree of positive or negative human social evolution along a social continuum. The social momentum, the impact of the human socialization process, and the resulting societal foundations and social hierarchies that are birthed are carefully scrutinized by researchers and experts within the social sciences. People must understand when measuring these elements that all societies are not homogeneous. Each society has it own mores, and from the outside, it can be very difficult for people to gauge with any type of accuracy and/or certainty the amount of social vexation that is occurring within a given society.

For instance, when people form an opinion with limited or no information and question the intervention of one country or countries into other countries and/or societies, they do not have the necessary information at their disposal to understand what critical factors and social dynamics direct this action and activity. As with anything else, uninformed opinions in this area can also create division and they can stall programs designed to help free the oppressed within humanity. There is a very delicate social balance within the continuum of humanity, and if the social scale begins to shift, those with the power to act must act, so long as the action is truly positive and for the greater good of the collective humanity. The true calamity for humanity would be in not acting when there is a need.

There are many social rings that exist within humanity and within the process of socialization. The social rings begin with a core center and then they extend outward. Within each social ring, there is a net energy balance that is yielded, and as the social rings become larger and more inclusive on the collective level, it is critical that the net energy balance remains positive. History has proven that when a negative energy balance exists within a social ring and it is ignored, even in a distant social ring, this will ultimately impact the collective humanity. Rogue leaders and nations can impact the collective regardless of their distance and their scope. It is the duty of those in power who possess the ability to ensure that humanity is protected and that the positive balance within the social continuum is preserved.

There are very powerful elements and mechanisms within the process of socialization at all social levels that can create chaos in society and they must be carefully measured in order to determine the present societal health. Positive societies and social systems must be unfaltering in their efforts to promote stable societies versus societies with social schisms that can lead to destructive and noxious societies.

The collective unconscious is shared by all innately throughout all time.

—Carl Jung

Because of this shared collective reality, people can be separated in time by thousands of years and can share the same social drives and the same ideas of those who came long before them. This social phenomenon can also unfortunately continue to perpetuate the cyclical and contaminated social errors found within humanity. In the New Testament, there is leadership guidance provided within Thessalonians: "Now we exhort you, brethren, warn them that are unruly, comfort the feeble minded, support the weak, be patient toward all men" (Thessalonians 5:14, KJV). If these simple rules are followed, humanity stands to evolve with a consistent effort.

Within the social sciences, tools, mechanisms, and measures have been continually created over time to help to detect and offset potentially catastrophic social phenomena within socialization. Because of the continual need for new and novel social tools, creative and innovative ideas must be continually harvested and *all* possible sources must be fielded. People and societies overlooking others based on their social position and/or their social role has been a fundamental human flaw and a social calamity since the dawn of time. One of the greatest tragedies in life and within humanity has been and continues to be that when a person or people know that they have the innovative social answers to contribute to society and they are either missed, ignored, or they lack the audience necessary to communicate their critical knowledge.

Having knowledge but lacking the power to express it is clearly no better than never having any ideas at all.

—Plato (427–347) BC

People must remember that even a *plebeian* can have the insights and solutions that can help humanity. There are still far too many cases within the process of socialization where people are overlooked based on their social position and social role and they are relegated back to their social status within their social system. This infected and contagious social process is again due to the human ego where the people in power positions either want to yield their own social solutions and/or to choose where the solutions will originate from. The human ego is a bridge to individual success and a barrier to the growth of humanity.

In Romans within the New Testament, the containment of pride is discussed: "For I say, through the grace given unto me, to every man that is among you, not to think of himself more highly than he ought to think" (Romans 12:3, KJV). Humanity doesn't need people with a strong ego to lead them, but rather humanity requires leaders who are able to identify those with solutions in order that those solutions can be harvested. When solutions are harvested, they can create systems that can help to stabilize the volatile elements that exist within the world.

The process of social reform was developed, it has evolved over time, and it is a stabilizing social mechanism to prevent the unhealthy systemic breakdown within a given society. When people see other societies that are revolting, what they are really seeing is the impacts of incessant societal oppression. When people within a social system are oppressed and they are overwrought beyond their social threshold level, this leads to social chaos. History has shown over time through wars, brutal leaders, and societal oppressions that systemic breakdowns in societies have led to dramatic shifts in the lives of individuals within those societies and also in the rest of the world as well. The world and humanity's continued existence relies on the movement of people and societies toward a more positive collective nature of cooperation for human progress, evolution, and survival. The process of *global unified cooperation* is a very difficult one because people are not quick to exonerate those who have bestowed fallacies upon them and/or who have forsaken them in the past. Social trust is not something that should be expected, it is something that needs to be *earned*.

Some people, some leaders, and some societies around the world do not believe in a collective social effort. This social ideology divide creates a fierce dichotomy and social conflict versus the creation of a positive collective affinity to establish amicable social relations. Leadership styles that are compartmental, self-centered, view only the small picture, are isolating versus linking, and which do not involve thinking across social spectrums, normally lead to severe social issues and potentiate social uprise. The ego fixation and the overconfidence in some leaders and societies have caused their eventual downfalls over the course of history. *The illusion of unanimity* is a social phenomenon that is created when no one else speaks out against a flawed ideology and a group or society just concedes that the decision rendered and, at hand, is unanimous. This social flaw can also elicit the social disease of groupthink within leadership and within societies and it can wreak havoc upon social systems. And in some cases, the flaw in the attitude of superiority lies within entire societies versus just the ruling social class. In the New Testament, the error found within the glory of men is outlined within Galatians: "Let us not be desirous of vain glory, provoking one another, envying one another" (Galatians 5:24, KJV). These social attitudes can lead to terrible outcomes for humanity and the collective.

Ethnocentrism is when a culture, group, or society believes that they are superior to others and this can build tremendous social tension between social elements, which can be either seen on the surface level or the tension may be lying dormant and can manifest in strength over time. There are several critical levels involved and the initial level is people's *core* nature (to include their personality, temperament, and core spirit, which can have a positive or negative net energy yield), and the next level is the crucial social element of *initial social embedding* (which is the initial exposure to an idea or concept associated with a particular group, which can have a positive or negative yield).

When a child or person is first given information regarding a group, this information becomes their *initial social embedding*. This initial social embedding can be masked and modified, but it cannot be eradicated. The initial social embedding will be exposed if the layers, which surround it, are perforated. The layers that surround the initial social embedding (ISE) are the *nurturing layer* (which is what a person is taught about society and life), the *surface layer* (which involves situational and audience variables), and the *response layer* (which involves surface attitudes).

What occurs within the *chain reaction* is that if a group which has a negative concept within a person's ISE creates a social conflict with that person on an individual level or on a group level within their knowledge at the *response layer*, the energy immediately attacks their layers. Based on the immediate audience and situation that is involved at the *surface layer*, a potential reaction can either be elicited or constrained. The *surface layer* may prevent a reaction due to the threat of reciprocal retribution, or the action may surface if it had a strong-enough internal impact. Within the chain reaction, the *core layer* and the *ISE layer* interact. Based on the net energy from that interaction, a positive, negative, or neutral force of energy will be yielded. If the core offsets the ISE then there will be no reaction, but if the combination of the force of action and the intensity of the ISE level combine and overtake the core layer, this force will perforate the *nurturing, surface,* and *response* layers and create a forward action. So, in essence, the pivotal factor is the ISE layer. If the ISE layer is negative, this can potentially override even the strongest of pure core layers. This social phenomenon again reinforces the concept of the need for humanity to maintain a positive social outlook. If a child's or a person's initial ISEs across social elements are embedded with negativity, they will be exposed to the potential to release negative energy regardless of the purity of their inner core layer. De Facto segregation is an element within society which is very real, and those that impose it may avoid punishment on earth, but they will certainly have to answer for their works later. In the New Testament and under the new covenant, all nations and all kindred are welcomed unto the Lord. It's appalling that Jesus gave this perfect example unto men and that they have ignored his commandment.

This type of social outlook (ethnocentrism) is still one of the major social flaws and social infirmities within humanity that extends from the smallest of social groups in a social system and broadens out into entire societies. This social course can lead people or groups into a feeling that they are the exception to all else and other social errors as well. In addition, this type of social outlook is also found to be morally repugnant and highly ignorant by the astute social community of intellectuals within humanity. And this social disease perforates into the minds of children and those who leave openings via their imbalanced ego, creating a layer of permeability. It is also a social paradox for those with more to feel superior to those with less.

No culture can live in its attempt to be exclusive.

—Gandhi

In the New Testament, James discusses how the humble are received and the proud are turned away: "God resisteth the proud, but giveth grace unto the humble" (James 4:6, KJV). People who look down on others and who judge them will answer to the one that is higher. There are various approaches and methods which study how social attitudes and social systems evolve over time and which attempt to find the root causes and their effects across the manifestations of social phenomena.

Within the nomothetic-idiographic approach in sociology, the *nomothetic* model focuses on the search for independent variables and relational links within phenomena, while the *idiographic* model focuses on complete in-depth understanding of individual cases. Reasoning is also applied within the study of social phenomenon. *Deductive reasoning* within the social sciences is top-down logic processing, which is taking the big picture and breaking it down into subunits. Deductive reasoning links premises to conclusions, if premise is true then the terms are clear, rules of logic are followed with a logical necessity. *Inductive reasoning* is bottom-up processing and is when an example or examples imply that they can be applied to a broader scope. The reasoning is trying to discover a *new* piece of information with incoming data to form a perception or output. Inductive reasoning involves *feature analysis,* which is used to build a complete perception.

Approaches from other sciences and fields can also be applied to the social sciences as well. In fact, it is ludicrous to reject the idea that concepts can be universal. *Aristotle* believed that "one who could connect the resemblances between two separate areas and be able to link them together is a person with *special gifts* within their cognition." *Genius* lies within seeing things from different perspectives, seeing a need that hasn't been filled, seeing the possibilities and going to multidimensional levels to find the ideas to solve issues. Problems and solutions can cross sciences, evolution tends to be repeated across the sciences, and creative innovations often use effects from outside the field where they were developed.

It is been said that "quantum results require quantum thinking" and humanity must always be looking for social solutions to improve in order to survive and move toward positive human evolution. Humanity has already spent far too much time fixing the identical types of cyclical and perpetual social issues and social calamities leading to chaos, when within it resides the ability to prevent this phenomenon.

Intellectuals solve problems, geniuses prevent them.

—Einstein

There are social solutions available which can prevent the subsistence of chaotic social phenomenon and it is only a matter of finding the fecund people with those solutions. In order to find these people and yield their ideas, people need to open up their minds to all of the possibilities and to also use all of the resources available across the entire social spectrum. But because of the *ego factor*, which exists within all social levels, even the leading experts in a given field will reject the concepts that are offered by novice people outside of their *ring of experts*.

The impact of the human ego is not immune to any social level within humanity. The perplexing thing about this social reality is that the social structures and social systems, which constitute the foundations of societies, rely on these very people to field the social solutions which will evolve humanity. This is the reason why humanity is not evolving. The progress and the forward positive evolution of humanity is being manipulated and controlled by those who have been elevated to social positions of social stature and/or power. As Einstein stated, our technology is exceeding our humanity and this is by the design of those who are in control. Those that are in social control know that if the populous is *educated* that humanity will evolve forward and that their social power and their edge will be eradicated. Because technology has taken over most of the world, the world must be warned about the potentially harmful elements that lie within technology. In the New Testament, Timothy discusses: "Avoiding oppositions of science" (1 Timothy 6:20, KJV). This message states that humanity will be deceived as it moves toward the reliance on science and technology and away from spirituality. The design also excludes the populous and is limited to a select group to control technology and to keep others out of that design loop. The spiritual message was to warn people that when technology so far exceeds their understanding and comprehension that humanity will not be able to evolve because it will be divided into *factions*.

The media and technology are two of the primary social forces that propagate this designed social petrifaction. These social bodies carefully conceive an illusory social conformity that humanity is moving forward, but in reality they are disguising the social reality that humanity is being pitted against each other in order to stall and/or freeze the evolution. The media and technology are influencing people to jettison forward so fast on an individual level that they won't realize and/or recognize the collective social impacts of their social actions. The only way for humanity to evolve forward is to work together on a collective level, and if people do not stop to realize that this ideology is being breached, the collective web of humanity, that has held together the positive energy force within humanity on the continuum, will disintegrate and the energy balance will shift over to the negative side of the continuum. For people to verify this complex concept and highly critical social reality on their own all they have to do is focus on *the high percentage* of individual messages being amplified by the media and technology versus the *minute level* of collective messages. This is all by design. There are people who are working for the collective effort, but the positive forward evolution of humanity is reliant on each individual to do their part as well. Those that are working for humanity continue to implement methods that can assist in the effort to be certain that the positive balance that exist on the continuum remains in place.

Soft systems methodology (SSM) is a concept from another field that understands that the world is an "open, dynamic, and interconnected system, and that breaking down the issues in the *human element* is very difficult" (i.e., social interaction [socialization], politics, individual perspectives, and more). Sociology and the study of socialization are highly complex social dynamics to breakdown because there is almost an infinite level of variables to consider.

Risk analysis is also used in many other sciences, and it can be carried over to the social sciences as well. Risk analysis involves identifying and managing potential problems, the probability of something going wrong, and the negative social consequences which could result. Risk analysis identifies issues and threats, both existing and possible. If people in societies used risk analysis starting within their smallest social ring and then this process was duplicated at every social level forward, this process in itself would elicit a positive social energy flux. Risk analysis doesn't have to remove the *human element* within planning, but preparation and identification can help to prevent chaos at any social level; thus, having a positive impact on the collective. There are many ideas and examples from other sciences and fields to explore which can also be carried over to the social sciences.

The failure mode and effects analysis (FMEA) business model includes steps that can be translated over to the study of socialization. FMEA involves spotting problems before a solution is implemented, risk analysis and cause-effect determination, predicting failures before they occur, looking at details and identifying systematically where the failures/errors are/could occur, measuring the severity (how critical), occurrence (how likely), detection (how easy to detect), and finally altering the design to eliminate or minimize the likelihood of failure. This would parallel with the process of social reform.

The ladder of inference from business entails the process of not jumping to conclusions and dealing with reality and the facts in order to abstract them. At the top of the ladder are actions, beliefs, conclusions, assumptions (which do not fail to consider alternatives), interpreted reality, selected reality, the drawn upon reality and facts (can be reviewed versus mental set and prior experiences). The *vicious circle cycle* involves the impacts when people jump to conclusions, miss facts, skip steps in the ladder process, and narrow their field of judgment. In order to be sure that the results of a measure are pure, people need to gather the true facts and reality, make sure to review each step of the ladder, make sure each step is making sense, ask questions (what and why, etc.), be careful to not sway over to natural tendencies, and not assume.

It is amazing that these concepts were designed and are effective in the business world and other areas, but that many people would rather go by their *ego* and/or their *opinions* within the process of human socialization and within the process of family life guidance. As family life guidance and human socialization are the *roots* within humanity, having flaws at these levels contributes to a negative flux of social energy within the collective continuum. Also whichever method is being used to measure social impacts can use correlative data. Correlations in data can be considered when examining the impacts of socialization. A *positive social correlation* is when the presence of one social factor predicts the presence of another. A *negative social correlation* is when presence of one thing predicts the absence of another. Determining the causal relationships and correlations within social systems helps to gauge when social reform becomes necessary.

One of the single greatest areas of study within sociology is discovering what causes the intense social divide between individual social approaches versus collective social approaches. The individual approach on the surface level seems to drive progress faster than the collective approach, but then humanity must ask itself what *human progress* really is. Is human progress technology and the accumulation of wealth or is human progress cultivating the human resources within humanity and sustaining the earthly resources which we have been given.

> *The greatest virtues are those which are most useful to other people.*
>
> —Aristotle

If the critical social decisions that impact the collective level are made by the few, humanity stands to suffer greatly. Matthew in the New Testament talks about seeking the wealth of the world: "For what is a man profited if he shall gain the whole world, and lose his own soul, or what shall a man given in exchange for his soul" (Matthew 16:26, KJV). Humanity must be cautious in its approach and it must not neglect the messages that it has received. The social divide over the ideology of individualism versus collectivism is something that is intensely debated and is it also strongly divided in opinion amongst individuals.

Opinion is the medium between knowledge and ignorance.

—Plato

Within individualism, the focus is on the success of the individual or an individual society, and the reciprocal benefits as measured by the perceived forward momentum of that society. Within the concept of individualism, society is willing to rely on individual self-regulation and also to try new innovative approaches to solve issues. Proponents of individualism stress that there is no morality without choice and with free will and within individualistic societies, this is very evident. Free will is a component within the design of life, but the media and technology are purveying their own image of what people's life path motives should be. Pure free will involves people reacting to the social stimulus that they encounter in their lives and choosing their corresponding life course. Pure free will does not exist when it is encumbered by excessive, focused, and intentional social bombardment. So, in essence, if people are being led by the media and luminaries to decide on their social life course and to make their life decisions, there is actually an *absence* of pure free will. This social phenomenon is actually a social paradox as the media would lead people to believe that they are running their own lives, but in reality people are being brainwashed by the perpetual bombardment of *alien* social influence. In the New Testament, James outlines the temptations of earthly lusts: "But every man is tempted when he is drawn away of his own lust, and enticed" (James 1:14, KJV). When individual goals do not consider the collective within humanity, this is when the divide infects the health of humanity and spirituality.

Individualism at the most basic social levels within socialization is an integral part of the self-discovery and self-identity process. The factor of individuation and potentially losing self-awareness in a collective group must also be balanced in the social equation. But when individualism is involved within the higher levels of society's super power structures, this is what can lead to chaotic and disastrous social repercussions for society and for humanity. If the collective good of humanity is not considered within the upper social power structures, this can alienate the majority of the people who make up society. Society was originally built up over time primarily with collective efforts of people, and although individuals with social power have helped to transform society over time, the impact of any critical social decisions on the collective good must never be overlooked.

In individualistic societies, people are normally taught to desire more, value living in the moment, people are always on the move, and people are always seeking action and worrying about the future. People in these individualistic societies typically are more aggressive, impulsive, and impatient. They seek public praise, invite competition, seek immediate gratification, possessions are valued, youth is glorified, pride and ego are the focus, a competitive edge is sought, and individual priorities are valued over human relations. The people in individualistic societies are normally very direct, are self promoting, they expect more, and they highly value accomplishments and awards. But one of the major issues within this type of societal approach is social judgment. Social judgments are cast very quickly in individualistic society versus people using the process of trial and error within social judgment. Matthew covers the error in casting judgment within the New Testament: "Judge not, that ye be not judged" (Matthew 7:1, KJV). Using a nonexperiential-based life approach to knowledge is a critical social flaw within interpersonal judgment and communication.

The only source of knowledge is experience.

—Einstein

Collectivist societies are always passively watching, listening, taking the time to rest, reflecting on the past, and visualizing. Humility and quiet recognition are valued versus showing off and holding treasures out for all too see. Any competition in collectivist societies is with self versus others. Other collective values are sharing, respecting elders and their wisdom, patience, universal equality, group security, the indirect personal approach, the use of contemplation, self-abnegation, and promotion of the collective group. Self is the conscious and unconscious aspects, personality, cognition, schemas, and core identity to include ego. The people in collective society's value wanting and needing less and gaining insight and knowledge experientially instead of having the social flaw of making immediate social judgments. Opinions are what lead to social judgment and this is why *unfounded opinions* are so damaging on any social level. Spirituality has a basis in both the growth of individuals and in the value of the collective. If the individual forsakes the collective, this is a flaw; and if the collective restricts the growth of the individual to prohibit free will, this is also a flaw. A strong spiritual foundation and the exploration of a pure conscience allow people to maintain the *proper balance* within these areas.

The collective reciprocal energy that comes from the social chemistry mix within socialization is very powerful and there is an energy continuum that this energy flows into. Forces such as social prejudice which is an attitude, and social discrimination which involves action, can also sway the balance of the social energy continuum. The *first law of thermodynamics* in the field of energy states that energy cannot be created or destroyed and that the sum is constant. This critical concept applies to the social sciences as well. Positive and negative social energy are being exchanged continually within the human dynamic of socialization. Society must maintain a positive balance in its social energy, if the energy continuum is altered and society becomes negative in nature, the effects can be profound as this has been shown over the course of history.

> *The world is a dangerous place to live, not because of the people who do evil, but because of the people who don't do anything about it.*
>
> —Einstein

Negative energy shifts within the societal continuum must be recognized and quelled or the collective social damage could become chaotic and irreparable. Social catharsis is the release of societal aggression, tension, and negative energy. If the impacts of socialization are not monitored closely then this social tension can cause social unrest, and if social catharsis (a healthy release) does not occur and the negative energy continues to build up, this can cause social chaos. If people are not content on a collective level, this effect can also lead to negative social phenomenon, this is why the social energy levels are watched very closely by social scientists. In the environment, the *law of tolerance* involves the maximum and minimum stress limits that an organism can tolerate, which is a direct parallel to human physical and mental needs, which if unmet can lead to a dangerous spillover effect of noxious negative energy into society.

> *Healthy discontent is the prelude to progress.*
>
> —Gandhi

However, the effects of negative social energy shifts have been studied intensely over time and there are several theories which point to the highly critical nature of closely monitoring social energy shifts.

The Chaos Theory is connected with the *butterfly effect*, which states that small differences or changes within a complex system can sometimes drastically alter predictions and outcomes, and can also create large scale phenomena. Edward Lorenz summarized the effect as "when the present determines the future, but the approximate present does not approximately determine the future." Chaos elements and the butterfly effect have been observed in social systems and in many other areas over time within trying to predict social activity patterns. In the chaos continuum, an acceptable error remains small, regular, and stable, while a large error can create *chaos*. Social chaos can be created by ignoring the social variance in the energy fluctuations within the socialization energy continuum. In the New Testament, the butterfly-like effect can be imparted as discussed in Romans: "For as by one man's disobedience many were made sinners, so the obedience of one shall many be made righteous" (Romans 5:19, KJV). This effect is why every individual truly needs to recognize their value within the realm of spirituality. The balance could literally lie within their hands.

Within the study of socialization, one major social phenomenon and social characteristic trend that needs to be watched very closely is referred to as the *dark triad* or *Machiavellianism*. This highly toxic and noxious social characteristic involves social dominance and it is carefully monitored within the social continuum. This social phenomenon personality type and social group uses cunning, deceit, and they are often found to be narcissist and/or have psychopathy. Within the balance of socialization, "the higher the percentage of *Dark Triads* that exist in society, the greater the shift in the overall societal nature will be, and the greater the risk of severe social harm will be posed." The social damage that can be done by this social group can be realized on any social level, and regardless of which social level the damage occurs, it becomes collective damage. This type of social agonist often uses their methods to exert a negative social energy force within their social agenda.

Force always attracts men of low morality.

—Einstein

Unfortunately the media only reinforces the actions of this social group and as people continue to follow the social influences of the media the Dark Triad group is able to *disguise* themselves much more easily within society. There are also many other critical social factors and elements that are studied in society. Societies are built up by the complex process of socialization and all of the components and elements within socialization can impact social systems, society, and the collective humanity.

Within the process of socialization, there are many factors and elements which contribute to the formation of social systems and societies. The social continuum is the balancing mechanism which weighs the impact of the various social factors and elements.

The level of social abnormality in society, which involves social maladaptive patterns which are unusual, are not social norms that are shared by a group or by society, things that disturb others, and whereby the behavior is irrational and makes no sense to the average person is studied and monitored very closely. If these social phenomena are not carefully monitored, the negative social energy set forth could have the potential to create social unrest and potentially social chaos. Unfortunately it is impossible for the social experts to measure the social abnormalities within every social ring within society, so humanity is dependent on the individuals within society to *assist* within this process. But the social conundrum surrounding the need for individuals to assist in the process is that they are not trained to concisely identify the elements that reside within those people who pose a social risk to the collective. Within the New Testament, Romans outlines a mechanism to assist in this area. If people are pure and they are walking the straight path then they are more able to recognize those who are not. Most often, those who have maladaptive social patterns seek the lust of the flesh whether overtly or covertly. "For they that are after the flesh do mind the things of the flesh, but they that are after the spirit are after the things of the spirit" (Romans 8:5, kjv). People building a strong spiritual foundation and walking the straight path can offer humanity many blessings. Being able to identify the *wolves* within the sheepfold is one of those blessings.

Because those with social abnormalities tend to group together and take action together, there are also other social phenomena that tend to occur. *Assorted mating* is another social phenomenon and it is the tendency for people to be in relationships and/or to marry people with similar issues which can lead to and/or can further contribute to their personal and/or social issues. Social mating is one social phenomenon, but along the same premise those in society who have similar personalities and/or who look to defy the social norms in the same fashion will also tend to group together.

> *Acceptance is required for self-esteem and identity therefore people will migrate toward acceptance if it is not elicited toward them.*

> —Maslow

The social elements of acceptance and social migration can transpire in all social levels within the process of socialization. In order to help monitor, balance, and evaluate the social energy continuum social foundations and social institutions were designed and developed over time to help guide and refine humanity.

Social institutions were designed to propagate and influence social norm agreement amongst the populous within the process of socialization. The social institution's primary objective was to gain social accordance and the secondary goal was to regulate the behavior of the people within society. The creation of social institutions was a necessary means to maintain social compliance within a collective social system. These social foundations and their social devices have remained concrete in their social force over time, and they have also become the fabric and social web to which all members of society are ultimately connected to. There are many social elements that impact people during their life course. The process of socialization involves a complete social metamorphosis. Each social level within the process of socialization is a different social cocoon stage. The family social influence in the *primary life social cocoon stage* is typically the most powerful social influence, but its influence can potentially be eroded by other opposing and competing toxic social forces.

School environments, the process of education, and spirituality when present are also very powerful secondary social elements, which can strongly begin to shape people's minds. In addition, peer social forces are highly dynamic social forces and they can either have a positive impact on a person or they can tear away at the foundation that was put in place during the primary life social cocoon stage. Peer groups within the process of socialization are normally a form of social relief for people from their primary cocoon stage of socialization. These peer groups also allow an opportunity for an individual to begin to interpret life and the process of socialization from their own unique and individual perspectives creating the emergence of free will.

Depending on an individual's core innate characteristics and the power of social influence that was cast upon them during their primary life social cocoon stage, peer interaction can dramatically alter a person's life course and their decision-making process. Individuals tend to identify with certain social elements during their life course with magnetic-like social force, and they will gravitate toward those social elements. Also individuals will begin to learn from their own associations and that is why peer influence can be such a powerful and critical social factor in shaping the final outcome of people's personalities. The peer level social interaction stage can alter the primary stage social forces for a period of time, but due to the normally transient and temporary nature of the peer interaction social stage, the social changes may not endure over the entire life course. For most people, the primary level social forces are generally more enduring than other social influences particularly where there is spirituality present and a person can always normally turn back to their primary social influences to reacquire lost social values that may have been eroded by toxic social forces with the support of their primary level social force network.

The process of socialization is very complex and people need to remain focused and positive on their social path. There are both internal and external factors than can inhibit a person's ability to navigate within socialization. Self-fulfilling prophecy is when a person's beliefs influence their actions, which directly leads to their predictions coming true. People need to maintain their value and belief systems, but they need not defeat themselves within the process of socialization. Ephesians within the New Testament discusses wearing the armor of faith for protection in the world: "Put on the whole armour of God, that ye may be saved against the wiles of the devil" (Ephesians 6:11, kjv). If people have a solid spiritual foundation, they possess additional strength to navigate within the process of socialization.

Socialization is the continual process of people breaking down individual social barriers and their acceptance of the social rules and norms that are in place within social elements and social structures. People begin breaking down the social barriers and begin working toward their attainment of a social role and a place in a social system within society. Social norms are the expected behavior in an environment, behavior variance is typically very identifiable, and disorders and antisocial attitudes can create a variance in the social norms continuum. Working against the social norms can have a severe impact on an individual's life course. Social obedience involves people changing their opinions, judgments, and actions due to authority and social norms that are present and not necessarily because of their agreement. There are some people who will adapt well within the process of socialization and there are others who will defy the system of social norms that exist around them.

Socialization is also the continual lifelong process of internalizing and identifying social norms, customs, values, group and societal ideologies, and the mechanisms by which societal continuity and balance are attained. Social values are the deepest level of social elements within any culture and they are engrained into the collective unconscious over the course of time. Social values are reinforced by social mechanisms and devices within societies.

Socialization involves and entails the social processes by which people can be propelled toward desirable social outcomes in the opinion of other people within their social rings and within society. All the social views within social groups and social rings are heavily influenced by the view of the even-more dominant societal superstructure. People can adapt and/or modify their own personal views to match the social norms of society and they can become acceptable (conformity) or they can potentially become social outcasts and/or social deviants by not conforming to the social norms within a society. The majority of people in society conform to the social rules in order to avoid social persecution. But at the same time, there are still many people who will practice their own social agendas within whichever social rings allow them to express their personal attitudes and beliefs. Some people will also often try to extend their personal attitudes from the social rings where they are being allowed to exude their personalities over to other social rings. These individuals are willing to take more social risks than others in society. Although in most modern societies, people are not completely restricted to the social rules in place, and their life courses are not completely predestined by their social environment which allows them to explore their free will existentially. Colossians within the New Testament outlines how increasing ones knowledge in God and walking upright can guide people on their life path: "That ye might walk worthy of the Lord unto all pleasing, being fruitful in every good work, and increasing in knowledge of God" (Colossians 1:10, KJV). Spiritual knowledge can guide people toward *respecting* the needs of others while maintaining their own beliefs and values.

As people continue to interact within their social rings and their social environments, the results of these interpersonal interactions continue to produce a collective social model. This social model that is cultivated over time ultimately determines a systems social norms, social values, and social outcome potentials. Each individual's social actions impact the collective social outcome. Within the socialization process, a person's ability to learn the social norms in a given environment and social culture influences their social acceptance and their ability to be inserted by others into a society's social structure system. A person's genetics, personality, temperament, education, life experiences, level of spirituality, and social environment can strongly impact the process of socialization.

Society and cultures are heavily involved in shaping people's mental perceptions, cognitions, customs, beliefs, values, religion, spirituality, language, and communication styles. These social factors strongly influence and shape an individual's identity and their social reality. *Structuralism* is a social paradigm where the elements of a culture must first be understood in relation to a larger societal structure. Humans interact to create this phenomenon, and intelligible social correlations are formed. A *pure trait theorist* would underestimate the role of the social environment in nurturing and shaping. Within the social sciences, there is now an *undisputed* balance between the forces of nature and nurture. Nature has the power to override nurture at any point, but nurturing has the power to change people. If there is spirituality present within the nurturing process, this can have a dramatic impact on people's life course. The social environment is anything that a person is exposed to in life. Everything that a person is exposed to during their life has some type of impact no matter how minimal, and it is the consolidation of all of these exposures that ultimately creates social force.

The use of words also creates social force and this is a critical area within the process of socialization. The *linguistic relativity theory* states that how words are used and framed impacts what people think within socialization. The element of language is tightly associated within socialization, plays a strong role within socialization, and labels can strongly impact people's perceptions. The framing of a social argument and how a problem is presented can set the social expectations and can heavily influence the social outcome.

Existentialism is the opportunity for individual exploration within socialization by free will and free experiences within life for people to authenticate their own existence. Social cognition involves a person's understanding of the social rules and concepts of social interactions including etiquette, verbal interaction, proximity (proxemics), gestures and motions (kinesics), and any interference between gaining a social understanding. The interference within the understanding of the social reality can create social ambiguity for people.

Social ambiguity can often arise in a person's pursuit of the social reality and higher knowledge. Individuals in society assign social understanding and value in their lives and their decisions are based on social context, meanings, and symbols. Social contextual meanings and symbols are often based off of perception and interpretation versus the use of logic and/or reason. But even logic and reason can sometimes have their own barriers and limitations. When people do not properly identify and perceive the correct social reality, social barriers can be created. Social barriers can inhibit the pursuit of people's personal social freedom. The inhibition of people's personal social freedom and a person's inner desires can create a feeling of restriction within their life and within the course of socialization. The net social energy balance resulting between human drive and social restriction can create a tremendous amount of energy and force.

The *interpretive paradigm* is a person's gradual social self-identification by the interaction with others to establish social structure and their role negotiation within socialization. Everything a person does during their lives has some type of impact. The full impact of a person's actions cannot really be measured at any given point because the consequences of their personal actions are infinite in their nature in the mortal existence and beyond within the realm of spirituality. The *normative paradigm* involves the interpretation of the societal norms that are in place and the expectations of others within a social structure. The first level of investigation within the social paradigm is discovering the procedures in which social situations are defined.

Each individual in life has their own unique abilities and traits that can help them navigate within the socialization process. The concept of *epistemological particularism* involves a person's ability and gift to know something without knowing how one knows that thing and also understanding that one's knowledge is justified before one knows how such a belief could be justified. Although a person may know the answers to a myriad of things in life sometimes with no discovery and/or acquisition being involved, they may face *fierce opposition* from others who simply cannot conceive and/or understand how this could possibly happen. An individual must understand that their abilities may not be accepted by others and that sometimes in life, ideas, knowledge, and innovation can be *repressed* for long periods of time until others are ready to embrace them. Receiving spiritual gifts and messages is discussed in Corinthians within the New Testament: "For one is given by the spirit the words of wisdom, to another the words of knowledge by the same spirit" (Corinthians 12:8, KJV). As discussed prior, people do not receive spiritual gifts on demand or by their idea of right of passage, but rather they are *bestowed* upon people.

Some examples of social and spiritual repression in history were Copernicus, Galileo, and a myriad of philosophers and spiritual leaders throughout all time. Their concepts were repressed for long periods of time by the existing power structures that were in place. This type of constricted oppression of social and spiritual innovation can happen on any social level, in any social ring, within any society, and the impacts can be far reaching upon the collective regardless of which social level they occur within. There are people who will tell others to *play their social role* in life, and this shortsightedness is not always necessarily due to the restrictor's level of intelligence, but instead is most often due to an attack on their social identity and their ego position. Throughout all time, people in lower social roles and social rings have been born with gifts and/or they have had gifts bestowed upon them. And their ideas and messages have been rejected and/or taken by others simply because of the disparity between the social roles within a social system. When this occurs within the realm of spirituality, the repercussions are even more far reaching. This social phenomenon is a perpetual social reality and it is highly repulsive because humanity continues to allow it. In the New Testament, Corinthians discusses how the wise work within their own vanity: "The Lord knoweth the thoughts of the wise, that they are vain" (Corinthians 3:20, KJV). Those who oppose spirituality and/or the growth of humanity will answer for their iniquities.

Many times people can be so vain that they believe their views are universal. *False consensus* is the belief that one's own individual knowledge and views carry over to others. Because of the fact that people in life are all unique in their ability and manner and that there are different individual social polarities that are possible, a wise individual will often have to both find the right time and audience to express their valuable knowledge. Determining the right time and audience can also be challenging. The vain lusts of men for power and control often prohibit the expression of social innovation and the conveyance of divine messages from conduits unto man.

Within the continuous exploration of the socialization process, people will continue to try and figure out the optimal ways to navigate through the complex social negotiation process. The *figure formation process* is how people attempt to manipulate or organize their social environment from time to time. Within the intricate process of social navigation, there is often conflict within decision-making process.

Conflict distinction is what Kurt Lewin (1931) described as social conflict that can create some vacillation, and in some cases, can cause distress in life. Lewin described several types of social conflict. *Approach-approach* conflict is the choice between two gratifications or positive social realities such as choosing from two ideal role paths. *Avoid-avoid* is conflict involving two threats or dangers and is normally a very disturbing conflict such as the choice between two social roles or social choices that are both unappealing. *Approach-avoidance* is a person wanting to obtain a social goal or goals, but fearing the possible negative outcomes, this conflict is often the most difficult to resolve within socialization. Approach-avoidance decisions can involve the choice for people to possibly have to alienate others in their social network (including friends and family) and/or have to separate from people in their social network via their achievements. The line that people have to walk within during the process of socialization between social fear and social confidence can be very delicate and miniscule in nature. Because of the complexities within social navigation, there can be a varied level of social confidence across people. Social preparation and social expectations are two components which play a very strong role in a person's social outcome. In the New Testament, Timothy speaks of enduring as a solider of Christ: "Thou therefore endure hardness, as a good soldier of Jesus Christ" (2 Timothy 2:3, KJV). The only path that is easy is the path of evil and sin. A solider of Christ will not trade their soul within the conflicts of life.

The *social judgment theory* states that all people have their social *anchor* positions within a range on each social or life subject, this anchor is linked to people's mental set/schema, which is part of their identity. The *latitude of acceptance* is social positions which are acceptable along one's continuum on a subject range. The *latitude of rejection* is social positions that are actively opposed by people within their continuum. The *latitude of noncommittal* is when people are not really accepting or denying, which is a social *stalemate*. There are five principles of social judgment and they are the following:

1. There are categories of judgment and an evaluation of the arguments.
2. The categories are used to rate and gauge the level of persuasion.
3. Ego involvement strongly impacts people's *latitudes*.
4. People's own personal persuasion distorts information in order to fit into their latitude.
5. Small changes are adopted, larger changes are rejected, and the choices are typically dependent on the personal social range and the personal anchor of the person involved.

In order to use social judgment in persuasion, a person needs to identify the position of the other person and then stay within their latitude of acceptance. In order for a person to fend off new ideas and defend their own latitude, they need to know their own latitudes and stay within them. Within social judgment, the rule is to always use logic and to explore one's core values before adopting any significant social and/or life change.

The *resistance to change* involves perceiving any signs of a threat, which can be active or passive, overt or covert, by an individual or group, and aggressive or timid in nature. A person must investigate the social drivers behind a social change, which can be beliefs, values, goals, perceptions, potential power, and social triggers. When people are trying to introduce social change to others there will often be gossiping and social testing that will be applied upon any social resistors. These social impacts can impact people and there are a variety of factors that can affect people. People's *biopsychosocial state* is the convergence of their thoughts, perceptions, social pressures, environmental stressors, emotional outlets, core values, and self-worth (identity). The convergence of these factors can help to identify a person's state of health and their level of social welfare. Within the process of socialization, there are many steps that lead up to and contribute to people's overall state of being. One other very powerful element within personal development and socialization is moral reasoning.

Kohlberg developed the *Kohlberg moral reasoning* model which involves social and life scenario judgments. In stage 1 of the model, the *preconventional morality stage*, children's/people's choices involve the considerations of obedience and punishment. Most children/people in life will try to avoid punishment and they will consider how various situations impact themselves which is called *conventional* thought. When people consider how others might view them, this is called *postconventional* thought or moral reasoning. Children and/or people normally progress through the stages in a stepwise and sequential manner via the socialization process. The next is stage 2, the *individualism and exchange stage*, where a child/person does what best serves their own needs. This is an early stage where children/people are still learning about their identity, the socialization process, and their role within it. After this, is stage 3, which is the *interpersonal relations stage*, children/people learn about the social rules, conforming, choices, influences, and personal relations. In this stage, children/people learn about the value of other people and the importance of their decisions that they make in during their life. The next is stage 4, the *maintain social order stage* where most people are looking out for society as a whole and are watching for signs and signals that point to any social abnormalities within society. Stage 5 is the *social contract and individual rights stage* where people consider their impact and the impact of others on social structures and on society. There are some people that do not get past stage 1, let alone get past stage 5 to progress toward the final stage, which is stage 6, the *universal principles stage*, where people begin considering a higher level of justice within humanity even if it conflicts with rules and laws that are established in society. People will *normally* build up their ability to make judgments and decisions over their life course. When spirituality is present, this force tends to increase the strength within the individual development process. Within the New Testament, Peter discusses people suffering for walking the path of faith and while working for the cause of good: "For it is better if the will of God be so, that ye suffer for well doing" (Peter 3:17, KJV). In those people that live in faith and in good conscience, there is an inner fire that burns for the cause of good, which cannot be quelled until good works are rendered upon those in need.

There are various stages of social preparation within the process of socialization that people move through during their life that help to initially mold them. Although depending on an individual's core personality factors occasionally *instinctive drift* influences some people to go back toward their original innate tendencies versus their acquired and learned social behavior from the nurturing process. Depending on the core nature of an individual, this can have a positive or negative social outcome.

In the *primary life social cocoon stage*, children have their core traits, core drives, and cognition sets, which can influence their attitudes and values. Children will normally exhibit social actions that correlate within their appropriate social groups. Within the primary socialization stage, children are mainly influenced by their family, their friends, by spiritual beliefs and values when present, and by the people within their social network. Children rely almost completely on their parents and/or caregivers in the *primary life social cocoon stage* to help prepare them for the future stages of socialization. Children can also be enamored and influenced by others in social circles or in society who have social *appeal*. Social appeal is something than can have a very powerful influence over both children and people in general. People with social appeal can include famous people, those perceived as experts, and also those who are popular, attractive, charming, humorous, highly skilled, and more. It is very important for parents to track the social elements that their children are drawn to. The media tends to create a very strong and profound appeal upon people and particularly the youth, which can potentially be of a negative nature. It is a parent's duty to try and quell the negative social influences, which create confusion and/or harm within the initial life stage. The youth are simply not equipped with the knowledge to evade the social evil, which is *planned* and *designed* to attract them. Parents must guide and direct their children to protect them from evil. One of the best ways for parents to protect their children is for parents to start building a spiritual foundation for their children while also explaining that there is evil in the world in order that their children are not *blindsided* by the negative forces within the process of socialization.

In this early *primary life social cocoon stage* of childhood and nurturing children normally are exposed to a select *control* group of people whom they will imitate and pick up the majority of their habits from *observational learning*. The people who children are surrounded by in their early years are where they get the bulk of their social knowledge and information from. Once the children are exposed to people outside of their original social control group, they will begin to see how others act outside of their original social experiences. While outside of their primary social environment, children will begin to see how other children act, how other adults act, and how adults interact with other children outside of their own original social control group. This social process will begin to perpetuate the idea formation in the children's cognition of social variance between social groups and social experiences.

Some children are *precocious* and they are able to perceive the behavioral differences amongst people at a very early age (advanced perceptual range), but many other children are not able to perceive these differences at an early age. And it is common that another group of children may go without these perception skills deep into their adult life and/or they may also never fully develop a high level of analytical skills or perception skills throughout life (perceptive range deficit). There is a continuum in which both children and people can fall within.

Hypertuned children are precocious and they can be either of a devious or pure core nature. These children have an *advanced perceptual range*, which far exceeds all other children. A hypertuned child has advanced cognitive abilities and they are also well aware of their moral core nature. While a hypertuned pure child will avoid immoral activities, a hypertuned devious child will gravitate toward the area of *moral turpitude*. The hypertuned devious child will normally be much more calculated than any other children that are devious. The hypertuned devious group is the group that is most likely to be *covert* in their actions, and it is also often difficult for untrained people to identify their category and/or their actions. Due to their avoidance of *childhood detection* many of these hypertuned devious children avoid the process of childhood intervention. This group can potentially go on in life to become narcissists that are willing to put their personal gain ahead of the collective good. If there is no intervention in childhood, this group can gravitate to social positions of power and positions, which put them in control of resources and/or money for exploitation. The hypertuned pure child is not a social risk factor, but they are often frustrated because many people dismiss them and/or their level of communication is a barrier for them at this early-life stage.

There are other children that have a *baseline tune*, which fall into the average range of perceptive ability and then there are also the hypotuned children that are *vulnerable to victimization* by both other children and/or adults because their perceptive abilities are far below the normal range. There is one more group which is the *zoned out* devious group. The *zoned out* devious group is the group that floats back and forth between the social reality and they are fully capable of harming other children that are vulnerable to victimization. The *anticipatory socialization* stage during childhood is the children's rehearsal for their future social relationships, and this can include the social modeling methods and techniques applied to the children by their parents, which can include demonstration, visualization, and/or experimentation over potential life situational social outcomes.

Parents and/or caregivers are the primary models of children's future encounters with others in socialization (including with authority figures). If parents do not explain and/or demonstrate to their children that there is more than one type of parenting model within socialization, (especially if their parenting style is *permissive/submissive*) their children may have a very difficult time in their social transition over to other social environments where there are varying levels of authority. There is also very delicate balance of how much information to give children (social blueprinting) and this is why there is so much variance between how different types of children are able to navigate within their lives. When spirituality is present in a child's life, this can help a child to have a better understanding of what behavior is appropriate within social interactions.

Planned socialization is a process that involves a parent's strategies and actions that are designed to train their children for the move and mobilization from the primary socialization level forward. These social actions can have a very profound impact on an individual's personality and on their life path. By creating a very strong primary socialization impact (social impact imprint), planned socialization can potentially offset the potential impacts of future socialization levels, which can typically erode a weak primary foundation. The social plan can be rooted in elements such as safety, education, family legacy, spirituality, and a myriad of other social considerations.

The continuum of child social preparedness ranges from some children being completely unprepared to deal with the existing social reality to the opposite end of the spectrum whereby some children are completely overprepared (social overload). Some children that are overprepared sometimes do not find as much enjoyment within their early social life interactions and/ or they do not do much self exploration within socialization. *Natural socialization* involves the exploratory nature of the young. The allowance for children's own self-discovery of their new environments is very important in their cognitive and social development, so the wisdom is in trying to instill a balance between the imparting of knowledge and the freedom of the children to explore and acquire their own knowledge within the natural socialization process. Children can potentially become bored and disinterested in a dull social environment if too much information (social crystal stimulus overload) is given to them too early.

In a *planned socialization* scheme, the results can vary widely depending on the balance of knowledge imparted, the cognitive range, and the personality traits of the children. The growth of the children can be restricted, impeded, or enhanced, but there is no way to generalize across children. The social parenting scheme of a parent successfully trying to be a *learning agent-social intervention mechanism* can be a very difficult process to measure with any accuracy. The balance between the self-learning social curve of a child and parent intervention is very delicate. Schemed interventions can be planned, continuous, reactive, and also fixed ratio or variable ratio. One of the risks with imparting too much knowledge upon a child is possibly limiting a child's own self-exploration. There are also certain people who intentionally program their children to operate under their designed social code, but this is potentially harmful to humanity on the collective level, particularly if they are programming their children to be social dominators. The more social dominators and the more socially aggressive people that there are within the social continuum, the greater the risk is that the energy balance in society could shift from the positive end of the continuum to the negative end. There is a reason why people are supposed to define their own life path with a certain degree of nurturing within the mix. In John within the New Testament, there is a discussion regarding the ramifications of people choosing the ways of darkness over the ways of the light: "And this is the condemnation, that light is come into the world, and men loved darkness rather than light, because their deeds were evil" (John 3:19, KJV). If social dominators breed their children to move toward the path of darkness, this has a very harmful impact on the positive balance within humanity. The people who work these iniquities should be *marked* accordingly.

If too much parental intervention occurs with children, this can potentially curb the limits on a child's creativity, personality, and spiritual growth. It is very difficult for parents to gauge exactly what kind of impact that they are having on their children because of the primary stage communication barrier, which exists between the adult level and the child level. Free will must be allowed by degree, but not without parental guidance and direction. Guidance and direction provide a child with a strong foundation. Without a strong foundation, a child can stray quickly off a fruitful path. The intention of *free will* is not to leave children to navigate within their course without adjustments. The people who choose to allow their children to navigate freely without a strong foundation are either *ignoring* the importance of guidance or they have *misinterpreted* the intent behind the entanglement of parenting and free will. Unfortunately the effect of parents not providing guidance to their children is often behavioral issues. Although there are some parents who ignore behavioral issues, the consensus is however that if a child is having behavioral issues within the process of socialization that those issues should be confronted and that there is a need for *intervention*. The social impacts of a child's maladaptive behavior patterns that are not modified have been proven historically to have significant impacts on the child (person), others in their social system, and on the collective level as a whole. In the New Testament, Timothy outlines guiding those who oppose themselves within the path of life: "In meekness instructing those that oppose themselves" (2 Timothy 2:25, KJV). So long as the *intent* is good, no parent or guardian should be questioned when they are attempting to *quell* the social impacts of a child or the children that are not growing within their life path and within their spiritual path. Unfortunately this is an area which can create intense friction and deep divides within society and humanity particularly when those without knowledge in the area cast their *narrow* and *uneducated* opinions.

For the hypertuned children who are able to perceive things at an early age on their own, sometimes these skills are a great blessing and other times these skills can be more like a curse. Hypertuned children who possess the ability to perceive and analyze things have an additional burden to endure not only during their childhood, but also throughout their entire lives if the abilities continue to manifest and develop. Most children spend there time thinking about personal social gratification and when they can get more candy or play with their toys and games. But for the hypertuned children with the gift of advanced perception (advanced perceptual range), everything that happens around them is carefully filtered and encoded, and the memories begin to be stored away for later access.

Once the *primary life social cocoon stage* ends, a child emerges from the social *chrysalis* and the *secondary life social cocoon stage* begins. In the secondary stage, a child exhibits behaviors as a member of a smaller group within the larger society. Their social behavior patterns are reinforced by the socializing agents that they are exposed to. This secondary socialization normally takes place outside of the home and children will begin to learn additional and potentially varying knowledge about the appropriate social situational actions and the social norms in life.

The expanded range of social learning at the secondary stage exposes the children to various social situations, and it builds up their social skills in order to begin using them within the correct context of the various social stimuli that are presented within the process of socialization. The secondary stage can be a small adjustment phase for a child, or it can also be a very radical and profound change for them based on their level of primary socialization knowledge, personal cognitive characteristics, personality, beliefs and values, and their level of social exposure. The more *appropriate* that the social exposure level is (of the depth and knowledge that the *primary life social cocoon stage* offered), the easier the transition for the child will be, by making social situations more predictable and allowing an easier social transition. As mentioned prior, it is not possible to define exactly what the *appropriate level* is, but things like parent education and training when paired with an *initiating* parenting style can bring people much closer to meeting with an *appropriate* exposure level. The secondary socialization stage can include social exposures such as school, church functions, activities, and more.

Within the continuing socialization process the hypertuned perceptive and analytical children will gauge the responses of what happens to them when they act a certain way or do certain things. And they will also continually appraise everything that others do and say, and the results will all be carefully monitored and stored for later recall. The advantage that these children have is that they are able to begin reading the other children and adults around them with ease. Hypertuned perceptive children are able to carefully take steps that will benefit them within socialization. The ability of these children to predict the behavior of both children and adults gives these children an important social edge. Normally the children who are highly perceptive are also very intelligent to begin with, so there is a big advantage for the children who are able to tame themselves behaviorally and they can begin to manipulate both children and adults from a very young age when they desire it and/or when they see the need. This process can become beneficial for humanity for the hypertuned pure children, and it can begin to become harmful with the hypertuned devious children.

Nearly all children learn how to manipulate other children and adults to a certain level or degree for rewards which is human nature. But the hypertuned children with a higher level of perception can separate themselves from the other children and create associations that will benefit them to a higher degree. Normally young children will cry, whine, and make sad faces, etc., and see how far they can take things to get a reward. But the hypertuned highly perceptive children can influence and dictate social situations by acting on what they have learned, processed and stored away, and then they can use the knowledge to their social advantage.

Hypertuned perceptive children carefully watch other children and gauge how their actions get punished or rewarded. By monitoring what is happening to the other children around them based on their behavior and their own behavior, perceptive children can systematically eliminate their own behaviors (as required), which were not beneficial and can play off of the other children who continue to behave in a manner which doesn't benefit them. These perceptive children can also manipulate the other children around them and the adults around them in many cases, especially when dealing with nonperceptive or nonanalytical adults. The fact is that everyone is born with a different set of cognitive and instinctual abilities and also with a different range of abilities. There are many skills within the cognitive range that can separate people. Within these cognitive ranges, there are some children who have more genetically inherited and acquired cognitive abilities than some of the adults that are either over their care or within their social system. This can create *cognitive dissonance* and social distortion for the adults who are not running on the same wavelength as the child or children under their care that are hypertuned.

Growing up, children see what is happening outside of their primary stage control group bubble. Children begin to see what the neighborhood kids are doing and how they are acting, and also how the neighborhood adults are behaving and interacting with other adults and the other children. Watching family members that are not in the control bubble also comes into play. Hypertuned highly perceptive children are able to define that people within their own family network typically tend to act a little more like the people in their own home control bubble than the neighbors and/or strangers (exceptions can apply).

The ability of these highly skilled hypertuned children to monitor, gauge, and manipulate people is just one of the skills set that these highly perceptive children will have in most instances. Normally people are born with and develop relatively parallel cognitive systems. Cognitive systems can include intelligence, logic and reasoning, memory, thinking style, perceptive capacity, and more. Hypertuned highly perceptive children also normally have a built-in and advanced pre-wired innate survival mechanism (instinctual sct), which is the ability to know what will get them in trouble or cause them harm without ever being told. Some children are possessed and armed with these pre-wired instincts that from a very early age separate them from many other children. The pre-wired perceptive ability is a fear mechanism. Many hypertuned highly perceptive children are able to understand from a very early age that cars, dangerous objects, animals, insects, etc., social situations, and their proximity to these things could possibly do them great harm. Some children just naturally know to stay away from water, dangerous objects, and also to stay away from certain animals, insects, and even from certain people and social situations. In very select cases, this instinctual activity can be a social phobia versus an intentional act to inhibit action based on instinct.

Some children also cognitively process information very differently from others and this can be either beneficial or harmful. A life example would be two young children riding big wheels down the street and one of the children recklessly skidding into the street off of the sidewalk. One child perceived the danger naturally and held up while the other child was focusing on the innate and primal thrill factor alone. There are other possibilities such as the child who stopped having a restricted range of temperament versus being instinctually advanced, and possibly the child who skidded into the street just not caring about the social outcome and was overriding their instinct in order to receive an adrenaline rush via mental stimulation.

All social scenarios can be measured over time, but for validity, they need to be measured in social clusters versus singular events, which can never be generalized. Processing social situations is just one element that can separate normal children from children with a higher level of perception. The child with the hypertuned advanced perceptive ability also begins to associate risks versus rewards (cost-benefit ratio) at a very early age.

Both the children who have these abilities and the parents who have children with these abilities have their own challenges to face. Some of the advanced children are able to play and interact normally within their own age range level or at least an age range level near their own age, but some end up acting more like an adult. Some of these children also don't interact well with other children, and/or they don't find other children within their age range to be interesting. The challenge for the parents of these children is deciding how much information to expose these advanced hypertuned children to and what type of information to expose them to. Childhood and all of the social choices and possibilities during the dynamic childhood stage are complicated enough without the added element of the constant analysis, which many highly perceptive hypertuned children naturally cannot escape in their life path.

Highly perceptive children begin analyzing every element that occurs within their socialization, every conversation they have, every conversation they hear, and then these children begin to correlate (associate) the information with other information they already have or know. They will then decode the information to see what all of the information means and how it will potentially affect them. In essence, this high level of perception can turn into a form of paranoia in some cases. Some possible ways to keep these forces from controlling and overtaking a young child's life and every thought they emit are through activities. In order to reduce any tension and/or stress that might be associated with fueling these advanced cognitive gifts, these children can get involved in activities that are highly likely to provide them with some relief from the steady and perpetual cycle of analysis that can haunt them if no one is able to see what is happening within them. There are many cases when a child with these abilities and skills is unable to describe exactly what they are dealing with to adults.

Being children can many times have these highly advanced skills at age five or less, it is often very difficult for these children to explain and/or communicate to adults *expressively* what they are dealing with because their external communication ability has not caught up to their internal *receptive processing ability* yet. And because the abilities came naturally to the child, they become systematic and it becomes secondary in nature. Many parents and other adults that come into contact with these highly gifted children simply don't realize what they are dealing with. Many people just think these children are simply bright or advanced for their age. Because there are adults that may never have a higher level of cognitive perception skills themselves (genetics and development), they simply would not be able to identify with these highly gifted children unless they became trained to identify them. The people that come into contact with these hypertuned children within their life path can have a wide variety of social influence on these children.

Most very young children don't come into a social environment and begin to immediately analyze the surroundings, the people in the surroundings, what background people in the surroundings probably come from, what words and what kind of words will likely come out of their mouths based on their appearance, and the aura those people are emitting. Unfortunately most people who come into contact with these highly perceptive hypertuned children do not know what they are dealing with and some of these children are molded to go onto to do negative things during their lives especially if they are *venal* in nature. The hypertuned devious child is the child that is most vulnerable to the temptations within the process of socialization. If the nurturing environment is either a negative social environment and/or uses the relaxed *permissive/submissive* parenting style, these hypertuned devious children can be molded directly and/or indirectly to go onto have maladaptive behavioral issues during their lives.

For the children that are not provided with the proper nurturing direction and guidance, their lives can easily be channeled into a negative social existence. Many skillful children who grow up without the proper guidance can go on to become future scam artist, master social manipulators, social miscreants, and even sociopaths, in whichever environment they fall into. Many of these children are not the type of children who get caught within their actions as they become more calculating with age. And there are also some children with these abilities that will have highly *resilient core personalities*, which can override the impacts of the nurturing process as well. During childhood, their range of manipulation can be very wide. Many of these children can easily manipulate and/or con adults with their *guile* who are unable to see below their surface level behavior and attitudes.

One of the biggest fundamental flaws within humanity is that people do not account for the potential of children to either cause harm as children and/or monitor them for future social violations as adults. A social paradox is that most people go along with certain social elements during their lives and ignore them and then when the same social reality comes back upon them or their family, they expect an *immediate social solution* to the issue. This social phenomenon shows the ignorance that had been bred in this area within society.

If these hypertuned devious children decide that they do not want to behave and/or follow the social norms, they will go to no end to first try and manipulate untrained, naïve, gullible, and/or *permissive-submissive*-style adult types to get what they want, and depending on their level of self-control, they may continually act out because they do not want to be controlled. Depending on the social outcomes from their youth, these children can potentially grow up to be highly manipulative in their personal relations, within their work, and they can also get into high-ranking social positions where they can impact the social masses on a financial, social, spiritual, and/or political level.

Depending on the combined characteristics of a child, they may potentially become a narcissist and/or sociopath if early intervention and the appropriate nurturing adjustments do not occur. These negative social scenarios are things that can potentially occur within early childhood socialization. If these matters are not handled and identified early within the socialization process, the collective harm can be potentially infinite. Although changes can occur in a person later in their life, people do not have a sudden *social metamorphosis* once they become and adult. The *intent* behind the behavior is always part of a person's core nature at any age.

Many of these hypertuned children do not *fully* realize what they have until they get old enough to know that it takes one to know one…*literally*. Normally social manipulators and social cons can identify one another very quickly and/or they can recognize other people who are highly analytical and who knows what they are up to. A highly analytical person can normally easily identify social manipulators. Some of the major factors in how these hypertuned children will socially develop within society are whether the children with these skillful gifts have a naturally built-in self-conscious and moral set, a spiritual foundation, a stable temperament, a stable personality (the nature element), and if the people around them during their childhoods reinforced good values systems and the proper parenting style (the nurture element). To reiterate the *permissive/submissive* parenting style is the *worst* parenting style according to all modern sociology and psychology models and therapies and for a very good reason. People not intervening in maladaptive childhood behavior can be disruptive to everyone within society.

> *Knowledge becomes evil if the aim is not virtuous.*
>
> —Plato (BC)

If society could train more adults to be able to understand these highly skilled children and their abilities, the power of positive reinforcement could be incredible. And if more adults became skilled in recognizing these children at early ages, many of these children could get help (if required) in order to be sure that their minds would not be constantly spinning out of control with constant analysis, and sometimes even social paranoia. Identifying these children, providing the proper guidance for them, and getting them help if their minds are spinning out of control at an early age is crucial. Imagine some of these hypertuned children constantly analyzing in-depth everything that was seen and heard from around age three to five into their later teen years, constantly, with no real knowledge of why their minds acted this way (without intervention) and/or that they are not alone in the world and there are others that have the same type of issues.

The mind of a child isn't the easiest thing to analyze, most often because their ability to communicate expressively is nowhere near the high level of early functioning that is taking place in the children receptively and internally on a cognitive level. Intelligence is something can be measured on many different levels, but *perception* is something that is much more difficult to measure, especially in young children, than math, language, reading, and other areas. When a young child sees something at age three to five and is analyzing not only that they see something that doesn't look right, but they are also analyzing why they are there, what the people around them are doing and saying, and if these people around them have enough knowledge to protect them from the situation, and if these people don't protect them from the situation, what will happen either now or in the future because of it. If the advanced thinking and social skills of these children could be properly identified and channeled then not only would the child benefit, but society could potentially reap the collective benefits as well.

These early-life complex social insights are the type of thoughts that a highly perceptive hypertuned child has internally, but many times that they simply can't expressively communicate. And unfortunately many adults are or would be unable to understand these children even if their communication level was better due to the adult's lack of training and insight in the area. Many adults also simply dismiss what children are saying because of their age. Other children typically trust those around them and don't have the built-in ability to analyze on their own, and some of these nonperceptive children will never acquire the ability to perceive negative and dangerous people and/or situations, even as adults (social danger perception). The group at the highest social risk level is the hypotuned group who are the most vulnerable to victimization.

Some of the only ways to find out what is going on in a child's mind is to observe what the child does or says, and how they interact with people. Many adults and parents will stop at a minimum level of effort and either will not take the time to dig deeper, or they are not advanced enough to recognize what is occurring. Some parents also simply ignore issues for whichever reason. Many different people have many different gifts in life, and as mentioned above, the gift of perception is not the easiest to recognize especially in children.

Some hypertuned children at a very early age can feel the negative aura energy coming off people and/or can look at certain people and see through their eyes (the eyes are the window to the soul) and know that there is something wrong with those people, at the same time are wondering why the adults around them are not protecting them from these people. It is common unfortunately that people will potentially sacrifice the safety and security of their children blindly for either need or desperation, and expose their children to the social and life consequences. An adult should do *thorough research* before leaving their child with anyone. Even with all of the historical examples that have transpired over time, many people still ignore these social truths and life realities in exchange for *social convenience*. An adult should never sacrifice a child's safety for anything and there are some adults who do this daily, and then they act like they were not at fault when something terrible happens (denial). The social coping mechanism of denial cannot salvage innocence lost or damaged. Some adults will never develop perceptive skills, which can be a cognitive limitation (genetic), but many others will simply turn a blind eye to danger for their own convenience at the expense of their children. These people are perpetuating this human social flaw by *sending the lambs to the wolves*.

There are also some very young hypertuned devious children who are highly intelligent, highly manipulative, and who will go after other young children because they pose the lowest risk to them and they are easy targets. These children are the *social aggressors* and their victims are *vulnerable to victimization*. As people innately all have the drives of aggression and libido (even at very young ages), just because the person is a child doesn't mean that they are not capable of doing harm to others at very early ages. The first group of people that these devious children will go after is the other children that are younger than them within their own home because they provide the *easiest access*.

Regardless of the social reality, many people will still say things like "but they're just a child," and they will feel sorry for a child with maladaptive behavioral patterns instead of intervening to help the child with the behavioral issues and protect other future victims. The way to help the child is to *intervene* and it is not by *ignoring* and/or *pacifying* them. *Permissive-submissive* parents and/or people are famous for ignoring maladaptive child behaviors. Their parenting style only works on children who have a *pure*-core nature. By people not intervening, not only is the child with the maladaptive behavior continuing to stall within their development, but other innocent children are being *victimized*. This terrible social cycle of victimization could be systematically broken if people would cast aside their faulty social beliefs and their narrow and shallow opinions which breed social ignorance.

There are child aggressors and there are children that are vulnerable to victimization. Personal *core characteristics* exist from birth; they do not just start once someone turns eighteen. This is a common excuse of people who ignore child behavior issues and their primary fallacy is that they claim that, "they're just a kid." This contorted social fallacy and thinking error cost both people and society. Many adults ignore these early childhood possibilities and some even encourage interactions between the children who have the major behavioral issues (the social aggressors) and other children (those who are vulnerable to victimization) in order for the child with the behavioral issues to *work through their issues*, which is exposing *innocent* children and society to potential harm. This completely flawed, ignorant, and irresponsible adult social behavior leads too many people in life being harmed and it perpetuates collective negative social impacts, which can harm people individually and society collectively.

Some children at very early ages understand that the adults that surround them are their guardians, but that their guardians will sometimes do things that expose them to things that are not safe or right. In some cases because their guardians feel sorry for people and/or that they do not want to offend their family or friends, children will then be exposed to negative and dangerous social situations. As an example, two young children are brought over to a relative's house by their mother to go swimming. There is other children playing in a filthy, dirty pool, thoughtlessly. The two highly perceptive children know that this social situation isn't right, but they also can sense that their mother doesn't want to hurt the relatives' feelings who his having the pool party. The two children are told to get in the pool by their mother who forces the children to go swimming. While looking at the pool before getting in, the highly perceptive children at very early ages were thinking about what the dirty water could do to them now and that swimming in the water could also cause something bad to happen later, without being explained. These types of social scenarios occur all the time within the process of socialization. Children are exposed to risks frequently. When people put their children in dangerous social scenarios at very young ages, they must realize that many young children do not have the cognitive range to fully assess the impacts.

The fact is that many people do not realize that there are children at very early ages with the advanced hypertuned mental functions of some adults. Because of this, many children do not get the proper guidance and/or intervention that they need, due to being surrounded by adults who are either unable to recognize the children's abilities and/or who ignore the signs of their abilities. This social flaw within humanity is something that can be repaired with the correct amount of *social inertia*, but people cannot continue to procrastinate if they want to change it. The next stage of childhood social development exposes children to an even more diverse level of information and people, which if negatively channeled can also be very threatening to society as a whole.

In group socialization, peer influence has a great deal of power, especially if primary socialization was not both concrete in foundation and abstract in preparation. Children's personalities can be heavily influenced within peer groups. Peer groups are critical during the developmental years of childhood and adolescence, they are more profound if the primary family group is not supportive, and peer groups are many times joined for mere acceptance. Negative peer groups often have lower demands and standards for acceptance, which can attract those who are having issues within peer bonding. Some peer groups can discriminate by any difference they perceive and can exclude people. Peer groups are an important social opportunity for an individual to experiment within their identity and develop their social role. The process of peer interaction and bonding can also have a very devastating impact on those that are rejected. Social rejection can potentially lead to long-term social issues. This is why it is highly important for a parent or guardian to ensure that they are *closely monitoring* the childhood socialization process. Parents do not need to know every detail involved, but they must be able to feel *the pulse* of the impact upon their child.

Social institutions such as schools have a genuine opportunity to intercede into the process of early childhood socialization, with the reinforcement of social norms and rules, teaching of human interaction and empathy training skills, and reinforcement of prosocial skills training and development. The educational system also has social exposure ramifications from the interaction of children with peer groups within the system. The social impingement created within the process of socialization within the educational system can vary widely depending on the individual child's core personality strength, their internalized nurturing phase value system extending from their primary social group, and the dynamic social situational context, which occur within a social peer group. The interaction of children within peer socialization can have a myriad of varying social impacts and outcomes.

Positive social interaction within the process of socialization can include the social elements of bonding, idea exchange, social euphoria, love, motivation, etc., and these types of positive social interactions can help to further enhance the strength of the mental constructs in children and also to improve their cognitive development. *Negative social interaction* within the process of socialization can include isolation, doubt, contempt, anger, distain, social plotting, and much more. The *net social energy balance* resulting from the social interaction ratio between the positive and negative social collisions can heavily dictate and influence social outcomes. The mental construct and/or the psyche of a person can be altered, impaired, and sometimes can sustain interminable dysfunction if the net social energy yield is not properly balanced. A person's *mental construct* and their internal *core resiliency* are major factors in mentally processing and weighing in this net social balance, which is critical to social outcomes. Once a child passes through the initial life cocoon stages of socialization and they shed their final early-life stage cocoon, they are then fully exposed to the *social reality* stage.

In the *social reality* life stage, which occurs after the antecedent childhood life stage, all the people that pass through a person's life path are social players in their life course and within the game of life. In the complex and dynamic process of socialization, social life outcomes and social values are determined in part by everyone that a person encounters during their life path. Each social player that a person encounters in their life path is a piece of the social puzzle within the grand scheme of their life, regardless of the level of social impact. Within the intricate process of social perception and interpretation, it is possible that within the almost infinite amount of social interactions that occur in the life path that some point will occur where there will be certain social stimulus that will be missed and/or miscalculated, which can have a varying degree of social impacts. In addition, the *veil of social comfort* that may have existed in a person's life during the childhood stage is frequently removed from most people once they reach the stage of social reality. Also, most people are protected by a veil of social comfort during the initial stages of life in order to offset the toxic and noxious elements that exist within the social reality stage. This veil of social comfort was designed to allow for the promotion of more *unencumbered* growth and development in the early-life stages. When people are exposed to a higher level of the noxious elements from the social reality in their early-life stages, this exposes these people to the social contagions before their core resiliency and their other social defense mechanisms have been allowed to solidify.

The process of socialization is the highly complex and dynamic life game of people forming their personal identities and seeking their social roles within social systems and within the overall social superstructure. Within the process of socialization, the alienation and forsaking of other people that were parts of a person's prior social stages can occur (which could include people's friends and family members). The social alienation and/or forsaking of people that can occur within the process of socialization are often a requirement for a person's passage and forward social progress. Sometimes these complicated social measures are calculated as necessary by the individual and they will make preemptive social adjustments, and there are other times where people are given social ultimatums as a social contingency for their social elevation. Another area which can be sacrificed within the process of socialization is spirituality. A person should be very *cautious* when trading social positions for their core spiritual beliefs and values as the impacts are potentially very far reaching. Ephesians within the New Testament talks about walking upright and reproving evil versus being drawn over into its lusts: "Have no fellowship with the unfruitful works of darkness, but rather reprove them" (Ephesians 5:11, KJV).

The social reality is the net measure from the social outcomes that are yielded from the continuous flux within the social exchange process and along the social continuum. The social energy yielded from social outcomes is registered at the individual social level in order for people to gauge their own social position and it is also realized amongst all of the other people within the social rings and social systems that are involved. The social reality is a social metamorphosis from which the social energy is always modifying, evolving, growing, and the dynamics within the social reality are continually being designated and categorized. The social reality is only navigated and understood through the use of social tools and mechanisms. There are social cues, meanings, signs and symbols, which are some of the tools that can help guide people within their life path toward social truths and realities.

The social reality involves people trying to understand how to assign the various social applications and categorizations that they experience during the process of socialization, which is a highly complex social process. Within the process, people assign social tags and social labels to the various social elements that exist within social systems. How a person is labeled within this process is a critical social factor for each person. People's individual interpretation of the complex and dynamic social tendencies, social rules and norms, complex social communications, and the actions of the other people within their socialization web must all be carefully analyzed and scrutinized.

Ultimately each person forms their own individual social exchange tendencies. Based on these social tendencies, each social encounter that people have can begin to modify their existing interpretation and their perception of their own social reality. Each life event and each social exchange in a person's life path creates a social ripple, which cannot be easily gauged and/

or predicted for consequence, as the social impacts are infinite in their social affect. In addition, each person must choose their life path very carefully as the process of socialization has many idiosyncratic social traps and social deterrents that can oppose people. These social traps can be traps that anyone can fall into because of the traps' social prevalence, or the social traps can be specifically set up and targeted toward a person or group. Social dominators and social wolves are the perpetrators behind the social traps, which target people on a specific level. When the social combination exist where a person is a *social novice* in the social reality stage and they are attempting to invade into its deeper levels, this will often result in that person falling into a social trap. Social ambition commonly leads to social errors, and as people gather more life experience in reading the social cues, they can become more adept in avoiding these social traps and social pitfalls.

In order for people to sustain a balanced social equilibrium within the dynamic social structure and also create a recognizable social foundation, which can be understood by all of those within a social system and society, certain factors are required. Each social ring, system, and society develops social elements, structures, and foundations in order to elicit the social cycle. Some of the necessary and key social elements that are present and which are established in the process of socialization are social factors such as *social norms, social rules of conduct, social roles,* and systems of *social language and communicative behavior.* Within the complex process of socialization, many people are embattled to find their way along their social path. When people meet with social dissidence and friction within their life path, this can potentially have a massive impact on their personal identity formation and/or in finding the meaning in their lives. People's individual interpretation, perception, understanding, and realization of their place within their social ring, social structure, within society, and within societies corresponding superpowered structures, can help them to stabilize their potential for self-discovery. People can begin to move toward their own self-discovery and their social potential by finding their place within the social *dominance hierarchies* that exist within each social level.

Social dominance hierarchies are the social pecking orders that are formed and established within the process of socialization. People will maneuver in many different ways based on many different internal and external factors in order to establish their own social roles within the social hierarchy. There are many covariant social factors, which can impact people's social paths and their social designation within the social hierarchy.

There are many social factors, which can play a pivotal role in the socialization process, and both the media and technology are potentially noxious social elements that can undermine the innate human need for people to interpret and navigate their own way within the social reality stage. The media and technology can *distort* the realization of a person's role or status within society by altering the course of the innate human drive and need for self-exploration and self-discovery. When the social elements of the media and/or technology are leading people and/or brainwashing them toward the social construction of what their identity should be, this social action is destroying and undermining an innate human mechanism, which is critical for individual development through free will and also for the sustaining of the core nature of humanity. In the New Testament, Matthew outlines how Jesus warned his apostles of the evil that they would face within their work. When young novices or the *sheep* are sent out into the world, they will come across these wolves also. The wolves can come by many colors and designs, but regardless of their appearances, their work is all the same and that is the work of iniquity: "Behold I send you forth as sheep in the midst of wolves, be ye therefore wise as serpents and harmless as doves" (Matthew 10:16, KJV). Because many people are so fixated on their personal quest for freedom and independence, they do not see the evil that is behind the curtain.

The impact of the media and technology has not yet breached into the inner level of most people's or societies core humanity, but these elements are continually eroding the *outer-protective limits*. Most people in life still possess their social boundaries and their core-invasion limitations, but these social elements are slowly breaking down these human barriers. The design of these social elements is to erode these essential human barriers over time versus using a brute force social attack, which would be blatantly obvious to people in today's more-evolved society. The nefarious design of the media is to make people believe that they are making their own social choices and this formula has been especially effective at the lower levels within the social continuum and it is also exacerbated by the influence of the upper class, which also drives people toward conformity to nourish their own social continuance. These social entities want people to sacrifice their personal beliefs and values for the chance of social elevation, but they do not offer the warnings that go along with this level of sacrifice. When people sacrifice their cores, they are making the ultimate life sacrifice. An increasing number of people over time are willing to risk their cores and to roll their *dice of life* in order to reach a life apex that few people can actually attain. If this social illusion, which is created by these elements by *dangling* desire, is sustained by humanity over the course of time, it will result in the destruction of humanity.

> *It has been appallingly obvious that our technology has exceeded our humanity.*
>
> —Einstein

The media and technology can rise up and they can interfere with this necessary and delicate life process of discovery, and they can also suffocate and reduce this innate human drive for free will by creating social ambiguity. Social ambiguity is a threatening social factor that can sometimes occur within and between the interpretation and perception of the various social elements that are woven into the social norms, the lie within social systems. The social ambiguity nemesis can potentially create unique behavior amongst the people within the socialization process.

These random and unique social behaviors, which are perpetuated by the influencing forces of the media and technology, are atypical and they will be interpreted, adjusted, and socially tagged within the already-existing system of social norms. The social consensus amongst the people in a social ring is required within the process of socialization and their agreement on a social consensus defines the social reality. The social reality consists of social norms and the social structure within a social system. This is why the ambiguous effects of the media and technology can be so profound. The media and technology can potentially modify human behavior with lighting quickness when compared to the normal curve of social evolutionary mechanisms. Even though the design of these entities is to create a social affect over time, they have instigated a social force that has changed humanity more in the last one hundred years than in all combinations of time in the past. The time is *now* to preserve the positive balance of energy that exist within humanity, and this can be accomplished by building back up the positive core value systems across people, and, in addition, sharing the gift and knowledge of the path of spirituality. People can not continue to procrastinate in this area as the *beast* is working twice as fast in the opposite direction.

But regardless of the sources of social influence, that are cast upon society and their force, people can still modify their own behaviors within socialization in order to try and reach their desired social outcomes. Free will does not involve people being completely led by a source such as the media, a false spiritual leader, a luminary, and/or technology, and people with a strong inner core and the desire to preserve humanity can endure. If people believe that they are truly living freely and existentially by following everything that the media and/or other sources tells them to do, then they are mistaken, for they are nearly *conforming* to the influences of the media and other negative roots. The media and its agents and elements depend on people's conformity for their own prosperity. These entities carefully *study* human behavior and they project their findings upon society to elicit their desired response. But people can *combat* the flawed forces of these social entities by conversely studying them carefully, marking them, and determining their own social response. In the New Testament, John talks about avoiding the lusts of the world: "For all that is in the world, the lust of the flesh, and the lust of the eyes, and the pride of life, is not of the father, but is of the world" (John 2:16, KJV). Regardless of a person's level of spiritual knowledge, logic and reasoning should be enough for a person to see that the world would be a wicked place to live if the forces of evil were able to sway the balance of the continuum of humanity.

People can govern their own social activity within their future social encounters based on the associations that were formed from their previous social encounters. People systematically harvest all of their past social events in their lives and these events are encoded into their cognition. People's social roles and their social statuses in the social hierarchy are determined within the social encounter system amongst the other people in their social systems. As people become more familiar with each other within social encounters, their social behavior will normally change and it can include and/or incorporate more casual, unique and more atypical behavior. When most people first meet others and engage into a social exchange, they are normally more reserved to a degree although there are always social exceptions. More complex people typically engage others in a more *stepwise* social fashion over time to protect more guarded and sensitive personal information. But there are some people who immediately divulge all of their personal information and their entire social repertoire within their first social engagement, but this type of social action can be very harmful within the process of socialization because other people can use that information as social ammunition against that person later. Also it is common for social information to be exchanged in the form of gossip that can also impact the course of people within their life course. People's social status, their roles, and their invitation to future social events can be obstructed by their inability to issue information in stepwise social stages. As social encounters occur with more frequency and exposure over the course of time, the social tendencies of the more complex people will shift and their information will be more freely exchanged.

The initial social encounters that transpire between more complex people within socialization can often be highly superficial and their initial interpretations can be based solely on their cognitions, which were formed from prior social encounters and social events with other people that have primed them to recognize social cues and identifiers over time. People's individual social perceptions and cognitions can have a very commanding influence on their life course and within the social exchange system as their cognitions can strongly dictate their interactions and social actions with other people. Social factors such as the appearances, auras, and the perceived backgrounds of the other people in a social exchange system are measured. These social measurements can be formulated into highly concrete personal perceptions within people's cognition and these perceptions can also be carried over into the very roots of the social system.

Within initial social encounters, more complex people typically confine themselves to the most basic level of communication, which resides within the preestablished social exchange norms. Complex people will normally always hold themselves back in social exchanges in order to follow the social design of the social interaction continuum. If the predefined social rules of the initial social encounters are not complied with, a person or people may be overtly or covertly removed from a potential role or roles within a social ring or structure hierarchy. The social deviation by people away from the social norms within social exchanges along the predefined continuum can lead to their expulsion from a social ring and also their exclusion from future social interactions within a social ring structure. The establishment of these social rules and guidelines allows people with social experience to gauge how adept the others that they encounter are within the social reality stage. This system allows the social dominator control group of people within a social ring, social system, social structure, and/or society to determine the placement of all other people within the system into categories. There are a very select group of people within each social ring level who choose which other people will be elevated. There are occasions where certain people will avoid social exclusion and/or elimination based on a layer of *secondary social factors* (which will be discussed later).

Social interactions can elicit many different cognitive associations depending on a wide variety of factors, which can include the physical traits of the other people, their language and communication styles, and much more. Preconceived and often fixed cognitive expectations are formulated at each stage of the social interaction process, which is part of social preparation. People who are equipped with a high level of self-monitoring capacity and metacognition capabilities are often able to anticipate what is required of them within social interactions much more easily than those who do not possess these highly evolved social mechanisms. These social mechanisms are critical tools within the social preparation process. Those who are not adequately prepared for the social reality stage and/or who try to move forward too quickly within it will fall into social traps and will be expelled from certain social considerations.

People must be socially advanced and be able to perform well over time in the stepwise and sequential evolution of social interactions in order to receive their desired social acceptance from others. Social acceptance into a social ring and/or into a social structure can be withheld from people who are not perceived as being acceptable to fit within the advancing socialization process.

Social elevation is a highly contentious process within the complex social maze of socialization. Social passage and elevation within social rings can be highly contested affairs especially if people seek to elevate into higher social rings. *Secondary social factors* such as a person's personality and their temperament are some other critical factors in the socialization process and they can sometimes compensate for other social deficits that a person may have within their social exchange repertoire. On occasion, a strong and desirable personality can overcome other social deficits in a person's social knowledge base, and they can be elevated within a social ring or system. There are additional *secondary social factors* (which will be discussed later).

Within the process, once a person realizes that they are being perceived as acceptable within a social interaction, they can begin to develop a strategy for gaining even more information within the social exchange. Via cognitive skills and/or with social priming complex, people will realize when they are *in*. By being perceived as acceptable by the others in a social ring, a person can much more easily begin to interpret and establish their social identity or role within the social structure. After a person realizes that they are *in*, this takes some of the social performance pressure off of them and they can then shift some of the energy that they were using to get *in* over to other cognitive systems. Once accepted by a social group, a person's identity and role within a ring or structure can begin to be refined over time and also certain elements of the person's identity can be either expressed or withheld (self-regulation) depending on nature of their future social encounters and exchanges. During the social personal identity formation process, each person within the social exchange system is also setting up and modifying their personal expectations of the others within the social structure. The energy within the system is always constant and only the people, who are able to maintain their adequate balance of social inputs and outputs, will endure within the system. The social exchange system and process requires continual social inputs and outputs from those within the social system. Regardless of a person's social role or status, one poor social exchange moment can literally impede and/or reverse a person's forward social momentum. It is critical for people to maintain their social energy and equilibrium.

An individual person's initial and continued accurate interpretation and perception of the collective social meaning system within the social structure can be a very difficult task to perform and maintain. In order for people to properly prepare and compensate for the changes, which occur within the complex system, they must always assume that their social opponents are ahead of them, and this will inspire them to stay socially prepared and hungry. Once a person becomes comfortable at any social level in the process of socialization, within the social reality stage, this personal comfort can lead to a social weakness that can be identified and later exploited by other ravenous people within a social ring or system. A person's efforts in trying to interpret the innate cognitive processes and intentions within each individual within a social system can potentially be very difficult and often a precarious task within social interactions. Each individual social interaction and each relationship amongst the people in a social system can be highly unique within the delicate social exchange system and this is why people can never stop preparing for social exchanges. In addition, social control must always be maintained or a person can potentially be expelled from a social ring or system at any point. There are also people who are operating within a social system that are using a system of smoke and mirrors within their social path. It is common that some people who do not possess the social skills and/or social talent that is required to elevate within a social system to use socially manipulative elements to ascend within the system. A *social façade* is one of the tactics that some people will use in order to try and elevate within a social system.

If a person is putting on a complete social façade, not only is the social facade likely to be detected at some point by other skilled people, but the person purveying the behavior is also creating a tremendous amount of social stress to combat just within themselves. Within the continual cyclical socialization process, which runs along an energy continuum, energy is a personal commodity that is continually required to maintain a social edge. When a person is putting on an act, they will eventually expire over time because their energy stores will not be able to offset the scrutiny of those who can sense the act. The act is a social diversion, not a social edge, as the act will lead to a social fall, but the edge will lead toward continued social elevation. *Social faking* or putting on a social façade includes people attaining social roles by dress, by false experiences and credentials, false associations, etc., in order to increase their social credibility, and being too persistently boastful is often what gives the social façade act away and a person can be destroyed socially due to putting on a social façade. There are also other social techniques that are used by those who lack the raw potential to elevate naturally.

Social flattery is also a social tool that *social yes people* (those who agree with social dominators regardless of the social impacts), *social coattails* (those who go as far as social dominators will take them), *social weasels* (those who survive only by providing social dominators with information regardless of the social cost), and any other scheming social climbers will use in their social exchanges to try and elevate by being ingratiating. These social fallacies will incorporate the social techniques of complimenting, listening attentively, and giving off body positive body language to others. Social flattery can be used by yes people and other deceptive type people with ease, but if a person that is not skilled in the area tries to use flattery, they are easily discovered because the social effect is very flat and not symmetrical. Those adept at using flattery will continually try to increase a social bond, improve their social status, and strengthen their identity. The core problem with all of these *manufactured scheming techniques* is that the tools are creating a *false identity* in these people and if a point comes along within socialization where the tools no longer work, the person employing the methods will be socially and personally crushed because they have no *true* identity strength. Social dominators know this social reality and they do not care, because they can continually just *reload* with new people who are willing to continue the cycle.

Social identity masks can protect a person, they can facilitate social interaction, they can hide anxiety behind the mask, and the mask can allow for social security and social power. Because many people are highly aware of their own social shortcomings, often when their social mask is removed, their true self identity is still not found, but rather another social mask layer is revealed (another false self-identity). Within their identity or their identities, people create social coping mechanisms and defense mechanisms to protect themselves versus their internal fear of being cast out of a social group. Social identity masks are developed by those people who prepare for the process of socialization, but that see themselves as not being socially relevant. Depending on an individual's ability to interpret their social reality accurately, the identity mask may be a better alternative to some than using the other scheming mechanisms, which erode people's core nature and their humanity away over time. Within people's identity, there are needs such as social belonging, self-esteem, fair treatment from others, and social approval. Different people will employ different types of social tactics in order to meet these critical internal demands.

The context of all of the social interactions within a social system are continually being analyzed by all the people in a social system, and this continually both creates and modifies the existing social order, social roles, and social structure. The social roles and social statuses of the people within a social structure are determined by the reactions of the other people to the stimuli, which each individual person presents within the social exchanges. The process of social analysis is continuous and the social decisions are determined when the social data reaches the social dominators who reside within each social ring and social system. Within the process of people establishing a social role or status, their level of social exchange is quantified amongst the entire social pool and the more dominant people in the social system rise to the top, which is where social categorization and labeling occurs. This is the social juncture within the social reality stage where the social power continuum is established amongst the social groups, within the social system, and whereby social order is formulated. Social rings, social systems, and societies could not operate with *fluidity* and *order* without the establishment of social order. Authority is of *paramount importance* and it is normally only the *type* of authority that is debated within social systems.

Some of the people within the social system will have in place already or will develop highly refined abilities to perceive what can generate them a higher social status and also more social influence within a social structure. Duplicity is another scheming social technique that can come naturally to a person or it can be developed, but in turn, duplicity can also be recognized by other experienced people through social interactions. Recognizing the abilities and the aura of other people can come about naturally within a person and the skills also can also be developed through priming in social exchanges within the social system. However, people that manifest these skills innately will always have a *social edge* in the area so long as they stay tuned into the social reality.

Some people will take advantage of others, by playing on multiple angles via duplicity within the social system. And occasionally people who possess these advanced social skills encounter others in social exchanges that also have these duplicity abilities. It can be very difficult for people to interpret these types of social exchanges. The ability for people to determine if this type of social exchange was legitimate or not or whether both people were just scheming is difficult for people to conclude with certainty. Social dominators will often employ these techniques if they possess them. These techniques are most dangerous within social rings and systems when social wolves employ them because social wolves typically leave *social peril* behind in their social wake. The social wolves will identify the social marks and they will exploit them. Social marks are the people within a social ring or social systems, which are not equipped to identify those, would exploit or attack them or those around them. James within the New Testament covers duplicity: "A doubled minded man is unstable in all ways" (James 1:8, KJV). The difference between the negative element and positive element is that the negative element works feverishly on their craft, while the positive element often loses track of the fact that the same social games and agendas have been played upon since the beginning of time. The negative element marks those that are good, that are not willing to seek after the lusts of the world, while the positive element fails to *mark* the wicked with the same ferocity.

When trying to interpret the myriad of stimuli that is presented within a social system, a person must use reasoning and logic to integrate the stimuli and form adequate perceptions. Trying to determine what logic the other people are using can be very difficult. In the reasoning process, there are differing elements that can be used to try and estimate a person's social intentions. Inductive reasoning derives conceptions from specific examples. Deductive reasoning is the process of reasoning from general statements to reach a logical conclusion. Deductive reasoning is a skill that develops without any training, although encoding and integrating the stimuli can be very complex.

A person must be able to recognize, learn, and determine which social skills to use in a particular social exchange. People must be able to recognize what standards are appropriate and adequate in a particular social setting. A person must try and carefully shape the impression that they are forming with others in an exchange.

Over time, a person will consolidate and build up their social methods for getting through more complex social scenarios, and they will also develop more advanced coping skills. Regardless of a person's level of social expertise, everyone develops their own set of coping skills as the process of socialization does inherently include an element of stress.

When people enter into social exchanges, they often are seeking to gather more information. They are also using their prior knowledge to link and condense all of their prior acquired information together. Understanding the verbal and nonverbal cues given off by other people is a social mechanism that allows for further growth and the additional value of people within a social system. People will mentally prepare themselves by anticipating their future social encounters, and they will develop a preconceived idea of the intentions of others. Social preparation can potentially help to keep people ahead of their social competition and away from the clutches of social dominators and social wolves. By playing out social encounters in advance (visualization), people can *prepare* for their critical reactions within social interactions, which can ultimately lead to their actual actions and the corresponding social outcomes.

In a primary level social exchange experienced, people such as social dominators will begin with basic questions and answers, which will only touch on the surface level of communication, and each person will try and interpret what the other's underlying intention is. Because these types of highly complex social interactions can often not be of a defining nature, people will sometimes wait until more information is obtained prior to forming their final cognition. Experienced people also often possess a predetermined knowledge base via their social priming from other social encounters, which allows them to generalize to a degree what the other people in a social exchange are after, based on their overall characteristics. The use of logic and reasoning will be used by a skilled person to determine the other person's underlying motive. These social experiences are all internalized and are transformed into consciousness for later use.

Social and societal systems are typically well organized, there is a social order in place, and the social order is based on the social relevance of people within a social value system. The social relevance and value of each person is well understood within each level of a social system. People are assigned social roles and social status within a social system based on the socially agreed concurrence of their social relevance and value. Some social roles can also be *inferred* between *select* people within a social group, and these roles may be unknown to others within the system. When these types of social scenarios occur, the people that are involved are in an inner *clique* social circle. Social cliques can create animosity within social systems when they are discovered. Social cliques are almost always revealed because at some point, a *weak* social link makes it into the inner social clique and reveals the existence of the clique by broadcasting their inclusion. The members of a social clique or inner circle will normally take turns probing prospective candidates to check for weaknesses before they are invited into the clique.

In the social relevance and value system, there is concurrence between people within a system who are under a shared social understanding. The people within the social system are then willing to act mutually with each other based on their established social roles, which creates social order and the social hierarchy within a social system. Without these social parameters in place, a social system would cease to function fluidly. In some instances where mutual agreement cannot be obtained, the social dominators in social rings or systems can resort to other social tactics to compel people to cooperate. Social dominators can threaten to withhold social elements from people, and they can dangle social promotion toward those who are willing to act in accordance with their social direction, and more. In the New Testament, Matthew outlines the plan of the wicked to dangle the lusts of the world before the just: "He also that received seed among the thorns is he that heareth the word, and the care of this world, and the deceitfulness of riches, choke the world, and he becometh unfruitful" (Matthew 13:22, KJV). If a just person is lost to the lusts of the world, they become unfruitful in the cause of purity. Within the social relevance and value system, there is a surface structure and also an underlying structure. The constant and continual perception and interpretation of the social reality amongst the people in social systems is altered continually by the acquisition of new information and also by outside forces such as the media and technology. This new social information can potentially bring about rapid social change and innovation. Social innovation can sometimes quickly change the social dynamics within a social structure. People's cognitive skills, verbalization skills and their unique styles are the keys for social innovation. But these individual displays and manifestations of social innovation are sometimes only acceptable in a given situation as they may be considered social defiance at certain points and times by certain people within the social exchange system. Social dominators will attempt to control the process of innovation at every social level. Social dominators will sometimes *take* social innovations from others to use as their own and there are other occasions where social dominators will *suppress* innovation because it conflicts with their own social direction.

The attempt at social and/or spiritual innovation by a person can have a positive or negative affect on that person's social growth within the social value system. Because of the social continuum of power, sometimes the social dominators place restrictions on which people can elicit ideas, innovations, and mechanisms of social change. Because of the element of ego and other factors, often the ideas coming from the lower levels within the social structure are either ignored, buried, or they are taken by the social power players and dominators as their own ideas. There are also some people in social systems that continually have their ideas taken by others, and they do not ultimately yield the social status and roles that they both *desire* and *deserve*. Social power brokers in social value systems will often do anything they can to maintain their social roles, their social power, and their social status.

Social innovation can be a step toward social progress; not only on a collective level, but on an individual level as well, and many individuals seek to get ahead in the social structure regardless of what it takes to get there. Many individuals within socialization also seek to get into the inner circle of the social power continuum. *Intergroup social competition* is the process of individuals trying to penetrate into the inner circle or *clique* of a group. *The intergroup continuum* provides individuals with social cues as to their status in moving toward the inner circle, these signals can be overt or covert. *Intergroup social identity* is the intrinsic motivation of people to achieve a positive self-concept and be accepted by a group or groups, individuals can *associate* and move toward a social group or they can *disassociate* and move away from a social group via their own social creativity and desired social direction. Dimensions within social groups are assigned as *value dimensions*. The decision for people to associate or disassociate with various groups can be very conflicting.

Based on people's core values, individual traits, personal dispositions, and needs and desires, they will either move toward certain social groups and/or social power, or they will be influenced to move away from them. Everyone has their own core innate preset *social threshold adjustment levels* that they will respond to when confronted by the various social stimuli that are presented within the process of socialization. If people are innately and naturally wired to be good and honest via their core, then their core and cognitive systems will begin to resist with *organic friction* internally if they are outwardly moving against the core of their very nature. This natural phenomenon is very difficult for some people to initially recognize and then later accept and also for many other people to comprehend. If people fight against their natural core value and organic system inclination, they will end up letting the oxidative stress *corrupt* their health. When people are confronted with this social phenomenon, it can create a tremendous amount of cognitive dissonance in their social direction and this is why a level of spirituality can benefit people at any level. Without any spirituality in their path, people can easily miss the early signs and symbols, which can point them toward their correct path. In the New Testament, Philippians outlines suffering within the path of pure faith: "For unto you it is given in the behalf of Christ, not only to believe on him, but also to suffer for his sake" (Philippians 1:29, KJV). The path of purity is not an easy one, but the blessings and rewards that extend from faith cannot be conceived by those who walk the wicked path.

Many people believe in the concept of the *just-world bias* and they expect naturally occurring consequences for people's life actions as result of an unspecified power or enigma that restores the moral balance (i.e., karma). Unfortunately some people do not play by these same social rules in the socialization process and within the social power continuum. Some people are only concerned with moving themselves into their desired social outcome without any concern for what happens in between. And unfortunately some people will evoke their own form of karma upon people based on their own opinions and social interpretations of people and social situations. *Social revenge* upon people within a social system is not karma—it is social retribution. In the New Testament, James warns against people judging others: "There is one lawgiver, who is able to save and destroy, who art thou that judgeth another" (James 4:12, KJV). People must be *cautious* in their actions as their own paths are also under the judgment of the one who is higher.

It is also common that people within the social power structure will operate under the *norms of reciprocity* whereby they will give a little of something to people in order to get a lot in return. Some people will also take anything that they can get to move ahead within a social system and they don't care that they are merely *social puppets*. There are also many other unsuspecting people in life that are brought into and enticed into malicious social confidence games and social scams. Socially adept and highly skilled people such as social dominators and social wolves will attack and prey upon the social marks. They will assail these vulnerable and desperate social marks based on their appeals to the vulnerable and desperate people's greed, dishonesty, vanity, opportunism, lust, compassion, irresponsibility, desperation, naiveté, gullibility, and more. These social dominators and social wolves will continue to prey upon the social marks and social lambs within social systems because they know that they can and they do not care about the collective whole. People can attempt to avoid these attacks, and they can also try and help others as well. In the New Testament, John mentions the apostles being the branches of purity and faith: "I am the vine, ye are the branches" (John 15:5, KJV). The same that applies to the apostles applies to any servant of faith who reaches out to help another.

Organismic self-regulation involves the creative adjustments that people make in relation to their individual environments for their personal equilibrium. A person's personal equilibrium can be disturbed by the emergence of need, by sensations, or by interest. These elements can derive from internal or external forces. Once something becomes figural (a priority) in a person's social field, it can be focused on. Skilled social dominators and social wolves will probe others within their social network to find out their needs and their interests in order to exploit them at the opportune time. Social insights can only be realized after examining people's figural patterns over time within their life course. Unfortunately some people can never escape their figural social patterns especially if there is no social support network in place for them to turn to.

In addition often, the people in social power roles such as social dominators will protect themselves from direct and potential social exposure by employing a layer of deniability and by using social *shills*, who are plants or stooges. These social shills do not identify to others who they are working for or reveal their true hidden agendas. The social shills are planted to gather information for the social power brokers or to help sway a group toward a move that is advantageous for the people in the social power structure via *group polarization*. Social shills, yes people, social weasels, social coattails, and others in the social structure, who are allies of those with power within the process of socialization, compete *directly* with those people that are intrinsically motivated and morally bound. So the life path can indeed be very difficult for the *good* and *honest* person. The wicked are discussed within Timothy in the New Testament: "Without natural affection, false accusers, despisers of those that are good" (2 Timothy 3:3, KJV). The wicked and evil lie in wait to damage the just. This is the design of life and the test of faith along the path.

But in order to win the social battle within the life path, people must not abandon their core-positive nature. The positive people in society must not yield their inner core values. People will know if the social energy balances ever shift from a positive to a negative flux on the energy field continuum, because when the social dominators and social wolves run out of social marks and social lambs to attack and they have to resort to attacking each other, it will be *clearly obvious*.

The plant shill social agents will work very carefully and often skillfully amongst the social marks and social lambs and they will withhold info, spy, and will also create a negative social undercurrent of fear on behalf of the social power brokers within social systems. Social shills can spread negative information regarding their social marks and targets and they can go the other direction and play the role of the social advocate and use duplicity to gain the favor of their target in order to get information. There are some other social tactics that social shills can use. *Incremental conversion* involves social shills pushing and nudging people toward their social agenda while *persistency conversion* employs guilt, hurt, and rescue games. The actions of social power brokers and their shills can be overt, which is obvious and direct, or they can include more covert actions.

Covert aggression is the use of subtle and discrete aggression by social manipulators, which is often undetected by others and also is often carried out in isolated situations with the victims or targets. *Covert intimidation* is used by social manipulators who will use guilt trips and shame in isolated conversations to gain power and control. Social manipulators are not obvious and they make it very difficult for others to validate their actions. Social manipulators also seek to find out personal information on people to use it against them and also to find their emotional buttons to gain social leverage and power. If ever confronted, a social manipulator will deny accusations, play innocent, will often play the role of the victim, and they will try and minimize their actions as not being harmful to others.

When social manipulators try playing the victim role, the manipulator flips things to appear that they have been wronged, and makes it appear that they were only responding to the actions of others. Manipulators will also try *playing* the servant role within socialization, normally with their superiors, which is a covert manipulative action to obtain personal objectives for themselves while masking their efforts as being out for another or others. Social manipulators are also always projecting the blame on others and always looking for *scapegoats* on all fronts to pass the blame upon in order to avoid any personal consequences. Social dominators, power brokers, and manipulators will avoid giving people around them the full and necessary information to be at a 100 percent level in order to protect themselves. They will then turn around and use the information that was held back as a reason to expel a person or people who do not comply with their social agenda.

Seduction is yet another method that social manipulators will use. The manipulators will prey upon people's need for social acceptance and their desire to achieve within socialization with smooth and cunning snakelike *social slithering*. They will use charm, flattery, and praise because they know that everyone likes to feel good about themselves and desires to be part of the collective whole. If the flattery doesn't match reality on the social scale, then people need to figure out what the manipulators are after in order to protect themselves and others. In any type of social exchange, people are always looking at the social alternatives. When anyone within a social ring or social structure consciously allows this negative social cycle to continue, then they become part of the negative social resistance within humanity. Many times, people become part of the negative social resistance to ensure their own prosperity and to protect the social dominators from social liability. These are the people that the positive social movement needs to expel from their social roles in order to replace them with people who are out to promote the collective good within society. The reason why there are social cliques in place is to protect these negative groups from being infiltrated and ousted. Within the process of socialization, people are always weighing the effects of their choices and decisions versus the realization of their personal goals within the life path. If there are too many people who choose the negative social path then humanity will suffer the consequences of their actions.

The social exchange theory of Albert Bandura involves a social cost-benefits analysis by people which includes tangible and intangible considerations as well as physical and psychological factoring. These personal assessments can influence the decisions that people make during their lives and within socialization. *Social influence* is a person's status and their position relative to power or influence. People who lack social power and/or influence within the social structure typically are dependent on those who do have power and influence to move forward within socialization.

Within the process of socialization, it is very difficult for many people to understand which type of people that they are dealing with, this is why the social manipulators have so much freedom to roam. Social manipulators are well aware that many people are unable to *detect* their acts.

Unfortunately because of the social naiveté and gullibility that exist in many social rings and systems, some people will be allowed to use a public persona disguise and they will have a hidden shadow personality. The public persona is used to disguise the true personality of a social manipulator from the public or from people who are outside of the inner circle or social clique. The people in the social inner circle will always protect the power brokers within the inner circle in exchange for social rewards, which can include the promise of social elevation. Within an inner circle, there are varying levels of power. The Big Fish are the top power brokers in a social structure or social system that are often arrogant, feel they can do what they like, and often can make other people feel extremely small. The Big Fish often use *pedestal standing* as their first measure to try and socially persuade people in their network to do what they want them to do.

A secondary social control technique that the Big Fish will use is *controlling the agenda*. When the social impacts are being considered, the Big Fish will employ all measures to protect themselves. The social power figure will control the order of the social agenda of social meetings including who will be there, they will perceive what people will be thinking, will apply group pressure, apply commitment pressure, and they will always try and decide the outcomes in advance (visualization). In addition, the people in an inner circle or social clique will almost always have their own social language and social codes as well. The people in the inner circle will also have their own secret conclaves to review their social agendas. When litigation, money, and/or power are on the line, the social dominators will seek to find *anything* they can to offset those who are attacking them and this includes using *fabrication*. A social challenger must realize that they are truly facing the social beast when they try to act on the behalf of the collective, but when people stop making these social attempts that is the point where the negative resistance will have won and when humanity will begin to *erode*. In the New Testament, Timothy talks about what will occur if the just stop fighting the good fight: "For men shall be lovers of their own selves, covetous, boasters, proud, blasphemous, disobedient to parents, unthankful, unholy" (2 Timothy 3:2, ᴋᴊᴠ). When the pure people of faith in the world stop fighting the good fight, the last days will have arrived.

Code switching is when people use a different language or different symbols and social cues within the context of different social settings. People who operate within an inner circle will use code switching when dealing with the different elements within their social network. Certain elements and social agendas are only spoken of within the inner circle and never mentioned to the people outside of the inner circle. A *special language* is used by the members of the inner circle to evoke emotional control, by the use of power words and evocative words, which are controlled by inner circle. Special words with special meanings in closed groups are commonly called *godwords*. In addition to the special languages, other tactics will also be employed by the social power brokers in social systems.

Mind control is something that is often employed by the agents of the inner circle within social power circles. These social agents will attempt to discredit others via the promotion and the impulse of illogical thinking, as the power of mind control lowers people's ambition, efficiency, and even their physical ability over the course of time. The mind control tactics can be done surreptitiously via stealth, in a clandestine nature, which is done undercover and secretively versus the overt nature of brute force social attacks.

Mentation can also be employed by social power brokers or members of their inner circle. Mentation involves techniques which are mind control elements that can be conscious or unconscious in their action. *Breaking sessions* involve agents pressuring people until cracking them in a group and then being kind to them as an individual to build trust with them. This technique can potentially turn a person to be obedient to the social agenda of the inner circle. Guilt is used to escalate the group and then the inner circle attacks any challengers and accuses them of being the issue. *Dangle elevation* is the social manipulation technique of offering people social elevation if the desired path is followed. But once people partake in the actions of the negative resistance, they are forever tied into their circle and correspondingly *trapped*. Many people fall into this type of social trap. *Identity destruction* pushes people out of their normal personality and into a lost and isolated state. This technique is used to exhaust people then to guilt trip them, creating social distance and social distortion. The goal is to reconstruct people and then to have them model the new desired way that they are expected to follow. *Fragmentation* is also often used to break down a larger social event into smaller subunits, as a group of small things (the power of numbers) seems more significant to most people and the technique offers a power broker more negotiables to use as social influencers. There are also still many social power players and social dominators that exist within humanity that would incorporate *indentured servitude* amongst the populous if they could find the path and if the path was not eliminated by those with more authority. If those in power over these social conditions ever yielded their authority, this is what could lead to social chaos and bedlam.

Those within humanity who yield great power should never fail to comply with their collective social duty to be a *social watcher*, unfortunately the elements of greed, the desire for personal and family protection within comfort and the earthly lusts for extended social power often erode this critical social function. In addition, *going along to get along* is a common social theme that people will often be presented with during their life course, but a person must define what *going along with* entails, as it may completely conflict with their personal core value system. Spirituality is another key life component that must be retained within humanity in order to maintain the positive energy balance that presently exists within humanity. There are varying degrees of spirituality, and humanity must not sacrifice the truth for worldly lusts. There are also other forces working against the unity efforts with the preservation of religion. Powerful forces are taking advantage of the present fragmentation within religion to break it down further in order to appease those who want religion to fade away over time. When and if the time comes where humanity has made this ultimate sacrifice, the *end* will draw closer.

Within the *realm of spirituality*, there are *true believers* who fully lead their lives based on the collective principles of their spiritual belief system and lead a life path of purity, which combines their spiritual beliefs with their inner core value system. The true believer group is a highly essential group within humanity, but they are very limited in numbers. A true believer has no doubt regarding the existence of a higher life meaning, an eternal existence, and everything they do in their lives revolves around this ideology. A true believer does not pick and choose when or what to follow along their spiritual path of faith as their direction is concrete and unfaltering. In the New Testament within Galatians, the Bible talks about the pure and just living by their faith: "The just shall live by faith" (Galatians 7:11, KJV). Although some people within humanity will try and convince themselves and others that they fall into this select group, there are actually very few who are able to reach and maintain this *earthly spiritual apex*.

Reaching this spiritual apex within the mortal existence involves *enduring* along the path of life with a clear conscious life effort and an unconscious purity within the core. People have to understand their true core state of being and gravitate toward their peak spiritual level. When people are moving toward their own individual spiritual capacities, this is recognized. In contrast, a *spiritual façade* is only recognized by *people* and the façade only confounds people's actual spiritual growth. In the New Testament, John outlines the rewards for those who have had faith: "Blessed are they that have not seen, and yet have believed" (John 20:29, KJV). Unfortunately there are many people within humanity who are requiring an *individual sign* to inspire their faith, but this is not the design. Hebrews in the New Testament also mentions the power of faith: "Faith is the substance of the things hoped for, the evidence of things not seen" (Hebrews 11:1, KJV).

Jesus lived and no one denies this, and his apostles did walk the earth after him. Many believed on him during his time and still more many carry on their belief in him. In the New Testament, Matthew talks about the gifts of seeing God. "Blessed are the pure at heart for they shall see God" (Matthew 5:8, KJV).

People must also understand that all men are *fallible* regardless of their spiritual level. In John within the New Testament, it explains that all men on earth, regardless of their spiritual level, have *sin* in their lives: "If we say that we have no sin, we deceive ourselves, and the truth is not in us" (John 1:8, KJV). The reason that sin can also occur at the apex of earthly spiritual levels is that no one on earth is perfect and all men are *fallible by degrees*. An example of the type of fallibility that could lie within the true believer group is outlined in the New Testament within Matthew: "When doest thine alms, do not sound a trumpet before thee, that they may have glory of men" (Matthew 6:2, KJV). Sometimes men forget themselves and errantly seek praise and attention for their good works and deeds, and this does not please the one that is higher. When people give, they should do such willingly and in humbleness. This is further explained within Luke in the New Testament: "Whosoever exalteth himself, shall be abased, and he that humbleth himself shall be exalted" (Luke 14:11, KJV). It's human nature for people to fall toward wanting attention and acceptance, but people need to be cognizant and be able to *reel themselves back in* when they sense that pride is overcoming them.

Next, there are those within the spiritual realm who are *driven believers* who have not received the fruits of their full spiritual message yet, but that are still living by the same principles as those who are true believers. The driven believers cannot be swayed in their beliefs and values by the others within humanity who dwell on the opposite end of the spiritual realm continuum, but they still need to locate and receive their full spiritual message. Essentially the driven believers have a pure core, but their conscious approach still has a *diminutive void*, which is why they have not met with the fruits of their spiritual apex. This void leads to fallibility and some poor earthly choices, but it does not cause any wavering in the purity of their faith and in their belief. The driven believer group is slightly larger than the true believer group within humanity, but their numbers are still paltry as compared to the balance of those within the entire spiritual realm continuum.

In addition, there are also those who are *neutral believers* who truly hope that their mortal existence has a greater life meaning, and this is the first group along the spiritual realm continuum that has the potential to freely and quickly break away from seeking a *pure spiritual path*. Neutral believers are those who tend to *pick and choose* which elements of scripture and doctrine that they will follow and also choose when they will walk the spiritual path. Where the true believer and the driven believer have acquired spiritual wisdom and walk the path of pure spirituality *every day*, the neutral believer will have *ebb and flow* within their spiritual path. In many cases, the neutral believer will walk the path of spirituality on the Sabbath day in full or in part, but then they will then pick and choose the other times that they walk the path outside the Sabbath day. These gaps within walking the path of spirituality are what create a layer of *spiritual permeability* and increase the propensity of fallibility.

In the New Testament, Matthew outlines that there is not true pure faith present when a person decides to *consciously divide* their time up along the pure path: "No men can serve two masters, ye cannot serve God and mammon" (Matthew 6:24, KJV). Mammon refers to the lusts of the world. John in the New Testament discusses the error within duplicity: "If we say that we have fellowship with him, and walk in darkness, we lie and do not the truth" (John 1:6, KJV). In many cases, the neutral believer is altering their path due to their audience and/or their environment, but this activity is not well pleasing to the Lord. In the New Testament, Luke discusses the importance of people professing their faith unto others: "He that denieth me before men shall be denied before the angels of God" (Luke 12:9, KJV). The admission and profession of faith is further discussed in Romans within the New Testament: "For the scripture saith, whosoever believeth on him shall not be ashamed" (Romans 10:11, KJV). People are not expected to be perfect in their words or in their actions because fallibility and free will are within the design of life, but when people *deny* their faith to others based on their audience and/ or their social environment, this action eventually opens up the doors to the path of iniquity.

True believers and driven believers need to seek out the neutral believers very actively along their paths before they are potentially tempted to *detach* from seeking the "pure spiritual path" and be corrupted by the forces of evil. All people within humanity need to be approached regarding the strength and need for a pure spiritual path, but the neutral believer group is highly critical because their core can still be pure, but yet they are *highly vulnerable* to become more fallible. As time passes, humanity continues to lose more people from the neutral believer group. The neutral believer group is the group which can decide the *spiritual balance* along the spiritual realm continuum because their numbers are still very significant. The neutral believer group also resides closest along the spiritual realm continuum to the other groups within the continuum. The position of the neutral believers along the continuum often allows them to carry more social and spiritual influence in helping the others who are positioned on the opposite end of the continuum to locate and/ or relocate their spiritual direction and path. The neutral believer group can often gain better access to those who have had their cores eroded along their life paths and can help guide them toward spiritual restoration, and they can also sometimes even pull people out of the *spiritual abyss.*

Once the neutral believer is able to reach someone who has fallen off, often this opens the door for others who have even more spiritual knowledge to enter in and begin assisting with the *restoration process.* There are some within humanity who question why people would actively seek out the workers of iniquity to try and bring them back into the sheepfold. Matthew in the New Testament covers this area: "They that be whole need not a physician, but they that are sick" (Matthew 9:12, KJV). When Jesus was asked why he was sitting with the publicans and sinners, he explained that those who were in need of restoration were in need of his attention. In addition, people must also be aware that there are angels who walk the earth. In Hebrews within the New Testament, there is a message regarding the need for humanity to be open unto all: "Be not forgetful to entertain strangers, for therefore some have entertained angels unawares" (Hebrews 13:2, KJV). Humanity must not forget that angels can be sent down to walk among the people and to sit with them. Even though the Lord sees all, he also calls upon his angels to help with his work. This is why there are passages regarding the need for people to be kind unto their brothers. If someone is struggling within this area and/or the Lord wants to test someone, he may send one of his angels to work on his behalf. In the New Testament, Luke explains that there is no reward for people *only* loving those that love them: "For if ye love them which love you, what thank ye have, for sinners also love those that love them" (Luke 6:32, KJV). Spiritual courage is needed on all levels.

True believers and driven believers typically have a more difficult time reaching those on the other end of the spiritual realm continuum because they are on a *different spiritual plane.* This does not mean that they are better than the others, but rather that their language, aura, and approach may not *smoothly transition* over as well as the others. The further people are apart on the spiritual plane, the more difficult it becomes for the others who reside on the different levels within the continuum to identify with them and recognize their needs. Sometimes there are *spiritual chameleons*, which can relate to anyone or at least a wider group within the spiritual continuum and these people can be very helpful within extending spiritual messages and in gathering the flock. Regardless of where people fall within the continuum and which people are able to reach the others within the continuum, there must be no more hesitation or procrastination within gathering the flock. The time is *now* for people to become the spiritual branches that they have been *called* to become. If the spiritual branches are not extended out then the balance of humanity cannot reach the fruits. Those who cannot reach the fruits cannot walk the path of spirituality.

The harvesting of the flock cannot be a *passive effort* and more branches are required to help the process of saving souls within humanity. Matthew in the New Testament details the need for more branches within the harvest: "The harvest is plenteous, but the laborers are few" (Matthew 9:37, KJV). And further, Matthew states that people need to pray for the harvest: "Pray ye therefore the Lord of the harvest, that he will send forth laborers into his harvest" (Matthew 9:38, KJV). A path to reaching one's spiritual apex can often lie within contributing to the gathering of the flock. In the New Testament, Matthew wrote of Jesus beginning the harvest: "Follow me, I will make you fishers of men" (Matthew 4:19, KJV). If a person reads this passage and is not truly inspired then perhaps becoming a missionary branch is exactly the *step of faith* that is required to propel that person toward their spiritual apex.

Next, within the continuum are those who are putting on a *spiritual social façade* overtly in public for their social persona, but covertly in design in order to elevate and/or propel them in their life path whether the gain is for social acceptance or other social elements and considerations such as social role, social power, and/or financial gain. The people in this group often feel that their membership or their lineage provides them with the *right of passage* and therefore they need only to offer kind words, display necessary gestures, and make their required appearances. But they are *gravely mistaken* because the spiritual design calls for faith and good works rather than purely the lip service of the tongue. In the New Testament, John discusses the need within the spiritual path for more than just the lip service of words: "Let us not love in word, neither in tongue, but in deed and truth" (John 3:18, KJV). If the spiritual social façade group fails to do good works in faith, they can be very harmful unto humanity. This spiritual social façade group is a very dangerous group because they can potentially *corrupt* others to follow their path of iniquity, which can further erode the net level of spirituality within humanity. In the New Testament, Hebrews details how there are some that are unclean that have *slipped* into the sheepfold: "The law maketh men high priests which have infirmity, and some are not pure" (Hebrews 7:28, KJV). When these people attempt to corrupt others, they can harm humanity. Therefore, people need to be very vigilant in guiding them toward the correct spiritual path, without this effort the potential for fragmentation and erosion is high.

But even though this group is harmful within the realm of spirituality, there is still the *potential* that this group's cores can be salvaged even though they are consciously exploiting the system of spirituality. A salvaged and refined core can cause the conscious to succumb to its force. These people are merely waiting for the right people, with the correct approach, and the proper message to intercept them before their cores completely erode. Often, the people who reside on the negative end of the spiritual continuum will tell themselves that they can only be influenced when they receive a *clear individual spiritual message*, but what they forget is that those messages are normally reserved for those moving toward a pure level of spirituality. Those who are consciously moving away from spirituality are diminishing their ability to receive a spiritual message.

The final group within the continuum is the *spiritual exploiter* who is false and overtly reaches out to people within humanity and becomes rich within their spiritual work. Matthew in the New Testament warns humanity about these false people: "And many false prophets shall rise, and shall deceive many" (Matthew 24:11, KJV). Acts within the New Testament also details that the false will come unto the sheepfold: "For I know this, that after my departing shall grievous wolves enter in among you, not sparing the flock" (Acts 20:29, KJV). Paul knew that the wolves would seize the opportunity to work iniquity. Anyone with a spiritual knowledge base, a truly pure conscious and pure core knows that the people who are becoming rich off of the *realm of spirituality* are working outside of the eternal design and they are instead working iniquity. In the New Testament, Matthew outlines the presence of these false people: "Beware of false prophets that come to you in sheep's clothing, but inwardly they are ravening wolves" (Matthew 7:15, KJV). Matthew further explains that these false people can be marked by their works: "Ye shall know them by their fruits" (Matthew 7:16, KJV).

These false people take advantage of the others within humanity that are blinded by their showmanship and ardent style. In the New Testament, Romans explains that these false people must be marked: "Now I beseech you brethren, mark them which cause divisions and offenses contrary to the doctrine which ye have learned, and avoid them" (Romans 16:17, KJV). In Romans, it is further detailed that these false people seek to fill their own worldly lusts: "For they are such serve not our Lord Jesus Christ, but their own belly, and by good words and fair speeches deceive the hearts of the simple" (Romans 16:18, KJV). Within Corinthians in the New Testament, the penalty for deceiving humanity is discussed: "But when ye sin so against the brethren, and wound their weak conscience, ye sin against Christ" (Corinthians 8:12, KJV).

These *false* spiritual leaders also attract those within humanity who seek to hear flattering words to gain the approval for their misguided life path. But the only approval that these people who seek flattering words are receiving is of *men* and of the *world* and so like the others they are also blinded. In the New Testament, instructions are made clear on how the gospel is to be rendered unto humanity within Corinthians: "For we preach not ourselves, but Jesus Christ the Lord, and ourselves your servants for Jesus sake" (2 Corinthians 4:5, KJV). In Galatians within the New Testament, being a true servant of Christ is further outlined: "For do I now persuade men or God, or do I seek to please men, for if I yet pleased men, I should not be the servant of Christ" (Galatians 1:10, KJV). In the New Testament, Ephesians further details how the gospel of the Lord is to be shared: "Let no corrupt communication proceed out of your mouth, but that which is good to use of edifying, that it may minister grace unto the hearers" (Ephesians 4:29, KJV).

This false group is the group within the continuum that will have to face the highest spiritual toll because they are *consciously exploiting* people to become *rich* and they *do not* truly believe as evidenced by their actions. Peter in the New Testament states that these false people have worked iniquity in the highest form: "For it had been better for them not to have known the way of righteousness, than after they have know it, to turn from the holy commandment delivered unto them" (2 Peter 2:21, KJV). Anyone that had pure faith and that truly believed in the true design of spirituality wouldn't be working the deeds of iniquity. These people have obtained spiritual knowledge and through their worldly lusts they have conceived a plan to become rich by infecting the Word of God. In the New Testament, Timothy reveals how the false people will seize the opportunity to become rich by offering false doctrine and gathering those who have grown tired of hearing the true doctrine: "For the time will come when thy will not endure sound doctrine, but after their own lusts shall they heap to themselves, teachers with itching ears" (2 Timothy 4:3, KJV). These false people will orate that they know God and that they are sharing his message. In Titus within the New Testament, the ways of the false are communicated: "They profess that they know God, but in works they deny him" (Titus 1:16, KJV). When true doctrine is altered, this should be obvious to people, but these *silver-tongued* and wicked false people create a blinding ambiguity over those who are tempted by the worldly lusts that are dangled before them. In the New Testament, Peter outlines the false people's plan: "For when they speak great swelling words of vanity, they allure through the lusts of the flesh, through much wantonness, those that were clean escaped from them who live in error" (2 Peter 2:18, KJV). People must mark these false people and escape from their *snare of iniquity.*

These wicked and evil people can easily be marked and flushed out if their flow of money is cut off. If they are exposed and their money is cut off, a very *different* kind of person will surface, and a wicked and shallow person will be revealed. The absolute worst area in life to be a social exploiter is within the *realm of spirituality.* But those who are truly *diseased* with greed will most often take the path of least resistance. These people know that they can become rich by exploiting people, and so they pursue their path of greed. These people become rich by twisting and contorting the Scriptures in order to flatter the masses by telling them what they want to hear versus extending the knowledge that the one who is higher had commanded. In the New Testament, Corinthians details how the false people become contaminated with iniquity: "What is my reward, verily that, when I preach the gospel, I may make the gospel of Christ without charge, that I abuse not my power in the gospel" (Corinthians 9:18, KJV). These sickened and wicked false people develop the belief that they should be rewarded for their work. But they are mistaken on two levels. The *true work* of the Lord is not done for the accumulation of wealth, and also when a following is gathered by abusing the power of the gospel, this will be punished. Paul explains within Acts in the New Testament that the true servant of the Lord seeks no lustful rewards: "I have coveted no mans silver, or gold, or apparel" (Acts 20:33, KJV). Those who gain personal wealth within their work are not true servants of the Lord.

This false spiritual group has passed the ultimate social boundaries within their wickedness and they have extended their social evil into the spiritual realm. The people who follow them are being sent down the *wrong path*. Their followers are being sent down the path of lusts and evil versus the path of life. Their followers also are led to believe that these false leaders are *blessed* because they can hold an audience and a following. Luke discusses this in the New Testament: "Ye have taken away the key of knowledge, ye entered not in yourselves, and them that were entering in ye hindered" (Luke 11:52, KJV). By leading people down the *wrong path*, these workers of iniquity are *hindering* their follower's opportunity to walk the true path of spirituality, which leads to life.

In the eyes of the one that is mightier, it is better to be poor, and rich in faith, by following the word rather than rich on earth and leading people toward the path of evil. These false people have made the determination that they would rather seek worldly riches than have eternal life, and they are leading others within humanity onto the path of destruction. It is not the people who will determine the fates of these workers of iniquity, but they will be called forward later to answer for their iniquities by the one that is higher. Luke in the New Testament conveys that the evil deeds of the wicked and their iniquities are known of the Lord: "There is nothing covered that shall not be revealed, neither hid that shall not be known" (Luke 12:2, KJV). These false people and spiritual leaders are buying their own time on earth and they are accomplishing their goal by *fleecing* those who are buying into their false doctrine and spiritual following.

Because Paul knew that the false people and wolves would come, he conveyed to the apostles for them to be certain that the same message was being delivered by all with no division. In the New Testament, this is relayed within Corinthians: "Now I beseech you, brethren, by the name of our Lord Jesus Christ, that ye all speak the same thing, and that there be no divisions among you, but that ye be perfectly joined together in the same mind and in the same judgment" (Corinthians 1:10, KJV). Within Ephesians in the New Testament, this was further explained: "That we henceforth be no more children, tossed to and fro, and carried about with every wind of doctrine, by the sleight of men, and cunning craftiness, whereby they lie in weight to deceive" (Ephesians 4:14, KJV). Jesus lived so that we could become more like him, and after he was gone, his apostles carried on his work in order for his doctrine to live on. When people ignore the true pure message and/or they create their own doctrine, the impact on humanity cannot begin to be measured as it is infinite in nature. The primary element on earth that has always led to a spiritual division is *worldly riches*. Because Jesus knew this, he spoke of this matter, which is outlined within Matthew in the New Testament: "Lay not up for yourselves treasures upon earth, where moth and rust doth corrupt" (Matthew 6:19, KJV). The message was continued: "But lay up yourselves treasures in heaven" (Matthew

6:20, KJV). Then was concluded: "For where your treasure is there will your heart be also" (Matthew 6:21, KJV).

Being rich does not preclude people from going to heaven, so long as their path to achieving the wealth was *pure*, and that what is done after the wealth is acquired does not involve *iniquity*. But because the freedom of wealth opens up the world to those with it, the doors of iniquity are also opened. In the New Testament, Timothy outlines the temptations that come with wealth: "They that will be rich, fall into temptation and a snare, and into many foolish and hurtful lusts, which drown men in destruction and perdition" (1 Timothy 6:9, KJV). If people begin to love their money more than their God then this leads to the path of destruction. People are warned within Timothy in the New Testament regarding the evil that can arise with wealth: "For the love of money is the root of all evil" (1 Timothy 6:10, KJV). Money most often changes people and this can cause them to feel *superior* to all of those people *beneath* them. In the New Testament, James makes a reference to how the rich can look down on those with less: "And ye have respect to him that weareth the gay clothing, and say unto him, sit thou here in a good place, and say to the poor, stand thou there, or sit here under my footstool" (James 2:3, KJV). Many times those with wealth will begin to despise the poor, which is caused by the *infection* that can come along with the evil of money. James discusses this activity in the New Testament: "But ye have despised the poor, do not rich men oppress you, and draw you before the judgement" (James 2:6, KJV). When people begin to love their money more than their God and to despise the poor, they can turn away from one of God's greatest commandments. The commandment of *charity* is a commandment that the Lord values as among the most high.

In Acts in the New Testament, Paul reminds people about the words of the Lord: "I have shewed you all things, how that so labouring ye ought to support the weak, and to remember the words of the Lord Jesus, how he said 'It is more blessed to give than to receive' (Acts 20:35, KJV). Paul continued his message within Corinthians in the New Testament: "And now abideth faith, hope, charity, these three, but the greatest of these is charity" (Corinthians 13:13, KJV). Paul added in Corinthians within the New Testament that people should not have an abundance, and that the less fortunate should be taken care of: "As it is written he that had gathered much had nothing over, and he that had gathered little had no lack" (2 Corinthians 8:15, KJV). Paul also warned that people should give *willingly* and *cheerfully* in humbleness versus being resentful of those with less: "Everyman according as he purposeth in his heart, so let him give, not grudgingly, or of necessity, for the Lord loveth a cheerful giver" (2 Corinthians 9:7, KJV). The reason that charity is so important is because the Lord gave himself unto the people by making himself poor that the *people* could become rich in *faith*. Corinthians speaks of the grace of the Lord within the New Testament: "For ye know the grace of our Lord Jesus Christ, that, though he was rich yet for your sakes he became poor, that ye through his poverty might be rich" (2 Corinthians 8:9, KJV). In the New Testament, it was outlined within Colossians that charity brings about perfection: "And above all these things put on charity, which is the bond of perfectness" (Colossians 3:14, KJV). The reason that people begin to hold back and despise the poor is because of their acquisition of *earthly knowledge*. But this is foolish because the truth is that wisdom lies in understanding the meaning of charity. In the New Testament, the purpose of charity was discussed: "Knowledge puffeth up, but charity edifeith" (Corinthians 8:1, KJV). Those in life who *complain* about the poor and believe that they are receiving blessings are *disillusioned* to learn that they are walking off the path when they do this. When a pure person with spiritual knowledge hears someone complaining about the poor, it's almost *nauseating* for them to hear the words.

In summary, the *realm of spirituality* is always in the midst of debate. But regardless of whether one has no faith or full faith, the application and use logic, reasoning, and morals lead people to the same destination as spirituality within the understanding of the dynamics of a good and pure life. If a person considers and envisions everyone within humanity being out for their own cause, ignoring those in need, and taking everything that they want, with the proper focus, that vision paints a very *grim* picture. The problem is that there are many people who don't care about having vision, but they instead charge ahead to try and capture the flag in life regardless of the cost. In order for the positive element to endure within humanity, those negative people need to be marked whether they claim spirituality or not. At the present standard and pace, chaos will occur because there are more people feeding into the negative element than there are feeding into the positive element. But if those within the positive element put forth the *equal energy* in this continuum, the negative element would be squashed. The world would be an even better place if the wicked were sent scampering into the corners versus the good. The take away from this section is that people can gauge where they are and where they want to be. In addition, people may take away a better understanding of where others lie within the continuum as well. There is no one on earth within the realm of spirituality that doesn't have a degree of *spiritual poverty*, and in order for people to receive blessings, they must realize their own spiritual poverty. This is explained in Matthew in the New Testament: "Blessed are the meek, for they shall inherit the earth." And just like Jesus and his apostles, those within the pure element welcome *any and all* people into the realm of spirituality. It's a blessing to everyone within the positive element to receive their brothers and sisters into the fold.

But because of those in life who seek to take the flag, the elements of greed, social control, and social power, manipulation have been played upon since the beginning of time. This pattern will continue to occur because the core characteristics of these negative people in humanity are continually passed along within humanity over time through genetics, which can overpower nurturing. And because of the harmful impact of this activity on humanity, this social phenomenon has been written about by many over time.

For example, in Shakespeare's *Julius Caesar* the complex social maneuvering and the associated character flaws are something that occur both in the piece of literature itself, in today's social reality, and also will continue to occur into the future. Some of the social themes in *Julius Caesar* include Caesar's inability to read people and/or the events that eventually led to his downfall. Caesar's *pride* caused him to ignore his wife Calpurina's dreams, and all the other signs and symbols that pointed toward his downfall. Caesar conflated his identity into one entity, his ambition and his fallacy of immortality caused him to ignore the social reality of the events occurring around him and to have no fear of his fate.

When leaders within the social power structures ignore the collective need of the people at any social level, history shows that ignoring these needs will eventually lead to social change. Leaders however will commonly attempt to keep the necessary social changes at bay through a myriad of techniques in order to maintain their social position, power, and influence. Change is not something that is welcomed within the social ranks of leadership.

Brutus in *Julius Caesar* was *conflicted* within the complexities of his motives, his conflicting value systems, rigid idealism (both a virtue and flaw), and commitment to principles caused his social miscalculations. Brutus was limited in his self-serving aspects and this caused his doom, by him ultimately serving no one. If a person is going to challenge power and battle for the collective, they cannot go halfway or they will be swept away, a person must stick to a conviction or they will be squashed in any social power struggle.

Anthony in *Julius Caesar* was an *opportunist* who was impulsive, improvising, and conducted himself with cold calculation by tailoring on both sides with *duplicity*. Anthony succeeded via his adaptability and his bargaining. There are many people in life who have the skill of duplicity, they will use it to their advantage, and many of them do not care which people fall to the wayside within their self-serving life path (social alienation), Anthony employed a more covert method with his duplicity.

Cassius the *nemesis* and a ruthless schemer had no private life, and he overtly challenged the social structure. There are other people in life that are very open about their desires and it is easier to plan around people who are overt versus those who scheme completely covertly. These character portrayals within *Julius Caesar* will hold true for all time in the social reality as well as these character types, which are hardwired into some people's personalities within society. There are many social theories that have been posed over time to try and explain why people act the way they do, how the socialization process works, and also some that search for life's higher meanings. Everything in life has its balancers, society must make sure that the negative energy forces never overtake the positive and this is ultimately the social duty of all people.

One idea regarding the *stages of socialization* within groups was posed by Moreland & Levine in 1982. They posed a series of socialization steps. The first step of the process was called the *investigation phase*, which entails a person's cautious search for information in their life. In this stage, an individual compares various groups to find a good fit, which they called *reconnaissance*. And while an individual is making their own interpretation, the groups that they are evaluating are estimating the value of the individual as a potential member, which they called *recruitment*. After the dual evaluation that occurs within this phase is completed, there is either an offer for inclusion into the group or a rejection from the social group. In order for an individual to get into a group, there are many social factors and considerations come into play.

The *socialization phase* involves an individual accepting a group's culture, norms, values, and perspectives, which they called *assimilation*. Within the process of assimilation for the incoming member, the group also adopts some aspects of the individuality of the new member in order to *accommodate* the new member's needs. If the assimilation occurs, then the *acceptance transition point* is reached and the individual can become a full member within the group. However, this process can be delayed if the group reaction is negative toward the individual or if there is division or group fragmentation. The individual may also react cautiously or they may misinterpret the other members if they perceive that they are being treated differently as a new comer.

The *maintenance phase* involves the negotiation of a group member's contribution, which they called *role negotiation*. Members will remain in this stage throughout their group involvement. Within group role assignment, some individuals are not satisfied with their role in the group, or they may fail to meet the group's expectations.

The *resocialization phase* is when the critical divergence point is reached and there are two possible outcomes. Either the differences are resolved between a member and the group, which they called *convergence*, or the group expels the individual, or the individual leaves the group on their own, either of which they called *exodus*.

Groups will also commonly have a *remembrance phase*, which is the process of the group members making sense of their time in the group, if a consensus is reached on what is considered meaningful time in the group, then a tradition is normally established. This social stage concept provides a sort of blueprint or guide within socialization. Because socialization is such a complex, dynamic, and evolving process, there are no exact steps that can be provided. This is why so many people have generated social theories over time.

There have been many different ideas on humanity and existence as it relates to life throughout time. The concept of *monism* involves a person holding onto only one type of belief system. *Pantheism* involves believing that all things are like God, while *materialism* involves believing that only physical things are real, and finally *idealism* involves believing that what the mind can conceive is reality. These concepts are all still woven into modern society, with materialism being the primary adopted concept within individualistic societies. People must identify and mark those positions held by others, but this can be challenging because of the *game of duplicity* that many people employ within their life path. People who are truly after material gain and do not have a spiritual foundation will often use and abuse others to get what they want.

Within the process of socialization, there are people working on different life philosophies and it is important to try and figure out what kind of people that one is dealing with. If a person is driven only in the area of materialism, their values may be very different than those who are more balanced and/or who are more spiritually driven and motivated. Within socialization, aligning with people that have similar core values is a goal, but unfortunately this goal is not always a possible social reality. This philosophical divide is often what drives people to their social decisions and alters people's life paths within socialization. These social event scenarios happen at the very lowest individual levels and social rings and they also extend to the very top of the social power continuum. Being a social value system does exist within the socialization process and people's core philosophies can have an enormous impact on their individual life courses, this creates the *conflict* within the overall direction of the collective society.

Foucault posed that, "There are periods of history that are not based on absolute truth, but rather unspoken assumptions of what is right and wrong and where new paradigms are created when old ones cannot explain or account for an explanation. And that an ideology, the set of conscious and unconscious ideas that constitute ones goals, expectations, and actions, creates peoples lives and builds their sense of identity." Although we are free beings in life, we are somewhat trapped into the ideology of our social structure. But regardless, the spiritual relationship with the one that is higher should never be forsaken.

Functionalism is based on people's function in a system and the role the mental state plays within a system versus their internal constitution. Within socialization people experience a variety of mental states. Functionalism evaluates causal relations to sensory stimulations. For example pain can be realized by different types of physical states. Mental states can cause and be caused by physical states. *Multiply realization* is when it is understood and multiply realized by other life forms in theory, that others can experience pain. Understanding that such (as in the *butterfly effect*) that other dynamics must be considered. *Dual state* states that mental states can cause and be caused by people's physical states. *Logical behaviorism* involves assigning meaning to people's mental states and their predispositions to act on their mental state. *Cognitive memory trace decay* is the occurrence or absence of stimuli, which can impact the retention or loss of memory and is affected by stress or emotion that in place while playing our social *role*. Pain produces the belief or mental state that something is wrong and creates the *desire* to get out of that state, which is *anxiety*. Pain can be physical or emotional. Pain produces *expressions*; each expression is a quantifier of causal relation, and if the stimuli all occur at once then they are *interlaced*.

Causation is a relationship between events that must be invoked to explain people's behavior. *Interest* is pointed toward subjects and is predetermined based on things people lack (i.e., self-identity), people can move in a direction within socialization to compensate for their perceived social weakness (i.e., their birth order can elicit an *inferior* feeling and social recognition can be the mechanism of compensation). Most people are never fully aware of the complex dynamics of their own personality.

Albert Bandura's *social identity theory* states that a person's *self-identify*, plus the *collective identity* (how self-identify interacts with collective identity), is used to form categorization via perception. *Collective identity* is a process that is shared and negotiated within a group over time to define, goals, and relations. Many different life dynamics have been considered over time and there are many approaches to try and explain life and socialization.

The concept of positivism involves people's sensory experience, and the philosophy that logical and mathematical treatments are the exclusive sources of all authoritative knowledge. Truth is in science and empirical evidence is the data received from these sources. Comte believed that absolute laws not only dictate the physical world, but also society and socialization. He believed that the physical sciences had to precede the study of human society.

Positivity is the degree to which phenomena can be exactly determined. The exactness of a science is in inverse proportion to its complexity; and astronomy, physics chemistry, biology, and sociology are all great phenomena. Comte's stages are the following:

1. Theological
2. Metaphysical
3. Positive

According to Comte, the *theology stage* was the central focus during pre-enlightenment. The *metaphysical stage* is the time since the enlightenment (i.e., logical rationalism and the rights of humanity). And the *positive stage* is the scientific stage, where individual's rights outweigh and stand over one person's rule.

According to Comte, the three phases involve universal rule in relation to society and its development and that each stage must happen in order for the other stages to proceed. An appreciation of the past and the ability to build on it toward the future was and continues to be the key in the transition within human socialization and also in the general progress of humanity. Comte said, "That from science comes prediction, and from prediction comes action. Since continual empirical data is being sought and learned, the 3rd phase can never be complete, and how would we know when that stage was reached."

Antipositivism is a theory that humanity's focus should be on norms, values, meanings, symbols, and cultural processes viewed *subjectively* versus the scientific and objective approach of positivism. In philosophy and sociology, people often debate the meaning of existence and the process of humanity's interactions within existence. Another philosophy that was rendered about how humanity works within existence is the *Seven Universal Laws of the Universe.*

The first law within the seven universal laws of the universe is the *law of mentalism*, which states that there is a universal consciousness that starts in the mind and that reality is a manifestation of the mind. Reality is passed along and across time and although individuals are able to create their own reality, ultimately people rely on a universal reality as their driving central force. The second law is the *law of correspondence*, which relies on the harmony between physical, mental, and spiritual realms whereby everyone is interconnected. Harmony with oneself radiates out upon the universe. The third law is the *law of vibration*, which states that nothing is at rest and everything is part of the life energy cycle. Everything that we experience through our senses occurs via vibrations even in the mental realm. The aura is the vibration that one gives off and its energy can be felt by others. The fourth law is the *law of polarity*, which states that opposites are actually two different extremes of the same thing and people can be on the polar opposite end of each other. In order for a person to move along the polar continuum, that person needs to change their vibration. The fifth law is the *law of rhythm*, which states that everything in life has its rise and fall and its flow, much like that of a pendulum. In our thoughts, the pendulum can swing us one way and then the flow of momentum carries it back in the other direction, unless we consciously alter the natural flow of the rhythm. The sixth law is the *law of cause and effect* states that every cause has its effect and that every effect has its cause. People's actions and their words create vibrations of momentum, which manifest over time and interact with other vibrations. The seventh law is the *law of gender*, which states that both genders possess the traits of each other and that these traits often lie dormant within people due to socialization and based on social rules. Being complete in life involves people understanding that this balance does exist and involves people seeking to find the correct balance. Because of people's varying auras, polarities, and the effects that they cause, and along with people's different levels of understanding; social ignorance, social divides, and social inequities persist.

Marx wrote extensively about society and human socialization. The *Marx false consciousness* concept focuses on explanations regarding social problems as the shortcomings of individuals versus the flaws of society. As individuals are born into the existing societal structure, this structure is part of the molding process. Marx stated, "That uprise lies latent in the populace." There are competing forces which exist in the world. The forces of self-aggrandizement and altruism, emotional and intellect, and gender all compete with each other in a perpetual cyclical continuum, which shapes both society and civilization. Marx felt that individual behavior is shaped by the larger social structure and that individuals continue to challenge the status quo over time. Based on this challenge to the social rules, the relationship between individuals within a social structure is a continuum. These social challenges over time become more quantifiable in their value as forces of change.

These individual actions can alter and/or change the social structure. The forces of individual and collective desire move along the continuum at a slower pace, but if this pace is delayed or stalled, it will normally create a peaceful rebellion (nonviolent struggle). If the collective desire is not recognized and is ignored, this can result in revolt. There are other social theorists that each has their own views about social cause and effect.

Durkheim saw the balance between crime and morality as an integral part of all healthy society, and that the collective conscious defines social evolution. Conflict is part of the human existence, and in order to have conflict, there must be polar elements amongst individuals and also within the collective society. The key is to make sure that the correct balance is maintained. Also a consideration must be made regarding social authority and power and how that power is maintained.

Sharp stated that if the subjects (people) do not obey, that the leader does not have true power, as power derives from the subjects of the state. Any power structure relies on the subject's obedience to the commands of the leader. Sharp's ideas have been very broad in world movements. Society is defined by inequality that produces conflict. This conflict can only be overcome by the fundamental transformation of the existing relations into new relations. Individuals and groups are agents of change. Exploitation and oppression of the people are forces that maintain the division of power and the division of labor. The suppression of individuals and people can suffocate creativity, which is the engine for social development and social change. People in power positions at any level will often suppress innovation in order to maintain their social role and/or their social power and also to stall the change that would impact their role or power.

The realization of human potential is what can transform society and social relations. Consensus does not preserve social order, it entrenches stratification (i.e., The American Dream). Weber emphasized the importance and influence of individual social acts, which can impact social relations and society as a whole.

Marx (1872) stated, "There is no royal road to science, and only those who do not dread the fatiguing climb of its steep paths have a chance of gaining its luminous summits." Marx focused heavily on the dynamics of the social classes within socialization and the interaction between the social classes.

Marx's concept of *historical materialism* focuses on the causes of development and change in human society by which humans collectively produce the necessities of life and is when society changes by means of economic activity. *Conspicuous consumption* is when people focus on their standard of living in comparison to others. Social classes involve the social stratification and hierarchical social categories within society. *Classis* is Latin and was used in Rome where the census categorized citizens by wealth. By the late 1700s, the word *class* was replaced by terms such as rank, order, or estate. Social classes have existed during all time and the social class balances have played a huge role within socialization and in social evolution.

Class impacts can also include an educational impact whereby certain people are able to be legacies within their families, and they will be channeled into an education that creates further and continued separation from many others in society. This educational impact can also create an *antipathy* toward educational acquisition in some groups, whereby the acquisition of knowledge is perceived to be beyond a person or people within a social class. The societal rank or role can perpetuate and can stagnate the mobility of the people and the social classes.

In work and employment, social alienation can occur within the ranks due to people's social class background, and due to this impact, people's satisfaction is often felt more by some people at the lower levels within the social hierarchy. *Class conflict* is the tension and antagonism between the social classes. Social class division can create antipathy, exploitation, and the inequitable distribution of wealth between the classes.

Consumerism in more recent history has given rise to social mobility and this upward mobility has increased with the increased numbers of people in the labor force. Within consumerism, an idea is planted in people surrounding an ideology that focuses on a perceived social flaw with an inability for a person or people to keep up, which can result in their dissatisfaction in life. This flawed ideology can also result in things like high stress levels, depression, and even suicide. *Social relative deprivation* is when people believe that they are worse off than other people in a similar group of people. Consumerism creates the powerful social element of *desire*. The affect of desire on people is to create a feeling that there is lack of something in their lives by creating a sense of loss and making people feel incomplete in their wholeness. Desire creates fantasy within people and an excess in fantasy can lead to a dull reality and people's fixation on their desires. A fantasized existence and flawed social ideology can distort people's reality. The social effects of the media, marketing, and technology were predicted long ago and those effects have transformed entire social models and societies.

The temptations of evil lusts are poured into humanity by these elements of iniquity. Those who claim that these elements are just giving the people what they want are obviously not from within the positive element of humanity and they also lack an understanding of spirituality as well.

An *idiom* for this type of social climbing is "Keeping up with the Joneses." Within this social phenomenon, people will identify others in their social structures as the benchmark for their social caste, they will then place themselves into a category, and if they fail, it is perceived as cultural inferiority. Some social theorists predicted what would occur within social systems based on the elements and conditions that were in place.

Marx proposed his theory on socialization and how the classes and social power can dictate social outcomes. Marx stated that *production relations* were required for existence, production, and exchange. Production is carried out through definite relations between people and some control the means of production. Relations are determined by the level of character of *productive forces* (the means of production, tools, technology, raw materials, knowledge, and the human component).

The modes of production concept states that the character of productive relations is determined by the character of productive forces. Shifting over time from ancient slaves, to feudalism (landowners and serfs), and to capitalism (capitalist and the working class). The exchange of labor for wages occurs with capitalist who control the means of production. From these relations, an economic base arises with laws, customs, culture, morality, and norms (way of thought), which constitute the ideological superstructure of society.

The superstructure of society concept states that the human means of subsistence, the division of labor, and class division is dependent on modes of production based on productive forces, society moves forward when the dominant class is replaced by a new emerging class (liberation is required for this to occur).

Marx's progress involves progressive stages and social relations.

1. Progress is social and driven by material production forces (Tech, labor, capital, and goods).
2. Human productive relations (Capitalist and workers).
3. Production relations progress dependent on production force.
4. Relations of production, development of forces of production, capitalism increases by the rate at which forces develop and stresses the accumulation of capital.
5. Both productive forces and production relations progress independently by the will of mankind or by strategy.

6. The superstructure is ultimately an expression of the mode of production (forces of relations of production).
7. State is position of ruling class, instrument to enforce preferred productive relations.
8. State power only transferred by social and political upheaval.
9. When relations no longer supports productive forces, revolution must occur as the historical process depends on class struggle, especially the organization and the conscious of the working class (it is not predetermined)

Marx and the other social theorists that have been mentioned are all correct whether in part or whether in the combination of their ideas. Humanity does desire conflict and this conflict is driven by an innate pre-wired drive, which is based off the tendency of people to prefer *choices* between multiple life elements within socialization, this can also be classified as the drive for free will. When people do not have choices, their core spirits and their energy can be severely impacted and/or altered. And also there is an underlying *root tension* in all people that is attached to their drive for choice. This root tension is much more prominent in some people than in others and this tension is not always seen or expressed on the surface level.

There are some people who have very low tension levels and drives within the social continuum, and there are other people who will do *anything* that they have to in order to relieve their inner tension. The process of socialization and people's individual desire for social climbing and/or social power are tied directly into their inner tension. The more concentrated a person's inner tension is, the worse the action potential becomes for other people within their social network and potentially even for society. In a social value system, some people are out for themselves and others are out for the collective good. The forces of social pressure can vary across people, groups, and societies.

Each person Goes through their own social matrix in life, and based on internal and external factors, they will all go in unique directions. Because there is so much variance between people and across situations, everyone simply cannot be generalized into a category. The social sciences group similar social elements within people and groups together and track the social evolution that occurs. Although broad generalizations cannot be made across large groups, the social sciences have evolved over time to be able to accurately diagnose issues within individuals, groups, and in societies. Because of the action potential that exists, even at the smaller micro social individual level, there is a need to watch for the signs and signals of negative social patterns.

Many people because of their innate core characteristics, free will, and ability to choose their path, and the options available within their path will either ignore or will remain ignorant as to the impacts of negative social patterns that occur on an individual level, in group levels, and within collective society. What many people also do not account for is the collective societal positive energy balance, which needs to be maintained for the sake of humanity. For every social issue that is ignored, there is a potentially powerful collective impact, which could be developing. Even ignoring one small issue can potentially impact a large number of people as mentioned in the *butterfly effect*. The *probability theory* states that random events can transform into patterns.

There are many different factors and elements, which are involved in people's ability to understand even the dynamics of the things, which are happening within them let alone in trying to understand the dynamics involved within the socialization processes within societies. A *visionary* is a person who is committed to growth, who looks beyond causes to problems, and who develops precise solutions for success. *Wisdom* is seeing life situations from a larger point of view. *Discernment* is the ability to understand the deeper reason for why things happen. *Discretion* is the ability to avoid words and actions that can create socially negative outcomes. *Creativity* is approaching problems with a new perspective. Finally, people's *opinions* (without experience, truths, and knowledge) are highly toxic and noxious to people within the path of life. People need to reserve their *uninformed opinions* to spare the world from the negative output.

Everyone in life has their own unique skills and abilities and some people are more gifted in certain cognitive areas than others. *Wit* is the natural ability of people to perceive and understand concepts with an exceptional level of intelligence. Some of the major forces, which can work either for or against people in their life paths, are their innate characteristics and abilities, their environmental factors, which can include their nurturing, education, one's social system, one's support network, spirituality when present, and the personally internalized impacts of literature, the media, and technology. Individuals must never forget that people are the *value* in the social value system. People must *combat* the negative social energy forces that conflict with their core values and threaten the collective good and evolution of humanity. And also, people must be cautious regarding people who look to exploit and/or erode spirituality. Spirituality is always *pure* on its own level and it is *people* who defile spirituality. The negative resistance and the negative forces in life are also the people who fall within the shallow end of the spiritual continuum. These forces only *pretend* to be spiritual if it serves their social purpose. People must work toward their own evolution, toward the evolution of humanity, and toward the preservation of spirituality as the negative social forces seek to destroy all of these critical life elements. Enduring within the positive life path can be excruciatingly difficult, but the rewards for doing it are greater than anyone can imagine.

communication

Verbal Communication, Language, and Speech

Humanity can only survive and thrive within its ability to effectively communicate. When there is a lack of concise communication, or if the communications that are either sent or received are in a format that is ambiguous, this can potentially cause chaotic effects between individuals, social rings, social systems, and societies. Historically there have been significant times and periods where unmindful miscommunications have caused severe relational impacts and lasting tensions between powerful people and societies in the world, which have had consequential and collective harm displaced onto humanity.

Within the ambiguity that can be found in interpersonal communications, there are certain words that can potentially have completely different meanings. The communicators in a social exchange must understand how their words and statements will be received, and they must also always understand their audience.

Verbal communication is the forward voluble activity of conveying meaningful linguistic information through the exchange of words between people using the verbal mode. Verbal communication requires a sender, a message, and a recipient. The process of communication is only complete once the message from the sender (communicator) is understood by the receiver. Reciprocal communicative feedback is also highly critical for the effective communications between communicating parties. A pattern of *one-way* communication at any social level can slowly lead to the deterioration of positive social relations between individuals, social groups, and social systems within the process of socialization.

The level of communication between parties does not always have to be completely balanced, but the social impacts of communications that are heavily in favor of one side within any social level along the continuum have been well-documented by the social sciences over time as fueling the potential for social issues and/or social chaos. Everyone has something to express and when people are not allowed to express themselves, this almost always builds up social stress and social tension. The impacts of these nonreciprocal communicative social relations can build up over time on a collective level and they can potentially impact many people.

Further, communication is the process by which meaning is assigned and conveyed in an attempt to establish a shared understanding between communicating parties. Misunderstandings can be avoided by people on both sides of the communication continuum taking the proper communicative precautions that can include people (receivers) reiterating their understanding of what was communicated to them, this can lead to the desired social outcome. And as mentioned prior, the sender (communicator) is responsible for understanding their audience and the potential impact of their words. Although within the process of communication, many times people (receivers) are afraid to let others know that they are unable to understand a communication. This social reality can be due to multiple variables and possibilities.

Unfortunately an extensive myriad of social realities are simply implied in life, and most people just assume that certain social requirements and social aptitudes are in place and that a social link exist between they and others based on people's assigned social roles and their social status. The possibility of others within a social communication chain having personal social deficits, are rarely calculated into the social equation. Many people just move fiercely forward within the process of socialization without any consideration of the potential social contextual outliers that may exist along their social path. This social oversight is one of the fundamental flaws within humanity, and it is abrading the forward positive evolution of humanity. The social *silver-tongues* and those who speak more eloquently often preclude those who communicate at less rapid speeds and at less intricate levels within the vernacular from participating within certain chains of social communication. When these people act in this manner, they contribute to the flux of negative social stress energy that deforms and disfigures the cores of their targets and also the core of the collective humanity.

One possibility within the communicative distortion in the reception of a message is that a communicator simply does not care what the level of their audience is, which points generally to a personality flaw within the sender (communicator) and ultimately this flaw is part of the communicator's own social incompetence because when others (receivers) are not getting all of the information that they require, they cannot possibly meet the social requirements that are being set forth. Due to the fact that many social leaders in social rings, social systems, and society are *type A* personalities, the social reality is that these social encounters and the communications within them will move at their desired social pace and will involve intense impatience with anything that impedes that pace. Type A leaders do not like to be harried and are often impervious to the demands of others. Being type A leaders are the predominant group in power at every social level, they need to be targeted by the forces of positive social modification and they need be compelled to adjust their social ineptness. Another fundamental flaw within society is that society has tolerated and enabled the type A personalities to dictate to groups and societies throughout all time that the social flaw resides in those that they lead, when in fact the true social flaw resides in them and in their own personal disdain for those who possess less social force and social agility. The social balance within this leadership continuum remains highly imbalanced because the type A personalities socially recruit and promote those who possess their identical social attributes. This social equation can be modified, but those who control the direction have refused over time to alter their social perspectives. The type A personalities use their social status and their social roles to influence those under them, while true leaders use a combination of social and humanistic acumen to inspire those under them. Type A leadership has accounted for a tremendous amount of societal stress throughout time, but yet the social factions, which could demand a social paradigm shift do not use their social potential to influence the adaptation within this fundamental human social flaw. Fear and aggression are the social mechanisms that have been used throughout time to maintain this social imbalance; and fear and aggression are negative energy sources that erode both people and the core of humanity. As evidence of this point, there has been modern literature put forth, compelling groups to use these social mechanisms to become social dominators and social power brokers. This course of *unseeing* and *callous* action does not break down the barriers restricting human evolution, but rather it makes the barriers more difficult to supplant.

Another possibility in communicative message distortion is that the receivers simply are putting on a complete social façade and that their time before being discovered is running out. If people keep acting as if they are understanding communications when this is not the social reality, they are not only hurting themselves, but they are also hurting others on a collective level. The social façade can potentially be based on a person's social role, intellectual disparity, biological issues, and sometimes can even be due to a person's desire to avoid any type of negative socially implied embarrassment.

If the social façade is due to the social embarrassment element, this could potentially be directly tied back into the challenge that exist when type A social leaders refuse to alter their *fervent* social pace due to any circumstances. Unfortunately many brilliant ideas and social opportunities are left behind due to this type of social scenario. Effective communication between people is very important in order to facilitate and generate action, create understanding, express ideas, and much more. Sometimes, there are also social and technical barriers that can block the forward flow of communication and the desired understanding of a communicative message.

Communication barriers can distort and modify the desired intention of the communicative message that is being conveyed and they can also create very undesirable social outcomes. There are many elements that can become communication barriers and some of these elements can include social and cognitive filtering elements such as: the context of the social situation, the level of attention that the receiver is offering, the cognitive abilities of the receiver to properly perceive and interpret the message content correctly, the various elements that are incorporated into the senders expressive speech and language outputs, the emotion of the environment, the mood of both the sender and the receiver, and more.

If the expressive communicative language that a sender is using is ambiguous jargon which doesn't apply to all parties, highly complex in nature, situational context that is not understood by all parties, this can also create a communication barrier. People should never assume that other people always understand their communications and this is a very common social flaw and a common communications barrier especially with type A social leaders. Within communications, there are certain elements that compose the foundation of forward dialogue and they are the underlying guide to human relations.

Words are an element within the human communication system that relay verbal communication. Words within language and in communication are context dependent and their intention and meaning are up to the individual interpretation of the end receiver. Words have a field or range of meanings and therefore word associations can trigger and elicit a wide variety of responses from different receivers. Some words within communicative language can provoke an immediate association of an opposite thought. This type of word association is called the *difference of opposites* (i.e., when a person hears the word *black*, this automatically triggers *white* as the colors are associated and enmeshed together).

Words within language and communication are subject to negotiation, contest, and struggle. This is why people need to be able to identify and adjust their communication link in order to get on the same social wavelength within a communication chain and be certain that they understand their audience within their communications. This process will ensure that all parties within a communication system will understand each other. Language is a system of signs and symbols (words), each with their own action potential. Language creates the meaning within communication through a series of differences or contrasts. The contrast in language is very similar to the contrast in other human social elements such as personalities and human conflict. Everything in life has its own unique and dynamic social balancers. Within language there are even more elements and components, which help to build the foundation of communication and also help to define meanings.

In communications, which are social interactions, people interact using a shared set of communicative signs and symbols.

These signs and symbols share three levels of *semiotic rules* in language. *Semiotics* (semiology) is the study of signs, which has two key elements, the *signifier* and the *signified*. The three semiotic rules are the *syntactic* rule, which applies to the formal properties of signs and symbols (words). The *pragmatic* rule applies to the relations between signs and expressions and the communicators. Pragmatics involves the role of context in interpretation and word recognition.

The *semantic* rule involves the relationship between the signs and symbols and what they mean. Semantics are the relationships of words, how they are used, and under what context. The *linguistic relativity theory* poses that how words are used and framed impacts what people think and how they perceived. Labels can also strongly impact people's perceptions within communication. People need only to view history briefly to see the impacts of how framing can impact people and societies. Many people and many groups will use framing and semantics intentionally (almost on a subliminal level), and depending on their audience, this can build tremendous tension and can potentially lead to a collective harm. In addition over time, words and word meanings can evolve.

Diachrony involves the impact of the change in meaning of words over time. Linguist (those who study language) sometimes fail to identify the *root cause* of word changes and the underlying reasons surrounding the change. Unfortunately in most things in life, it is more convenient for people to explore and solve only the surface issues and it is also human nature to stop ahead of reaching the root of an issue, challenge, or mystery of humanity. This is the social reality and this social flaw is something that hinders the forward evolution of humanity. This social flaw occurs at all levels within humanity and across all human social spectrums. In language, the *signs/symbols* are the words, the *signifier* is the sound that forms the word, the word is the interpretation of the meaning of the signifier, and the *signified* is the concept or meaning that is indicated by the signifier, which varies between people and context and which can change over time. The concept or meaning can stabilize with habituation over time and it can also be cued by thoughts, and images. *Syntagm* in language and communication is when the signs (words) occur in sequence to create meaning (the flow of words). The *paradigm/paradigmatic* relationship in language and communication is when one sign can be replaced by another (i.e., a, the, that). The *conceptual map* is when meaning is realized in language and communication by coordinating the signs (words) within the conceptual map. Both the signifier and the signified are needed to create the conceptual map. Words and their meanings must be categorized and stored in cognition memory docking in order to reference them later.

A *mental lexicon* is psycholinguistic comprehension and competition. A *lexicon* is a word catalogue and grammar system, inventory of *lexemes* that are used within syntactic structures, inflectional rules, and derivational rules. Lexemes are different forms of a word (i.e., run, runs, ran, etc.) The use of lexemes is governed by the laws of grammar. A *polyseme* is a word or phrase with different but related senses (i.e., to *procure* aligns with *to get*, and *understand* aligns with *I get*). A *phoneme* is the smallest unit of sound in a language, the English language has forty-four phonemes. A *morpheme* is the smallest grammatical unit in language. *Morphophonology* is the study of sound changes in morphemes. *Morphology* involves the identification, analysis, and description of the structure of given languages and the linguistic units (root words, intonation/stress, implied context, etc.). Languages can be varied within their structures.

The English language is a fusional language with inferences in its word relations, and the patterns of word formations formulate the rules. Other languages can vary widely from the English language. The Chinese language uses unbound free morphemes and depends on word order to convey meaning, with the exception of *mandarin*, which uses compounds with mostly bounded roots. Another factor that plays a role within language and communication is the *accent*. According to linguistics and psycholinguistics experts, the accent is the most difficult thing to duplicate. *Proactive interference* is when a person's existing cognitive schema is *blocking* the integration of new formation into their existing schema or a new schema formation (i.e., in learning a new language). During the language developmental stages, there is a critical learning period.

The *critical period theory* in language, states that for (tone, pitch, accent, etc.) that the *first language* acquisition must occur by the time the cerebral lateralization in the brain is complete at around the puberty stage, and that language acquired after this will be slower and less structural. There are different ranges of capabilities across individuals as with most human elements, but this theory generalizes the standard language impact. There are also other milestone ranges within language and speech. The *telegraphic speech* milestone range states that by age two, children are normally able to produce at least two words, at this two-word stage. This milestone area also involves the beginning of syntax formation within language. There are scientific fields that study the various aspects of language and communication within human development.

Neurolinguistics and *psycholinguistics* study the human cognitive abilities of comprehension, production, acquisition of language, neural mechanisms, and analysis of brain activity and biological structures. Phonetics and phonology involve understanding how the brain understands sounds. Phonological disorder is a language and communication deviation and the inability of a person to produce speech at their age range. The study of language and communication involves identifying the brain structures and mechanisms involved in the speech production process.

Brain lateralization relates to the two brain hemispheres and that certain mental processes occur in various areas of these hemispheres. Language occurs on both sides of the brain—grammar and vocabulary on the left side and emotional content on the right side. Brain modularity is determining which brain modules are involved in specific functions. Noam Chomsky posed that there is a specific area in the brain for language or a *module*. There are many factors and mechanisms that are involved in language and speech production within communication.

Dysarthria is a neuromotor speech disorder, which affects the muscles that help a person to talk and pronounce words. Any of the speech subsystems can be affected (respiration, phonation, resonance, prosody, and articulation). Thus there can be impairments in the intelligibility, audibility, and efficacy of vocal communications. The cranial nerves that control these muscles include the trigeminal nerves motor branch (V), the facial nerves (VII), the glossopharyngeal nerve (IX), the vagus nerve (X), and the hypoglossal nerve (XII). Neurological issues from damage to the central nervous system (CNS) or peripheral nervous system (PNS) can hinder control over the tongue, throat, lips, or lungs.

Within speech production itself, there are many various components that come into play and correlate to how speech is produced in each person.

Fluency is the forward flow of speech in communication and fluency can be impacted by many different factors. *Abduction* is the ability to spread apart the vocal elements and breathe and *adduction* is being able to bring together the vocal cords for voiced sound and fluency. The diaphragm allows a healthy breathing pattern and flattens and lowers during inspiration. *Articulation* is the ability to make words from buzzing a sound in the larynx and *aphonia* is the inability to vibrate the vocal folds to produce sound, which is *disfluency* or the blockage of forward speech flow. The larynx is the primary voice producing area called the voice box, which houses the vocal folds. *Phonation* is when the vocal folds' vibration resonates to the vocal tract and articulators. The vocal tract is the area between the larynx and the lips. *Registers* are the pitches produced by the vocal folds and vocal tract movements. *Pitch* is the loudness of the sound produced. Men having a larger larynx and vocal folds allowing for more vocal intensity. *Intensity* is the level of vocal power. *Intelligibility* is the ease of understanding a person's speech based on their volume and articulation. A *decibel* is a unit to measure sound. With the ability to produce sound people can adjust their production levels. Voice *inflection* involves having ups and downs in the voice pitch versus only a monotone pitch. It is common in social systems that people often find a monotone pitch very unappealing. Voice *intonation* involves when the voice pitch or stress is rising or falling. Intonation is used normally to stress important or highlighted elements within communication.

The *Lombard effect* involves a person raising their voice during communication versus other competing voices in an area. The *timbre* is the quality of the vocal output. Voice quality is not only important in the field of music, but it also can impact people within their interpersonal relations, within social groups, and in their careers. Some people are naturally drawn to people with certain types of voice pitches on one end of the social continuum and some social roles discriminate against people based on their voice pitch on the other end of the social continuum. There are various types of vocal outputs that people can have based on a variety of elements.

The chest voice/chest register is the voice resonating through the sternum and trachea area, which is most common in males, while females speak normally in either mixed or falsetto pitches and with a head voice. The *head voice* is what females typically use, while males use the chest voice as mentioned prior. *Falsetto* is a higher-pitched voice register and in male speech, falsetto may be undesirable. This social reality has to do with social expectations and social norms that have been established over time. A person's level of confidence, self-esteem, and their perceived identity can also play a role in their voice pitch and vocal output. Some people will modify their voice pitch on their own to accommodate their perceived or desired social identity and sometimes those who lack confidence will speak under their breath. These voice elements can also impact a person's social roles and social value within the process of socialization.

The *habitual pitch* is the daily pitch that is used by people around others when and where the context of the social situation does not dictate the use of other pitches or a person's optimal pitch (ideal). People will change their voice pitch sometimes widely across different social situations. Depending on how many different social scenarios a person is involved in within their life path, the *switch-pitch* effort can become very exhausting. If people are extending too far away from their natural voice pitch range and creating social facades, these efforts can potentially lead to oxidative stress, which cannot only impact their voice, but can also affect their overall health. For everything that can occur correctly within speech production, there are also a number of elements, which can inhibit people's speech production.

The glossopharyngeal cranial nerve (CN9) elevates the larynx and pharynx via the branchial motor (vocal folds for pitch and volume), which also protect the trachea (airway). Vocal folds produce phonation via vibration (voicing). If the glottis is open, this will produce a voiceless action or a *faucalized* voice (hollow or yawny). A closed or blocked glottis produces a harsh voice. There is a *sweet spot* that can occur called a *modal voice*, which is at max vibration, with a combination of airflow and glottal tension. Speech pathologists use a register to identify phonation and the modal voice is one of four which they use. Voice pitches can sometimes also be considered to be social deficits (i.e., negative, weak, passive, etc.). It is a sad fact in humanity that people can be judged across all human social elements. Individualistic societies often are highly judgmental within socialization. When people judge others based on a singular social component or element, they are potentially sacrificing a myriad of other social talents and gifts. This social reality is yet another social flaw, which impedes the growth of humanity. There are also some more production errors, which unfortunately can impact people within the process of socialization and in the social value system.

Bleat is a voice pitch with excessive physical tension in the voicing creating a fast *vibrato*, while *breathiness* is when the vocal folds do not completely meet, so air is in the voice. Vocal *fry* is a low pitch, where the vocal cords open and close and are popping, while *hypernasal* is a nasal and oral honky voice, which involves trouble closing off the back of the throat (velopharyngeal area), and excess airflow through the nose. *Jitter* is a varying pitch in the voice with a rough sound. *Spasmodic dysphonia* is where there is a strained voice or no voice, and when the vocal folds clench tightly, while a *glottal attack* is when the vocal cords abruptly are brought together, and there are audible clicks on the vowels. Many of these elements are referred to as *paraverbals*.

The *paralanguage* includes such elements such as voice lesson quality, emotion, and speaking style, as well as prosodic features such as rhythm, intonation, and voice stress. Some paraverbal elements can include a person's message duration, the number of words they use, the speech rate, pauses such as filled pauses (i.e., umm and ahh), unfilled pauses with silence, repetition with repeat words or statements, forgetting or contradiction, speech errors (i.e., using the wrong words, combining words, omission of words), response latency (delay in answers), and response speed (people still have to evaluate a quick statement for details). Some people will try to speak quickly to *sound/appear* intelligent and/or intelligent people will speak quickly to avoid having their words and statements broken down in social situations. It is common that social leaders will use the speed technique. For people that are quick on their feet and intelligent, they are said to have wit. Wit is the cognitive natural ability for people to perceive and understand things with an exceptional level of intelligence. *Repartee* is a person's cognitive facility to answer questions swiftly and cleverly. There is so much social variance that exists between individuals that there are specific social science fields dedicated to studying the effects of these communication and speech production differences and their social effects.

The social impacts of people's voice pitch, voice output, and communication styles have become so scrutinized over time that certain people go to speech pathologists on their own to adjust their voice pitch in order to get into certain careers. Some people also see speech language pathologists (SLPs) in order to like their own voice better as some people cannot stand the sound of their own voice and/or the voices of others. In addition, there are some people that cannot find any enjoyment in music. *Amusia* is a condition where people find music completely unappealing. Around 4 percent of people in a given population has this condition and in places like China where *pitch* determines the meaning of some words, people with amusia cannot properly distinguish the meanings properly, which impacts their ability to communicate effectively. Some famous people in history with amusia were Sigmund Freud, Ulysses S. Grant, Teddy Roosevelt, and Charles Darwin.

For those people that are fortunate enough to have a healthy ability to produce speech and the cognitive ability to communicate on a highly effective level, their social abilities can be strengthened even further with the acquisition of knowledge. Often, the people who become masters of their language will use power words within their social repertoire. With the command of a language and the use of power words, people can often dictate social outcomes. If a person or a group has a social agenda, they can use these power words to influence others. Socially dominating people in leadership, sales, marketing, politics, and other roles and areas where people are trying to win influence over others, will all become the students of words, language, and communication styles. These people can then exert their social force over the social masses because of the fact that many in society are not refined in these areas. But people can begin to offset the potentially adverse impacts of these social efforts by becoming *educated.*

Power words can be studied and they can be put into categories in order to influence people. An example would be within the human element of the desire to be safe, for safety, the words *safe*, *secure*, and *sound* can elicit the feeling in people that they are getting something that will provide them the safety element. To elicit the social element of greed, the words *cash*, *deserve*, *money*, *more*, and *free* can be used. To elicit the feeling of control, the words *easy*, *guide*, *proven*, and *best* can be used. To reach people on a personal level, the social element of identity can be applied through the use of words such as *you*, *approved*, and *favorite*. To build the element of *trust*, the words *certain*, *proven*, *scientific*, and *truth* can be used. Power words can capture people's attention and they can elicit an emotional association and response. These commanding social tactics are designed to bring people's subconscious social platforms into a conscious reality.

Some other power words that are frequently used are: save, discover, guarantee, health, love, need, suddenly, now, announcing, introducing, improvement, amazing, sensational, remarkable, revolutionary, compare, bargain, and hurry. Some children's power words can include the following words: last chance, magic, challenge, just arrived, and bargain. The science and knowledge of the impact of words and communication is used today for much more than the original intent of human betterment and social evolution.

People must remember that social dominators and social wolves know who their audience is by studying them, so it is only fair that the people also know who the communicators of these messages really are as well. In a social paradigm shift where the social knowledge and information is balanced out more evenly, the social dominators and social wolves would lose much of their social ground unless they were found to be truly worthy and to be relaying social truths and realities to the people. What most people in society do not realize is that these social tests can be run either way. The people in society owe *nothing* to the people who are trying to persuade them toward a social direction.

Communication is the fundamental need and the core element of humanity and the elements of communication are closely monitored in parallel with the study of socialization as they go hand in hand.

Where communication goes, humanity goes. A common social misconception is that past civilizations changed over time purely due to innovation and/or leadership, but the social reality is that only through the power of communication were the people that were being oppressed able to change the world and also help to evolve certain oppressive social elements within humanity. What people must also remember is that certain innate negative social elements within humanity carry over through the course of time in certain people and they have never gone away. These negative social characteristics can lay dormant within certain people, and they are always ripe to be harvested if the proper social conditions are ever presented. Genetics have ensured that although people can be enhanced naturally over the course of time in certain life elements, the choice to evolve the nature of humanity is a *conscious* choice that is made by people instead of something that is naturally occurring. If the core nature of humanity had evolved over time such as other organic and biological elements, society would be well ahead of its current state of evolution.

When the collective good of the people and/or humanity is not being taken care of, people turn to communication to alter the course of socialization. The first thing that social dominators and/or social restrictors will do at any social level to offset the power of communication is to cut it off. Modern social dominators can also use technology to intercept communication and/or to distort communication to either promote a unified cause or to hinder a unified action. The only way to be certain that the collective need and good of humanity isn't diminished is to be sure that communication networks are never completely severed. People must not let the negative forces within society confound their ability to reach each other in order to propel the positive evolution of humanity forward.

COGNITION AND ABSTRACT THOUGHT

Thinking, Memory, Learning, Perception, Problem Solving, and Personality

The resources of the humanity are within its people, and humanity depends on the process of social harvesting of people's resources for its continued social evolution. Humanity's foundation strongly relies on the strengths and talents of individual people that ultimately can contribute to the growth of social systems. The growth of social systems fortifies the strength of the collective level. These ultra-critical human characteristics that are sought and mined need to be continually harvested in order for humanity to reach its full potential. There are certain crucial human characteristics that are found in select people, which are highly critical to the continued evolution of humanity. Humanity must leave no stone unturned in finding its valuable people resources and there are a variety of human resources in which value can be discovered.

There are certain people within humanity that possess uncommon and exceptional personal characteristics. A *visionary* is committed to growth, looks beyond causes to problems, and develops precise solutions for success. People with *wisdom* can see life situations from a larger point of view. The characteristic of *discernment* is the ability of people to understand the deeper reason for why things happen. The power of *discretion* is the ability of people, leaders, and societies to avoid words and actions that can create negative social outcomes. *Creativity* is the ability for people to approach problems with new perspectives.

The true sign of intelligence is not knowledge, but imagination

—Einstein

Fecundity is the capability for people to produce intellectual and novel creative productivity with abundantly imaginative output. In order for people to properly express (communicate) their capabilities and gifts to others, they will also need to possess some other important covariant characteristics.

Wit is the natural ability of a person to perceive and understand concepts with highly exceptional intelligence and repartee is their facility to answer questions swiftly and cleverly. In order for social harvesting to transpire, there has to be resources available, and the people with the resources also need to be able to communicate and extend their available resources to others. This process can be troublesome when harvesting from the *uncouth*. There are many different human factors and variables, which exist across individuals that can differentiate the potential for social mining and harvesting opportunities.

Cognition is a covariant social factor, which involves the mental processes of thinking, knowing, and remembering concepts, which are a mental grouping of people, things, and/or items. A *cognitive map* is the mental blueprint for cognitive mapping, routing, and docking. Another substantive factor within social mining and harvesting is people's mental construct. The mental construct is a person's *psyche* to include their motivation, anger, personality, intelligence, love, attachment, honesty, and not all of these elements can be measured with a high degree of accuracy. In order to have a positive yield in human harvesting, many covariant factors must align.

A covariance is a related factor, which can be positive or negative, where one factor is dependent on the other for social procurement. In order for human harvesting to occur, there are a number of covariant mental elements, which must manifest and exist together in unison in order to yield the action potential and the collective benefits necessary for social progress and social evolution. There are some major organic systems, which are higher order systems that incorporate the various covariant elements and factors that are necessary for social harvesting.

A major high-level organic system is the *self*, which is a person's mental conscious and unconscious aspects that includes their personality, cognition, schemas, and core identity to include their ego. The *schema* is a component of the self and it is involved heavily in covariant social procurement. The schema is a combination of a person's cognitive organic system and their conceptual framework for information. People's social actions and their behaviors are organized tightly around and they are heavily influenced by these covariant factors. The schema also impacts the integration and processing (encoding) of new information into the *mental set*. People can either accept new information as supportive to their schema, or they can deny information which doesn't support their existing schema. The schema and mental set are higher order organic systems, which are composed of many other additional covariant elements.

Within the higher level organic systems, a person's *mood* is formulated, which is a social element that correlates to people's overall feeling or mental state. The impact of the mood can be profound on the continuum of social harvesting. A steady and positive mood can elicit the yielding of tremendous social resources when coupled with the other positively related and parallel cognitive covariants (i.e., creative fecundity). When these covariant elements are working in unison, they can produce colossal amounts of social procurement. While on the other end of the continuum, there are negative considerations. Mood disorders are prolonged and intense mood shifts, which can create functional difficulty, a decline in perception of daily life normalcy, depression, and more. No matter what the action potentials are of the other social and cognitive covariants, the mood covariant can inhibit the process of social mining and harvesting. Mood congruent behavior is when a person's expressed actions are consistent with how they feel. However, many people rely on using defense mechanisms to manage their daily life. Unfortunately the mood covariant component can heavily alter the action potential of the other underlying covariants. Everything in life has its balancers.

> *The excessive increase of anything causes a reaction in the opposite direction of something else.*
>
> —Plato

Intelligence is also a very important covariant element, which involves goal-directed adaptive behavior and derives from innate (genetic) and social influences. Intelligence can be measured via testing. Intelligence tests are used are used to evaluate reasoning, comprehension, judgement, and potential. For accurate measurement, the test must have a reliable and valid design. The tests can predict achievement, strengths, and weaknesses. For any psychometric test, the examiner must be well trained. The results of IQ tests are also commonly related to self-worth. IQ tests are typically a combination of innate ability (genetic) and environmental exposure to include education. IQ tests, however, can be inadequate on a multidimensional level, it is difficult to pinpoint core success drivers, only a sample of a person's attributes are measured, and they do not take into account the complexity and immediacy of real life complex social scenarios (i.e., using fluid intelligence).

The IQ can be measured via the mental age (MA) and the chronological age (CA). By dividing the MA by the CA and multiplying by one hundred, the IQ is determined. An aptitude test is another measure of ability or potential that is commonly used. According to historical research, which has been labeled as the *Flynn effect*, the cumulative human IQ has been rising steadily over the past century, but unfortunately due to the need for positive unison (chemistry) between the covariant factors, which include cognitive abilities, intelligence in itself is just an isolate within the social harvesting equation.

The collective IQ in social systems is continually measured and a *normal distribution on IQ curve* is the habitual trend pattern that occurs. The breakouts of the curve by percentage have been historically (with one hundred being average intelligence and central point) 2.5% at 55–70, 13.6% at 70–85, 34% at 85–100, 34% at 100–115, 13.6% at 115–130, 2.5% at 130–145 (the highest distributions center around the average IQ of 100). The bell curve seen within the IQ distribution is also seen in many other scientific areas including within the area of genetics. This social balance is also a strong parallel to other social factors within the continuum of humanity such as personality, social polarity, and even conflict. There is a balance in everything within humanity. Social harvesting can occur within the different levels along the curve, but the quality of the harvesting is dependent on the cumulative impact and positivity of the covariant cohesion (chemistry). Due to some of the deficits within the older types of IQ tests and the limitations in the range of intelligences measured, different types of intelligences were posed in more recent history.

Crystallized intelligence involves knowledge being acquired and developed over time and is *not* a strong predictive indicator, but rather a measure of current aptitude. However, vocabulary is one of the primary components within many IQ tests and people's vocabularies are stored within the crystallized memory docking areas. *Fluid intelligence* is abstract, situational, and is used in critical thinking. When people possess a strong positive covariant combination of crystallized and fluid intelligence, this is when the social harvesting process can yield a much higher level of human resources. These people are the gold standard within the social procurement spectrum. Unfortunately in many cases, these people are taken advantage of by social dominators and they have their ideas taken from them with little or no reciprocal *social equity*. From a moral and ethical standpoint, everyone should be entitled to receive the social equity from their personal resources. *Emotional intelligence* is a person's own assessment of feeling intelligent, their awareness of their emotional behavior *self-monitoring*, and their empathy for others. Even more social procurement can transpire when additional layers of intelligences are compounded together in people. There are certain people who are considered *rare breeds* who possess multiple levels of intelligences. Because of the fact that people are so diverse within their abilities, other intelligences have been recognized more recently in history.

Multiple intelligences are other intelligences that were posed by Howard Garder, and are as follows:

1. *Musical intelligence* involves people with excellent patterned thinking and recognition.
2. *Naturalistic intelligence* involves people who are at one with nature and patterns with nature.
3. *Interpersonal intelligence* involves people who are adept at people skills, assessing emotions, perspectives, and conflict resolution.
4. *Spatial-visual intelligence* involves ability correlated with patterns, puzzles, and art.
5. *Linguistic/language intelligence* involves excellence in writing and speaking.

6. *Logical intelligence* is being exceptional with concepts, reasoning, abstract ideas, and analysis).

7. *Body/kinesthetic intelligence* involves proficiency with hand-eye coordination, dancing, sports, and doing things with body).

8. *Introspection/self-reflection intelligence* involves being skilled in self-monitoring, metacognition, analysis of theories and ideas, and aware of own drives and emotions.

Some other cognitive covariant elements are the *primary mental abilities*. The seven factors are: word fluency, verbal comprehension, spatial visualization, number facility, associative memory, reasoning, and perceptual speed. The Wechsler Adult Intelligence Scale (WAIS) is one test used to measure these factors. There are also other intelligence tests, which can include the four most common IQ tests: the Stanford-Binet Intelligence Scale, the Wechsler Adult Intelligence Scale, the Wechsler Intelligence Scale for Children, and the Wechsler Preschool and Primary Scale of Intelligence.

The WAIS-IV is for ages 16–89 and the WISC-IV is for ages 6–16. *Object assembly* and *matrix reasoning* is for nonverbal (NV) reasoning. *Digit symbol coding* is for short-term memory (STM) visual motor speed. *Picture arrangement* is for NV understanding of sequential social interactions. *Picture completion* is when the brain fills in the missing parts. *Figure weights* are for fluid intelligence on quantitative and analytical reasoning and perceptual organization. *Visual Puzzles* are for spatial reasoning, integration, and mental flexibility. *Vocabulary* is still widely considered the best overall measure of intelligence (a variable that needs to be factored in with the vocabulary element is how much reading has occurred surrounding the time of the test).

For the standard measure of IQ, a score of 10 would be *profound mental retardation*, 25 would be *severe mental retardation*, 40 would be *moderate mental retardation*, 55 would be *mild retardation*, 70 would be *borderline mental retardation*, 85 is a low average score, 100 is an average score, 115 is a high average, 125 is superior, 130 is gifted, and 145 plus is genius level on IQ.

The Kaufman Adolescent and Adult IQ Test (KAIT) is for ages 11–85 years old, and is a fluid and crystallized measure. The fluid aspect involves problem solving and reasoning, which are not influenced by education or culture. The Kaufman Assessment Battery for Children (KABC) focuses on development and neuropsychological changes, specific to adults and adolescents, the KABC focuses on age 11 and under. The Gf-Gc theory focuses on the difference between fluid and crystallized IQ, the KAIT is influenced by Piaget's theory of cognitive development and the formal operations stage specifically (adolescence) where complex mental operations and manipulation come into play. The KAIT is also influenced by Luria's theory of planning ability, which is that developmental changes early in adolescence influence decision-making and problem solving, inhibitory control, and planning (executive function).

There is a KAIT core battery and expanded battery. The fluid core focuses on logical steps, sequential reasoning, long-term memory, mystery codes, induction, and rebus learning. The crystal core focuses on knowledge of words, language development, double meanings, language comprehension, auditory comprehension, and listening ability. The expanded element focuses on visual processing, culture knowledge, auditory delay recall (memory), and rebus pictures. There are also mental illness (MI) subtests available.

The KAIT strength is that there are visual and auditory formats, different context, active, and engaged. The design allows for more accurate tracking of intelligence changes between adolescence and adulthood.

The three IQ scores are:

1. Composite
2. Fluid

3. Crystallized

The mean 100 with a standard deviation of 15, there is high reliability and validity. The KAIT is often used to measure gifted children.

Kaufman Short Neuropsychological Assessment Procedure (K-SNAP) is for ages 11–85 and is for mental function and neurological damage; it has cultural neutrality, takes 20–30 minutes, and is a *preliminary test only* for impairment. The test measures alertness, attentiveness, and environment orientation. *Gestalt closure* is used, visual closure, simultaneous process, partial inkblot completion, and four-letter words are used to solve problems and make plans. Although intelligence is a driving factor in producing novel social solutions, intelligence is only one covariant within the covariant harvesting system mixture.

The mixture (elements) and quality (chemistry) of people's covariant elements and factors can vary widely from person to person and they can even evolve within certain individuals over time. One of the primary social flaws within society is that many people believe that their proficiency in one particular area extends across into other areas. There are *very few* individuals who possess the quantity and quality of covariant factors to be fecund across multiple life areas. There are also many people who believe that their *credentials* alone place them into this social category and this social flaw can be costly because it is common that people will offer faulty social solutions outside of their area of individual expertise.

Once we accept our limits we can move beyond them.

—Einstein

The body and mind work together in order to create organic system homeostasis and biological harmony. Dualism is the function of the body and the mind making the person or the self. When the essential covariant components of the body and/or the mind are not in balance, a wide variety of impacts can be realized such as with mood. The *cognitive dissonance theory* involves a person having inconsistent cognitions and cognitive patterns, which can lead to mental imbalances and this can have an impact on other covariants. Due to all of the covariants within the cognitive mix, these imbalances (chemistry) can occur with some regularity.

Within the system of *cognition*, the covariant of *thinking* involves *parallel processing*, which is the ability of the brain to do many thought processes at once (i.e., in driving, there can be multiple stimuli occurring all at one time). *Mental acuity* is the sharpness of the mind when thinking and it involves memory, focus, concentration, and understanding. The *mental set* is another major organic system and it is tied together closely with the schema. Within a person's mental set is their central tendency to approach problems the same way by basing their social approach on what is perceived as working. Once people form their schemas and their mental sets, they are normally very rigid in their social positions regarding any changes to their actions or belief sets. Unfortunately it is common that people become *unalterable* in their social positions, which are a social deficit when there is no flexibility. Each social position has a range of polarity that runs along a continuum and when people become fixated on one specific area along the continuum with no flexibility, this can potentially become a social flaw. Some of the forces at work within this potentially inhibiting social rigidity are *proactive interference*, which is the negative influence of old memories on new information. *Retroactive interference* is when new material impacts the recall of older information and this leads to competition and unlearning (this can be a positive or negative). *Belief bias* involves people believing only things that are consistent with their prior beliefs, which is vacuous and omnipresent in humanity. The human ego is often the social barrier between people reaching the zenith of their intelligence range.

The learning and knowledge that we have is at the most but little compared with that of which we are ignorant.

—Plato

Functional fixedness is when people block new information, new ideas, new concepts, new uses for objects, and have the inability to see new uses for an object and/or different ways to use objects or ways to solve problems. Within this social deficit, concepts are only seen in terms of their *face functionality*, this is a narrow and limited social range, and it can inhibit the problem solving process. The evolution of humanity and the process of social harvesting are reliant on people being flexible within their social continuums. This adverse social phenomenon is a major social flaw, but people who are fecund can produce social solutions where others are more limited in order to maintain the positive flow of social harvesting. These personal cognitive limitations and social entanglements can start very early in people's lives.

Commonly children by age seven will normally assign uses and meanings to things, objects, and to ideas, which limits their creativity for other uses and this is a major restrictive element of people's growth potential, and it is also a direct result of the negative social power of *conformity*. In addition to social conformity, there are other factors which can also create *social paralysis*. *Output interference* is when the act of trying to recall something interferes with the original information stored. There are so many covariant variables in play within the organic system that can potentially impact cognition, that many people will experience fluctuations in their cognitions and their cognition patterns which is *cognitive dissonance*. There are some people however that have the systematic organic aligning of all of their covariant elements. These individuals are able to develop additional cognitive skills and abilities.

Metacognition is the ability for a person to control their thoughts, to know about how their self-cognition and the thoughts of others are interplaying, and being able to enhance these perceptions over time. Research and theories over time have pointed toward the consideration that there are different modalities involved in the cognitive processes, which can vary widely across people and across brain modules.

Anatomical left brain cognitive processes involve abstract learning and the left brain pattern in certain people points to their tendency to seek details, logic, analytical communication, objectivity, ideas, qualities, persuasion, and critical thinking. The *linear learning and thinking style* aligns with left brain thinking style, and it entails a structured approach, which is predictable and stepwise, and seeks planning, detail, routine, and these people are highly receptive to the communication of details.

The *anatomical right brain* cognitive processes involve the concrete learning style, which entails learning via the five senses, the right brain pattern points to being intuitive, thoughtful, subjective, sensitive, creative, and seeing the bigger picture. Right-brain thinkers can also be *global strategic thinkers* who are impatient with linear subjects and want the access to information right away in order to relate it to their overall goals. These people like to do, try, feel things, and are receptive to concepts.

Divergent thinkers are commonly the fecund group within society and they are always searching for multiple answers, concrete experience, and reflective observation, are imaginative, have ideas, see different perspectives, enjoy brainstorming, and are highly creative. *Convergent thinkers* are normally only thinking toward one social solution, use abstract conceptualization and active experimentation, practical application of ideas, deductive reasoning, decision-making, and problem solving. This critical thinking style is looking for a single correct answer.

Assimilators use abstract conceptualization, reflective observation, and use inductive reasoning and bottom up logic. *Accommodators* use concrete experience and active experimentation, trial and error versus thought and reflection, and are actively engaging in the world and doing things versus just reading about them and studying them.

People's cognitions are filtered within *representational systems*, which impact how they filter all of their information (i.e., through the senses). *Metaprogrammers* examine how others around them operate and filter information, which allows them to clarify their beliefs. *Chunking* is a way of filtering all of the social stimuli that surrounds people. A *meme* is information that is passed to people over time via ideas, sounds, and/or songs for self-perpetuation. Certain social information is resilient and is selected to carry forward and pass over time by penetrating through the various social filters that reside within the other competing social stimuli. The organic system of cognition and covariant relations is also heavily tied to the brain capacity and brain development. Certain covariant elements can have a very profound impact on others within the system.

The *executive function* (EF) is a highly important cognitive function (commonly considered the highest function) and it is primarily orchestrated within the prefrontal cortex of the brain. EF is heavily involved in the cognitive functions of planning, staying on task, impulse control, and more. Being EF is impacted by other covariants, its functions, if altered, can limit the social processes of individuals and also the process of social harvesting and procurement. The development of the EF can also vary widely across individuals.

The prefrontal cortex is a highly stress sensitive area in the brain and it can be impeded by stress which can be part of the impacts of mood. Mood is one of the covariants, which can impact a person's social output. The biological stress response element floods the prefrontal cortex (PFC) with the *dopamine neurotransmitter (NT)* causing the PFC functions to diminish. The *trigger* is a state of *dysfunction* in the areas of interpretation, emotion, and reaction. This organic dysfunction can limit the capacity for thought and reflection and instead can create *automatic* reflexive reactions. The development of the EF normally beings in infancy, and there is generally a spike of neural activity in the PFC between the ages of two to six years of age. The EF curve can continue into the young adult years of the twenties, in some cases peaking at around age twenty-five. There are also some people in life who never attain a higher level of EF. There is a continuum that people fall within in this covariant area as well.

Due to the impacted or underdeveloped EF within the PFC and emotional response centers, people may need external cues and reinforcements to supplant the normal functioning of the PFC for self-regulation. There is often a narrow window of *cognitive flexibility*, which is the ability to change one's mind, one's schema (views), one's adaptation level, ability to solve problems, and find creative solutions (fecundity), in cases where the EF is inhibited, EF is not properly developed or EF doesn't develop properly in the PFC.

The *inhibitory self-control* function is such as Freud's superego, which involves appropriate social impulse control. The ego is the filter within the cognitive organic system according to Freud, and this filter helps people to avoid maladaptive feelings and habits which derive from the ID. With a solid equilibrium in the PFC and when emotional centers are balanced by the ego, planning can be achieved, one's schema can be modified, and instead of giving into social temptations, one can begin to strategize and set goals.

When the mental organic systems are beginning to function properly, the working memory improves and the ability to hold thoughts and relate them into one's schema is enhanced. *Self-awareness*, self-monitoring, and metacognition (if present) can all begin to operate and/or improve, and a person can also begin to regulate themselves and understand what is happening around them. Metacognition is the highest level of self-awareness, which typically isn't achieved until later years, but it is the ability to monitor one's thoughts as they relate to the perceptions of what one thinks others may be thinking. Metacognition is something that is developed over time in most cases and not everyone develops this advanced mental skill.

A properly developed EF also allows for reflection in the moment. A dysfunction in the EF can create issues with perspective, judgment, and social control. Social *inhibition* is the hesitation and the blockage of social action and/or emotion in social scenarios, which is the opposite of social facilitation. Social *suppression* is the conscious control of and over desired social impulses. If the EF is functioning properly, other covariants can be effectively utilized. Reason or rational is having a sound mind, the ability to exercise reason, and the use of the conscious thought process to solve problems. There are many different aspects to reasoning. *Concrete concepts* involve reasoning that is situational, unique, cannot be generalized, involve literal interpretation, and are immediate versus abstract. *Conceptual concepts* is reasoning, which involves patterns, links, complex situations, set priorities, uncovering, formulation, drawing inferences, applying crystallized knowledge to fluid situations, and addressing underlying issues.

Deductive reasoning (is top-down logic processing) involves taking the big picture and breaking things down into smaller subunits. Deductive reasoning links premises to conclusions, and if the premise is true then the terms are clear and the rules of logic are followed with a logical necessity. The *general principle* applies to a *specific case* (trying to prove something). Deductive reasoning requires logical and rigorous proof, and relies on initial premise being correct. The *idiographic* approach from Gordon Allport (1937) can be associated, and it is the intellectual tendency to specify the meaning of individual contingent, unique, and often *subjective phenomena* as *qualitative*.

Inductive reasoning (bottom-up processing) is when an example/s imply the application to a *broad scope* (i.e., trying to discover *new* piece of info). Inductive reasoning involves *feature analysis*, which is used to build a complete perception. The *nomothetic* approach of Gordon Allport from German philosopher Wilhelm Windelband is the intellectual tendency to generalize *objective phenomena* as quantitative data, and to understand how the world works around us. People's tendencies and outlooks can vary widely based on their covariants.

The concrete active style constitutes around 50 percent plus of the population. The concrete active type follows guidelines, structure, sequential patterns, questions their own intellectual ability, they are dependent on others for judgment, they seek immediate gratification, lack of abstract thinking, are engaged on a sensory level, and they prefer being in a group. The concrete active type may also use social masks to hide their style and/or social deficits within the style to protect their social status and social roles. The *abstract reflective* type constitutes around 10 percent of the population and this type uses their imagination, sees the big picture, is open-ended, has autonomy, values knowledge, dislikes ambiguity, enjoys diversity, and puts their theories into practice. This group is where many of the fecund people within the social continuum of humanity derive from. The *concrete/abstract hybrid* roughly makes up the balance of the population. Regardless of what type of a profile that a person falls into, everyone encounters the cognitive matrix of encoding.

Assimilation involves people encoding new information into their existing schema; however, most people subjectively incorporate new information into their existing mental set and schema. Being people are rigid in the views and their personal social anchors and social polarities, their subjectivity can minimize the amount and/or the impacts of any new information that they take on. *Accommodation* is altering one's existing schema with new information. *Equilibrium* is the balance between the cognitive forces of accommodation and assimilation within the schema and mental set. People's social attitudes are integrated and formed within this affect-cognition-behavior system, which is highly dynamic because people's attitudinal elements can be altered one by one. Regardless of whether one attitudinal element is altered or many, the affect of a single change (like the butterfly effect) can impact a person's entire schema structure based on what the changing/shaping element is and how the overall social anchor and social polarity is impacted. There are also some more forces that play into personal cognition.

Attribution is the process of attributing social events based on factors, variables, which can incorporate both internal and external biases and inferences. *Self-serving bias* is attributing positive outcomes to personal factors and negative outcomes to external factors, which is associated with the concept of *locus of control*, which can be internal or external. An *external locus of control* is the belief that outside social forces and factors control ones social outcome. This type of locus can create a loss of feeling of control, befuddlement, and in some people hopelessness, if it dominates their social reality. One of the core elements in a person's personal and social identity is to have some amount of personal control on their life path. An *internal locus of control* is where a person feels that they control their own destiny versus an external locus of control whereby someone feels that external factors control their destiny.

The locus of control can potentially change over time within individuals based on their own social experiences in their life path. Although it is very important for people to have a feeling of control over the various social aspects of their lives and not vacillate on their locus, it is also important for them to recognize the social obstacles, which may have inhibited their personal efforts. Personal failure is directly related to self-identity and a person should not *solely* attribute personal goal and life failure to themselves if *outside* social factors indeed were validly involved. In society, the negative element can set traps for people and they can also create social pitfalls. But people must be able to clearly identify when this occurs in order to properly attribute social failure. Correct social attributions must be accounted for and new goals must be set. In order to be certain that people are making the correct social attributions, they can use different methods. *Introspection* involves self-reflection in order to gain personal insight; the issue is that changing/evolving internal personal feelings can potentially impact the insights and ultimately the associated attributions. One of the fundamental social flaws in society is when people lead others to believe that they are completely in control of their social destiny. This porous and flawed social instruction leads to people becoming socially defeated within the process of socialization. People must instead be instructed to understand their personal attributes, their social ranges, and to prepare for social contingencies when social obstacles interfere with their life course and/or their social direction. In addition, people do not have to be completely reliant on outside sources for their social direction. With an education, a positive support network, and with the correct balance of cognitive covariants in place people can potentially begin to formulate their own concept of the social reality. People do not have to be *scientists* in order to develop their own social theories; however, if they want to apply any generalizations to their theories, they *must* follow the same path as scientists do.

Those who know how to think need no teachers.

—Gandhi

A *social theory* is developed and posed when observable social events and the scientific method are used to help organize these *observable events*. Predictions are made to make connections to comprehensive social principles. Theories are not as specific as a *hypothesis*, as theories are rather more *general explanations* about behavior and events, although there are still certain steps involved to make theories valid and to avoid conjecture.

The *scientific method* is needed for *cause and effect* and involves the manipulation of the independent variable (IV) to impact the dependent variable (DV). The first step is the hypothesis or prediction, then second comes defining the method of study, third comes the analysis and explanation of the findings, and finally the reporting and sharing. Cause and effect cannot be reached if extraneous IV factors confound the results. *Outside interference* is the chief inhibitor of reaching cause and effect. This is why *certain people* and *select things* need to be *removed* in social experiments and for that matter also within people's lives when they are trying to find a correlation. If there are social *influences*, which are impeding a process and/or confounding the validity of a test, those influences *must be removed.*

In a *true experimental design* people must manipulate the IV and observe the social effect on some behavior or cognitive process in order to elicit the DV. Random assignment and controlling the external variables are the factors which are required. A true design *must* have *manipulation* and *random assignment* to establish *cause and effect.* The *hypothesis cycle* has the following stages: deduction, prediction, observation, test predictions, and induction. A hypothesis will be more detailed than a theory.

Validity is critical in the experimental design, it is crucial in measuring an effect having validity, and just because something is reliable does not mean it is valid, cause and effect must be clearly shown. The *replication* of a test must be possible, if a test or experiment can be replicated then it can become *reliable* and broader generalizations can be made. *Reliability* is the consistency of the measure, the ability to be repeated with similar or equal results and in order to be *valid* something must also be reliable. People and scientist can also both make the same types of errors within their results.

Type I hypothesis/theory error is a *false positive* or an *alpha error*, which involves rejecting the *null* hypothesis even if true. The null is the opposite of the desired outcome that test was looking to show cause and effect for (i.e., if the test was set up to measure the impacts of an IV on behavior for a desired DV, and the DV was not elicited/realized, not accepting the opposite/null is a type I error). The *type II error* is a *false negative* or a *beta error*, which is accepting the null when it should be rejected, this is the process of *changing* what the *original intent* of testing was trying to identify. People can try and measure social variables in the context of their lives and/or in the lives of others. There are also other covariant aspects that are involved in social harvesting that can further influence the social outcomes in a positive or negative way.

Learning is another covariant element and there is a *critical period* within the learning development process. Certain cognitive and social elements must be learned within the ideal or necessary learning stage in order to correctly acquire the desired and typical normative development. EF also can be incorporated into this critical period. Within learning, people can focus on strengthening their underutilized styles to expand their social potential. In *standardized learning*, the potential of certain individuals may be highly limited within the multiple intelligences that are possible. Because of the typical educational structures that have been in place over time, many people use standardized learning methods versus using their own personal learning style strengths. Because groups over time have fought for this social ideal, Individual education plans (IEPs) are available for people who require a modified learning agenda. Continued learning is highly important in terms of continued development. There are many elements that exist and operate together within the organic system to elicit the process of learning.

Plasticity is the ability for nerve cells (neurons in the brain) to change through new experiences and learning even into adulthood (although there may be variance from one person to the next genetically). *Learning perception* is the foundation of people's personal strengths and learning styles. *Learning concrete* is learning registered via the five senses. *Learning abstract* is the incorporation of outside ideas, qualities, and qualities unseen. *Learning sequential* involves linear and logical learning. *Learning random* is learning via memory chunks. The learning styles may also be combined (i.e., concrete sequential, abstract random, etc.). *Learning with learning disabilities* (LDs) is for those with different styles and/or abilities that can get an IEP to help them learn at their own pace and with the proper repetition. There are also some other learning approaches that have been formulated.

Auditory learning is repeating and oral activities such as debates or lectures. *Empirical learning* is learning though the senses (observable). *Kinesthetic or tactile learning* is hands-on, role-play, projects, movement, and exploration within learning. *Pedagogical learning* is learning through teaching and education. *Visual learning* is learning via pictures, event time lines, diagrams, handouts, slides, etc. Kolb designed a learning inventory.

The *transformation of learning experience* (Kolb) involves a learning style inventory LSI. *Concrete experience* involves specific experiences and sensitive (feeling). *Abstract experience* involves logical analysis and intellectual understanding (thinking). *Reflective observation* involves observing perspectives before judgment (watching). *Active experimentation* involves risk taking, action, and influence (doing).

Kolb also discussed the *experience grasping approach* or *experience transforming approach*:

- *Do and Feel* = Accommodate
- *Feel and Watch* = Diverge
- *Think and Watch* = Assimilation
- *Think and Do* = Converge

Learning can evoke different outcomes in different people. The learning process can tap into people's ability to form an *insight*. An insight is when a solution comes about from a novel realization, which is the opposite of trial and error. A fecund person can come up with solutions and insights with consistency and quality over time. Insights are the highest form of learning, by being able to figure out social solutions to achieve the desired social outcome. One of the other most important covariants in organic cognition is memory.

Memory is something that is continually studied because of its social impacts. The *cerebral cortex* is a thin outer layer on the hemispheres, which is the information-processing center, and processes new *declarative* episodic memories, new movements, and it is also a motor and sensory cortex, to name a few of its functions. Within memory, *effortful processing* involves having the necessary attention, effort, practice, and rehearsal. *Encoding* involves using the sensory input for memory storage, the information is broken down and consolidated for recall and decoding at a later time. *Data* is the information collected, which can be qualitative or quantitative. There are also many more impacts on memory.

Overshadowing is when multiple stimuli are present and one stimulus produces a stronger response. The *serial position effect* is when the first and last things experienced normally have the greatest level of recall, which is a primacy and recency effect. The *primacy effect* can influence memory; it is the first thing/s experienced, whereby the *recency effect* is more influenced by more recent experiences. The *recency effect* is memory bias toward recent stimuli or recently improved recall. There are mechanisms of memory acquisition, encoding, maintenance, and retrieval.

Consolidation involves reconstructing a memory, creating pathways, and gathering pieces. *Recognition* is the identification of information in memory versus the more difficult process of *recall* (i.e., a multiple-choice question versus fill-in-the-blank questions). *Recall* involves bringing something from memory into conscious awareness, which is a very difficult mental process. Recall is cue based (i.e., perfume—first-odor associations are privileged in brain representation for pleasant or unpleasant) there is a direct neural link to the hippocampus for olfactory, but for information, recall is more exploratory and difficult (i.e., fill in the blank).

Retrieval is the recall of events, images, and feelings of which some are more difficult than others. *Constructive recall* is where the memory schema is stored, if details are lost, and other details are submitted to fit within the existing schema.

The *cognitive map* is the mental blueprint for cognitive memory mapping, routing, and docking. Memory *decay* is when sensory and short-term memory fades, but the decay is not of a critical nature. Sometimes people can feel like they are reliving a moment. Deja vu is when memory retrieval cues are fired when people are in a similar or familiar environment to that of the original memory acquisitions. Ed Tolman posed that *latent learning* is mental mapping and learning that can occur even without rewards and it can manifest and appear later. Latent information is almost unrealized processing and retention, and acquiring and storing the information to be used later with no way to detect that the information is being stored until it manifests and comes out. Elizabeth Loftus, a memory expert, posed that the *mis-information effect* is when memory is altered by the emotion surrounding the information acquisition, and that suggestion leads to *false memories*. *Emotion* involves physical arousal, expressive behavior, and conscious experience. A *flashbulb memory* is the sudden onset of a memory from an emotionally charged moment or event that suddenly comes about. Memory is a very powerful cognitive covariant device, which is a critical component within the social harvesting process.

There is also a tremendous amount of strength in people *doing* things. In memory, most people remember around 10 percent of what we read; 20 percent of what we hear; 30 percent of what we see; 50 percent of what we see and hear; 70 percent of what we see, hear, and discuss; and 90 percent of what we see, hear, discuss, and practice. There are several different types of memory.

Declarative memory is explicit and long-term memory that is divided into semantic and episodic memory. *Semantic memory* is idea, meaning, and concept. *Episodic memory* is recalling past events. *Procedural memory* is the how-to-do memory, and is not impacted by damage to the *hippocampus* such as the other types of memory.

The memory function involves encoding via perceptions and sensory inputs. Some of the areas of the brain involved in memory are the hippocampus (which is involved in spatial navigation, the limbic emotional system, and both short-term and long-term memory, the frontal cortex, and the medial temporal lobe). Memory storage involves sensory and short-term and long-term memory aspects including time, place, and environment. Humans can normally handle seven to twenty items within twenty to thirty seconds in their STM. When paired with association and impact, the STM is encoded into long-term memory. Retrieval is based on the level of attention at the time of encoding and *retrieval cues* are used for recall.

Memory functioning is reliant on strong neural synapse connections and strong neural connectivity and conductivity within the neural network. For instance, if the level of *acetylcholine* (a neurotransmitter in the brain) is low then brain function can deteriorate, acetylcholine is a neurotransmitter, which is released and flows throughout the synapses for proper brain function. Humans typically lose about 5 percent of our hippocampus cells per decade starting normally around age thirty to forty. The hippocampus is the routing center for the initial memory acquisition phase and a conduit from STM to LTM storage.

Things that can influence memorization are also the emotions surrounding the memory. People can use tools like mnemonic devices, associations, and writing (for imprint memory). The *method of loci* is a mnemonic device where one visualizes items they learn in *spatial locations* (i.e., using a landmark to remember an item). For long-term memory (LTM), *proteins* build *memory docks* in our neural synapses, but disruption after *consolidation* can impact recall and the memories themselves. *Synaptic consolidation* occurs within the first few hours after learning, then *systems consolidation* is the process whereby memories are no longer reliant on the hippocampus for the memory docking, and this process can allow the memories to become independent of the hippocampus within weeks to years along a continuum. *Reconsolidation*, which stabilizes a memory trace of initial acquisition and can make memories labile, able to undergo change, again through the activation of the memory trace, and may be a factor in long-term memory. If reconsolidation is the recall mechanism the existing synapse docking could be impacted and the memories themselves.

The drug *propranolol* is used to treat some bipolar patients and some people with post-traumatic stress disorder (PTSD), the drug helps to block *norepinephrine* (an excitatory neurotransmitter) and it can change or modify the quality of a memory. The effect for people with PSTD is that the memory trace may be bad to *scare* in order to avoid the traumatic memory associations that they have encountered and consistently revisit via memories and dreams. Memory formations can be broken down even further.

For cognitive memory, the *three box model* entails (Sensory input > Short term STM > Long term LTM = encoded and retrieved, not encoded, or retrieval failure from LTM). *Sensory memory* in general is typically held for split second, some sensory memory is encoded into working memory and some by selective attention. *Iconic memory* is split-second visual (i.e., photo image, eidetic memory), which is photographic, highly detailed, and normally lost after STM by most people.

Echoic memory is auditory three-second to four-second audible memories (sensation and emotion), and are typically stored longer than *iconic* or (visual) memories in the short-term memory, which fades quickly. There are states which can impact both STM and LTM.

Selective attention is stimulus filtering, when people don't pay attention to everything and only certain things are processed into permanent LTM. Sensory interaction is the influence of interaction and interference amongst the competing sensory group, vision typically dominates over the other senses as far as memory influence.

STM is typically ten to thirty seconds in duration, and normally people can store (7+/-) units or chunks of information, *Miller's magical number* for STM is (7+/- 2 units). Short-term memory is estimated at ten to thirty seconds, the next *consolidation* must occur with items in STM in order to integrate into LTM; most people can store seven to ten chunks of information into their STM. Memory tools and devices can improve memory performance. Mnemonic devices such as expansion (i.e., planets; "my very excellent mother just served us nine pizzas" involves the first letters of planets).

LTM include *episodic* (i.e., sequential, dates). *Semantic memory* is crystallized memory such as stored facts, categories, etc. *Semantic encoding* research shows that associative learning encoded and stored in semantic memory encoding (ideas, meanings, and concepts) is stronger than in *auditory* or *visual*. *Procedural memory* are skills and use memory, the how-to-do memory, and is not impacted by damage to the hippocampus such as the other types of memory. There are various mechanisms used within memory retrieval.

Explicit/declarative are memories people think of first via active retrieval.

Implicit/nondeclarative memories pop into mind. *Implicit memory* is called the *skill memory* for which no recall is needed (i.e., riding a bike and/or performing a repeated function). Damage to the hippocampus in the brain often does not impact implicit memory. There are also some other important factors involved in memory.

Context is very important in memory encoding (emotion). Memory can also be impacted by people's state dependent level of consciousness/awareness for retrieval. For constructed memory/ recorded memories, some can be false. The *re-learning effect* allows for the speed of memory re-acquisition. *Mood-congruent memory* involves the mood at encode and mood at recall. *Interference* involves competing memories, *retroactive* new information interfering with the past memories and *proactive* where old information prevents new info encoding. Long-term potentiation involves neurons that can strengthen neural connections and neuronal sensitivity via firing, *plasticity*. Automatic processing is learning memory, which is automatic and can inhibit an automatic *response*. The *adaptation level phenomenon* reduces the tendency to respond. The *mere-exposure effect* is similar to the *adjustment level phenomenon*, it can be positive or negative, can change over time, and people often prefer *old stimuli* to *novel stimuli*. The *misattribution of memory* is one of the *four sins of memory* according to Schacter at Harvard. The four sins are remembering information, but being wrong about the source, changing faces, placing a face seen in one place over to another (criminology), and identifying people. The *misinformation effect* involves false memories, altered memories, and can produce many different versions (criminology). Memory is an integral organic covariant that is strongly related to another important covariant, which is perception. Memory and perception are closely tied together in affect.

Perception is the collection and integration of sensory stimuli and the degree by which the stimuli will elicit both emotions and reactions from the interpretation as a unique event or from stored cues as a similar or recalled event. Perception is a critical tool in how emotional and behavioral patterns are learned and formed. There are many different perceptual elements that factor into people's level of perceptive capacity.

Synthesia is the perception of something with multiple senses at the same time (i.e., hearing a sound produces simultaneous visualization, or smelling aroma produces visualization). *Perceptual adaptation* is the filtering out distractions (i.e., filtering out noises in focus). *Perceptual constancy* is the ability to recognize a person, place, or object, even though some of the cues within the stimuli have changed between exposures and/or over time. The *perceptual set* is being able to see or perceive something based on one's prior experiences which would be *priming*. Priming is acuteness to stimuli due to past exposures either real or imagined. *Visual capture* is the tendency of people to allow visual images to dominate their perception (i.e., people want to perceive in movie theatres that the sound is coming through the screen versus from the speakers on the side walls). *Attention* is a person's level of focus within the present variables in a given scenario. *Continuity* is a person having perceptual organization in lines or patterns. *Self-monitoring* is the perception of the environment and the modification of a person's thoughts and actions in order to mirror what is occurring around them. This process is done via metacognition and/or priming and these skills can be evolved over time in certain individuals. In order for the perceptual process to fire, a certain amount of stimuli must be present.

The *absolute threshold* is the smallest detectable intensity of a stimulus that can potentiate the firing of the perceptual neurons in the brain. *Appraisal* involves the environmental stimuli appraisal and the evaluation to potentially elicit emotion. *Arousal* incorporates the element of the *adaptation level phenomenon* to a given scenario or scenario type and either elicits or inhibits the sympathetic nervous system (SNS) arousal (BP, HR, etc.) which is tied to the element of emotion. As priming and habituation can weaken the impact of certain stimuli in people over time with exposures, the SNS is less likely to fire. But regardless of whether the SNS was activated or not, there are *cell assembly traces* of cortical neurons that remain after exposure to a perceived stimulus.

A *threshold* is defined as the minimum amount of a stimuli needed to detect a change at least 50 percent of the time and is the smallest amount of stimuli that can be detected (i.e., for vision under the right conditions, a candle or light can be seen from miles away). *Subliminal stimuli* occur below the minimum threshold limits for nearly all people. There is a wide variability from person to person on both perceptual *sensitivity* and *interference*. The *difference threshold* is when the change is noticed and this is called the *just noticeable difference.*

Weber's psychophysics law states: "the change needed is proportional to the intensity of the original stimulus" (the more intense that a stimuli is, the more intense the change needs to be to notice any difference). Some of Weber's physical constants are that hearing decibels have to be increased by 5 percent or above to notice a difference, vision by 8 percent (intensity of light), etc. *Visual perception* can have major impacts on the process of integration and inference. *Proximity* involves stimuli being perceived as belonging to a group if close together. *Similarity* is when stimuli are perceived as belonging to group based on the appearance. *Continuity* is perception that based on a stimuli's form, it is perceived as belonging to group. *Closure* is the use of top-down processing and gap filling to complete a visual perception. As perception is tied directly into memory, there are also other mechanisms that interplay between these covariants.

Association is a cognitive mechanism whereby one idea brings about a thought *association* of another concept, event, stimuli, and a learned connection brings about a conditioned response and/ or stimulus. *Situational cues* are context cues that convey through people's perceptual capacities that an action will occur, and priming aids in the development of interpreting these cues. There is a high level of variance in the levels of perceptual capacities across people, and in some cases, there are mechanisms which can create perceptual conflict.

Cognitive dissonance is disharmony within the process of cognition, which can potentially create conflicting thoughts or a conflict in understanding, which is expressed most often through body language. Some people can detect when cognitive dissonance is occurring with others and they can modify the interaction in order to realign people back onto the same wavelength of understanding. Cognitive interference is one of the major factors which can lead to cognitive dissonance.

Proactive interference is when people's existing schema is *blocking* the integration of new information into a new memory formation in their schema and/or a new schema formation from developing. Many people have very strong cognitive anchors and social polarities, and these elements can inhibit any modifications to these people's cognitive systems. The *spotlight effect* is a social phenomenon that involves the tendency for people to think that other people are focused on their social actions. This effect is tied directly into the element of identity and it correlates to the social polarities that exist within people's identities. People want to feel that their social views and social roles are being recognized by others and this is also tied into the ego. Within the social harvesting process, as people's abilities are unified in their covariant strength, the impacts can begin to have a collective affect on social systems and society. When powerful covariant cognitive elements such intelligence, reasoning and logic, thinking, memory, perception, and more are combined together in harmony, they can yield tremendous social action potential. But when these covariants are not in tune, the impacts can have the very opposite effect and can inhibit forward social momentum. When in tune (harmony), the covariants can help to solve social problems, and when out of tune, they can contribute to and create social issues.

In problem solving normally, there is some type of social issue or argument that needs to first be defined and then rectified. The *basis of argument* should entail logic, which is derived from a set of predefined statements. A *premise* is an assumption that something is true, and in logic, an argument must have a set of at least two declarative sentences (propositions), and a conclusion. The *rule of inference* is a transformational rule, construction of deductive proof, and rule of detachment, if *antecedents* are not in error then the *consequent* is not in error. If P implies Q and P is true, then Q is true. The rule of inference would be similar to *deductive reasoning* where the elements must align in order to make any social generalizations. One of the major issues in problem solving is how a problem is framed.

The element of problem *framing* states that how a problem is presented can rigidly set the social expectations and can also drastically influence the social outcome. There are many different principles that can be considered within problem solving. The *four legs* approach involves considering the following problem factors: outcome, sensory, awareness, flexibility, and action. The *outcome* consideration is to know what is wanted. People must clearly define the problem and then identify the ultimate goal. The *sensory awareness* consideration involves metacognition, and understanding the climate of the problem environment. The *flexibility* consideration takes cues and tries to move closer to desired outcome. The *action* consideration states that if something isn't working that massive action is required. Although these steps may seem elementary on the surface, they require a tremendous amount of cognitive power to apply them, and people should always try to emulate those who are adept at solving problems.

Critical thinking involves consideration, evaluation, and in-depth conclusions versus ambivalence. *De-centering* is people considering multiple aspects of a situation and allows for insights to come about versus the decision-making error of thinking that all situations are analogous. *Insight* is when a solution comes about from an extemporaneous novel realization, which is the opposite of trial and error and a fecund person can come up with solutions and insights. Insights are the highest form of learning, by being able to figure out solutions to achieve a desired social outcome. Few people are capable of high-level critical thinking and/or in producing advanced insights, this is why social harvesting occurs. In order for people to produce these insights and solutions, their covariants within their organic cognitive system must be primed and functioning at a very high level or their output can be fatuous.

Idea generation extends from fluid intelligence, which is abstract, situational, and involves critical thinking versus *crystallized memory*, which is acquired and developed knowledge over time. Idea generation and insights involve fluidity in thought, seeing things differently than others (in many people, their first thoughts can bias their thinking), and the incorporation of randomness. There are many people in society who excel in learning material and then both retaining the crystallized material and using it. But the people with the gift of having *amplified fluid intelligence* to pair with their crystallized intelligence are the truly fecund people in society.

This social disparity is one of the major societal issues extending from individual interpersonal social relations all the way up to the top level of societies along the continuum. There are many people who are *obtuse* in society and that refuse to recognize that certain people possess higher levels of cognitive ability. Due to the social elements of jealousy (a component of identity and ego) and polar interference (where some people are unable to visualize), the people with these special gifts are sometimes ignored, mistreated, and/or they never receive the credit for their ability in their life path because others take the credit for their ideas. There are businesses and foundations that reap the rewards that they extract from the fecund via their designed *pyramids of innovation procurement*. Social dominators will take these ideas from the fecund, and in most cases, there is no social mobility for the fecund, but most often the social dominators are given credit and they experience social elevation in this convoluted and ambiguous social game. In social mining and harvesting, the correct process is to utilize and recognize the ability of people and not to find ways to diminish people. Unfortunately the fecund are often at the mercy of capricious people in society. People who hinder the process of social mining and social harvesting have a very finite cognitive range and they are inhibiting the growth potential of the collective humanity as just *one* fecund person can potentially radiate a social concept or concepts, which could potentially evolve humanity via the *butterfly effect*.

The difference between genius and stupidity is that genius as its limits.

—Einstein

In problem solving, people must decide on their own social perspectives, and then come at the issue from another perspective (i.e., attack the problem as a doctor or a lawyer would). Unfortunately due to many people's finite cognitive restrictions, these people are unable to naturally take on different perspectives, and in turn, they should *walk the walk* before criticizing others. In order for the people that have a narrow or closed off social perspective to realize the error in their ways, they should walk a mile in the shoes of others for perspective, either figuratively or literally. *Meeting the need* involves people trying to meet the needs of others versus only going from their own social perspective.

Problem solving involves decomposing the whole issue into parts, the mind automatically connects and fills in sequential gaps (i.e., when people read mixed up words, and the neurons in the brain are actively scanning for the first and last letters or the *framing* of the words). Problem solving and creativity works the same way. People use their cognitive networks to search for new connections, for solutions, and creating new synaptic channels to solve issues. *Seeing beyond* is reversing a concept, exploring the concept for its latent potential, and seeing a use for the concept beyond the original intention. Genius is seeing things from different perspectives, seeing a need that hasn't been filled, seeing the possibilities and going to multidimensional cognitive levels to find insights and solutions to problems. *Lateral thinking* is the process of turning problems into opportunities. *Concept extraction* is starting with the basic conceptual links, expanding the links outward, and then thinking of different means to increase, decrease, or neutralize an action potential. *Focus* is a person's intuitive drift toward the unexplored possibilities within a problem.

Problem solvers are able to identify sub-goals within major issues, which are smaller and more manageable units, in order to fix the whole problem. Problem solvers are open to all the possibilities at hand in order to arrive at solutions. There is wide continuum of sources that can potentially elicit solutions. The fecund and the gifted normally are operating on a completely different *wavelength* than most other people, and therefore, it is common that many people will elicit critical comments toward this group. The actions and the thought patterns that derive from this group may *seem* irrational to the majority of people, but when the fecund are communicating within their own group, these offerings are considered *normalcy*. The fecund must *never* let the others in society alter their social course.

There is no great genius without a mixture of madness,

—Aristotle

Many times problem solvers will also have a *gut reaction* when there is an emotional component that is activated and impacts social judgments and decision-making. *Intuition* involves the rendering of an immediate insight without observation, which is a *gut feeling* or *hunch*. Sometimes *priming* over the course of life can create more instances of intuition within people. *Instinct* is the innate pre-wired cognitive circuitry, which directs and guides typical human behavior. If a person is correct based on their internal cognitive processes a high degree of the time, this should be recognized as a gift. But there are social forces that can work against people with these special gifts because so many people *cannot* conceive how and why only certain people have these abilities. There are also external resources that have been developed over time which can help people formulate solutions.

An *algorithm* is a step-by-step set of well-defined instructions, which create a formula for a solution and a rule that guarantees an answer. Another external example is using a *fishbone diagram*, which is a tool that helps people to investigate the most likely causes of a problem and then calls for the testing, measurement, and the formulation of concepts, in order to talk through toward a new strategy and/or solution to an issue. Regardless of whether the ideas are elicited from internal sourcing or external devices, innovation is always in high demand. *Innovation* is the process of interlacing ideas and actions in order to integrate them into practical and effective use and/or to solve issues. If people are working on larger systemic social issues, there is a period of time that is involved in the adoption of innovation. Unfortunately positive social innovations can be strongly impeded by the negative social forces. The negative social forces will resist social innovation if they perceive that they will become obsolete and/or that they will lose social power and influence.

The *diffusion of innovation* involves the rigorous process of formulating how to spread innovation across a wide social spectrum and have the innovation adopted. Diffusion involves the movement of an innovation across the social spectrum to the lower concentration of the adopters (users). Once the penetration level of innovation reaches a certain number of adopters, the rate of diffusion will increase. In social systems, this diffusion is highly critical in order to offset the action potential of the negative social factors.

The *diffusion of innovation* according to Everett Rodgers works in normally well-defined stages. The social factors involved in the diffusion are awareness, interest, evaluation, trial, and adoption. In the stepwise process of innovative diffusion there are about 2.5% of people in the spectrum who are the innovators, then the next 13.5% are the early adopters, next are the early majority at 34%, and then the later majority at 34%, and finally the laggards compose around 16%. Once the social penetration is made to the early adopters, the rate of growth accelerates quickly. Technology and access are social elements, which can potentially alter the normal diffusion curve. Within the element of innovative diffusion, the adopters can become uncertain and this can impact the curve. In the environment, the trophic level is a concept that encompasses the laws of thermodynamics, where energy is diffused at lower rates as the energy passes through its diffusion cycle. Much like the trophic concept, the diffusion of knowledge and/or innovation can work in a highly parallel way. Whether one is dealing with energy transfer or the diffusion of knowledge and/or information, the transfer rate will never be at 100 percent.

Signal detection theory involves decisions under conditions of uncertainty and involve active versus *passive* decision-making within the sensitivity index. This theory can be applied to social systems and social innovation. Social *targets* are things that are correct or wanted within social systems versus social *distracters*, which are the incorrect or unwanted social elements. When social innovation is being introduced via social diffusion to try and eliminate negative social elements, there can be different social outcomes. Within social retrieval people identifying the *innovative targets* would be a *hit*, while people identifying the *social distracters* would be a *false alarm*. Social distractions, interference, and competing negative stimuli can impact people's correct social detection. The factors are called the social *response criteria*. A false positive is when people think they sense what is *not there*. A false negative is when people miss a stimulus that *is there*. There are so many social factors which can potentially impede innovation and the forward momentum of social systems that the diffusion curve has not been accelerated over time.

In innovation, the process of *managing ideas effectively* entails research, new systems and processes emerging, taking risks, and eventual change. In order to *manage risks* within innovation, people need to identify ways to properly manage them. If the impending issue/s is too difficult to change or eliminate through the exhaustive efforts of innovation, people must accept the risk and then determine the risk factors. As social factors typically evolve in a cyclical fashion, many social issues can potentially be eliminated before they begin or at early onset. Social decision errors are one of the primary social elements, which contribute to social decline and/or the loss of forward momentum within the evolution of humanity.

Social decision errors arise from dubious personal and group beliefs and findings and often include a *logical fallacy*, which is an argument using illogical reasoning and a failure to understand the implications of the facts at hand. Faulty and/or illogical reasoning can be factors in decision errors, and people can also consciously dictate social outcomes to fit within their own narrow and limited social perspectives. *Self-fulfilling prophecy* is when people's beliefs influence social actions and which leads to their predictions coming true. This social activity is *forcing* a social agenda upon others and ultimately onto a social system. Sometimes people's social agendas do not go as they planned or desired and when things do not materialize into their desired social outcomes, they will make false claims. These false claims can hurt the people within their immediate social ring and the social impacts can also potentially radiate out into other social rings. It is impossible to accurately measure the impact of even a singular human social decision error as the social ramifications can be infinite.

Hindsight bias occurs after the fact, when an event or ordeal (social outcome) is over, and people think that they predicted the actual outcome, when the outcome is already determined. The *base rate fallacy* is people judging an outcome while *ignoring* prior knowledge and *belief perseverance* is rejecting something even if something is *proven* and *known*. Many social decision errors are tied into people's identity and to their egos. *Confirmation bias* is people ignoring information that contradicts with their own social schema disposition or the results that they were looking for within a social outcome. *Discomfirmation bias* is people agreeing only with what supports their own social beliefs. If people become comfortable and adept within social manipulation and in having social outcomes transpire within their own continuum of social perspective, this can have a massive negative impact on people and on social systems. This type of social behavior is a common contagion that opposes the growth and development of humanity.

Perception and habituation work together, and the more adept people get at doing something the less likely they are to look at process from another perspective. Also the expertise of people in one area/s does not carry over to all areas in life. In addition, one set of social conditions may vary dramatically from another set of social conditions and people can try and transfer their own social and life experiences over to other areas as a generality versus examining the variance between the social areas. The *conjunction fallacy* states that just because something can happen in a different circumstance, doesn't necessarily make it more likely to occur in other areas. People need to show empirically across many areas (repeatable) how their social concept can appear in different social scenarios in order for their ideas to be generalized and to become reliable and valid. *The law of small numbers* states that there is an error in assuming that a small sample is representative of a larger population.

> *An expert is a person with few new ideas, a beginner is a person with many.*
>
> —Einstein

But the ideas of the beginners must contain social truths and realities versus shallow opinions. A narrow social perspective can confound the action potential for human progress and evolution regardless of whether it comes from a plebeian (common person) or an expert. There are also many other factors which can lead to social decision errors.

The *ambiguity affect* is when people prefer the known to the unknown and *social anchoring* is when people base their social estimates on only their *known* social anchors. The *availability heuristic* is when recent events seem more likely to people and this dictates their social decisions and actions. The *bias blind spot* is when people don't compensate for their own social bias. Many times people also have a *bounded rationality*, which is limited logic and reasoning within their social decisions. The impact of a bounded rationality can lead to the *neglect of probability bias* in people, which is not using risk management, contingencies planning, and is a black-and-white approach. If people have a bounded rationality, their ability to consider social probabilities and that those social probabilities can change over time can be nonexistent and any efforts to discuss these social elements with them can be futile. The confluence of these covariant social factors can have highly derogatory social impacts.

The *illusory correlation* is when people assume false correlations (i.e., birds of the same feather flock together [not always]), and believing a relationship between variables exist when no true relationship exist. Another example could be a bad experience in a relationship leading to the correlation that all future social experiences will be the same. The mood covariant can elicit *mood-congruent judgment* errors where people's mood biases their judgment, and their distorted ideas can lead to poor social decisions and actions. *Psychological accounting* is a component of mood and involves people framing their social decisions by the direct consequences of their choice and by ratios versus direct absolute amounts. The context of a scenario and the *stage of the motion/action* can impact their social decisions. Choices can be *framed* in terms of consequences, but people must think beyond the immediate consequences of a social decision. The mood element is closely tied into people's identities and the ego within their identities.

The human ego can create social overconfidence in people and this can lead to *egocentrism*, which is the focus solely on one set of social perspectives. Being *compartmental* is being self-centered, only seeing the small picture, being isolating versus linking, and not thinking across the full social spectrum, which would include the perspectives of others. Being compartmental is a common social flaw in people at many different social levels including high levels of leadership. The *overconfidence barrier* exists when people become overconfident in their own judgment. When people's social predictions exceed *the 80-percent level*, people can naturally become overconfident and they can get a *god complex*. It is not *healthy* to get a god complex, but it would also be *unwise* to ignore the ability to accurately predict social outcomes. In order to try and bring this type of person down, people can ask them a question about something they don't know, but they can come back and say that is not in their area of expertise or within their scope. Some people do not have the ability to formulate the correct social answers a very high degree of the time and these are the people who are normally contentious toward those who *can* predict social outcomes with regularity. The key is for the people with this special gift to still go through the correct thought process and cycle regardless of their accuracy level, so that their ego doesn't lead to a social decision that can potentially create a large social error and potential social chaos. It is important for society to find the fecund people who are able to predict social outcomes within the process of social harvesting.

On the other end of the social continuum, there are some people that believe that they are right all the time and they just forget about, dismiss, and/or use hindsight bias about the times when they are not correct. As an individual, if a person considers the reasons that they may be wrong and with more practice, before long their confidence will more closely match the accuracy of their social decisions and predictions.

The *fundamental attribution error* is the overestimation of the strength and quality of people's own personal dispositions. This can include their self-perception and their perceptions of others in social systems (i.e., the *actor-observer* bias). *Depressive realism* is the tendency of mildly depressed people to make social judgments that can occasionally be more accurate that those who are not depressed, being they are *less egocentric.* The social impacts of the ego in individual people can also often inhibit the progress of social rings and social systems as well. The ego can be a toxic social element, which can become a noxious social contagion. Over the course of time, the people with the strongest ego have traditionally tried to influence the direction of their own immediate social ring and also the direction of the other social rings and social groups to which they interact within.

Conventional group meetings have historically been dominated by egotistical people and this creates even more social pressure for people to conform. *Social climbers, yes people,* and other followers of the *social dominators* can directly contribute to the restriction of social innovation. Blocking can also occur in groups, which is when social power figures (social dominators) interfere with the social concepts and ideas that are formulated by people in a group, who are not *chosen* to generate the ideas and concepts. This social action can cause blocked ideas to be forgotten and lost, which can stagnate social innovation. When social power figures (social dominators) are exerting their will upon a group, there are symptoms that will appear. *Groupthink symptoms* can include when the cognitive element of rationalization is ignored and then despite to the contrary conflict in information, the group goes with the presented social idea or concept, and somehow justifies the social decision. In order to avoid the pitfalls of groupthink, people must create a process to avoid groupthink.

In order for social innovation to occur, people must check on the assumptions behind their decisions, validate the decision-making process, and evaluate the risk involved with a social decision. People must explore the social objectives and alternatives, create tests for assumptions, reexamine the rejected points, use an outside resource for a fresh look (consultant), process information objectively, and must develop at least one social contingency plan.

Brainstorming is a great way to begin generating ideas and to avoid traditional groupthink.

The brainstorming process should be free, open, and nonjudgmental. Research has shown that individual brainstorming yields the highest quantity and quality of innovative social ideas. Once the ideas are generated, they can be brought into a group where the ideas can be expanded upon, by others who sometimes have more experience and expertise in channeling and finalizing social ideas. Brainstorming makes people feel that they are contributing to the innovative effort. Even within the brainstorming process, there are still times where the person or people who contribute the ideas are not given credit and this is another social flaw that exists within society. If a person is responsible for generating the majority of the innovative ideas, they should be socially elevated instead of not being accepted into the group, which finalizes the innovative approach.

Within the brainstorming process, the ladder of inference can be applied, which states that people should not jump to conclusions, must deal with reality and facts, and then they must abstract the potential solutions. The top of the ladder is actions, then beliefs, conclusions, assumptions (do not fail to consider alternatives), interpreted reality, selected reality, the drawn upon reality and facts (can be reviewed versus mental set and prior experiences). There are impacts when people jump to conclusions. The vicious circle cycle involves the tendency of people to jump to conclusions, miss facts, skip steps in the ladder process, and narrow their field of judgment. People must gather the true facts and the social reality, make sure to review each step of the ladder, make sure each step is making sense, ask questions (what and why, etc.), be careful to not sway over to natural tendencies (drift), and not assume. Also people must not fall into groupthink, they must watch for the signs, validate any risks before concluding, test the validation, and be able to repeat the techniques to build confidence. Within cognition, all the other covariants ultimately rely on the final element, which is the personality. The element of personality can profoundly impact people and society. The impacts of individual personalities on society and human evolution are infinite.

The personality can be defined as a person's unique consistent pattern of thinking, feeling, and actions, which define their core behavior patterns. A person's temperament is an equally potent element and it is an aspect of the personality that people are born with. The characteristics of people's temperaments are innate and enduring. The temperament is embedded into people's core emotional construct (i.e., calm and reserved or anxious and nervous). The temperament typically is something that is very difficult to modify in people as well as the personality. Many people in society still do not recognize that these core human elements are both biological in predisposition via genetics and that they are also consolidated at very young ages. With nurturing, a person's surface actions and behaviors may appear different over time, but the elements of personality and temperament are the *roots* of all behavior and they are both hardwired into people on a genetic level and they are consolidated very early in life.

The *phenotype* is the genetic code for people's physical, psychological, and biological makeup that can be measured. Genes inherited in addition to the environment is the phenotype and the *genotype* is just the genes consideration. A genetic *trait* is an enduring personal characteristic, which can include dispositions and can give rise to behavior patterns (i.e., curiosity). A personality *chiasmus* could be that you can take a person out of a social environment, but you cannot take the personality out of a person. The personality can be impacted by internal and external factors, which can include birth order, family size, and many other factors. Gordon Allport, a personality psychologist, developed the *trait theory of personality* with three levels of disposition.

1. Is the *cardinal trait*, which is the *dominant* trait
2. Are the *general traits*, which are present in most people

3. Are the *secondary traits*, which are situational traits and they can also be masked depending on the social scenario.

Longitudinal studies find that people's core and cardinal personality traits stay with them throughout their lives with elements such as anxiety levels, friendliness, a desire for exploration or a lack of, being some of the most fixed personality traits. People's circumstances, roles, and issues change in life, but their personalities and temperaments are hardwired innately (genetically), and the foundation is embedded very early in life.

Meta-analytical studies show that there are links between personality types and both emotional and physical outcomes. There has been links shown in studies between *neurotic* personality types and issues such as headaches, asthma, arthritis, ulcers, and heart disease. For instance, the trait of shyness can sometimes lead to a high level of isolation and this can contribute to biological impacts such as stress and depression, which, over the course of time, can contribute to a shorter life span. The personality can also definitely dictate and influence life choices and social outcomes.

Within the personality, there are also life and death drives according to Freud and others, which are the source of people's instincts, and they maximize gratification while minimizing guilt and punishment. The psyche (mental construct) lends a greater amount of energy to receive positive social energy than negative social energy because of the adverse impacts of negative social energy and its abundance in availability. People consciously and subconsciously protect themselves from the oxidative stress of negative social stimulus. People's identities require social acceptance, and if social acceptance is not yielded, their identities can begin to erode over time. Defense mechanisms are used to counteract the force of negative social energy and prevent social exhaustion and/or social burnout.

According to Freud, *Eros* is the life drive to preserve and create life, while *Thanatos* is a drive toward aggression and death. This is the balancer where fear, hatred, anger are stored, which lead to antisocial acts. People can become fixated and they can develop a drive imbalance and this can create the desire for people to repeat their actions, which can be tied to *instinctive drift*, which is a move toward innate tendencies and away from nurturing and learned behavior. Even with the most potent nurturing, there are very powerful pre-wired elements that are embedded into people. The *drive-reduction theory* (Clark Hull) states that there is tension and drive to fulfill biological needs for homeostasis, which are primary, and that the secondary drives are learned. The *opponent process theory* states that there is a baseline normal state in people, and then if people's social actions occur away from their baseline, people will eventually feel an *opponent process* to return to their baseline. This is not only a physiological impulse this is primarily a mental impulse. All of these psychological concepts point to the inner drives that are present in people and that these drives can potentially run astray. When people are not able to balance their own social drives within socialization, intervention is required. Unfortunately many people in society still dismiss these social realities because of their narrow, rigid, and inflexible schemas.

An estimated 10–15 percent of adults in the US experience symptoms of at least one personality disorder. Factors that contribute to personality disorders are internal and external and can include genetics, personal relations, level of sensitivity (construct), abuse history, life trauma, and more. While most people have a mixture of central and secondary personality traits, cardinal traits are relatively rare. Cardinal personality traits would be highly polar traits such as being a *narcissist* on one end of the personality social continuum pole or being *angelic* on the other end of the personality continuum. Freud's *libidinal dynamism* is the early prelinguistic identity struggle that people encounter in life, which is a desire for people to join the whole beyond the self and is termed the *jouissance*. If this element is left unchecked, emotion will control and overwhelm people, society helps to control this social element via social mechanisms such as the process of education and the application of social norms. Jouissance normally depletes with age as language is acquired and enjoyment can come from escapist fantasy.

As adults, if the level of jouissance is not reached, this can lead to narcissistic behavior, which involves in part an adoration of a perfect self-image. *Narcissist cathexis* is the investment of high amounts of personal energy into the self and then interpsychic and all instincts that don't discharge outwardly are turned inward, which is *repression*. The *narcissistic personality* is self-centered, arrogant, exploitive, lacks empathy for others, and admiration is sought. Narcissistic characteristics can further include people having no true strong social bonds (superficial and masked interpersonal relations), the use of reduction, their envy seeks to destroy the good objects of others, their fear of extinction is high, the signs of ageing cause severe distress and anger, self-exaggeration is in excess; and there is deception, lying, seeking excessive attention, belief in superiority, delusions of grandeur, they are irrational when they don't get what they want, there is love of self, and a strong investment of libidinal energy into the ego (narcissistic cathexis).

In a social environment, narcissist will use, abuse, and discard people, they will also use flattery and recognition to keep people off balance. *Primary narcissism* occurs normally from six months to six years of age, and prevents *psychic damage* during the formation of the *individual self*. *Secondary narcissism* is choosing self-gratification over adhering to the social norms, being this can alienate other people this level of narcissism can be pathological if there is no empathy for others. *Cerebral narcissism* is when people's intellectual abilities give them gratification. *Somatic narcissism* is when people's body, beauty, physique, sexual ability, and conquests provide them with gratification. *Inverted narcissism* is when people project onto other narcissists, keeping distant yet close, and they experience social gratification through the narcissism of others vicariously. This can be a form of sadism as well.

Sigmund Freud posed that the *first five years* of life are crucial to the development of the adult personality, the identity must be controlled to satisfy social demands, the ego and superego balance the demands of gratification into acceptable social channels. The individual must have their needs met to move onto the next stage, but there can also be an issue where an individual is too well satisfied and becomes reluctant to leave the psychological benefit of a particular development stage where there is *overindulgence*. *Fixation* is not moving past a stage. The *twin evils* in child nurturing are *pampering* and *neglect* and overindulgence would qualify as pampering.

Ego strength is people's ability to maintain their *identity* versus internal and external social factors, which can impact the ego. People continually are exposed to various elements within the process of socialization and the maintenance of the ego is what allows people to endure the process. *Instinctive drift* is when people move toward their innate tendencies versus their learned behavior from the nurturing process. A *fixed-action pattern* is a social action that is not contingent on the social environment and the actions are instead tied to internal tendencies. (The individual Freud life stages will be seen later in the book)

Psychotherapy/psychodynamic therapies focus on a belief that the conservation of energy is essential in brain function and *homeostasis*. Healthy people can adapt within the process of socialization and are able to maintain their psychic balance. But some people are not able to maintain a healthy psychological balance (i.e., in people with psychological disorders such as *anxiety neurosis* [PTSD]) when their psychological anxiety leads to physical symptoms.

Within the mind, the *conscious* elements, the top level or the surface level according to Freud, interplay within the ego, superego, and the identity. The preconscious (stored info to summon), the subconscious (priming, mere-exposure effect, not thinking about, but behavior reflects the stored information), and unconscious mind (where people are not consciously aware of some memories and includes the identity and repressed aspects) can heavily impact the conscious mind. Traumatic life social events that reach the preconscious can result in shame, and if events reach the unconscious or subconscious then are brought back into conscious, this can cause varying behavior. The *unconscious mind* drives later behavior. There are also many other elements within these foundations.

The *reality principle* is the negotiation between the identity and the social environment. The *pleasure principle* is the driving force guiding the identity, seeking pleasure and the avoidance of any pain, as pain is more available in life whether emotional or physical, and can lead to social *avoidance*. Social avoidance and isolation can lead to stress, depression, and even a shorter life span. A large component within the balance between pleasure and pain is socialization. Everyone is hardwired to desire social acceptance.

Social desirability is the part of the internal social construction mechanism of the self to be positive on the social scale. If not believed to be desirable, this can create *cognitive dissonance* (conflicting thoughts in the mind within interpretation), and cognitive dissonance can arise in the decision-making process. Interpretation is how we perceive perceptual differences. The level of cognitive dissonance proportionately increases by the impact level of a social decision. The *need to belong* is something that Maslow stated was an innate pre-wired psychological need. Acceptance is required for people's self-esteem and their identity; therefore, people will migrate toward acceptance if it is not elicited toward them. Unfortunately social migration can result in a positive or negative social outcome. Desire is a very powerful innate drive, which involves the need for social connections and also other needs of the self in order to feel whole. This is why the media, marketing, and technology have had a profound impact on society. When wholeness is perceived from external sources such as these social elements versus a more intrinsic value system, this can lead people and society down a vicious social path. Especially when coupled with a narrow support system.

Desire is the feeling of lacking something, a sense of loss, an incomplete wholeness. Desire creates fantasy, and fantasy leads to a dull reality, a fantasized existence can blur reality and can cause severe psychological impacts. All people are different both on internal and external levels, yet society continues to convey the completely opposite message. Not all people are athletes, models, geniuses, etc. due to the genetic factors. But being that society is part of the identity process, people must prepare themselves for the social matrix that has changed drastically especially in recent history within socialization.

Identification is the process of people forming an identity and this can extend to the point where people may copy others, and be dependent on relations. *Introjection* is when the people take on the behaviors and attributes of others (i.e., a child does this with parents for their *persona* [outward appearance]), and this is the way the *ego* and *superego* are constructed. The primitive version is incorporation. *Incorporation* is making something else part of the self. The formation of identity and self involves an *outer/inner world* and the inputs and outputs of interactions. *Internalization* is when the ego installs, it is integral to sense of self and personality (high level concept), and it is shaped in combination with predisposed genetic traits. *Identity* is the sense of self, self-perception, and the use of defense mechanisms when things begin to attack one's identity versus blaming self identity. Identity masks can protect a person and can facilitate social interaction, anxiety can be hidden behind the mask, and the mask can allow for social security and power. And often, if the identity mask is removed and the true self is not found, but rather another identity mask layer (another false self), a person has created many layers of identity protection to offset their social anxiety. By creating social masks, people are risking their very essence which is being eroded over time.

Self concealment involves people hiding their negative traits from others and if people become too self-concealed, it's possible for them become anxious, defensive, and depressed. This type of life can perpetuate and create a passive-aggressive personality type in people. When people are too self-conscious and they are so concentrated on self-focus, they can get to the point of fixation, which is very unhealthy for the psyche. By concealing themselves and putting on social identity masks, people are not applying the fundamental social requirement of *self-disclosure*, which is highly important in interpersonal social relations, and is a critical element for long-lasting intimate love relationships. The chemistry between people can never fully develop if one or both of the people in a social relationship are concealing their true self. This is why people see others that are in relations that have such fantastic chemistry, because the people with the chemistry are properly matched because they are not *concealing* their true self and the personalities combine and connect like magnetic social force. There are some cases where the people behind the identity masks are out to hurt people. Due to this, there are entire sciences devoted to discovering these people. Although sometimes these people just cannot contain their own delight. The *duper's delight* is a quick grin (delight of deception and control) with the upturn of the mouth, creased eyes, and head often thrown back. But people who discover a duper must be careful not let the duper know that they have been pegged by expressing their own duper's delight.

Carl Jung, a personality psychologist, developed the concept of the use of the persona (the public image) and the shadow (the opposing and sometimes evil personality side). The people who employ these tactics are surreptitious in their actions by hiding their true demeanors. Because of social masks and social concealment, many times people are not able to recognize the opposing personality that is hiding behind the mask. But people can become more adept at recognizing social masks by focusing on certain social and physical inconsistencies.

For instance, people cannot fake their countenance in certain facial characteristics and in *morphology*, which is the study of these physical dynamics. Scientific research has identified that the face naturally uses twenty facial muscles just in order to smile. *Ballistic trajectory* is the natural physical reaction via the brain that elicits reflexes to symmetrically appear, peak, and fade versus having a rigid offset. The (neurotransmitters) NTs in the brain are designed to work, with proper functioning, in a smooth fashion. There will be *cohesion* in the pace of both verbal and nonverbal action. The *speed of onset* will be smooth in transition versus rigid and delayed, and *apex overlap* will separate interlacing of emotions, complex distortions of the face, it is very hard to fake individual faces and even harder for multiple. Every action or inaction that is displayed by people is part of their identity. Personal identity is one of the most critical covariant factors to each individual within humanity and also for the potential impacts on the collective society.

Within their identity, people create coping mechanisms and defense mechanisms for the internal fear of being cast out of a group. Within identity, there are needs such as belonging, esteem, fair equity from others, and approval. People with personality disorders can also play games where they desire to be persecuted and then seek support to break out. Some people will also prey on other people who have disorders and they will be supportive of them in exchange for their loyalty. Within the process of forming the identity, the self is also being consolidated.

The *true self* is a realized sense of integrity and wholeness while the *false self* relies completely on the external compliance with social codes and the anticipation of the demands of others in order to maintain social relations. A *functional false self* will allow the true self to override it when the right time comes. A *dysfunctional false self* involves forced compliance versus loving adaptation, and the false self starts overriding true self. The constant tension and stress involved in the development of the self can sometimes lead to personal and social dysfunction.

Alfred Alder stated that ultimately the formation of the self and identity are the *social responsibility* of all capable people. If these elements are not formed properly, people can develop *inferiority complex*. Within this complex, often people look to control others to feel less personally inadequate as a form of *compensation* (Freud). Alfred Alder pointed to the social comparisons that were made for people as a child, their mental limitations, and social bias as being factors that can lead toward this complex and further yet a *neurosis*. Also the importance of birth order where dethronement, center, and overindulgence of youngest can be factors, typically the middle children are most well adjusted in families. Yet another social factor is the parenting style and the twin evils of pampering or neglect.

Congruence is people moving their real self toward their ideal self and ultimately toward self-actualization. The *ideal self* (Carl Rogers) is used to depict the difference between the real self and the ideal self. The ideal self must be set as realistic or the real self cannot possibly move toward and/or obtain the form of the ideal self. This self balance can be impacted by factors such as social models, experiences, and societal demands, and great dissatisfaction and disappointment can be realized if the variance is too wide between the two elements. Parents, guardians, and other people in children's lives can set them up for social failure by setting unrealistic goals and self-images.

Positive self-regard (Carl Rogers) poses that people have two fundamental psychological needs, positive self-regard and moving toward self-actualization. Positive self-regard is the feeling of having and giving love, affection, and respect. Reaching self-actualization involves the complete and full evolving and development of a person.

Integrity (Erickson) states that a certain level of integrity is essential in a meaningful life, while people dwelling on things that haven't gone right or regrets can lead to their *despair*. Despair is also very unhealthy for the psyche (mental construct). In order to offset the impacts of socialization, people often utilize defense mechanisms.

Repression is blocking memories from conscious awareness. People will use a myriad of defense mechanisms to protect their psyche. *Denial* is not accepting an ego threatening truth. *Displacement* is the redirection of issues onto another. *Projection* is believing that others share one's opinions. *Reaction formation* is people expressing the opposite of how they actually feel, and they may even partake in an organization to express that opposite. *Regression* is returning to an earlier state or earlier comfort behavior. *Rationalization* is explaining an unhealthy behavior or feeling in a rational way and avoiding the true reasons for the behavior (i.e., blaming others for a result or stating that ones true intentions were different than actual), this is to prevent anxiety and harm to self-esteem and identity. In success or failure scenarios, people tend to give themselves credit for success and blame others for failures and the creation of false benefits stem from an undesired result or occurrence.

Intellectualization can include the intellectual, unemotional study of a topic as a distracter to a reality (i.e., with a medical diagnosis, people focus on the intellectual component to reduce their anxiety). Freud stated that this involves distant perspectives, abstract thought in order to avoid any matter than can become an unpleasant thought as a defense mechanism by removing oneself emotionally from a stressful scenario in order to elude anxiety. *Sublimation* is the extended efficient handling of a conflict between the need for satisfaction and the need for security without the perturbation of awareness. It is the only way people can get part of their satisfaction and also feel secure. People can offset their inappropriate social tensions by channeling their frustration and tensions into a more acceptable social goal or activity like art. Sublimation is considered to be a *healthy* defense mechanism.

Activities allow for the release of energy, which is social *catharsis*. When people are not able to maintain a healthy psyche, they can seek therapy in order to regain their psychological balance. If people do not seek an intervention and they continue to remain in a perpetual cycle of the use of any unhealthy defense mechanisms, they pose a risk to themselves and potentially to others within the collective society.

Psychodynamic therapy is a highly effective form of therapy that is used to help people return to a healthy psyche. Although psychotherapy sometimes is beyond one singular approach, it is not *eclectic*, because it has its own *self-efficacy*. There is an alliance between the patient and the therapist, who both need to have positive expectations. There must be quality and attention. Psychotherapy identifies the underlying conflict, such as repression. Dream analysis is also normally part of the therapy and can assist in reducing people's emotional reactivity. The goal of the therapy is to ameliorate troubling symptoms for relief and to increase the capacity for self-observation. Psychotherapy seeks to identify the corrective emotional experience and to focus people on mastering the old negative experiences. The aim of therapy is for patients to let go of their unhealthy parts of the self. There is a *credible reason provision*, which is based on the idea of personality and change. Psychoanalysis is the primary curative therapy, while medication and other methods are adjunct therapies.

Psychotherapy can be used for people with many different issues. The key is for the intervention to take place prior to extensive psychological damage occurring.

Psychosis is a radical change in personality and a distorted or diminished sense of objective reality and can include people who are unable to distinguish reality from the unreal. Psychosis also normally involves an inappropriate and confused manner and behavior. There can be disorganized speech, noises, patterns, and incoherent periods. There can also be unpredictable situational behavior and also disturbed motor behavior (i.e., catatonic). *Abjection* is the deep horror from stimuli caused by a breakdown in the meaning between the subject and the object. Abjection is the stage of leaving unity and toward a sense of separate self. In adulthood, abjection is the threat of returning to an abuse state (where they exist).

Depressive position is the balance of anxieties that can extend from childhood. *Projective identification* allows a person to emphasize with others and move parts of the self into others in order to understand them. This type is gentler and more cooperative than paranoid schizophrenia. Schizophrenia is a prominent mental disorder and its impacts are far reaching. (There will be much more on psychology later in the book)

Personality typing is commonly used to identify people's personality traits. There are several models that are designed to identify the different aspects of people's personalities. Personality typing compares people to an index of organized information about others, and then compares people's past as a predictive indicator of the future (qualify and quantify).

Some commonly known personality types are the *type A* personality, which typically feel pressure, agitation, competitive, ambitious, and are generally a higher risk for health issues. The type A personality can be *authoritarian* (controlling) and they often don't listen to explanations, will jump to conclusions, and refuse to provide explanations. The type A personality can also be *aggressive* and have an overtly aggressive attitude and behavior. The *type B* personality is more relaxed and easygoing. The chameleon personality type is a hybrid and is highly adaptive across environments. The type B and chameleon personality types can sometimes be *passive-aggressive* if they form negative attitudes and develop a passive resistance to others, passive-aggressive people can sometimes hold in their tension and the releases can be potentially toxic to themselves and others around them.

There is also a *paranoia continuum* within personalities, which ranges from a misinterpretation of cues on occasion to the complete social system interaction impact. The *paranoid personality disorder* (PPD) condition involves the absence of any evidence, motives, intentions, and this pattern of thinking without these factors can lead to hostility and social isolation where a person doesn't trust others. There are many elements within socialization that can lead people toward becoming more cautious in life and for certain people who are predisposed to being paranoid in life, their continuum is much smaller and their level of trust can be diminished much more quickly and can potentially lead to PPD. (Psychology will be covered more in-depth later in the book)

Some of the personality tests that are commonly used include the *Strong-Campbell Interest Inventory* (SCII) by Holland (traits of high risks secondary students), Kuder Occupational Interest Survey (KOIS), Strong Interest Inventory (SII) for career and educational assessments using *Holland Codes*, Jung Myers-Briggs Type Indicator (MBTI), Harrington-O'Shea Career Decision-Making system, and the *SkillScan* to identify skills and work on skills.

The Holland Codes are occupational themes which fall within the Realistic, Investigative, Artistic, Social, Enterprising and Conventional (RIASEC) hexagon: *realistic* (doers), *investigative* (thinkers), *artistic* (creators), *social* (helpers), *enterprising* (persuaders), and *conventional* (organizers). Research shows that people flourish in career environments of interest. The six themes relate to a person's *resemblance* to a theme versus an exact match, as there are many personality patterns. The US Department of Labor/Employment and Training Admin (USDOL/ETA) uses this testing. Vocation is an expression of personality. There are 720 patterns within a Holland hexagon.

The *big five personality traits* that are typically focused on are: extraversion, agreeableness, conscientious, open to experience (creative), and emotional stability or neuroticism. The big five factor model traits (expanded) are *extraversion* (talkative, energetic, assertive, and ambitious), *agreeableness* (sympathetic, kind, affectionate, trusting, cooperative, and tolerant), *conscientious* (organized, thorough, methodical, dutiful, dependable, and careful), *emotional stability* (calm, relaxed, confident, easygoing, and steady), and *openness to new experiences* (wide interest, imaginative, insightful, cultured, creative, and broadminded). The two easiest scales to fake personality on are *neuroticism* (anxious, moody, and insecure) and *conscientious* (methodical, dependable, and organized). Lie indicators will plug in questions that deal with typical traits that are *undesirable* such as being envious of other people which is a common personality trait.

Carl Jung, the father of *analytic psychology* stated that the *collective unconscious* is shared by all innately throughout all time. He identified eight personality types. The Myers-Briggs Type Indicator is used to identify the type. Some test have also have *lie scales* built into the test for *deception* for reliable, unemotional, and agreeable people. The Jung types are *introverts, extroverts,* and the quantifiers of *feeling, thinking, sensation,* and *intuition.* Which form the following possible combinations: extrovert-thinker, introvert-thinker, extrovert-feeling, introvert-feeling, extrovert-sensation, introvert-sensation, extrovert-intuitive, and introvert-intuitive.

Factor analysis is a *psychometric statistical method* used to describe variability among observed, correlated variables in terms of factors. Personality, attitudes, and beliefs can be measured for postulation of *mental ability* or *G* or *generalizability (G) theory.* Measuring of fluid and crystallized intelligence (verbal intelligence) and sixteen personality factors were derived from factor analysis. The *three-stratum theory* includes use of psychological test, school marks, and competence ratings. The three strata represent narrow, broad, and general cognitive ability to identify stable and observable differences among individuals in the performance of tasks and *nerve-firing rates.* Using research to derive theories and use empirical evidence. Linear combinations are drawn off of potential factors. With three factors: self-attitude, performance, and soma (body) disturbance. *Fluid intelligence* is gf, *crystallized intelligence* is gc, *general memory* and *learning* is gy, *broad visual perception* is gv, *broad auditory perception* is gu, *broad retrieval ability* is gr, *broad cognitive speediness* is gs, and *processing speed* is gt, which can be called *flavors*. *Content validity* means that items representative of what is being tested for validation. *Concurrent validity* means that testing concurs with prior existing standards. *Construct validity* is the degree to which an internal variable is measured.

Cattell, a personality pioneer, identifies sixteen main personality traits, which everyone shares to a degree.

Sixteen PF Personality Questionnaire

1. Abstractedness (imaginative versus practical)
2. Apprehension (worried versus confident)
3. Dominance (forceful versus submissive)
4. Emotional Stability (calm versus high strung)
5. Liveliness (spontaneous versus restrained)
6. Openness to change (flexible versus rigid)
7. Perfectionism (controlled versus undisciplined)
8. Privateness (discreet versus open)
9. Reasoning (abstract versus concrete)
10. Rule Conscious (conforming versus nonconforming)
11. Self-Reliance (self-sufficient versus dependent)
12. Sensitivity (tenderhearted versus tough minded)
13. Social Boldness (uninhibited versus shy)
14. Tension (impatient versus relaxed)
15. Vigilance (suspicious versus trusting)
16. Warmth (outgoing versus reserved)

Another Personality Typing Matrix is the Sixteen Myers-Briggs Type Indicator (MBTI) Matrix by Carl Jung.

- E—*Extraverted* prefer group activities, energized by social interaction

- I—*Introverted*, reserved, solitary activities, find social interaction exhausting
- N—*Intuitive*, imagination, ideas, focus on what might happen
- S—*Sensing*, observed in practical matters, focus on what has happened
- T—*Thinking*, tough, follow their minds, suppress feelings, focus on objectivity and rationality
- F—*Feeling*, sensitive, follow their hearts, focus on harmony and cooperation
- J—*Judging*, decisive, prefer clear rules and guidelines, eager to commit, seek closure, value deadlines
- P—*Perceiving*, probing, prefer keeping options open, reluctant to commit, relaxed about their work, seek freedom

Introverted Intuitive Thinking Perceiving (INTP)—Introverted thinking with extraverted intuition. under 2 percent of all people and often, philosophers, professors, designers, etc. Socrates, Newton, Jung, and Einstein. They will look for an environment where their creative genius can be explored and do not care about social expectations or the usual goals of job security. Have no difficulties noticing patterns where others cannot. They possess the most logical precise minds and can notice the most subtle discrepancies. When the mind is resting, they may seem to be floating off, or they may be deep into thought or having an internal debate.

The thinker has internalized rationality and logic, and uses intuition in dealing with external events, develops theoretical possibilities of how things could be improved. Have ability to analyze difficult problems, patterns, and come up with logical explanations. Clarity is sought; therefore, knowledge is continually sought. A feeling of personal responsibility to solve problems often comes about within INTPs. Existing rules are ignored and personal definitions are applied with objectivity. They seem dreamy and distant to many others, and prefer more complex activities. They interact well with others unless they believe that their firmly held beliefs have been challenged and/ or violated. INTPs can be initially shy around new people, but once they are comfortable with people they will open up. INTPs do not prefer subjectivity, and often are not well-equipped to meet the emotional needs of others. Social rebellion may impact their creative potential. If the INTP doesn't work on their emotional side, they can become very critical and sarcastic of others. Sometimes INTPs well-constructed ideas are not well understood by others. It is important that the INTP makes their ideas understandable or the ideas will have no value. INTPs tend to be restless and temperamental, with very complex character. A lot of scientific breakthroughs have been made by INTPs, and if allowed to develop their ideas, society can be enhanced.

Jung Functional Preference

- Dominant—Introverted Thinking
- Auxiliary—Extraverted Intuition
- Tertiary—Introverted Sensing
- Inferior—Extraverted Feeling

Introverted Intuitive Feeling Judging (INTJ)—under 2 percent of all people, they are natural leaders; however, they tend to stay in the background, but as leaders they are objective and adaptive, which makes them effective because they are able to change things that aren't working well. The scientists have very evolved intuitions and are convinced that they are right about things, use logic and rationality for external world, ideas and strategic planning, focus on observing the world and generating ideas and possibilities, mind constantly gathers information and makes associations. Are tremendously insightful and are very quick to understand new ideas. Application of concepts is most important. (Do not follow ideas as far as they can like the INTP). INTJs value systems and organization. INTJs are driven to make their nonlinear (abstract) concepts and ideas understandable. They are always scanning ideas and concepts, expressing judgment, and planning contingencies. INTJs, like INTPs, need to develop their emotional side to better connect with other types. They will be misunderstood if they do not develop the ability to express their insights. Sometimes the INTJ will blame others for their lack of understanding versus their own inability to properly express their ideas. If the ability to express their ideas isn't developed, they can seem to be arrogant, aloof and reserved, and to be an elitist. INTJs can become abrupt and short with people and can become isolationists, if they do not develop their expressive side. INTJs are long-range thinkers and dislike ambiguity. With stress, INJTs can get absorbed in the minutia of the details more so than with normal activity. INTJs have insight into the big picture.

Jung Functional Preference

- Dominant—Introverted Intuition
- Auxiliary—Extraverted Thinking
- Tertiary—Introverted Feeling
- Inferior—Extraverted Sensing

Introverted Intuitive Feeling Judging (INFJ)—1 percent of people; the most rare of all types—introverted intuition with extraverted feeling. *The protector*, feelings and value systems, gentle, caring, complex, artistic and creative, order is important, and creating the best systems for getting things done, they are intuitive, but cannot pinpoint the detail why, although they usually know they are correct, uncanny ability to understand through feelings they get about people and things, others scoff at their abilities to predict events, so they carefully choose whom they share things with. INFJs are deep, complex, can be secretive, and sometimes difficult to understand; they are sensitive to conflict and cannot tolerate it very well. Due to their nature, they can either internalize stress, which can lead to health problems later or they can become agitated with charged anger. Because of their ability to predict things, they may be stubborn to adopt the ideas of others. They have high expectations of themselves and frequently of their families, which can manifest into being hard-nosed and stubborn. They don't believe in compromising their ideals. They are however patient, devoted, and protective, and forms strong bonds with their families. In careers, they do not like detail, because of their depth life can be difficult within interactions.

Jung Functional Preference

- Dominant—Introverted Intuition
- Auxiliary—Extraverted Thinking
- Tertiary—Introverted Feeling
- Inferior—Extraverted Sensing

Introverted Intuitive Feeling Perceiving (INFP)—introverted feeling with extraverted intuition. *The idealist* focus on making the world a better place for others, finding out the meaning of life, truth, and underlying cause, are good listeners and put people at ease. They are caring and can be expressive, but can still be somewhat reserved. Do not like conflicts and will go to great lengths to avoid it, can be irrational and illogical in conflict situations. Because they don't care about what is right or wrong, they just don't want to feel bad. They understand other people's problems and genuinely want to help them. They are generally flexible and laid-back unless their value system is attacked, they will engage in the details if they are protecting what they care about, sometimes do not notice the mundane things in life. They do not like to deal with hard facts and logic, they also do not like impersonal judgment or having to use it, if angered will start trying to throw out facts even if they are inaccurate in an emotional outburst, sometimes their high ideals and controlling aspects doesn't work in groups, they must balance their ideals versus the requirements of every day living to be happy, they have a wonderful ability to express themselves on paper, often appear in social service professions, working toward public good and not having to use hard logic, often don't give themselves enough credit.

Jung Functional Preference

- Dominant—Introverted Intuition
- Auxiliary—Extraverted Thinking
- Tertiary—Introverted Feeling
- Inferior—Extraverted Sensing

Extraverted Intuitive Thinking Judging (ENTJ)—extraverted thinking with introverted intuition. *The executive*: Born leaders, want to take on challenges, quick judgments and ability to gather impersonal information, constantly scanning for opportunities to fix things, can visualize direction, have little patience for error, don't cater to people's feelings, have difficulties seeing outside their own perspective, can be forceful and overbearing without considering others, must get in tune with thinking side or can suffer applying logic within their insights leading to poor decisions, will also become dictatorial and give orders and directions without sound reasoning for doing so and without consideration for the people involved, will hide their emotional side for fear of sign of weakness, excellent verbal communication skills, forceful and dynamic. They are career people, but want their homes and families to be in order.

Jung Functional Preference

- Dominant—Introverted Intuition
- Auxiliary—Extraverted Thinking
- Tertiary—Introverted Feeling

• Inferior—Extraverted Sensing

Extraverted Intuitive Feeling Judging (ENFJ)—extraverted feeling with introverted intuition. *The giver:* People focused individuals, special talent for bringing out the best in others, satisfaction from helping others, able to persuade people. They can also get under people's skin to get the reactions that they want and can be manipulative with their power. Do not do well along. They are a little more reserved than other extraverted types. They act in a chameleon-like manner amongst others at their own level. They highly value the needs of others and their thoughts. Even when around others, they can feel lonely if they are not sharing enough of themselves, don't like ambiguity and are fussy about their homes. Counseling is a good path, they do not like dealing with impersonal reasoning. They do not like logic and reasoning. They want very close intimate relationships, can be worried, sensitive and judgmental if they don't develop their characteristics fully.

Jung Functional Preference

• Dominant—Introverted Intuition
• Auxiliary—Extraverted Thinking
• Tertiary—Introverted Feeling
• Inferior—Extraverted Sensing

Extraverted Intuitive Thinking Perceiving (ENTP)—extraverted intuition with introverted thinking. *The visionary:* Understanding the world they live in, quick to size up a situation, have a deep understating of their environments with depth. They are flexible and adaptive, resourceful problem solvers. They get support they need to fulfill their visions. They come up with ideas, but often don't finish what they start, can be visionary and enterprising if they fully develop their characteristics. They enjoy verbally sparring with others within debates. This is the lawyer type who can use quick logic to act upon situations, the more personal or human element is not considered by the ENTP, this can cause personal and social isolation. They are creative, clever, curious, but if not fully developed can become stressed and lose their ability to generate ideas.

Jung Functional Preference

- Dominant—Introverted Intuition
- Auxiliary—Extraverted Thinking
- Tertiary—Introverted Feeling
- Inferior—Extraverted Sensing

Extraverted Intuitive Feeling Perceiving (ENFP)—extraverted intuition with introverted feeling. *The inspirer* inspires and motivates others with passion. Being they like projects, they can change paths with regularity. They live on a value system and onlookers may not see them as pointed in their direction. Everything they do must be in line with their values, intense with highly evolved values. They must stick to their projects or will never achieve larger successes, can understand others very quickly. They do not enjoy mundane tasks and this can be frustrating to family members. They can become manipulative if they go the wrong path, but most will not use this path because it doesn't align with their value system, can make errors in judgment. In relationships, they do well with others who enjoy change. ENFPs can be hard for children to understand because of their inconsistency, and they may bounce back and forth on parenting style, but within their value system, they enjoy flexibility and are productive with limited supervision. They do not like to be controlled or labeled. They often experience muscle tension due to feeling of being constricted. They must remain centered and must follow through.

Jung Functional Preference

- Dominant—Introverted Intuition

- Auxiliary—Extraverted Thinking
- Tertiary—Introverted Feeling
- Inferior—Extraverted Sensing

Introverted Sensing Thinking Judging (ISTJ)—introverted sensing with extraverted thinking. *The duty fulfiller:* Interested in security and peaceful living, have sense of duty, follow through on task, organized and methodical, loyal, faithful and dependable, are upbeat and fun, obey the rules and plans, may do everything by the book, can be taken advantage of because of sense of duty and ability to produce, not into abstract theory, good with facts but unwilling to accept ideas which don't align with their own perspectives. They will not stop supporting their own ideals, can have issues expressing themselves. They may take other people's efforts for granted. They take care of their family, but may have issues expressing their love. Under stress, they may be heavily impaired and can become irrational with the negative outlook.

Jung Functional Preference

- Dominant—Introverted Intuition
- Auxiliary—Extraverted Thinking
- Tertiary—Introverted Feeling
- Inferior—Extraverted Sensing

Introverted Sensing Feeling Judging (ISFJ)—introverted sensing with extraverted feeling. *The nurturer:* Warm and kindhearted, wanting to believe the best in people, harmony and cooperation. They are obvious to others, remember things that are tied to their value system, do not like change. They do best by doing things and being shown the practical application, good with aesthetics, space and design, and also with picking out a good gift. Will often not express their own true feelings, which can cause them to be bottled up, has difficulty saying "no" and can become overburdened. They intensely dislike conflict. They are sometimes taken for granted, a lack of positive feedback with result in becoming discouraged and possibly depressed.

Jung Functional Preference

- Dominant—Introverted Intuition
- Auxiliary—Extraverted Thinking
- Tertiary—Introverted Feeling
- Inferior—Extraverted Sensing

Introverted Sensing Thinking Perceiving (ISTP)—introverted thinking with extraverted sensing. *The mechanic*: They like to understand the way things work, good at logic and like to use on practical applications, not interested in theories without a practical application, and like to take things apart to see how they work. They thrive on action and adventure. They do not believe in following the rules and become easily bored. They believe in equity amongst people, but not in following the *system*. They need to be alone to sort through information, they like to make quick decisions and cannot stand to be behind a desk. They are not tuned into how they are affecting others, may have emotional outbursts and share very personal information. They are capable of being patient, happiest with action which involves use of logic and technical skills, don't like to be confined.

Jung Functional Preference

- Dominant—Introverted Intuition
- Auxiliary—Extraverted Thinking
- Tertiary—Introverted Feeling
- Inferior—Extraverted Sensing

Introverted Sensing Feeling Perceiving (ISFP)—introverted feeling with extraverted sensing. *The artist*: Very sensory, artistic sense, rebel versus anything that conflicts with values, quiet and reserved and difficult to get to know well, may hold back their ideas, put energy into focused tasks and are kind to people. Like animals and nature, the ISFPs may seem carefree, but they are actually very focused internally, learn best in a hands-on environment and do not like abstract thought or impersonal analysis including logic. They are constantly gathering info on others and interpreting the meaning, they do not like to lead or be led, can be perfectionists, and can take life too seriously.

Jung Functional Preference

- Dominant—Introverted Intuition
- Auxiliary—Extraverted Thinking
- Tertiary—Introverted Feeling
- Inferior—Extraverted Sensing

Extraverted Sensing Thinking Judging (ESTJ)—extraverted thinking with introverted sensing. *The guardian*: Like things running smooth, clear standards, and believes and expect others to have the same outlook. Value competence and efficiency. They are self confident and aggressive, and naturally go into leadership roles. They are great at devising plans of steps and action. They are straightforward and honest, which can be taken as demanding and insensitive. Fun at social events. Need to balance logic versus emotional sensitivity. If bogged down, can start to feel undervalued and isolated, can lock up their emotions and communications if stressed, which otherwise stream with ease. Believe in security and social order above all else. They must see the value in others ideas to partake in them.

Jung Functional Preference

- Dominant—Introverted Intuition
- Auxiliary—Extraverted Thinking
- Tertiary—Introverted Feeling
- Inferior—Extraverted Sensing

Extraverted Sensing Feeling Judging (ESFJ)—extraverted feeling with introverted sensing. *The caregiver*: Love people, turn information on people into supportive judgment, bring out the best in others, good at reading others and their points of view, like to be liked and for things to be pleasant, likes to make people feel good about themselves. They are hurt by indifference and don't understand unkindness, will go out of their way to be pleasing toward others. The more nurturing their environment during youth, the more they will offer. They will look for ways to support their social views and/or moral transgressions. They can turn to control and manipulation and can be dangerous as well. They may become depolarized and not be in tune with the cost of their actions. They are manipulating others to get what they need, but in their minds they believe that they are following a code of conduct. They like structured environment and do not like abstract concepts. Males of this type will be masculine, but can show their sensitive nature as well.

Jung Functional Preference

- Dominant—Introverted Intuition
- Auxiliary—Extraverted Thinking
- Tertiary—Introverted Feeling
- Inferior—Extraverted Sensing

Extraverted Sensing Thinking Perceiving (ESTP)—extraverted sensing with introverted thinking. The doer: Straightforward risk-takers, pay little attention to introspection or theory. They look at situation, make choice, and move on. Can perceive people's attitudes and motivations. They can pick up on little cues, which go unnoticed by most others such as body language. They will go along the outskirts of guidelines, getting it done supersedes the rules. They go by their own code versus the *system*. Fast-moving fast-talking people. Their manner may hurt others, although they can be fun to be around. They go off of facts and logic and do not take people's feelings into account. They do not trust their instincts and do not trust the intuitions of others as well. Does not particularly like education particularly when it involves theory and abstract concepts, although they may be brilliant. They may see classes as going nowhere. Make good salespeople. Great at getting people excited and getting things started, but sometimes lack follow through.

Jung Functional Preference

- Dominant—Introverted Intuition
- Auxiliary—Extraverted Thinking
- Tertiary—Introverted Feeling
- Inferior—Extraverted Sensing

Extraverted Sensing Feeling Perceiving (ESFP)—extraverted sensing with introverted feeling. *The performer.* They love people and new experiences, center of attention, relish drama, and live in the present, can often sense something is wrong with others, can give practical care, not greatest advice givers because they don't like theory, can become fixated on overindulgence and gratification, may avoid looking at consequences. They are the life of the party and the show, genuine acceptance of others. They do not like being crossed. They like to talk away through their issues, which may not resolve them. They can go with the flow although they do not like routine. They do not like theoretical thinking and avoid it. They like to learn by doing and learn by interaction. Like aesthetics food and drink. They make things fun and get people energized. They can easily connect with children and small animals, which is not found in many other types. They need to avoid the pitfalls of living in the moment.

Jung Functional Preference

- Dominant—Introverted Intuition
- Auxiliary—Extraverted Thinking

- Tertiary—Introverted Feeling
- Inferior—Extraverted Sensing

There are also color psychological associations. The color *purple* points to striving to be better, being spiritual, emotional, seeking knowledge and answers, providing knowledge, and being self-critical within the reflection upon self-identity. *Red* points to passion, energy, people focus, power, and control and fluctuating temperament. *Yellow* points to education and business, wanting others to know about you, leaders, methodical, detailed analysis, stubborn, others can be suspicious of motives, hide stress, reticent (not revealing one's thoughts freely), and dressing nice. *White* points to purity, shyness, and being outspoken. *Pink* points to seeing the best in others and situations, intelligent, being reserved, and don't share sometimes. *Black* points to detail; look for the mistakes of others and find them so they can be repaired; black is a *repelling* color when worn. *Blue* points to lower trust level, order, can be moody, emotional, and codependent. *Green* points to healing, helpful, having secret thoughts, harmonious, and caring. The color *orange* points to the appreciation of nature, sports, being helpful, seeking adventure, being impulsive, learning, and a belief in entitlement.

Situational psychology can also be used to assess the personality.

Scenario A (All events occurring at the same time)—What does one choose to do first? The baby is crying, there are clothes outside on a line and it starts to rain, the doorbell rings, the phone rings, water is running in the sink. If someone chooses to get the baby first, it points to family orientation. If someone gets the clothes first, it points to sexuality. If someone gets the water first, it points to wealth consideration. If someone gets the door first, it points to friends or company. If someone gets the phone, it points to career focus.

Scenario B (Childhood room description)—Describe the room; how the room makes you feel, describe the furnishings, do you want to leave the room? A pleasant room points to a good childhood, strong description of furnishings points to good memories. Wanting to leave the room points to a desire to leave and grow up.

Scenario C (Seaside)—How many people does one see and how close are the nearest people? If there are lots of people, it points to being very social. If there are just some people, it points to comfort with social outings. If there are a few people, it points to content with being alone. If there are no people, it points to the avoidance of social situations. If the people are far away, it points to being quiet. If the people are close, it points to be social.

Scenario D (Driving)—If you follow partner's navigation and get lost, what would you say? Would you say that "I thought you knew", "It's okay", "I should have paid more attention", or "It's my fault"? The first response is unforgiving or dissatisfaction in unrelated area, the second response points to easygoing and understanding, the third response points to insecurity and a tendency to bend over.

Scenario E (The Oasis)—There is a box on the road, what's in it? Choose a place to live, where would it be? While you are wandering you notice a village or an oasis, which would you choose? If you lost everything, what would you do? It's Sunday, what are you going to do? Who do you turn to in a tight spot? What age would you choose for the rest of you life? Twenty-four hours to live, what do you do? If you could save one thing from a fire, what would it be?

For the box, if one chooses nothing of value, it points to being out of luck. If something valuable chosen, it points to good fortune ahead. If nothing is in the box, it points to practicality. For the place chosen, if one chooses present home, it points to comfort. If a faraway place is chosen, it points to being a dreamer. Indecision points to no strong connections. Choosing the oasis points to being impulsive, not liking rules, and procrastination. Choosing the village points to responsibility and being a finisher. If one lost everything and chooses to start fresh, it points to responsibility for actions. The Sunday activity points to spending habits, spending points to not being a saver. Staying at home points to being more frugal. If in a tight spot and one fixes things themselves, it points to self-reliance. If one chooses a friend or family, it points to insecurity. If one only seeks advice, it points to being a realist. The choice of age chosen; if one chooses childhood, it points to wanting no responsibility. If one chooses their present age, it points to maturity and confidence, people over forty tend to choose ten years younger than present age typically. Twenty-four hours to live; if spent with family and friends points toward emotional attachments, spending alone points to discontent, going to activity or party points to being composed. Saving one thing from a fire, one will choose from sentiment, materialism or practicality (i.e., a laptop or planner).

Scenario F (The Cube in the desert)—How big is the cube? What is the color of the cube? How far away are you from the cube? How big is the cube compared to the desert? Can you see inside the cube? There is a ladder by the cube, is it leaning on the cube or supporting the cube, and how close is the ladder to the cube? There is a horse by the cube, what is the distance between the horse and the cube, and is the horse tied to cube or not, and does the horse have a saddle? There is a storm coming, is the storm close? Is the storm big or small? Is the storm passing or staying? There are flowers by the cube; how many flowers are there? What is their color and how do you feel about the flowers? The size of the cube is one's ego, the colors of the cube (see color chart in example to follow later), and the distance to the cube is the level of self-understanding. If the ladder is leaning on the cube it means people turn to you. If the ladder is supporting the cube, it means that you turn to friends. If the ladder is close to the cube, it points to closeness with friends. If the horse is close, it points to close to oneself. If the horse is saddled, it points to wanting to control things. The color is self-impression (see color chart to follow later). The storm points to an obstacle in life, issues, the size and duration point to the severity and the outlook. For the flower, if the flowers are close to cube, it point to closeness with children or others. For the color (see color chart to follow later).

Scenario G (Walking through the forest)—What do you see and how do you feel? What kind of trees are there? Is it bright or dark? There is a path, is it visible? How many paths? Wide or narrow? Well-traveled or isolated? Easy or obstacles in the way? There is a bear, does the bear see you? Do you ignore and move on? Walk around? Go back and hide? Fight bear and win? Fight bear and get wounded? Or indecision? There is a key, describe the key and what does it unlock? The forest resembles world perceptions and emotions, the size of the trees is the influence of one's parents, the light or dark points to how one feels about their childhood and interactions, the path points to adolescence and whether one was prepared or not, if multiple paths there were choices available, the width of the path points to whether there is room for emotional growth. If the path is well-traveled, it points to support and if the path is isolated, it points to very little support. Obstacles on the path point to feeling that circumstances preventing the growth. The bear refers to dealing with problems. A playful bear points to being stress free while a mean bear points to stress with no solutions in sight; if the bear hasn't seen you, it means no daily stress; if the bear noticed you, it points to some stress; if the bear comes toward you, it points to high level of stress; if you go toward the bear, it points to be pragmatic and direct; if you avoid the bear, it means that one is nonconfrontational or indirect in decision-making; ignoring the bear means little stress upon setbacks; if one attacks the bear and wins, one is highly confrontational and seeks to dominate; if one attacks the bear and loses, one see oneself as having no way around stress and that they will never overcome it. The key points to work-related interest. The key's appearance points to how others see you. The function points to one's goals. If the key opens a place, it points to solving challenges; if the key opens multiple things, it points to career uncertainty; if the key opens a castle, it points to wealth; if opens a locket, it points to addressing people's needs; if the key is useless, it points to no positive outlook; if one is not sure, it points to no direction and/or goals.

Scenario H (Superhero)—Choosing a superhero power. Fly, time travel, invisible, x-ray vision, change forms, read minds, see future, and super hearing. Flying means big picture, free from routine tasks for a career maybe a pilot, government, research. Time travel points to finding causes to mistakes, curiosity about people, and a career in research or human behavior may be in order. X-ray vision points to seeing problems and getting to the root, seeing what others cannot, career in physics, politics, math, medicine. Changing forms points to sociable, career in hospitality or entertainment. Mind reading points to guessing thoughts, career as counselor or psychologist. Seeing the future points to adventure, creativity, and career as explorer, scientist, or inventor may be in order. Super hearing points to following patterns, following events and being nosy, career as a reporter.

Scenario I (A room without a chair)—Remain standing, ask for chair, set own chair up, ask interviewer for chair, create an imaginary chair. Remain standing means submissive, asking for chair shows initiative, setting up own chair shows lack of social cooperation, ask interviewer points to cooperation and finding a solution, imaginary chair points to a sense of humor.

Scenario J (Jungle)—Do you rush in or evaluate? How many candles are glowing in the hut you find? Is the table in the hut square or round? How many chairs do you see? There is a jug on the table, what is it made of? How much water is in the jug? There is a waterfall outside, how fast is the water? There are swans by the waterfall, how many are there? Rushing in or evaluating is for relationships? The candles represent generosity, a square table means stubborn, while a round table means flexible. The chairs point to hospitality, the composition of the jug relates to the heart, the level of water relates to love, the waterfall relates to libido, the swans relate to amount of friends wanted around.

Dream psychology can also elicit much about personality.

In *dream psychology*, people can learn what various elements symbolize or represent within socialization, and then in their dreams, those symbols are associated with their inner desires. Reoccurring dreams point to unresolved issues, unhealthy behavior patterns, and unexpressed emotions in wakeful reality. For dream analysis or *dream work* can create insight into the range of feelings involved. Dream analysis can identify contradictory and inconsistent sides of a client. *Chimney sweeping* (Freud) in *psychoanalysis* a patient talks about random early experiences, unconscious dreams and hidden desires, fantasies and unfulfilled desires, making the unconscious conscious can help change pathological behavior. *Latent content:* A dream's latent content are the underlying, hidden, true meaning, which is censored by subconscious to protect versus real meanings. Freud believed that if he could get the latent content that he could identify the problem and resolve the conflict. *Manifest content* (latent and manifest) are the parts we remember is the *actual content* versus the *latent content*, which is the *underlying meaning*. *Resistance* (Freud) is a disruptive response on a sensitive topic, whereby the source and/or root of the underlying condition may be close; with resistance, someone may either make a joke or get angry. If *buttons* have been hit. Some common dreams that are realized by people:

> *Abandonment*—can point to needing to leave past attitudes and events behind, can also point to a feeling of being neglected or overlooked.
> *Abduction*—being manipulated by someone or by circumstances, lack of control in life
> *Absence*—if someone or something cannot be found in the dream, it can suggest that what is being sought is already lost

Abuse—if you dream that you are abusing someone, suggest that there is a feeling past actions will come back to haunt you, and a feeling of regret

Acceptance—to dream about being accepted, points to self-esteem issues

Accident—what happens in the dream and the reactions of others is important, it can point to anxiety, guilt, punishment, reflections on own activity

Acting—means that you are putting on a front in reality

Addiction—to dream about this points to an obsessive behavior

Adultery—sexual urges and desires repressed, if about another relates to a fear of abandonment or fear of not measuring up to expectations

Backstabbing—insecurity or ruthlessness dependent

Balance—being off balance signifies not being certain of options and choices

Barrier—obstacle to growth in emotion or expression and/or resistance to change

Camouflage—hiding true self, or blending in order not to be noticed

Captive—captive in some aspect of life

Danger—pessimism, depression, or that one needs to be more cautious alternatively

Darkness—feeling of being lost and ignorant of the unknown

Death—seeing the dead points to fixation and movement toward resolution of stage, seeing yourself dying points to the death of a part of you versus the physical death

Defeat—to dream of defeat means that you are headed in the wrong direction

Defending—self or another points to underlying hurt

Depression—points to inability to make connections and depression in reality

Desert—loss and hopelessness

Destruction—chaos and self-destruction

Detest—detesting a person in a dream, resentment and aggression, based on treatment

Eating—if alone, can point to loss, loneliness, and depression

Embarrassment—signifies hidden weakness, lack of self-confidence

Faceless—seeking to know self or others

Falling—lack of control and failure if frightened, or confidence if not frightened

Fear—anxiety related to goals

Fictional character—escape from own reality or take on their characteristics

Fighting—inner turmoil

Gate—passing and achievement or restrictions and obstacles, if there is a gatekeeper then need to watch who is let into your life

Ghost—repression, fear or ghost's acts, unresolved feelings, fear of disconnection

Giant—trying to overcome opponents or inferiority complex

Hair—can point to vitality, or weakness, or confusion, depending on the context of dream

Harass—if self is being harassed, feeling helpless; if seeing someone else being harassed, it points to need to be more supportive

Hate—repressed aggression and fear of confrontation

Ignore—points to overlooking some important life aspect

Illness—despair and lacking coping ability and self-pity

Immobile—feelings of being trapped

Impotence—fear of losing power

Isolation—if one is always alone in dreams, this can point to feeling isolated or being in a transitional point or phase

Jail—restrictions or feeling of guilt

Jealously—vulnerability, weakness, guilt in reality

Journey—self-discovery process

Jumping—points to need to go for goals

Jungle—points to inhibition of self

Key—keys can have positive or negative implications, either for unlocking possibilities or feeling of being locked out of them

Killing—on the verge of losing self control; if it is someone known, this is repressed aggression; if it is an unknown person, it can point to killing off old aspects of self

Kissing—a symbol of love or desire, and who and what is being kissed points to which aspect is involved

Ladder—the direction and position are the keys, pointing to moving forward or being restricted or losing ground, and also if anyone else is helping or hindering

Laughing—insecurities and acceptance

Leader—either shows that assertion is present or should be realized

Leaving—if self leaving things behind, if others can point to feelings of rejection

Machinery—can represent mental functioning, reflect on how the machinery was operating and its condition, it may point to a need to repair self-elements

Map—either clearly seeing way to goals, or if hard to read means difficulty

Nudity—points to exposure of self or others depending on context

Oasis—searching for an oasis points to insecurity and overwhelming circumstances

Obedience—if not obedient points to insecurity and rebellion

Obsession—points to a need to take over a difficult life situation

Oldness—can point to idea of unyielding ways and rigid thinking being reflected upon or can point to concerns about vitality

Operation—points to feeling that something needs to be removed (i.e., habits or people)

Pain—being too hard on self or others

Paralyzed—points to being emotionally paralyzed with situations

Park—temporary escape from reality for renewal

Path—clarity or obstacles

Quicksand—points to getting too comfortable in a situation and not paying attention and misjudging what is coming next

Race—how one performs is an indication of what is being experienced, one may need to speed up or slow down to properly set and/or realize goals

Rain—points to cleansing and renewal or can point to sadness and despair

Rainbow—hope

Reaching—emotional void or reaching for something that one cannot have or desire

Recurring_dream—unresolved issues, unhealthy behavior patterns, unexpressed emotions in wakeful reality

Reflection—can point to identity crisis, how one feels others perceive them, or the reflection of one's true self

Sabotage—indicates that there is something that one is ignoring, or if one is sabotaging others then there is conflict between the subconscious and the ego

Sadism—repressed anger being explored

Scar—deep-seeded insecurities, struggles, painful memories, holding one back

School—if out of school, it points to insecurities and inadequacy

Superior in dream—seeing superior in a dream means that someone is holding power over you and making you do things that you don't want to do, feelings of restriction, there will be obstacles that have to be overcome

Target—eyes on a goal; if missing the target, symbolizes missed opportunities; if someone else takes the shot and hits your target, it means that one feels that others are taking the credit

Taste—if a bad taste then something in life has to be reconsidered

Teasing—insecurities

Teenage—struggling for identity

Undercover—points to one hiding their true self

Unknown—person can be hidden self, dream helper who can offer insight; if it is an unknown place it, symbolizes that one is not ready for change if one is lost in dream

Vandalism—repressed anger and passive-aggressive tendencies

Vehicle—mode, course, and type identify one's feeling of control over life

Victory—confidence in abilities, sometimes must visualize success before achieving

Violence—can point to issues with self-aspects or unexpressed anger and rage

Visitor—something new is coming

Voiceless—lack of identity and personal power

Waiting—how one is feeling while waiting is the key; and if one keeps someone else waiting in a dream, they are taking advantage of someone else

Walls—dependent on the context of what is happening with the walls and what kind of walls, if any, are present; the range can go from freedom to obstacles to lack of privacy and exposure

Warning—something in reality needs attention and to be recognized

Washing—washing oneself can point to esteem, but specific to body part can point to other things such as washing hands can point to the need to confront an issue

Waste—overextending oneself and investing too much

Water—symbolic of the emotional state depending on its appearance and the context, pure flowing water is spiritual and peace, while muddy waters means emotional conflict as well as drowning in water

Waterfall—renewal

Waves—tranquility and renewal

Weapons—defend and protect others, or hidden aggression to hurt others

Welcome—being welcomed points to be accepted, welcoming others points to being trusting

X-ray—need to look beneath the surface of person or situation

Yelling—if heard represents repressed anger; if not heard, it points to a feeling that one is being overlooked

Youth—if seeing other young people in a dream, this points to a fresh outlook, and if seeing self as young, this points to regrets and disappointment about missed opportunities

Yourself—watching yourself; by analyzing your actions, one can see the reflection of how one feels about behavior during reality

Thinking (intent) leads to behaviors and actions and social outcomes are determined by these factors. The collective of humanity is impacted by every social action and reaction that occurs. It's important for people to realize the magnitude of their own social actions and the affect that they have on society (the butterfly effect). When people realize the power of their social affect, this understanding enables humanity to evolve.

Behavior

Behavior, Attitudes, Actions, Goals, and Attraction

Human behavior involves the fusion of a highly complex set of organic functions and there is a very wide variety of variables and factors that can impact behavior. Most people can go about their life course within a normal behavioral continuum while other people can face a much different set of social challenges based on their individual life factors. Life factors such as biological elements and predispositions (genetic), the nurturing system (guidance network), cognitive systems and perceptions, emotional outlets and support networks, core values (personality, temperament, and spirit) and self-worth (identity), spirituality, social pressures, environmental stressors, life goals and more are all combined to identify a person's state of health and well-being that plays a pivotal role in their social actions and outcomes.

> *Human behavior flows from three main sources, desire, emotion, and knowledge.*
>
> —Plato

Modern biochemistry research has shown that inner conflict and even a simple social conversation can impact people's brain chemistry. People are constantly changing over time, but these changes can range from a torpid pace to a more rapid pace along the organic continuum. Within the process of socialization, these biological impacts can potentially manifest into negative emotions. Emotional pain can be repressed and a person's lack of honesty regarding their core inner feelings, when combined with making negative perceptual social assumptions, can lead to erroneous thinking within their cognition. The root and core of illness is a person's lack of self-esteem (identity) when combined with a feeling that they lack control over their life and that their world is out of control. When emotions are repressed and social catharsis does not occur, this can damage and alter people's minds and their bodies. There has been a long running debate between the social elements of nature and nurture over time, but more recent neuroscience research has shown that some people are in fact naturally predisposed to a greater risk of illness and the impacts of life stressors due to the nature element.

In the *nature-nurture issue*, it is now recognized that traits are passed along via genetics and that nurturing can help guide people away from their predisposed traits and their associated maladaptive patterns, so long as the pre-wired genetic traits (nature) do not override the nurturing efforts. A genetic trait is an enduring characteristic, which can include dispositions and can give rise to maladaptive behavior patterns. Also genetic trait core resiliency is much stronger in some people than in others, and this has been shown through the course of time through various studies. In addition, it is now undisputed that there are genetic predispositions (nature), the *human genome project* and other neuroscience research has proven this.

The personality is a person's unique consistent pattern of thinking, feeling, and actions, which define their core behavior patterns. The temperament is an aspect of the personality that people are born with which is innate and enduring. The temperament is related with people's *core* emotional construct (psyche). People can be calm and reserved or anxious and nervous. The temperament typically is something that is very difficult to modify within people. The nurturing social element is also a very critical element within human behavior, but it also can produce a variety of social impacts depending on the people, the context, the choices, and the environment.

Reciprocal determinism (Albert Bandura) incorporates personal factors and environmental factors into behavior development and states that, "An environment can impact a person and that a person can impact an environment." It is common that people do not recognize that every person and everything within a social environment can have a potent impact on the social impacts being generated. Behavioral outcomes can have covariance where related factors, positive or negative, one dependent on the other, can impact behavior development. Some of the crucial elements to be considered within early social nurturing are the desired method of parenting (initiating/authoritative), which is considered the best, the personalities of the parents or caregivers, the personality of the child or children, the developmental level of the child or children, the signs and symptoms of any early maladaptive behavior deficits, the impact of the social environment, and more. Unfortunately many people are inflexible and highly rigid within the course of their nurturing choices and applications. One social nurturing process that is successful in one social circumstance does not extend to all other circumstances, as each social situation has its own unique variables. People cannot generalize their own social experiences directly over to other social situations.

One of the more common social flaws within nurturing is to adopt the *permissive/submissive* parenting and nurturing style based on the advice of others. This style is considered the worst parenting and nurturing style for good reason. Because of the high variability within each social circumstance, having this approach can be detrimental to everyone involved and even to the collective society. If this style is chosen and used with a child or children with resilient and maladaptive core nature elements, this potentiates social peril in the near term or long term. In addition, the twin evils of social nurturing are pampering or neglect. If the permissive/submissive nurturing style is chosen, this falls into the pampering element. Giving a child or children everything that they want and exactly when they want it is potentially setting them up for social defeat and it also contradicts all common social norms and expectations. Much more on this topic will come later in the book.

The social methods that people are filtered through as children will have a profound impact on their social course as adults. A *codependent* is considered someone who enables unhealthy and/ or maladaptive social behavior, and also the further denial of the behavioral issues. The permissive/submissive parenting style via its social pampering is only masking any underlying behavioral deficits, which ultimately will surface later. The permissive/ submissive style also does not properly confront negative and maladaptive social behaviors that do manifest and become observable. This permissive/submissive style is reinforcing a negative behavior and is highly illogical. There are also other social effects that are elicited with this parenting and nurturing style.

The *overjustification effect* is when an expected external incentive such as treats, money, prizes, pampering, etc., decreases a person's intrinsic motivation to behave properly or perform a task. This social effect undermines the intrinsic motivation, which is the most important element within human motivation. People must realize that all human behavior develops uniquely and it is impacted by both biological and social environmental factors. Geberth (criminologist) stated that, "No one acts without motivation." *Antecedent conflict* involves issues from childhood that are brought out during adulthood. This can be related to the repression of issues, which occurred during childhood and it can also be fueled by the *pampering* of children within the *twin evils* of nurturing. Children who get everything that they want as children can continue to believe that they are entitled to these same rewards as adults. These people's core natures can be repressed and then as adults, their true nature can be revealed through their overt or covert attempts to yield social gratification. Based on the nature and nurture elements and the social environment, people form their schemas and their social attitudes.

Attitudes are a component of the schema and they are integrated and consolidated within the *affect-cognition-behavior system*, which is dynamic because attitudes can be altered one by one and can potentially impact the entire structure of a person's schema. People develop their attitudes and then those attitudes must contend with the social reality. The social reality entails *social norms*, which are the expected behavior in a social environment, behavior variance is typically very noticeable, and disorders and attitude issues can create social *variance* and turbulence within the social ring environment. *Prosocial behavior* involves following the social norms, behaving within a range of the social continuum, and helping others with no thought of any social reward. Altruism is considered the internal motivation and the behavior action itself is the prosocial behavior that is observable. *Agnostic behavior* is antisocial *contest behavior*. There are two main types of social cores. There is a pure social core and a devious social core. Based on each individual's own core type and cognitive system range, where there are no limitations in EF, people can decide their own course of social behavior.

Discrimination is the process of people learning to do things and behave within social norms based on the social conditions. Intelligence and reasoning within cognition would point a normal individual toward social behaviors that elicit harmony versus pain. *Preparedness* is biological predisposition and is why some people are able to navigate the life course much more easily than others. *Metacognition* is the process of people controlling their own thoughts, knowing about how self-cognition and the thoughts of others are interplaying, and enhancing these perceptions over time in order to properly discriminate and manipulate behavior in social environments. The *Premack's principle* states that more probable behaviors will commonly reinforce less probable behaviors in situational context (i.e., a parent telling a child that they cannot play their video games on the weekend if they do not behave during the week). The *response deprivation theory* states that the deprivation of activities *normally* will elicit behavior reinforcement within a desired behavior because most people *value* the opportunity to even go about their normal routine activity. However there are many people that are highly resilient within their core nature and their *nature side* will continually override their nurturing social environment. *Incentives* are elements that can be applied to change behavior and they can be either positive or negative stimuli, which motivate behavior. There are people however that are completely resistant to any and all behavior-modification techniques. These are the people that need to be *monitored* within the process of socialization. If this group is left unchecked, both the individuals within their immediate social rings and the collective within humanity can end up paying the social toll.

Instinctive drift is when people go back toward their primal innate core tendencies versus maintaining their learned behavior and where *conditioned behavior* reverts to *instinctual behavior* regardless of the social scenario and/or the social consequences. There are certain people that have a core nature, which will erode the social protection layer that a solid nurturing process can construct. The *probability theory* states that random events can transform in patterns. When a behavior pattern continues to manifest and then repeats itself then the action can become *statistically significant* and the behavior patterns are highly unlikely due to chance. If a person is consistently confronted regarding their antisocial behavior patterns and they are given social consequences, this sometimes can create *habituation,* which is a person's decreased responsiveness to a social stimulus due to repeated exposures. The exposures can be positive, negative, or neutral. In order to offset habituation, the social consequences can be altered and/or manipulated by the parent or caregiver. In the process of people trying to determine what is causing the negative behavior patterns, they can look for potential correlations.

A *positive correlation* is when the presence of one thing predicts the presence of another. For instance, if there is a social influence that is associated with a person's antisocial behavior, that influence should most likely be removed. Sometimes this can involve removing a friend or a family member from the person's social environment and social circle, which can create alienation. This social alienation can potentially be very emotional and stressful, but it is unfortunately part of the social reality, and negative social influences that are impacting a person's growth and development within socialization must be removed. A person's character cannot be built when there are *competing* social elements in play. Other people have *no right* to influence learners, to *ignore the social norms,* and/or to *undermine* a parent or caregiver's right and ability to guide their learner toward prosocial behavior. The permissive/submissive style people are often the culprits in this type of social activity. These people will only judge the social situation at the surface level without examining all of the social variables, and they will also interfere along a wide continuum that can range from suggestions up to applying social pressure for conformity to their social demands. Many times, these permissive-submissive people will also try and use any social influence and/or social power they have to dictate the social outcome of events on their terms. They can use *dangle elevation* as a method. Some people will use money as a social influence method and others will threaten people with false and unfounded accusations.

A *negative correlation* is when the presence of one thing predicts the absence of another. For instance, if a person only acts out around certain people then the parent or caregiver can begin to formulate that the person's antisocial behavior is more likely due to an attitude than some type of biological or emotionally rooted element. Normally with biological or emotional elements, there are more consistent and enduring maladaptive social patterns. If the maladaptive behavior patterns become fixed, this can become highly problematic for the parents and/or the caregivers.

Fixation is when a person is rooted in a developmental stage and/or is their inability to adopt new social perspectives or ideas on a subject, issues, or their environment. And on the opposite end of the growth and development behavioral continuum spectrum is *maturation*, which is when a person is coping and acting in an emotionally appropriate way for their age within the process of socialization (prosocial behavior). *Maturity* incorporates a person's ability for social reasoning, coping, reactions, crisis management, and more, which are all factors that are indicators of their level of maturity. Part of maturity and becoming whole is having *empathy*, which is an emotional projection, which places people into the place of another or other people. The lack of development of empathy in a person is often an early warning sign to indicate potential negative social issues. People must also understand that *regret* is only an intellectual response and that *remorse* is a sincere emotional response. People in society without true character are immune to remorse and they only regret when they are caught in their devious acts. People with character and maturity inject their positive social energy into society, which bolsters the evolution of humanity. Ultimately there are innate core elements, which uniquely drive and motivate the behavior of each individual.

The *life and death drives* (Freud), which include aggression and libido, are the source of people's instincts and they maximize gratification while minimizing guilt and punishment in order to protect the identity and psyche in order for the maintenance of mental homeostasis. Eros is the life drive to preserve and create life while Thanatos is a drive toward aggression and death. This is the balancer where (fear, hatred, and anger) are stored, which can lead to people's maladaptive antisocial behavior and acts. People can become fixated within the negative element and they can develop a desire to repeat their antisocial behaviors and acts. There are other channeling social forces, which can also dictate behavior, which are needs and desires.

Needs, according to *drive theory*, are the root of people's core inner drive system that motivates them to act in order to satisfy their basic needs and maintain homeostasis on a basic level and then to seek out their inner desires on the next level.

Desire is an inner sense of lacking something, a sense of loss, incompleteness, lack of wholeness. The fear of loss, incompleteness, and lack of wholeness can motivate and lead people toward the greed of acquisition. Desire creates fantasy, and fantasy can potentially lead to a dull reality. A fantasized existence can obscure reality, and if the fantasized needs are not met, which are typically highly atypical and unrealistic, people can potentially experience emotional disturbances to their psyche's and mental construct. The imagined can alter the reality. Needs and desires are often developed when people compare themselves to others and/or base their overall worth within the social value system, which is highly imbalanced. Many things that the media and marketing promote are based on the accumulation of wealth and the sacrifice of the core human value system. These social elements influence people to believe that they are not good enough and once they are able to engross people into their fictitious social unreality, people can become trapped within their social web. People need to determine their own social identity and calculate their own measure along the social continuum. Needs and desires are critical social elements that impact people's life paths. There have been several models of human need posed over time.

The Hierarchy of Needs (Abraham Maslow) states that needs are *pyramidal*.

1. Base of pyramid *physiological*—food, water, etc., for general homeostasis
2. Safety and security—resources, family, health, etc.
3. Love and belonging—friendship, family, and intimacy
4. Esteem needs—confidence, achievement, respect for others, and respect by others
5. Self-actualization—morals, creativity, problem solving, lack of prejudice, acceptance of facts, one can have more *peak experiences* once one has reached and/or is close to self-actualization

The pyramidal elements can be somewhat intermixed, but in order for people to be whole, they must have built upon basic needs and have added other life qualities. Self-actualization is the apex of the pyramid and cannot be realized without achieving wholeness. People have needs and desires that they are motivated to obtain, but in order for people to obtain the higher-level life components, they need to also evolve on a cognitive and spiritual level as well.

The *Kohlberg moral reasoning* model for scenario judgment also has stages.

- Stage 1: Preconventional morality (obedience and punishment)—fixed, to avoid punishment (how situations impact themselves) or *conventional* (how others might view them) or *postconventional* (moral reasoning)
- Stage 2: Individualism and exchange—does what best serves own needs
- Stage 3: Interpersonal relations—social rules, conforming, choices, influences, relations
- Stage 4: Maintain social order—looking out for society as a whole
- Stage 5: Social contract and individual rights—impact of social structures on society

- Stage 6: Universal principles—justice of humanity even if conflicts with rules and laws

People can identify where they stand within the stages, and they can also form perceptions of where the others around them are as well. Although temporal things can temporarily fill the voids in people's schemas, all of the social models that have been posed and reality in itself point toward what is required to reach (the apex of life). There are some people who have imbalances within their schemas; however, that will deny these social truths and realities regardless of all efforts to guide them toward the wholeness that is inherent within reaching the apex of life.

The aim of the wise is not to secure pleasure, but to avoid pain.

—Aristotle

The *drive-reduction theory* (Clark Hull) states that people's inner tension and drive is to fulfill biological needs for homeostasis, which are their primary drives. While the secondary needs and desires are learned, it is also possible that the secondary drives can become highly habitual and can become primary drives. People in their life courses will normally continually appraise their social value within the social value system. The process of social appraisal and evaluation elicit emotion. Emotions can be very powerful and they can lead to behaviors and actions. Sometimes people's emotions can lead them to behavioral ranges that are outside of their normal behavioral continuum.

The *opponent process theory* states that there is a baseline normal state within people, and that when actions occur away from their baseline, people eventually will feel an opponent process to return to their baseline behavioral range. People with behavioral and emotional issues who are unable to return to their baselines state will sometimes require an *intervention* and if behavioral patterns become maladaptive then the level of monitoring and supervision will need to be increased. There are a myriad of elements and variables that are in motion during people's personal development when each person is forming their identity. Based on individual internal factors and external factors, people's paths to finding their identities can differ widely. The process of identity formation cannot be generalized as it is unique to each individual.

The identity is people's core cognitive conceptual understanding of how they relate to their social environment. Within identity, there are needs such as belonging, esteem, fair equity from others, and social approval. If people do not feel that their identity and their self-concept are socially *appropriate*, they will often put on a social façade and will wear identity masks. These identity masks can protect a person, they can facilitate social interaction, and they can hide their anxiety behind the mask. Within the formation of identity, people also create coping mechanisms and defense mechanisms because of their innate internal fear of being cast out of a social group.

A *defense mechanism* is a mechanism used to reduce anxiety, which can include *repression* (burying memories into the subconscious), *regression* (resorted to more childlike attitudes and behaviors), *denial* (ignoring any factual or obvious realizations), *compensation* (covering up weakness or desires through gratification in other areas), but the compensation does not resolve the underlying conflict. *Overcompensation* is characterized by a superiority goal, while *undercompensation* is a demand for help and leads to a lack of courage and fear. *Midlife crisis* is a person's compensation due to their lack of psychic energy required to maintain their psychological defenses and it normally occurs in men more frequently than women (it is strongly tied to ego). *Sublimation* is acting out aggression and inner tension in a socially acceptable form such as through art. *Rationalization* is making excuses to conceal true motivations as a fallacy of reasoning to avoid a true explanation, which are self-serving and reassuring, and is often used for addictions. *Reaction formation* is taking the strong direct opposite stance often publicly of one's inner true feelings and beliefs. The formation of the identity and the self are strongly related to the need for social acceptance and to have social desirability.

Social desirability is the social construction of the self by people in order to be positive on the social scale. If people do not perceive that they are desirable, this can create *cognitive dissonance* (conflicting thoughts in the mind). Unfortunately many people have distorted views of themselves due to internal or external factors. A common way that people produce errors within their social perception is by making social comparisons that are not realistic. If the people in a person's nurturing network or social ring are influencing them to set their expectations to high, their ideal self goal will be set too high for their real self to reach. The media can also create this socially destructive social error by claiming that people must all be elite to be of any social value. *Somehow* the world survived for thousands of years on its own before media outlets were created. There is a social continuum for many different social elements, and the media does everything that they can to convince people otherwise. Greed drives the media and this greed propagates the stress levels within people, within societies, and within humanity. People can offset the external forces, which bombard the social world by becoming more self-aware. *Self-awareness* involves people being aware of their life purpose, existence, self-concept, and self-esteem. Once people become more self-aware, they are better equipped to navigate within their life course. Part of the process of socialization, and establishing one's social acceptance is obtaining a social role and a social status.

Social roles are a set of situational expectations and expected social behavior as expected by a person's position in life in both their immediate environment and in society as a whole. *Self-efficacy* (Albert Bandura) involves people taking on challenges, having interest in activities, commitment to interests, having resiliency to setbacks, and without self-efficacy, confidence is lost quickly. Self-efficacy is developed in people when they believe that they will be able to accomplish tasks within their social roles. A person's belief that they can complete a future task or solve future problems should be set (only slightly above their natural *ability*). If the *social bar* is set too high for people, this can lead to psychic disharmony within their psyche (mental construct). Parents, caregivers, and other influences can literally set people up for social defeat by contributing to the design of goals, which are not realistic, and also there should be goal contingencies that are formulated as well. *Self-fulfilling prophecy* is when people's beliefs influence their actions, which ultimately leads to their predictions coming true, and this can result in either positive or negative social outcomes. If people are able to navigate successfully within socialization, they may eventually realize some social influence and/or social power.

Social influence is people's status and position relative to their power to influence. *Social leadership* is the ability of people to energize a social group.

Social loafing can occur within social groups, and this is the tendency for some people to loaf and let the others take more social initiative. If people are not able to navigate to their ideal or desired social level within socialization, this can create inner tension, which can then lead to frustration.

> *Strive not to be a success, but rather to be of value.*
>
> —Einstein

When people are placing all of their energy on their perceived level of success, *frustration* can occur when the internal tension and aggression are not released via social catharsis. This manifestation can lead up to a heavy concentration of negative energy, which can later explode outward. A social explosion can have negative social impacts on the person who explodes and it can create social disharmony amongst any others that experience the release as well. A person's social role can be impacted if they cannot properly manage and control their frustration. If a person is not able to control their frustration, this can lead to stress.

Stress causes a strain on the adaptive capacity of people and threatens their well-being. Things like personality, perceptions, physical health, strength, having a spiritual foundation, and more can all impact the stress response in people. Stressors can be internal or external, acute or chronic. Many people can fluctuate within their ability to perceive their social reality and this can create social stress. There are different methods that people will use to gauge their social status.

The *gut reaction* is one primary method of social evaluation that many people go through life using within socialization. There is an emotional component in gut reactions that play a prominent role in social judgments and in decision-making.

The Five Principles of Social Judgment:

1. There are categories of judgment and evaluation of arguments
2. The categories are used to rate and gauge persuasion
3. Ego involvement impacts *latitudes*
4. Personal persuasion distorts information in order to fit into latitude
5. Small change adopted, larger rejected, typically dependent on range and anchor

People must identify the social position of the other people, stay within their own social latitude of acceptance, know their own latitudes and stay within them, and use logic before adopting any change.

> It is the mark of an educated mind to be able to entertain a thought without accepting it.
>
> —Aristotle (384–322 BC)

Self anchoring involves people having control over their emotional state, when achieved, this allows for their energy to be spent on the positive gain for others and for social influence. The impact of how words are used and the way that they are framed and spoken can also create social influence. Within the process of socialization, there are many decisions and choices that people are faced with and conflict can arise.

Conflict distinction (Kurt Lewin, 1931) states that conflict can create some vacillation within the life path, and that in some cases, conflict can cause distress. Lewin posed several different conflict approaches. *Approach-approach* conflict is the choice between two social gratifications such as choosing between two different social paths or roles. *Avoid-avoid* is conflict involving two different social threats or dangers, and it is normally disturbing such as the choice between losing different social roles or values. *Approach-avoidance* involves people wanting to obtain a life goal or goals, but fearing the possible social outcomes that could occur in conjunction. This type of conflict is often the most difficult to resolve for people. People in life must choose their personal positions, their social approaches, and they also must be able to understand social dynamics, which include attaining social rapport.

Social rapport entails the elements that are involved within personal interactions and it has four levels.

1. The nonverbal actions and their affect
2. The affect of vocal tone and paraverbals
3. The affect of words themselves
4. The level of intrinsic beliefs and values, cognitive sensory acuity, the skills of matching and mirroring, which allows people to pace and lead others, understanding the impact of others postures and gestures, and more.

A person's *stance* can evoke innately driven emotional responses in both the self and others, the five stances are:

1. Placater—placate others so they wont get mad, and the placater doesn't get hurt
2. Blamer—seems strong to others, and they don't feel weak
3. Distracter—changes the subject, if ignored they will go away
4. Computer/super reasonable—analytical, use intellectuality to disassociate from the emotions of conversations
5. Leveler—tell others the truth of how things are in the moment

Social *pacing and leading* involves people socially calibrating themselves to the necessary level within a social interaction, identifying the stance of others, and then acting upon their cognitive social appraisal. Each social stance serves its own purpose.

When people are dealing with a *blamer*, they can use the *placatory* stance in order to shift the person's view over to their own view, but they must be cautious as this can cause a backfire and create a higher blamer response. When people are dealing with a placator, they can use the *blaming* stance to balance them out, but this can potentially cause a stronger placatory response if the placatory feels threatened. When people are dealing with the computer stance, they can use the blamer or placatory stances, which will cause the computer to switch to one of those stances and then a person can recalibrate to the appropriate response stance. When people are dealing with the distracter stance, they can use the computer stance until the distracter switches to the placatory or blamer stance, but people must be careful as a stronger distracter response can come out. If people stay at the same level as the other people in social interactions, they will not yield any results within their attempts to pace or lead social outcomes. In order for people to be able to pace and lead within socialization, they must actively learn about all of the different types of people that they may encounter in their social systems.

The different types of people that compose a social system can produce many different types of social behaviors and social outcomes. Some of the different types of people that can be found in social systems can include people who are *compartmental* that are self-centered, see only the small picture, are isolating versus linking, and they do not think across the board. These people are typically the *social dominators* who see others as beneath them. This is a common flaw within all social levels and is also a common leadership hierarchy and leadership flaw. *Social pessimists* can be overly defensive and they can create a negative social vibe within the social energy field; however, this social pessimism is a very common social characteristic, and, in some cases, it is an expectation within certain social rings. It is common within the process of socialization to come across social groups that have the expectation for everyone to be pessimistic, and when an optimist enters into the social ring, they are ostracized if they do not conform to the social standards of the group. *Emotional people* can fail to be calm and rational, they can rush to social judgment, they tend to offer illogical opinions, and they often make ill-informed and shortsighted decisions. The *social dreamer* will often go with the social flow with no inhibitions, and their course depends on whether they are dialed into reality or if they are more socially detached. *Social realist* are always analyzing, organizing, categorizing, and connecting social stimuli, but they can often spurn innovation if their views become too hyperanalytical. *Social floaters* conform to the present social wave, and they will take the path of least resistance in an effort to avoid social conflict. *Social pacifist* does not engage into social issues and often their social position creates the level of comfort for them to avoid having to be more engaged. *Social critics* or *hard chargers* are always attacking the social norms and offering their different social perspectives. *Social marks* and *social lambs* are the targets of *social dominators* and *social wolves*. It is common that many people are social marks, and they don't even realize it, as this is within the design of the social dominators and social wolves. *Spiritual superiors* believe that they are above all others and fail to see the error in their flawed view of the spiritual ideology. These *spiritual superior* people are actually *inferior* because they fail to recognize that the wisdom within the spiritual continuum lies within understanding that everyone has voids within their spiritual knowledge and their spiritual strength. *Meekness* is when people are able to gather the wisdom to understand that they are not all knowing and that they are not above others within the spiritual realm based on their own terms, as this judgment does not lie within human hands.

These different types of people can also produce strong social tendencies, which can manifest into social errors. There are social behavior tendencies, which are social accounting errors that can manifest in people over time and can have powerful social impacts. Like with most things within socialization people's personalities, egos and social identities are heavily involved.

Pluralistic ignorance is when people are continually looking for external social cues on how to act. This type of social error takes away from the social dynamic of individuality, which is required to build accurate social dynamics within social systems. In addition, if people are choosing the wrong type of social leads, this can potentially create social chaos. Self-serving bias is when people take the credit for only their good social outcomes. The bias involves people attributing the positive social outcomes to their own personal factors, and their negative social outcomes to external factors. This type of outlook produces diminishing social returns and can also lead to social alienation if people move toward a complete lack of social accountability. If a social system has a perpetual cycle of the negative energy extending from external blame, this could potentially lead to a high degree of social tension and also could possibly create social chaos in a social system. If people in a social ring or social system continue to not accept any personal fault directly, they ultimately will erode their personal identity indirectly.

The *fundamental attribution error* is a failure for people to consider the role of the *situational factors* in social context and is the overestimation of the strength and quality of their own *personal disposition* (i.e., the *actor-observer* bias). The actor-observer bias is when people are observing social actions, and they are rating the social actions based on internal versus external factors. People are making their social assessments based on their internalized opinion and they are not considering what may be happening with the actor. This bias can be offset by people not making judgments on singular behavioral events and instead basing their social assessments on behavior *clusters*. If behavior clusters are involved then the social nature of the actions of others can more accurately be defined.

Belief bias is when people formulate illogical conclusions in order to confirm their preexisting beliefs. *Belief perseverance* is the tendency of people to maintain a belief even after evidence is provided that contradicts and rejects their belief, even if something is *proven* and *known*. There are some people that do not like to be wrong, some that cannot accept truths because their deeply implanted core social anchors are impacted, and still more who won't accept truths because they fear that the truths are impacting their identities. It is common that people will not accept fault and/or admit that they are wrong to avoid the pain of social error. *Confirmation bias* is when people look for any evidence that confirms their own beliefs and ignore contradictory evidence, ignoring information that contradicts with their schema disposition or the results one was looking for in a social scenario (experiment). Some people will go to extreme measures to try and protect their own social views and social anchors, and some people can become so fixated that they can become delusional.

The reason so many people are not able to accept social, life, and spiritual truths are due to their *functional fixedness*. Functional fixedness is when people can only see people, objects, concepts, etc., only in terms of their *face functionality*. This is a narrow and limited cognitive range, and it can strongly inhibit the social problem solving process. People who are limited within their cognitive range will also often reject other people who are *fecund* and who can produce social solutions and find different ways to use objects and/or solve problems. Some people simply cannot conceive that there are other people who can see into other cognitive and social dimensions and some people are simply jealous of the fecund. If these people would become more educated in how human capabilities are acquired, they would better understand how this social reality exists and they would not be so contentious against it.

The *false consensus effect* is the tendency of people to overestimate how many people share their personal social beliefs. When people are considering social realities, they may reflect and think that others must be thinking the same type of things. This social phenomenon is directly tied into personal identity and also into social acceptance. People both want to be correct, and at the same time, they want to be socially accepted. With a false consensus, people on their own cognitive level and on their own terms are able to internally achieve both. But this effect is harmful on the collective society because their consensus is false. *Hindsight bias* is a very common social cognitive accounting mechanism that occurs when an event or ordeal is over already, and then people think that they predicted the outcome, when the outcome is already determined. This is a cognitive defense mechanism, which people use to protect their psyche and identity from the perceived negative energy of being wrong and/or having to consciously reset their social latitudes and/or social anchors. Although people may refuse to consciously absorb social realities in the present, subconsciously and unconsciously, a person's internal cognitive systems automatically adjust by a varying degree over time.

The *illusory correlation* is when people believe that a relationship between social variables exists when no true relationship does exist. Within social cognitive accounting, people will sometimes develop a fixed correlation, which is in error. In essence, this process occurs when people take any negatively associated social stimuli event within a social system and then they generalize a singular social event over to a perceived absolute correlation. In order for a correlation to be valid, there must be repeatable social clusters in order to make a generalization. These social cognitive errors are social *misattributions*, which are based on faulty cognitive inferences. For all of the faulty cognitive accounting errors that can occur, there is also the potential for cognitive balance. When people are moving toward more accurate social cognition, there are also a variety of social indicators for positive cognition. There is so much social power that can be realized when people realize their own personal limits and begin to think more positively. People are actually restricting their own potential by being shortsighted and having narrow cognitive flexibilities. Jealously is often the vicious psychological beast that impedes the transition of people from restrictive cognitive thought over to the cognitive liberation and forward positive momentum of open-mindedness. There are many positive cognitive elements that can be realized by people.

Adaptation is the social cognitive ability that is necessary to adapt to social changes via the exposure to social experiences and new information, and this ability is highly critical for personal growth and development. *Assimilation* (Jean Piaget) is people taking in new ideas, information and/or experiences and incorporating them into their existing schemas and knowledge base. *Accommodation* (Jean Piaget) involves people revising their cognitive schemas via flexible cognitive adaptive ability in order to incorporate new information into their existing schemas, which will be altered and/or changed. Some people are able to do this much more easily due to their level of cognitive flexibility. *Acculturation* is the process of people encoding these new ideas into their existing cognitive structure. *Adjustment* is when people alter their present course and/or their present behavior in order to reach a level of cognitive *balance*. Within cognition and socialization, a balance must be maintained. When imbalances occur, these can create potential negative social affects. A social affect is cognitive feelings, emotions, and moods that can result from the various social stimuli that people are exposed to, and the social affect can be either positive or negative.

Restraint bias is a person's belief that they can control their natural urges and the social *affect* of those urges. The social fallacies that can occur within this cognition are.

1. Weak evidence
2. Not feeling the urge at the moment
3. Not remembering how powerful a given urge can be

People must remember that *availability* is what creates the social urge. Often those people who claim the greatest amount of personal social control *fail* within their social restraint due to their *false* sense of control and the *denial* of the social reality. If people want to control something or to give something up, the best way to accomplish this is to *remove* the availability. Removing the negative energy and/or the negative social influence is what leads to the restoration of the proper organic balance.

With *perception and habituation*, the more people get adept at doing something, the less likely they are to look at a process from another perspective. Also people's expertise in one area or areas does not carry over to all areas in life. In addition, one set of conditions may vary dramatically from another set of conditions and people can try and transfer their own experience over to other areas as a generality versus examining the variance between areas. In problem solving, people must decide on their own perspectives, and then be able to come at the issues from another or other perspectives. People must not jump to conclusions on social affect, and they must deal with the social reality and the facts in order to abstract solutions. People also must not fail to consider alternatives or they will miss facts and they will skip steps. Sometimes within the process of trying to solve social problems, elements will surface naturally.

A *blessing in disguise* may fall upon people within their problem-solving efforts that they can use to find social solutions (i.e., a person with social issues comes within a person's path in order for them to gain more understanding and ultimately this will help other people). A *social feedback mechanism* is a tool that can help people to chart behavior patterns. A journal or a charted point system (i.e., such as a *force field analysis* chart, which is used in behavior [stats], can be implemented to help people find their own personal social deficits and/or the social deficits within others). When people are trying to understand social behavioral deficits and issues, they can utilize an *intermediary*, which is the *blessing in disguise*. They can utilize this person to carry out the functions of social deficit exploration and discovery. In Teoriya Resheniya Izobreatatelskikh Zadatch (TRIZ) innovation, there are applications that can be carried over from one field to another.

The element of TRIZ self-service can be applied to behavior as the social deficits and issues of the blessing in disguise can be used to study their behavior and this knowledge can later help others. The TRIZ element of *concentration/consistency* can also be applied over to the behavioral realm with its correlation to the removal of negative social influences. There has to be a concentration and consistency in the development of prosocial behavior and positively charged cognition. Negative social influences are *strong oxidants*, which are noxious and they can negatively erode social and behavioral progress. Unfortunately there are many people within humanity that believe that they are eliciting *positive affect* when they are actually creating a *negative affect* within the area of reinforcement. When these people enter into the design area, they must be *extracted* in order to reach the outlined goals. When people are trying to solve issues, they must set goals.

Goals must have long-term vision and short-term motivation. People must be able to see the big picture, be able to break down the larger picture into smaller units, and they must not delay in their process. In order for people to effectively reach their problem-solving goals, they also need social *enablers*, which can include the maintenance of self-confidence, the reassurance from others, mental rest (being fresh), environmental changes (respite) when possible, and the injection of some relief within the process, such as having some fun. Within assessing behavior, the risks must be factored in.

Managing risks is a highly critical step within the process of trying to identify social and behavioral deficits. Identifying ways to manage risks can help to protect versus errors, omissions, and social chaos. If a social behavioral element is too difficult to change and/or eliminate, people must accept the risk and then determine the risk factor. Unfortunately with behavior, many people are either unable to make these assessments and/or they do not go through the process at all. There have been many studies done on behavior over the course of time to try and help society to better understand the underlying mechanisms, which drive people's motivation.

Some social psychology experiments that have been done over time include the *LaPiere study*, which studied *attitudes* and the finding was that attitudes do not always predict behavior. Behavior can derive and manifest from other elements. The *Festinger and Carlsmith study* studied *cognitive dissonance* (disharmony or conflict in understanding, which is expressed most often through body language), and found that changes in behavior can lead to changes in attitudes. The *Rosenthal and Jacobson Study* studied *self-fulfilling prophecy* (expectancy can impact the outcome) and found that one person's attitude (positive or negative) can directly elicit a change in another's behavior. They also found the effect of "favoritism" to be profound on social outcomes.

Sherif studied the impacts of *superordinate goals*, which focused on people putting their differences aside to work on a unified goal. And found that social progress can be realized. When people put the collective need ahead of personal needs, social growth can be realized. *Darley and Latane* studied the *bystander effect* and found that when there are more people around in a social scenario, it is less likely that any one person will help someone that is in need. People will look around and look for social cues versus acting.

Asch studied *conformity* and found that people with groups of three or larger generally loathe to contradict the group and that they have a tendency to choose something that is incorrect versus correct in order to conform, which is used on conformity and task importance in social psychology. This is related to the inner drive for social acceptance.

Milgram studied *obedience* and found that people tend to obey authority figures regardless of even their intrinsic moral constructs. This correlates in the opposite direction to people with behavioral issues, as their tendency is to defy authority figures. *Zimbardo* studied *roles and deindividuation* and this was based off of the college guard experiment where the guards became abusive. This example correlates with any social and/or workplace mobbing where *deindividuation* occurs and people follow along with the group. Often within these groups, people take their social cues from people who are social sadist. Social sadist will claim that they are enacting *karma* upon others when in reality they are only leading a social agenda, which is typically retribution or social payback. There are many different types of people and correspondingly there are a wide variety of potential personalities within the social matrix. However, there are several specific personalities that are generally correlated to prosocial versus antisocial behavior.

The personality traits of extraversion, agreeableness, being conscientious, being open to experience (creative), and having emotional stability versus neuroticism are generally accepted as some of the core traits to predict people's behaviors. Carl Jung, a personality expert, posed that people who do not have these qualities will have a *public persona* while in reality and being hidden is their *shadow personality*.

The *Barnum effect* involves those with the shadow personalities (social dominators and social wolves), relying on other people within socialization to be *suckers* (social marks and social lambs). This is where the adage of "a sucker is born everyday" comes from. People need to be very cautious of others who are quick to analyze them. *Self concealment* involves people hiding their negative social traits from others. Because of the fact that social chaos can potentially occur within society if there are too many *shadow people* on the loose, there are dedicated social sciences that are used to detect and identify those shadow people and the balance of them in societies. In order to detect these shadow people, there have been tools developed over time.

There are primarily four *lying domains*, which are *comfort-discomfort* that includes anxiety, stress, body language, and speech. *Metronome* is rhythmic tapping and indicates anxiety. *Masking* involves masking body language to deceive others on motives and intentions. *Emphasis*, which is exaggeration in speech and body language, deemphasize critical points, the use of diversion (which is a technique used by manipulators to change the focus via distraction), the use of an eviscerate story, which involves the deprivation of essential details, and using equivocation and editing point to deception (equivocation is ambiguity arising from misleading use of word or words, semantic shift on words and/or syntax, often people trying to deceive will us *switch referencing*, which is the change of semantic meaning of a word in an additional statement from that of the preceding semantic use of a word). *Synchrony*, using *mirroring*, which is matching cadence in sync with another (this is often effective in gaining trust and empathy; it gives off an unconscious feeling of affirmation and is part of *neurolinguistic programming*). Being out of sync with the self and interviewer and contradicting previous statements points to deceit. *Perception management* is being friendly, dressing nicely, people saying things like "I would never harm a fly" (personality trait identifier), trying to control the body, and having palms up on purpose. There are also many more elements that extend out from these lying domains.

In detecting liars and social deviants, there are typically clusters of behavior that can point to their lying and manipulation, which can range over a continuum. *Clusters* are a system of evidence within body language; the more reliable a cluster of cues are the more chances of reaching a *valid* assessment become. The range of actions can include a rigid restriction of their NV behaviors and a modification in their normal flow of paraverbals and voice pitch. Examples of paraverbal modification can be changes in their forward fluency and can include message duration (brief or will increase to control, number of words, short sentences reflect care in preventing detection), speech rate or cadence (can go from slow to quick), filled pauses (fill gap with umm, ahh; also can look away and around), unfilled pauses (refuse to respond), pitch or tone (pitch rises from tension in the vocal cords), repetition (repeat statements, forget, or contradict), response latency or hesitation (delay in answers is a cue to lying, the truth normally comes quickly, but people still have to evaluate a quick statement for details as well), speech errors (using the wrong words, combining words, omission of words). Liars can also extend their overt forward actions that are too purposeful such as spontaneous offerings of information which are led with words such as "well" or "actually."

Liars will also sometimes use excessive talking to fill time (indirect avoidance), and they will sometimes provide precise details in order to try and point to their innocence. A liar will also often say nothing, have a varying eye gaze, and/or will say they do not remember. There are also social action patterns tendencies. *Submissive actions* can include self protecting, lowering, remaining still, keeping head down, keeping eyes wide, smiling, hair touching, ear tugging, becoming pale, sweating, and small and micro gestures. *Aggressive actions* can include face tightening, fist balled, facial flushing, personal space invasion, touching, gestures, a mock attack with body or object, sudden movements, and large gestures. There are general elements that can be used as guidelines to further assist in the detection of liars.

The *six universal/primary emotions* are happy, sad, fear, disgust, surprise, and anger. Although people can be nervous simply based on a social interaction, a deeper level of emotion elicits a greater physiological response and activates the SNS. Deceptive body language can include behavior cluster elements such as sweating, physical nonverbal movements, especially around mouth and eyes, and also can impact voice pitch/tone and cadence, which is a paraverbal. Anxiety can be revealed in body language and via facial expression *clusters*. These clusters can build a system of evidence within the combinations of multiple-associated elements. Watching for the *adapters, barriers,* and any *cognitive dissonance* is the key.

Adapters are small anxiety state signals, fake surprise (holding face), touching neck, scratching the nose or neck, distancing (folding arms), arousal such as sweating (face, palms, etc.), dilated pupils, and gulping are strong emotional signs of discomfort. *Barriers* can include holding body still in a rigid position, having hands clasped and lips folded inward are self-hushing techniques. Additional adapters can include rubbing hands is a self-comforting mechanism, gripping hands under arms is a sign of insecurity, a tight-lipped smile is a sign of dislike or disgust, a pasted smile that doesn't extend to the eyes is a sign of insincerity, biting lips is a sign of tension and/or suppression, a cross-body shoulder scratch is a signal of nervousness, hands interacting with objects is *leakage* (cues that are giving away truth and emotions surrounding the truth, leakage can be both V and NV, micro gestures can give away the emotions and cannot be controlled) and are a sign of deceit, pressure, and doubt. Palms up and fingers up is defensive; palms down shows control or authority; steeple fingers forward signals a barrier; interwoven clenched fingers is sign of anxiety or negativity; thumb clenched inside fist is a sign of frustration or insecurity; touching the nose is sign of lying or anxiety; pinching the bridge of the nose is a sign of negative evaluation; fingering ears is a sign of comforting or indecision; neck scratching is a sign of doubt or disbelief; hand clasping wrist is a sign of frustration; crossed legs can be a sign of disinterest; and wide-parted legs (splayed) is sign of unconscious arousal or aggression.

Positioning is also very important within questioning and reaching the truth, sitting at a forty-five-degree angle versus face to face is less threatening, this is part of *proxemics*, which is position relative to person, thing, or object. Some people will even employ pseudo-infantile gestures, which are childlike acts conducted to avert attack and gain sympathy. There has always been a human effort to detect social deviants and modern technology now continues to evolve the process with automatic recognition systems to try and detect things before they happen as well as use in the general detection effort.

Neurocomputation and automatic recognition of spontaneous expression is elicited by the Facial Action Coding System (FACS), which measures action unit intensity. There are forty-six component movements in the facial muscles. The actions can reveal emotional states, and situational states (interest, boredom, confusion, and comprehension). The action is similar to voice phoneme and context detector actions of other detection systems. Expression is measured via the unit intensity. To measure genuine versus faked pain, the truth versus lying, etc. The system can also be used to detect the onset and remission of depression, schizophrenia, and other psychopathy. Other common measurements are for suicidal versus nonsuicidal and intoxication. However individuals can differ widely on the amount of wrinkling and movement for a given facial action within the facial action units. There is also wide variability in head pose, speech presence, and facial muscle constellations within natural behavior. *Micro gestures* are *physiological* body, facial gestures that are microsubtle and involuntary can give away the true emotions that are being concealed, a camera can catch these down to one to a fifteenth of a second, pupil dilation and contraction, corners of mouth twitch, are hard to control and hard to detect. Paul Ekman agreed with Charles Darwin that human evolved genetic species traits for facial expressions were *not* dependent on social learning. Some actions do have their unique parameters.

With *fear*, there is normally a series of action clusters that include an inner and outer brow raise, the eyelids raise upper, the *corrugator* wrinkles between the brows, lower eyelid tightens, the lips stretch on the sides, the jaw drops, although the reaction, may not always include all of these action subunits. Within *expression*, it is very difficult to code the dynamics of the expressions (the activation and movement patterns of the muscles as a function of time). Generally *spontaneous expression* has a fast and smooth onset with distinct facial actions peaking simultaneously, and with *symmetry* versus *posed expressions* which have slow and jerky onsets and lack symmetry. The root of emotions and the corresponding facial actions are the *neural pathways* and there are two distinct neural pathways that radiate (innervate) facial expression, each one originating from a different area of the brain.

Volitional facial movements originate in the *cortical motor strip*, these actions involve real-time voluntary control, are less smooth with more dynamics, and are not symmetrical. *Involuntary emotional facial movements* activate in the *subcortical areas* in the brain, and these facial movements are synchronized, smooth, symmetrical, consistent and reflex like. This is due to the neurotransmitters in the brain that are designed to elicit this activity. Some involuntary actions can include anger, contempt, disgust, fear, happiness, sadness, surprise, and these are all smooth and ballistic in their action. There are both hardwired internal and externally learned facial expressions.

Biologically driven versus socially learned facial behaviors. Most behavior is learned and displayed under conscious control, and has culturally specific meanings that rely on context for the proper interpretation, but not all expressions are universal across cultures. For example, the *orbicularis oculi* eye action differentiates spontaneous versus posed smiles. The wrinkles, bulges, and shape changes define action units.

The four factors in facial expression are *morphology*, which measures sincere emotion versus fake emotion (i.e., *orbicularis oculi eye muscle* cannot be consciously manipulated easily, and the face naturally uses twenty facial muscles to smile). *Timing or speed of onset* are true emotions last about half a second to four seconds, then the emotion is either released or held, rigid and delayed action versus smooth transitions points to deceit and insincerity, microexpressions are too short, and *holding* also points to fake emotion. *Symmetry* if an emotion is faked, their will be *left dominant facial tendencies.* Asymmetrical facial expressions are a sign of mixed signals.

Cohesion is the pace of verbal and nonverbal interaction, the movement of the body correlates to the rate of speech; also pace, pitch, cadence and slips are keys, gesture slips involve conflicts in thoughts versus gesture (cognitive dissonance). *Apex overlap* is separate interlacing of emotions, complex distortions of the face, and it is very hard to fake individual faces and even harder for multiple. *Ballistic trajectory* is when actions appear, peak, fade versus rigid offset (this is innervated from neurotransmitters in the brain, which are designed and work with proper functioning in a smooth fashion). Facial expressions and actions are all key behavior and deception indicators, but the eyes are generally the most accurate element within the matrix.

Eye behavior is a key element, eye construction can be analyzed for image, auditory, kinesthetic/feeling construction, right-handed people (left brain) general look left to construct and left-handed people (right brain) typically look to the right to construct, shifty eyes (frustration) and gaze aversion are signs of discomfort, looking up and to the left are signs of lying (fabrication) using the brain to create details, looking down and away is a sign of guilt, eye fluttering is *cognitive processing* and is often associated with fabrication if it varies from normal eye movement, the normal blink rate is twenty times per minute, faster blink rates particularly much faster blink rates indicate arousal (emotional stress) and are involuntary contractions of the eyelids via the facial nerves motor neurons, emotions from the *limbic system* stimulates the reticular-activating system (RAS) aka the *extrathalamic control modulatory system.* This area is connected to the *reticular formation* and is responsible for arousal (somatic motor control relay), eye flutters *animated blinking eye* can occur from situations such as love, stranger anxiety, deception, etc. An *eye flash* can signal that a fact has been hit on or that something is getting to close to fact. Pupil dilation can point to desire or allure (the pupil dilates in dark lighting). Because of the fact that there are so many social manipulators and social deviants in society, the science of detecting deception and behavior will continue to evolve. Social manipulators can create social chaos both consciously and unconsciously. The collective social harm that can be done by social manipulators is infinite in nature.

Social manipulators and social deviants prevaricate deliberately, and they are most often not obvious within their social ruse. These people will put on a disingenuous front around all of the strategic people that they need to keep fooled. They make it very difficult for people to validate their mendacious lies and their insidious actions. Social manipulators will seek to find out as much information as they can on people in order to use it against them later and revile them. The social manipulators will also find out directly or indirectly about people's emotional buttons to gain social power over them in order to subjugate them. If a manipulator is ever questioned about their actions, they will deny all accusations and will play innocent versus offering any redress for their social actions. There are various methods that social manipulators will use to weave their web of social manipulation.

Playing the servant role is the covert manipulative action of social manipulators to obtain objectives for themselves while masking their efforts as being out for another or others. *Seduction* is when social manipulators give the false impression that they are amiable in their nature and use charm, flattery, and praise because they know that people like to feel good about themselves and to be accepted. Even the other social manipulators who may have social ranks above the person using the social seduction tactic will take the flattery, which is a repulsive thought for the positive element within humanity to digest. Many social manipulators are narcissist and narcissists are fueled by their own self-image. When it comes to social dominators, social wolves, and social manipulators they will group together in social chains, and they will carefully recruit others to ensure that their group's chain is protected.

Covert aggression by social manipulators is very subtle and discrete aggression, which is often undetected and also often carried out in isolated social situations with the victims or targets. When the manipulator has an agenda, they will wait until they can get their target all alone so there are no witnesses. The manipulators will use groveling and look for the signs of emotional cowering on people to see if their methods are having the intended impact. *Covert intimidation* is when social manipulators are inconspicuous in their approaches and they use grievous guilt trips and shame in isolated conversations with their targets in order to gain social power and control. *Shaming* is when manipulators use sarcasm and put downs to gain social control or dominance over people, manipulators will continue the negative social barrage over a period of time in order to break people down and they will do it very subtly.

Projecting the blame involves a social manipulator always looking for *scapegoats* on all fronts to pass the blame upon. Social manipulators will carefully select and assign the people under them to carry out tasks that are unethical, illegal, and immoral. In addition, these haughty social manipulators will intentionally not give people all the information and/or tools that they need in order to attain full success. Because the social manipulators understand what all of the social pitfalls and social traps are, they will exclude the provision of key elements to others (scapegoats) in order to ensure that their own social position is secure. They will also subtly relay to other key people upline in their social chain that there are things that their scapegoats need to improve on outside of the knowledge of the scapegoat and then via disparaging the scapegoat, the manipulator will be able to act upon that *preconstructed* foundation when and if they need to. If a social manipulator is caught in their devious actions, they will first attempt to play directly to the individual who caught them in the course of their act. Social manipulators will see if there is any way to offer a social recompense to make the situation go away. Depending on the outcome, the manipulator will quickly move to other methods if required. Some people are prepared to trade evil for evil, but this is a sacrifice that the positive element in society needs to refrain from.

Guilt tripping is when a social manipulator tries to reverse the fields and play off of someone's morals to save them and their family from shame and harm. *Empathic sensitivity* is used by highly perceptive social manipulators in reversal-type scenarios. Within their attempts to avoid any social pain, manipulators will also employ other protective tactics.

Selective inattention is for the *plausible deniability* protection of a social manipulator, which is when the manipulator is deliberately unaware of a situation or acts that occur around them and they act like they didn't see or know anything about them, and thereby the social manipulator can believably deny knowledge of an event or actions, this is why only *conversations* are held versus manipulators doing things in writing, which is an effort for their reduction of their potential liability and damages. *Plausible deniability* is when a manipulator can believably deny any knowledge of a conversation, event, or action. The social antecedent to *plausible deniability* is the covert and subtle actions of the social manipulator, which include selective inattention. In order to avoid a *command failure*, the social manipulator will assign the blame to a chosen scapegoat. Often when the manipulator is finally cornered in, they will turn to other tactics.

Playing the victim role is when the manipulator flips things to appear that they have been wronged, and makes it appear that they were only responding to the actions and attacks of others on them. *Minimization* is when a social manipulator tries to minimize their actions as not being harmful. Social manipulators will use their wit (the natural ability to perceive and understand complex social situations with exceptional intelligence) and their repartee (the facility to answer swiftly and cleverly) in order to continue their life path of social manipulation. Social manipulators are often *silver-tongues* who can talk their way out of anything. Many leaders within all levels, social rings are chosen on the front end because of this social attribute. And being social manipulators are able to articulate so eloquently their command of words often dominates the offerings of any people that oppose them. It's also common that those who are reviewing a social affair will *despise* having to listen to the broken and nervous commentary coming from those who are opposing the social manipulators. An example of this would be in a courtroom scenario where lawyers are competing in some cases versus novices. Because the lawyers are well-educated, trained, and have *silver-tongues*, they can both dominate their novice opponents and also create social appeal to those listening. Unfortunately within the process of socialization, *appeal* can offset *truth*. In addition in many cases, those reviewing the content of social affairs are present to limit liability and to determine which person or people in the social equation will net the highest amount of social liability in the near-term and the long-term. This is also a disturbing social reality and is what most often occurs when there is a *David versus Goliath* social scenario. There are many different social impacts that social manipulators can have on people, society, humanity, and deception can have many colors.

The *four colors of a lie* are: gray, white, black, and red. A *white lie* is when other people benefit via a liar's social pitch. A *gray lie* is a lie that helps both conspirators and normally these types of lies occur within the inner circles of social rings and social systems and they are the most frequent of the lies. The *black lie* is the worst of all the lies as the narcissist social manipulators benefit while all others lose. The *red lie* is based on spite and revenge, and occurs without a review of the social consequences to the liar themselves and the liar and others all lose. There have been studies conducted and theories posed as to why people continually try to dominate in social systems and manipulate others.

Alfred Alder stated that *social responsibility* was the task of each individual. *Inferiority complex* is often involved in social manipulation as a root cause and this involves people compensating in ways that makes them feel superior. The *reality principle* (Freud) involves the identity's inappropriate sexual desires and aggressive urges and for manipulators, sociopaths, and psychopaths, they can lack control in this area via fixation on the *pleasure principle*. People will release their inner tension and anxiety through social power and manipulation as a *catharsis*. Social dominance and social sadism has occurred throughout time and a concentrated pattern of social manipulation can be harmful to society on the collective level of humanity.

The dark triad or Machiavellianism (social dominance) involves the cunning, deceit, and narcissism/psychopathy of social manipulators. The higher the percentage of dark triads in society, the greater the energy shift in the societal nature will be and the greater the social harm. Normally manipulators will enjoy weaving their web of power and deceit and sometimes they can be caught in the act of their enjoyment.

Not even manipulators can control all of their actions and if a social manipulator has achieved an important social agenda, their smile may even form into a *rictus*, which is a fixed and gaping grin that is intentional and overt. The social manipulators will do this because they are narcissist and sadist, and winning and achievement aren't enough. They must also smear the fact that they got away with their deceit into peoples faces. There are different stages within narcissism.

Primary narcissism (Freud) is natural and it occurs early in life between six months to six years old, and prevents *psychic damage* during the formation of the *individual self*. *Secondary narcissism* is self-gratification over social norms, and this can be pathological if there is no empathy for others. *Cerebral narcissism* is when intellectual abilities give gratification to a person. *Somatic narcissism* is when the body, beauty, physique, sexual ability, and conquests given gratification to a person. *Inverted narcissism* is vicarious projection onto other narcissists give gratification to a person. There are certain characteristics that apply to narcissist.

Narcissistic characteristics can include a person having no *true* strong bonds, the use of reduction, their envy seeks to destroy the good objects and relations of others, their fear of extinction is very high, any signs of ageing cause them distress and anger, self-exaggeration is used, deception, lying, seeking excessive attention, superior belief, delusions of grandeur, irrationality when they don't get what they want, extreme love of self, investment of libidinal energy into the ego (narcissistic cathexis). In a social environment, they will use, abuse, and discard people, and they will also use flattery and recognition to keep people off balance and off their social tracks.

Narcissistic personality disorder (NPD) is an enduring pattern of nonconformity, deviant behavior, problems within perception and interpretation of self and others, intensity and duration of their feelings, poor *true* relationships with others, inability to control their impulses, patterns of grandiosity, a need for constant admiration, and a lack of empathy. In Greek mythology, Narcissus fell in love with his own reflection. NPD is a pathological self-absorption. A narcissist lives in a dream world of success, genius, power, and vanity. They often feel special and feel that they can only be understood by high level or high-status people. They demand excessive praise and feel entitled to automatic favorable treatment. Most narcissists are social manipulators and they are exploitative of others and with no empathy. They have a cycle of envy of or for others and they are extremely arrogant. They often feel that their problems stem from the stupidity of others, and they lack general appreciation. There are some subtypes as well.

The *emotional subtype* is unstable and self-dramatizing. The *craving type* is needy and demanding. The *paranoid type* projects their own contempt upon others and they are hypercritical and jealous, which is projected onto others. The manipulative type uses lies and manipulation for gain. The *phallic* types (almost all male) are very aggressive, athletic, are exhibitionist and show off their manliness.

The root causes can potentially be arrested development or a defense versus psychic pain. Freud states, "That in infancy that all infants feel they are the center of the world, and that failure in the *secondary* stage means that the child did not attach to the parents" (The Freud stages will be broken down later in the book).

From the 1960s forward, there was a social flux and a correlational trend between society and mental patient intakes, and a general increase in *narcissism*. Also, the media's continual societal bombardment via the information highway with social brainstorming and shaping, which influences people on what success means and reinforces social boasting and exhibitionism versus social modesty can lead to the impact of *inferiority complex* and the social impacts that stem from this social complex. Also in the social dynamic of parenting, people started trending to be less family focused and child oriented and more self-centered and career oriented. Being that in the realm of behavior, most people will repeat the behaviors that they have watched this social trend carried forward with the children. With each passing decade, the trending has led to a more concentrated focus on *individualism.* This is also a timeframe where there was a social paradigm shift and a decline in the rate of spirituality within the population. People were drawn away from their spiritual foundations via the attraction of the media and technology. These social lusts where prophesized well ahead of their creation. People were warned not to be blinded by science. In an individual world, people are enticed to forsake the natural inclination they possess for spirituality and trade this off for the worldly lusts of social gratification. When people choose this social direction, they bury their natural inclination and then when they finally are advanced in age, they realize an inner thirst that can no longer be quenched by temporal things. This is a feeling that is experienced by everyone who loses touch with their natural spiritual inclination. This feeling is not simply some organic element this is their soul emerging from the depths in which it was confined within. Because of many covariant social factors, personality disorders have steadily increased over time. Personality disorders can both reflect and can influence cultures and society. Grandiosity is the most critical *identifier* of the NPD.

Other factors of NPD are relationship issues, attraction to power positions, an unrealistic idealization of others and equally unrealistic devaluation of them, the assessment of others based only on their social usefulness, hypersensitivity to rejection and/ or criticism, an unstable self (self-praise and self-contempt), a preoccupation with image versus the inner reality, and emotions based on self-pity versus any regret for social actions. Kernberg's three levels for NPD state that the NPD must have:

1. The talent to pull it off, the NPD is well concealed, which allows for attraction and persuasion.
2. Their functioning is moderate, but they are lacking.
3. There may also be legal, anxiety, impulse control, and other comorbid issues.

The SCID-II is a measure for NPD and the narcissistic personality inventory (NPI) has 223 items and is also used. Another major social issue on top of NPD is APD.

Antisocial personality disorder (APD) is when people are impulsive, have little regards for others, and the condition is first seen in children, then in adolescents, and into adulthood. The extreme of APD is people being either *sociopathic* or *psychopathic* in their social behaviors and actions. In those with APD, there is no real guilt or shame, deceit and manipulation are used to get what is wanted, there is superficial charm and APDs have well-developed verbal skills that mask the inner indifference (con artist and social manipulator), APD people are also often people with higher intelligence and they may elude detection.

All psychopaths have APD, but not all with APD are psychopaths. Neurological tests can sometimes miss the diagnosis. Children with conduct disorder (CD) and who are *hyperactive* before the age of ten, run a greater risk and *lax inconsistent parenting* increases the risk such as the permissive/submissive style. Approximately 3 percent of all males have *psychopathy*, which is the extreme on the continuum. *The Hare Psychopathy Checklist* is the gold standard for the initial diagnosis. There must be three out of seven social factors for the diagnosis. The social factors list can include: frequent illegal acts, conning and manipulation, impulsivity, aggressive, lacks regard for the safety of others, frequent irresponsible behavior, and no evidence of remorse. The only semblance of remorse that the APD has is for being caught, which is the intellectual response of *regret*. CD precedes an APD, which begins before the age of ten years old. Treatment for the severe end of the continuum can include a long-term structured residence placement where the privileges are earned and they are unable to find victims. Relapse (recidivism is frequent).

Hare Psychopathy Test

1. Superficial charm with a smooth and slick style, smooth lies, and cool under pressure, with seamless transitions, distracts from questioning with charm, will attempt loving gestures and actions, and can be mesmerizing.
2. Grandiose, self-worth with cocky and superior overtones.
3. Bored and requiring stimulation-taking risks, finding most things *mundane*, constant need for stimulation. They will often encourage others in their network to antagonize anyone who isn't under their control and/or who are easy prey and whom is below them. To avoid a trail of deceit, sometimes the sociopath will distance themselves from those who have caught on to them.
4. Pathological lying with dishonesty and manipulation, will lie for personal gain, will use analogies and metaphors to cover for fabrications, and will make comparisons that have nothing to do with a line of questioning. Will point finger at others. Will fabricate details and make up believable stories on the spot. They will play on emotions to reestablish complicity with the investigator by attacking the other person as a subterfuge (deceit to achieve goal). The web of the sociopath's mind control is spun around all of those around them. A grain of truth is normally added within their web of lies to focus on in the event that they are caught.
5. Con artist and manipulative with a lack of concern for others, will use circumlocution and talk in circles when asked a direct question or will divert to another subject, or will turn to flattery for a diversion. Their methods can cloud reasoning and dull the intention behind the

examination. Evasion is used to talk in generalities and about anything but their own actions.

6. Lack of remorse for actions and often a disdain for victims, will use slander toward others and will try to invalidate their claims, will often protect their own misdeeds upon those that are being hurt, and will often malign spouse openly.

7. Shallow effect with limited depth, and coldhearted with limited range of feelings.

8. Callous with a lack of empathy and lack of consideration.

9. Parasitic lifestyle with low level of responsibility and exploitation of others, using people for personal gain or for financial needs.

10. Low behavioral controls, easily annoyed, irritated, angered, makes threats, and will make random threats openly.

11. Sexual behavior is out of control.

12. Early behavior problems beginning under thirteen with lying, theft, etc.

13. Lacks realistic long-term goals and long-term direction, has failure to execute goals.

14. Impulsive and easily tempted, the urges create an unpredictable nature.

15. Irresponsible with a low level of loyalty, failure to honor commitments.

16. Failure to accept responsibility for own actions, low conscious level, denial and antagonistic manipulation.

17. Lacking strong personal relationships, relationships are superficial.

18. Juvenile delinquency and manipulation, exploitation, antagonization of others.

19. If criminal charges, revocation of probation or terms of release.

20. Criminal versatility amongst types of crimes and pride in actions

Society has norms in place, which make it difficult for those with personality disorders to follow. A personality disorder is a severe disturbance in the typical behavior tendencies in an individual, and usually involves more than one area of the personality. There are almost always social issues involved, which impact those with personality disorders in their daily lives. Personality disorders usually develop during childhood and appear first in adolescence or early adulthood, the disorders can produce *ego-syntonic* behavior (considered appropriate to the individual) and this is one of the major issues.

Being people don't feel they are doing anything wrong, this can cause their behavior patterns to be inflexible and very difficult to change. Personality disorders are ongoing, persistent, and involve rigid coping and adaptation. A person's mood is one of the major elements involved and also a major indicator of issues.

Mood is a person's overall feeling or mental state. Mood disorders are prolonged and intense mood shifts, functional difficulty, and a decline in perception of daily life normalcy. *Mood congruent behavior* is when expressed actions are consistent with how one feels versus using defense mechanism to manage daily life. *Burnout* is the mental fatigue from stress and/or distress, which can arise during the socialization process. *Negative symptoms* are thoughts, feelings, behaviors which are *absent* or *diminished* in people with MIs (i.e., apathy, decreased motivation, poverty of speech or brief, *anhedonia* is the inability to feel pleasure, and a lack of emotional experiences. *Positive symptoms* are thoughts, behaviors, perceptions in people with MIs, but that are not present in the normal population (i.e., hallucinations, delusions, bizarre behaviors, these are common in schizophrenic patients). There are so many dynamics within behavior that it is very difficult for people to navigate within the social matrix and find other people who share their characteristics. In the complex system of socialization, people will eventually gravitate toward personal connections that relate to their own behavioral characteristics and/or desired qualities of social appeal. This could be labeled *social drift*. In addition to the social magnetism within behavior, people have other personal characteristics that they are also drawn to by their own innate organic and cognitive systems.

People have their cognitive set, their behavioral set, and they also have their physical characteristics, which are traits that they acquired via genetics. There are a number of physical characteristics, which are involved in social mobility and social attraction. Muscles and the physique are some of the key elements that impact people's social performance and their social mobilization capabilities. Based on genetics, people can be propelled to various areas along the existing *social value system continuum*. This social category can have a strong social impact on behavior. As a result, there are certain people and certain groups that will gravitate toward a feeling of social superiority.

Genetic physical characteristics are highly correlated into physical performance capabilities and into the social attraction matrix. Physical form and physical ability are cornerstones within the social attraction spectrum. Also physical ability can propel people within the social spectrum through social foundations such as sports/athletics, and physical performing arts. Genetics predetermines the range and limitations of these social factors in *advance* of the process of socialization. All people fall into a range within the *physical continuum*. Body shape, muscle balance and action potential, and performance are some of the elements which factor in.

Within the muscle category, the muscle balance in humans has a mix of *slow twitch* and *fast twitch muscle* fibers, which is normally at a ratio of around 50 percent to 50 percent. But Olympic athletes, other top-performing athletes, and performers who perform in events, which require more explosions often possess as much as an 80 percent level to a 20 percent level of fast twitch muscle fibers to slow twitch. People who are athletic are often propelled through the social continuum as they typically have a great deal of social *appeal*. Athletes and performers are members of society who normally generate a massive amount of social appeal. It is common that people in society are intrigued with the physical gifts and ability of these people. What people must remember is that those with this unique genetic mixes were *born* with these traits. There are still many people in society who try and *compare* themselves or their children with the people in this elite *genetic* category when the expectations are unrealistic. When people make these comparisons, they can set themselves or their children's *life bar* too high and this can create social defeat. The process of socialization is complex enough without people adding in unrealistic life bars. In addition to muscle performance, there are also different physical structure elements which relate to how people fit within the *social attraction matrix.*

The body type is a primary component in social attraction, and there are several different identifiable body types for both women and men that tend to be associated with various types of appearance and performance capabilities. Sometimes people can also have hybrid of different body types such as an *ecto-mesomorph* body type where the upper and lower parts of the body can be mixed types. For example a man who has a large muscular upper body and thin legs or conversely a man who has a thin upper body and massive legs.

The *somatotype* is the baseline type of body shape for humans. The ectomorph, endomorph, and mesomorph body types are more often used and associated with males. The *ectomorph frame* for males is a light build, with small joints, long thin limbs with stingy and lean muscles, and thin shoulders. The ectomorph type typically has a fast metabolism, they find it difficult to gain weight, and eating at night before bed can offset muscle via *catabolism.* The *endomorph frame* for males is a solid bone structure, but soft muscle tissue, which can gain fat very easily. The endomorph is typically a shorter build with shorter arms and legs, which are normally very strong and a lower calorie intake along with cardio is required to stave off fat gain. The *mesomorph frame* for males is a large bone structure, large muscles, naturally athletic physique, and is typically the best body type for building muscle. The mesomorph has strong and well-defined muscles and gains muscles and weight much easier than the ectomorph. Fat can be gained quickly so the calorie intake must be monitored.

Women commonly have other identified shape definitions. The *diamond shape* for women is thin shoulders, a wide midsection, and thin hips. The *hourglass shape* is wide shoulders, a thin midsection, and wide hips, which historically had been considered to be ideal for women, although in modeling, the demand can be varied. The *rectangle shape* for women is where the shoulders, midsection, and hips are all wide and uniform. The *rounded shape* for women is larger and rounded shoulders, midsection, and hips. The *triangle shape* for women is thin shoulders, a widening midsection, and large hips. The *triangle shape inverted* for women is wide shoulders, a thinning midsection, and thin hips. The body shape and physical appeal is one of the major factors in social attraction. People must remember that there is a *wide* continuum within genetics and also that there are only a *select* group, which falls into the elite range. When people set their expectations to an unrealistic level, this is a formula for social defeat. Unfortunately although the actual percentage for those that fall into the elite category is dwarfed by all others in society, the *media* continues to *brainwash* people that anything less than being elite is not socially acceptable. If the media was the friend of the people, they would not be sending this type of message. The media is not concerned about people's health and well-being, but rather they seek to confound people within their social façade of lusts. This socially calamitous *brainwashing* by the media leads people to have envy, jealously, self-doubt, and to seek unnecessary surgeries that creates a vast amount of social stress within society. In order to verify this social reality, the only thing that people need to do is explore their own thoughts. People have been warned about vain lusts within the realm of spirituality throughout all time, so when the media is promoting the opposite, a person can easily gather on their own whose design the media is promoting. People need to protect themselves from this evil bombardment by realizing the social reality and focusing on their personal gifts and attributes.

Social and innate attraction is hardwired into the organic systems of humans and it has been carried within humanity throughout human existence over all time. From babies to small children to adults, the laws of attraction are realized at all levels. Even at very young ages, humans are drawn to pleasant facial stimuli and symmetry. Humans are naturally hardwired and are immediately impacted by visual stimuli and the connection of the stimuli to the libido life force drive. Humans have an inner core drive to both procreate and be in a social relationship, these biological drives can be satisfied by other means, but ultimately, if these true pure drives are not being met then the defense mechanism of repression is being used, and this will impede the psyche (mental construct).

Humans tend to select mates based on the highly powerful primary surface level instinct for attractiveness and sexuality based on the visual stimuli presented. The laws of attraction point to both the emotional and physiological reactions that people have as a result of the stimulus presented by those who possess the desired qualities that are innately embedded into the human mind (cognitive system).

Secondary social learning and conditioning can modify the human primal attraction instincts and can create secondary attractive appeal, but the tendency is to always go back to the primal core instincts *attractive drift*. Secondary factors can be things such as similarity (physical, personality, emotional, spirituality, aura, etc.), proximity (social, environment), reciprocal thinking (cognitive), personality (sense of humor, mood, etc.), security (physical, income and financial worth, etc.), and more. Social attraction also occurs along a continuum and the impacts can vary across individuals along this continuum. Social relations can develop, manifest, and can occur outside of the primary attractive instincts, due to secondary attractive appeal levels or other factors, but people must be *cautious* of the social factors involved in their social bonding selection. If people extend too far outside of their innate core organic selective attraction range continuum, then they will likely be predisposed to continue to seek their *primal inner core desires* regardless of their existing social bond which is attractive drift. Without a spiritual foundation to help combat these elements, this social reality can be a very dangerous social challenge for people.

This inner core drive is a force that can continue to pull people toward what they want and desire deep in their unconscious. The mental imbalance caused by this social phenomenon could become a continuous *polar psychic pull*, which many people are not able to understand or control. When people begin to dream about other people then their innate core psychic demands are not being met, and in some cases, people can also fulfill their needs *in vivo* whereby they act on their core primal instincts physically *regardless* of the relationship that they are in. This highly complex social scenario produces negative social energy on multiple levels and has an adverse impact on humanity. This is why a spiritual foundation is a critical element in life. A spiritual foundation can help to defeat these negatively fueled inner lusts, which are often promoted by external forces, which increase the risks even further.

The fact and the social reality is that most people, if not everyone, will be attracted to the elite end of the social attraction spectrum on their primary level, but that they themselves may not align along the social continuum within that attractive level. The psychology of cognitively recognizing which social attractive level one is within and potentially having to accept the social limits within the attractive continuum from which they can select can be an adjustment in itself for people. It is also common in the human condition that people continually go back and forth in their own personal attractiveness assessment, and this action can include being accepting on a healthy level of one's range of personal attractiveness or the personal attractiveness assessment can extend out to an unrealistic and unhealthy end of the attraction continuum, which can be pathological. The media is responsible for exacerbating this social issue and flaw.

If a person believes they are much more attractive than others perceive them, this can potentially set them up for social defeat, and if this maladaptive social pattern is continued, it can be very damaging on many levels. If a person doesn't believe that they are as attractive as others perceive them, this can also create an unhealthy outlook and can limit the social bonding pool for those people, which is in essence a form of social defeat. People will often describe themselves as less attractive or more attractive to others based upon their emotional state and/or in combination with their personality and perceived identity.

Reserved and introverted people will often describe themselves as less attractive to others, particularly if their emotional state is in turmoil. Extroverted, aggressive, and confident people will often describe themselves as more attractive to others than most people perceive them. In some cases, the laws of attraction do seem quite magnetic. *Assorted mating* is an attraction phenomenon, which is the tendency for people to be in relationships and/or to marry people with similar social realities, social issues, and/or social perceptions, which can potentially lead to further issues for one or both people. This is a social phenomenon that has persisted over time, and it is also a reason why there are certain elements of *genetic selection* that are perpetuated instead of being selected to be eliminated.

It is a social reality that people never stop assessing their own personal attractiveness level, nor do they stop assessing the visual stimuli presented by others. And in the course of life as people age, it is often very difficult to determine where one has shifted on their own attractiveness continuum, and how they are perceived by others. This is why people continue to seek social acceptance cues from others within socialization even when they are in a correct or adequate social bond range for their own attractive level. The need for social acceptance is hardwired in humans, both in the assessment of how one is perceived on a visual level and at the next level which is human relations. Some people will argue that there are not any innate predispositions within a social attraction continuum and/or that attraction levels are not set along a social continuum, and further, they may state that most people do not look astray for acceptance, but the social reality is that these elements are hardwired into humans and the social phenomenon is part of the human condition.

The people arguing versus these pre-wired innate social conditions can potentially set others up for severe social adjustment issues if they are reinforcing to those people that they are at different levels outside of their actual social attractive ranges along the attraction continuum. This social decision-making error and flaw is why con artist continually prey on people within the world of modeling (they rely on the people who do not accept the social reality of the laws of attraction), when the reality is that there are a very miniscule number of elite level attractive people in the world that are models. Parents and individuals themselves can also play into this area, which can create social defeat and an impaired range of determining social attraction acceptance levels. People need to understand that their *genetics* determines the restrictive limits of their personal attraction and that each person has a finite level of attraction that they reach along the social attraction continuum. There is nothing anyone can do about their core genetic characteristics naturally. When people have a foundation within spirituality, they can offset the negative forces along the life path by being aware of their own personal value and the blessings which they possess. People have been warned that envy, jealously, and making comparisons to others can cause harm within the life path. But being many people dismiss these matters, many of them fall into social traps and social pitfalls.

This social reality is why people will turn to cosmetic surgery and other surgical procedures to modify their existing genetic makeup. The thing that people need to remember is that just like with a social identity mask, which hides a person's core identity and houses it behind a fake public persona, a *cosmetic identity mask* does not change the *fixed mental state* behind the cosmetic mask. The mental state is fixed because the images of the self are permanently stored in memory. The cosmetic mask and the social mask both only *modify* the social reality by the acquisition of whichever temporal social stimulus is being sought. People who acquire their social desires through these external transformations may fill their social void, but their psyche will never be fully satisfied because their desires were obtained through a social illusion fueled by lusts instead of true personal qualities. People who engage in this vicious cycle detach and fool themselves into thinking that their needs are being met. As the social acceptance they are receiving is superficial, a desire is being met, but not a need. People must strongly consider their own level of ability to handle these highly complex cognitive choices and issues. Cognitive dissonance is a common occurrence when it comes to the evaluation of attraction within the attraction continuum. And cognitive dissonance can lead to highly irrational social decisions and both short- and long-term personal harm and stress. Because people can become so befuddled regarding their perceived level of social appeal, they can also modify their appearance in other ways as well. Some people will look for social attention through body piercings, tattoos, hairstyles, and more. People must take the time to really evaluate who they are trying to appeal to and the personal, social, and societal costs of their actions. When people have a spiritual foundation, they can avoid conforming to the social bombardment that they must contend with within the process of socialization. In the New Testament, Corinthians guide people and explain this area: "Know ye not that ye are the temple of God, and that the spirit of God dwelleth within you?" (Corinthians 3:16, KJV). The message continues within Corinthians: "Now the body is not for fornication, but for the Lord" (Corinthians 6:13, KJV). Corinthians further detail: "Know ye not that your body is the temple of the Holy Ghost which is in you, which ye have of God, and ye are not your own?" (Corinthians 6:19, KJV). Corinthians then explains that everyone is a vessel to glorify him. "Glorify God in your body, and in your spirit, which are Gods" (Corinthians 6:20, KJV). Spirituality can be a highly effective guide for people, but people can go in many different directions to define their social course within the attraction continuum. As far as general attraction, both sexes have similar core-attraction mechanisms, although each sex also has some unique variability as well.

Within the primary surface level of physical attraction, it is common that men tend to prefer some basic core physical characteristics, which can include having a shorter companion that has a symmetrical face, which is youthful and, to a degree, baby like, with full features in the eyes, lips, and cheekbones. Men are also naturally attracted to an hourglass figure with full curvature in all of the features. The attraction continuum between the other physical variables can vary widely across individuals.

Because of the genetic variance that exists within humanity, there are a minute number of individuals on the planet that have the full-elite spectrum of attractive elements. There are few instances of people having a combination of the perfect figure, a perfect skin tone, perfect hair, a perfect face, etc. The fact is however that even models doubt their own level of appearance and social attraction level and this is a social reality. Many people still do not realize that this human flaw of doubt exist in everyone including the elite within the continuum.

Men will be inclined earlier in their life to focus almost completely on the beauty elements and aspects within the attraction spectrum, and then later, within *attraction evolvement*, their inner drives will be modified and they will be open to other strong secondary physical factors that can balance out the attraction equilibrium within their cognition. Over time, men will be attracted to the physique of women on a much higher level than they were inclined in their earlier stages. This adaptation phenomenon is an innate tendency.

The physique can strongly compensate for the other features, which they originally were compelled toward. This is due to a psychic shift from a purely innate cognitive desire to see beauty to an *attractive fusion* with their inner drive for libido. This is why men will take *positive social attraction acceptance cues* from a much wider range of women along the attraction continuum that women do with men. Women are naturally much more *specific* and overt within their *true attraction position* than men. Although a social paradox is that women may often be in social relations with men who are *outside* of their true attraction range continuum for secondary factors.

Women have a much more narrow *cued attraction acceptance threshold*, which means that they only want men that fall within their social attraction guidelines to provide social attraction cue stimuli to them within socialization. This consideration defies all of the laws of probability, nature, reason, and logic, because it is purely based on the emotional element within the cognitive set. It is common that women will turn there heads away, will roll their eyes, will make a grimace, etc., if they are receiving social cues (visual stimuli) from men that they do not want to have looking at them. These overt social reaction cues are outside of any verbal communication and/or forward gestures by the men, they simply extend from unwanted eye contact within social settings. These social reactions are mechanisms that have been fueled by the negative social contagion of *superficiality*. Men can also be superficial, but historically they are generally open to a much wider continuum for attraction acceptance.

Within the process of socialization, eye contact is a normal activity and also people are naturally and innately drawn to others who are attractive. It is also highly illogical that if people dress *scantily* that they only expect certain people to take notice and this is *social reality denial.* The people that are so self-absorbed with these social considerations are commonly the same people who will be in crisis when their beauty begins to erode and decline with age. Some of these people will also be the first ones to seek cosmetic surgery in order to try and recapture their social edge.

Women commonly tend to seek taller companions with facial symmetry, facial distinctiveness, facial masculine dimorphism, a strong jaw which represents sexual maturity, attractive eyes, thick and appealing hair, and a strong physique. In essence, most women are also attracted to men who have some feminine facial qualities and are *pretty-handsome* to look at. Women, just like men, will also normally evolve over time to incorporate the physique as an attractive force social equalizer. Based on a wide array of factors and covariants, people will engage into relationships.

Although it is common that many people simply fall into relationships, people must do their very best to carefully choose their social mates within the highly complex dynamics of socialization. Intimate relations should not be interchangeable, although the social trend has been created and the collective impacts have been realized, if the proper care is put by both partners into social selection, the probability of a long-term successful relationship is greatly increased.

There are actually *soul mates* within humanity for everyone, but unfortunately people frequently misattribute the *coining* of the existence of soul mates such as they do with karma in other areas. A soul mate is someone who is running on the same *life vibration* or frequency in their aura, which creates the magnetic bonding and there is always a physical element of unity as well. Both of these life forces—soul mate and karma—are social enigmas and natural forces and neither is a *selected* force, although people commonly confuse this principal. Two people must realize a *shared* social magnetism within a social attraction energy connection or the social bond will be very weak. As mentioned prior, there are different social attraction forces that compel people toward others along the continuum. Both men and women can get hurt and be damaged in social relationships, but the fact is that women typically have more social power in selecting their social mates than men. The social paradox to this social reality is that because women are more specific than men, they limit their choices by seeking the top end of the spectrum.

There are many girls and women who seek out a male companion based on their attraction appeal and they detach themselves from the social reality and probability that their will be emotional damage which will likely result. This social flaw is even more prevalent in adolescence and early adulthood. Those with attractive appeal will learn that they have social appeal via socialization, and many of those people will not be able to control their innate core urges and ultimately they will not be loyal. Even though this same social cycle has repeated itself from the dawn of time and it omnipresent everywhere, people continue to ignore this painful social pitfall and then they often act like they are surprised and/or shocked on the back end of the social decision. Women are even more predisposed to beauty than men. The *caudate nucleus* in the brain has been related to the emotional response from visual beauty (neural correlates which can include romantic love). Women tend to have a larger caudate nucleus than men and women's senses are often more acute as well.

Regardless of the derivation of a social impulse, when people are rolling the social dice and gambling on a social level, they need to be able to understand and accept the social odds. Unfortunately even if the writing is on the wall, many people ignore these social cues and the advice from others to pursue their social desires. People must be prepared for the social reality that *taking a chance* means that they are really taking a chance. People must visualize both sides of the social equation in order to try and gauge how painful the potential social rejection could be for them. This social phenomenon happens in both youth and in adulthood even though people's cognitive abilities are normally stronger as adults. There are some people who refuse to learn from their maladaptive social patterns and they instead forge on in being devastated time after time.

The issue is that the emotion behind desire is much stronger than the emotion behind need and neither one of these elements incorporates the cognitive covariants of logic and/or reason. The social dynamic of bonding is one of the most difficult areas for people to put logic and reasoning in front of emotionally driven decisions. These brain functions are often distorted when they are overtaken by the power of emotion. Another set of social dynamics that have become a perpetual and cyclical issue in society is people becoming intimate outside of a bond and also becoming intimate at very early ages. In the New Testament, Corinthians provides guidance in this area: "To avoid fornication, let every man have his own wife, and let every woman have her own husband" (Corinthians 7:2, KJV).

When people begin having intimate relationships at very young ages; this social dynamic impacts the people in those relationships and the collective society within humanity as well. It is common in life that people want to act on their biological drives (libido) and have relations just because of their physical preparedness and their innate attraction, but the cognitive component, which involves the emotional element is something that most people are not ready for, even as young adults.

There are so many people within humanity that are emotionally scarred and/or crushed in their youth based on sexuality and the processes of socialization that interplay within relations and the collective damage is tremendous. To have scars from intimacy prior to adulthood is highly irrational within the consideration of logic. People simply do not consider, or are incapable of considering, the full ranges of social consequences within their activity. In order to have the deepest relations, people must share the deepest levels of their self, and when people do this, they are exposing themselves to the potential for pain. Once a person has completely offered out their emotions into a bond, they can be crushed if that bond is broken. This is why extending these elements outside of a lifelong commitment can be so devastating to people especially for younger people who have not yet built up a stronger set of coping skills in their lives. If people actually had all the answers and knew it all within their youth then there would be no forward and empirical evidence of any psychic damage. This social phenomenon within youth is a social flaw that is one of the most difficult social issues to contend with. And because these issues carry over into society, they must receive even more attention. Timothy within the New Testament warned of youthful lusts: "Flee also youthful lusts, but follow righteousness, faith, charity, peace, with that call on the Lord out of a pure heart" (two Timothy 2:22, KJV).

There is a perpetual flow of the negative emotions and psychic damage that persist because of these lustful engagements that is driven by emotion and it's very obvious that people did not anticipate the harm that their actions were enabling. Intimacy is completely governed by the ability of people to manage the emotional elements that are inherent. The carryover affect of this premature lustful activity is tremendous. The negative social energy from the emotional damage is carried forward and released upon the collective society within humanity. As every social action has a subsequent reaction and consequence, other people within humanity can end up bearing the negative energy, which is carried forward as well as the initiators of the social damage.

The social damage that is done is infinite in nature, but the solution is always available as intimacy is a personal choice. Being that the higher EF are not in full flux and motion at these early ages, young people should seek wise and trusted sources to aid them in their important social decisions. This is why a spiritual foundation is so important for guidance. People are simply not ready within their emotional maturity to be involved in intimate relations at early ages. Social evolution has pushed this maturation process forward as the social norms have changed. A conscious effort over time by society to alter the life stage range in which people should begin to engage in intimate affairs has resulted in an organic modification in the reduction of mental preparedness and social maturation. The fact that people are biologically around ten years ahead of their emotional capacity to govern an intimate relationship is certainly a very troubling and perplexing life obstacle. Because of these social truths and facts, there are some people who have *severe* emotional reactions when a social bond is broken. There are those that spiral into a deep depression and still others who become manic in their actions. Experiencing intimacy during youth can even transform some people within their very nature and they can become *polyamorous* (seek multiple partners). And some people that cannot accept a bonding division after being intimate can become obsessed social stalkers and more. The repression of the innate biological libido needs of people is also something that needs more attention as the means of catharsis chosen by some people is often also very damaging to the psyche. These social elements have led to a social and societal impasse within the area, which needs more attention and social action. One additional area of particular concern is why society allows older teens to socially prey upon the younger variety. Some people may be familiar with the phrase: "Start em' young." This social attitude should be appalling to anyone who falls within the positive element within humanity, and they should mark those who speak this language.

And as far as human behavior and organic systems, once people have had more than one physical intimate partner in life, they can permanently *erode* the protective psychic layer that protects people and provides the organic drive within the innate human instinct to have a singular relation. The innate desire to have a singular *monogamous* relationship and its cognitive maintenance is not a conscious choice, and this is a very complex psychic device that is innately pre-wired. People may think that they can control this eroded psychic element within their cognition and psyche, but what they are actually doing is simply repressing the dormant energy. This cycle can also profoundly impact the level of *attractive drift* that occurs while people are in their new relationships. Once a person has had more than one intimate partner in their life, they will always have some element of attractive drift, which occurs within their unconscious. This drift is magnified even more if there was already a trace of the drift action potential present during the initial intimate social bond.

In modern society, it has become atypical for people who engage in very early intimacy to remain with those partners throughout life. When people get the sensation of having multiple intimate partners into their cognition, this psychic alteration and damage often can become irreparable. Once a person has become *polyamorous*, this type of cognitive dissonance and psychic damage can lead to things like married people having affairs, being in open relationships, and becoming swingers within socialization on the far end of the social-bonding continuum. These are all the elements of fornication that have been warned against since the beginning of time. This is why within the realm of spirituality that people are given instruction to be married and to remain with that partner for life. These instructions are to protect people against the damage that fornication purveys. Also within the modern human drive social metamorphosis process that is a continual cycle within the process of socialization, it has become much more frequent for women to pursue younger men and this has been labeled the *cougar society*. In the past, men have been recognized as seeking out younger women, and in modern society, this activity is being balanced out. The societal changes that have occurred within the last fifty years are manifesting at light speed. Some of the societal changes are occurring so rapidly that their social impacts cannot begin to be measured. Humanity stands to suffer greatly if people do not find and implement social solutions to quell the damage that his being thrust upon it by the forces of iniquity and evil.

Due to the social impacts of people's life choices, socialization can potentially become even more complex. Making personal and social assessments can become much more difficult. Although social assessment and social feedback are normal within socialization, people can easily become aware of whether they are just looking or whether there are more complex cognitive issues arising. If people's SNS is activated continually when they are processing appealing visual stimuli within socialization then this can lead to cognitive dissonance and potentially *psychic libidinal damage*. The lower the concentration of psychic damage that has manifested and is present, the better the chances are of potentially being able to rebound and recover with *bond rechanneling* is. Bond rechanneling involves a person moving back toward their original innate organic core desire to bond within a sole person. Regardless of all the truths and realities that are known already, people are continually searching for ways to define the forces of social attraction.

> *Personal beauty is a greater recommendation than any letter of reference.*
>
> —Aristotle

Unfortunately, this is a social reality and this is a root of evil that leads to a cycle of envy, jealously, anger, and maladaptive social action.

One social attraction model is the ATRAK model, which poses that there is an elite level ten, which composes well under 1 percent of the population. The next level is the *highly attractive* level nine, which composes around 5 percent of the population. The *attractive* level eight composes around 10 percent of the population, followed by the *moderate attractive* level six to seven, which composes around 20 percent of the population, then the *average attractive* level five composes around 35 percent of the population. Once a person determines their *ATRAK* level, they will move through the social attraction stages.

The social attraction stage of *realization* involves people discovering their personal level of attraction within the social matrix. This stage normally occurs sometime between the puberty phase and young adulthood. Once a person realizes their attraction level or range, they will move into the *exploration* phase in order to fully test their limits and their level of social desirability within socialization. This phase typically occurs between adolescence and young adulthood. After the exploration phase, people will move into the *consideration* phase in which people decide how they intend to utilize their social appeal. This phase typically occurs during young adulthood; however, it can occur earlier if the social environment and social forces create the necessary force to release it prematurely. The consideration phase is a critical phase because if people become too egocentric regarding their social appeal, which could include them entering into a social clique, then they are potentially setting themselves up for a larger fall later within the social cycle because of the social affect of superficiality. After the consideration phase, people move into the *application* phase in which they exert their social mobility direction. The application stage still allows a person to redirect their social approach prior to reaching the next stage in which their social appeal will begin to decline. People must carefully consider their social options or they can be crushed within the other later phases. After a person has moved through the initial stages, they will reach a point within the cycle where their social appeal reaches an apex and then they will encounter the initial stages of *attraction decline*. During the *deterioration* stage, people will either be content with their lives as they enter a new chapter or they will become harrowed by their new social reality. The deterioration phase can vary widely in age range. Some people can begin to decline in their late twenties and others do not see a decline until they are in their forties or fifties although the latter is highly rare. This is all based on a combination of genetics and the impacts of the environment. This is the stage where those who allowed themselves to become egocentric will seek any remedy they can find to alter the course of the social reality. This is also a social stage where the people that may have been mistreated by these people will relish their decline. If people are unable to escape their desire to be young again, this social flaw leads into the *fixation* stage. If people cannot accept the social reality of aging and they have been too egocentric toward their attractive level of social appeal, there is a chance that this state of fixation will carry forward with them over time and can result in a number of maladaptive social patterns. The most troubling stages for people are the deterioration and the fixation stages, which occur during the decline phase of physical attraction. If people are hypercritical of themselves and others within the initial stages based on superficiality, there is the risk of immense psychic damage in these later final stages. If psychic damage occurs as a result of oxidative stress, people can become highly irritable and intensely vindictive toward others and especially toward those who are young and vibrant. These people will be especially sensitive when they see social flirting happening within their midst. People who have become vindictive and that hold social power will often use it to control their social targets.

From the deepest desires often come the deadliest hate.

—Plato

People's attraction levels can be either positive or negative within the process of socialization. There are groups of people that form social cliques and social rings that have similar attraction levels. When people enter these elite and exclusive social groups, they tend to *deindividuate* and take on a persona of exclusivity. Many times, the socially elite groups will feel superior to others in society and will look at all others as socially inferior. These social groups will mock others behind their backs covertly, and in some cases, they may be so bold as to be overt in their actions. The social pitfall and social trap that this social attitude creates is a much more intense social crash when people migrate toward their decline at the midlife point. The more intense the internal and external social scrutiny is within the element of social attraction, the more profound the social crash will be. When people misuse and abuse the application phase within social attraction, the *inverse psychological reaction* will proliferate rapidly in their psyche. This social phenomenon could be labeled *karma* as it is a natural occurrence and not *social retribution*. Those who are highly superficial are most often the ones who have the hardest time within their decline phase.

Because of the fact that attraction involves so much emotion within cognition, there are other cognitive covariants that are paralyzed during the attraction process such as thinking, reasoning, logic, perception, and more. As the two major life drives are aggression and libido, and both are fueled with emotion, this is why the social dynamic of attraction is perpetual and highly damaging to humanity on a collective level. The only social cure is for people to engage in more reason and logic within their social decisions and to incorporate a spiritual foundation in their lives. A social paradox within attraction and socialization is that, that many parents will tell their children to conduct themselves one way and then display the complete opposite behaviors. This is why the youth social stage is equally complex for most people as the adult social stage. People are bombarded continually from so many difficult angles within youth, and they do not have the life experience to fully comprehend the impact of their social choices. As mentioned prior, genetics determines people's traits, dispositions, and plays a very prominent role within the process of socialization, mate selection, and the life path. In conclusion, people must be very cautious of how they treat others because there are earthly considerations and spiritual considerations that apply to those who forsake the others within humanity.

GENETICS

Genetics, Cellular, and Embryonic Development

People inherit their traits through genetics and the traits that people inherit ultimately will have a very large impact on their life paths and on the process of socialization. Human traits are present at all levels within people from their physical outward appearance and extending out to many other areas as well, including deep within people's organic cognitive systems. Although some people may not think that the human interaction and socialization process begins until the forward expressive and receptive communication stage arrives, in actuality and in the social reality, socialization begins before birth. The life path final destination is certainly not predetermined at or before birth, but based on genetics, people's life courses and obstacles begin to immediately be channeled in. (This will be discussed much more in depth later in the book) Evolution is the process whereby genetic traits are carried forward within a species over time.

Evolution involves the change in a species gene pool over time. *Internal evolution* involves random mutative changes. *External*

317

evolution involves changes due to environmental pressures. *Stability selection* is a factor within evolution where the extreme traits that are within a species are eliminated (i.e., more babies being born around the average birth weight and having less outliers on the edge of the curve). In the *normal curve*, aka the *bell curve*, there is a central tendency, which occurs around the height of curve, there is also a reoccurring phenomenon in psychology and biology in this area, (i.e., the average height falls central and the outliers to the sides), also for IQ and many more things, the 68-95-99.7 rule aka the *three-sigma rule* is the associated statistical rule. *Disruptive selection* is when evolution selects extreme traits that pass on. *Genetic drift* is when there is a move away from the normal gene pool. One of the most important psychic and cognitive components that are passed down along a continuum is human instinct. *Instinct* is an innate pre-wired circuitry, which directs and guides human behavior. Being instinct is inherited along a wide continuum there are varying degrees of behavior. *Evolutionary psychology* studies the patterns of natural selection and behavior that is selected to carry on. *Heritability* involves the relationship of how much people are like their mother and/or father as far as their genes and behavior. People get their traits through DNA.

Deoxyribonucleic acid (DNA) is repeated subunit molecules that encode the genetic instructions used in the development and functioning of all known living organisms. Along with ribonucleic acid (RNA) and proteins, DNA is one of the three major macromolecules essential for all known forms of life. Genetic information is encoded as a sequence of nucleotides, which are nitrogenous bases (guanine, adenine, thymine, and cytosine). Any of these chemical bases, G (guanine which is double-ringed purine), A (adenine which is double-ringed purine), T (thymine which is single-ringed pyrimidine), and C (cytosine which is single-ringed pyrimidine) can attach to the sugar. These bases are not alive and can live for thousands of years. Three nucleotides make one *amino acid.*

A *nucleotide* can only have one of the four types of bases. Information is read using the *genetic code*, which specifies the sequence of the amino acids within proteins. Nucleotides each have five carbon sugars a phosphate and a nitrogenous base (i.e., adenine). This code is read by copying stretches of DNA into the related *nucleic acid* in RNA in a process called *transcription*. Within cells, DNA is organized into long structures called *chromosomes*, which direct and control all life.

Humans have twenty-three chromosomes, twenty-two pairs are called *autosomes* and the twenty-third pair of chromosomes is called the *sex chromosome*. A female has two X chromosomes and a male has an X chromosome from the mother and a Y chromosome from the father. Some traits like *color blindness* and *hemophilia* are carried on the sex chromosomes, these are called *sex-linked traits*. Most sex-linked traits are found on the X chromosome and are called *X-linked traits*. If a male has a defective X chromosome, he will express it, while females have another X chromosome, so they can *mask* the other defective X. When a defective X chromosome is masked, the masked X is called a *carrier*. Within this process, certain traits can be carried and also a trait inheritance can skip a generation. In every female cell, one chromosome is activated and the other chromosome is deactivated during embryonic development

A *Punnett square* can be used to map chromosomal outcomes. A *karyotype* charts the chromosomes. Within *heredity and heritability*, people's traits are the characteristics produced by factors called *genes*. A gene is a segment of a chromosome. *Chromatin* is unwound DNA strains that are associated with proteins. The stages of *mitosis* are: *prophase* where chromosomes appear after *chromatin coils*, the nucleus breaks down and then elongated microtubules grow from the *centrioles* and the outer *nuclear envelope* disappears. *Metaphase* is when chromosomes align in the *equatorial middle* of the cell. *Anaphase* is when the *mircrotubules strands* pull sister chromatids apart at the *equatorial middle* of the cell. *Telophase* is when chromosomes arrive at each pole of the new cells *chromosomes* house cellular DNA and are the highest level of organization in genetic material and are within the *chromatin*. DNA and protein are tightly bound. The position of a gene on a chromosome is called the *locus*.

Chromosomes have a short arm and a long arm, a locus is a specific location of a gene on a *DNA sequence* or a chromosome, at a given locus, an *allele* can be *variant*. The *gene locus* is located on the X chromosome, males have only one copy (hemizygous), males more frequently are color-blind, have *fragile X syndrome* with mental retardation and *autism*, and some other traits. *Huntington disease* is when only one dominant allele is inherited. Children with a parent with Huntington's disease have around a 50 percent chance of getting the disease, which has an age onset typically around thirty-five to forty-five. Genes can be dominant, codominant, or recessive. Codominance would be the equal expression of both alleles with AB blood type.

Traits are passed down and some traits have very high levels of heritability. Physical traits called *phenotypes* typically have very high heritability at around 90 percent. IQ is heritable at around 50 percent to 70 percent. Temperament and personality also have a very high correlation rates in heritability. Temperament and personality along with instinct are critical areas within the cognitive system for personal development and behavioral control. The *genotype* is which alleles are possessed. Genes are *polygenic*, which means that genes can *interact* to have small effect on each particular trait.

Diploid entails there being two sets of chromosomes in multicellular organisms, there is a copy of each gene called an allele, on each chromosome. If both alleles are the same, they are called *homozygotes*. If different, they are called *heterozygotes*. If an allele is missing, it is called *hemizygotic*. If both alleles are missing, it is called *nullizygous*. *Zygosity* is the degree of similarity of alleles for a trait.

An allele is a variation of a gene and can mask the trait expression (phenotype) of another allele at the same locus. A variation of the sequence of allele will be fatal to an embryo. One allele is inherited from the male and the other from the female and can be a disease. A *mutant* allele can be passed and/or a *carrier* allele when an individual inherits *recessive alleles* from a single *gene trait* (i.e., cystic fibrosis or albinism). *Isoforms* involve the creation of different proteins from the same gene (coding region), with small genetic differences between alleles (genetic variation or alternative form of the same gene).

Within DNA, *adenine* always binds to *thymine*, and *guanine* always binds to *cytosine*, this predictable pairing is called *base pairing*. Hydrogen bonds link DNA strands. Two hydrogen bonds are needed for the *adenine-thymine* pairing and three hydrogen bonds are needed for the *cytosine-guanine* pairing.

DNA directs the manufacturing of proteins via RNA. Enzymes are involved in the reading and replication process. The *helicase enzyme* unwinds DNA into the *replication fork*. There are specific sites for replication called the *origins of replication*. *Topoisomerases* are enzymes that prevent DNA tangling and cut and rejoin to the *helix*. DNA *polymerase* performs nucleotide addition to existing strands. RNA *primase* catalyzes the synthesis of the RNA primers and is needed for the addition to the naked strand. DNA *ligase* produces a continuous strand after leading, lagging, and binding the *okazaki strands* to fill in the pieces. Hydrogen bonds form between new base pairs, leaving two identical copies of the original DNA molecule.

Transcription factors control the transfer of genetic info from DNA to RNA. DNA is transcripted at the nucleus and then RNA translation occurs at the *cytoplasm* for protein formation. RNA is single stranded. The five carbon sugar of RNA is *ribose* versus *deoxyribose*. The base *uracil* replaces *thymine* in RNA. There are three types of RNA. *Messenger RNA (mRNA)* copies information from the DNA strand. *Ribosomal RNA (rRNA)* makes up part of *ribosomes. Transfer RNA (tRNA)* shuttles amino acids to *ribosomes* to the correct location at the correct time by reading the mRNA. *Protein synthesis* involves transcription, RNA processing, and translation. During transcription, DNA is partially copied.

During the *translation phase*, there is a search for ribosomes via *codons*, the three bases, which correspond to one of twenty amino acids. Certain amino acids are specified by more than one codon, and these are called *redundant*. MRNA attaches to the ribosome and waits for the correct amino acid to come to the ribosome. TRNA enters and one end of the tRNA carries the amino acid, the other end is called an *anticodon* and has three nitrogen bases that can pair with the codon in mRNA. *Initiation* for protein synthesis is the AUG codon and this is the code for the amino acid *methionine*. The anticodon UAC is the shuttle for methionine, which attaches and helps the *P-site*. The *A-site* is for the attachment of new tRNA and gets filled. The *E-site* is for exit out of tRNA and binds free tRNA before it exits the ribosome. The three phases of translation are: initiation, elongation, and termination. The ribosome holds everything in place while RNAs assist in assembling polypeptides. A polypeptide changes before becoming a protein.

During initiation, the ribosomes have three binding sites, the A-site, the P-site, and the E-site. Initiation involves the DNA being unwound by the helicase enzyme. Special sequences called *promoters* begin in single strand, so only one of two DNA strands is copied. The *sense* strand is the template, the other dormant strand is the *antisense* strand and its copying is completed after the base pairing to termination. RNA processing moves out of the nucleus for processing and modification and there are more nucleotides present than needed. *Exons* are portions of DNA that specify the portion of a sequence of a protein (codes for polypeptides), *introns* are spaces between that do not code. Introns must be removed and are extracted by RNA proteins called *spliceosome*. During elongation, polypeptides are formed via *linkage*. At termination, *stop codons* signal for the process to end. Stop codons are (i.e., UAA, UAG, and UGA). Mutations can occur via *gene rearrangements*, and other factors such as *base substitutions*. A nonsense base substitution is early termination during protein synthesis. A missense base substitution is an altered codon, which produces a different amino acid. A silent mutation offers no detectable change within protein synthesis.

Gene rearrangement can include deletions, duplications, inversions, translocations, and environmental factors. Deletions involved the loss of DNA or genes, single base or a larger part of DNA. Insertion can involve a complete *frameshift* and can be devastating. Duplications are an extra copy of genes, unequal crossing during *meiosis* or chromosome rearrangements. Inversions involve the orientation of regions, the gene, or gene sequence in gene expression, and chromosomal inversion. *Translocation* is when a portion of two different chromosomes on a single chromosome is in two different places, they break and rejoin in a way that sequence or gene is lost, repeated, or interrupted. *Polymorphism* is a slight difference in DNA sequences. In order to help detect and combat genetic defects, the human genome project was designed and launched.

The human genome project was the first genetic mapping and the completion of the project occurred in 2003 after a cost two billion dollars. *Nano sequence devices* are speeding up the process of individual mapping, and they are making the process more affordable. The *list of loci* is the *genetic map*. *Gene mapping* determines the locus for biotherapy treatment. *Genetic testing* can be done at any age of a born child.

Gene therapy is a process to combat defective genes and it allows normal genes to take over for defective ones, the functioning gene is transported via a *deactivated virus* to the cell nucleus of the defective gene. Using one's own stem cells or marrow and delivering cells to the body, after gene therapy delivery. Scientific research is also moving toward combating disorders and harnessing bodies own ability to grow and heal. An example of healing would be *hypoplastic left heart syndrome* where there is no function in the left ventricle of the heart and the standard treatment was rerouting the circulation, so the right ventricle of the heart could also take over pumping blood to the body's organs and extremities. Due to overworking, the right ventricle, around 30 percent of patients don't survive to adulthood. With the new procedure, the obstructed valves are opened and the malformations are repaired to divert the blood flow to the left ventricle versus away from it. This action triggers a bio response to promote healing and tissue growth, this procedure has been effective on some of the patients and has been promising.

Gene sequencers sample for different genetic mutations for a drug that can treat the defective genes (i.e., for *tumor growth*, there are over 280 different genetic mutations, and around 70 percent of test find a mutation that there is a drug on the market for and/or a drug in the trial stages). Researchers have always wondered why the immune system hasn't treated tumors as invaders. Tumors protect themselves by hijacking the body's natural brake for the immune system. Most solid tumors—colon, lung, breast, and prostate—use the same mechanism to hide from the immune system. Genetics also play a highly prominent role in mental disorders and human behavior.

There are genetic factors within mental illness and mental disorders. Determining the etiology or cause for biological psychiatry issues and their gene identification for psychological diagnoses are not quite as exact as many with many medical diagnoses.

The *degree of penetrance* is the frequency and the level of genetic and heritability risk in a family group by percentage. Genetics are of a highly familial nature. The *genotype* is the sum total of genetic material from parents. The *phenotype* is the observable signs and symptoms, appearance and behavior, from the interaction of genotype and phenotype. *Behavioral phenomenon* is the likelihood of behavior and developmental disorders. The three genetic casualties are:

1. Genes govern organic causes of disorders.
2. Genes are responsible for abnormalities before and after birth.
3. Genes may influence susceptibility to nonorganic disorders (predispositions). The *quantification* of genetic defects is calculated (i.e., *heritability* and *schizophrenia* can be as high as 80 percent and *autism* can be as high as 90 percent.

Schizophrenia and *Alzheimer's* are both *polygenic* where their expression is determined by more than one gene. Huntington's disease is *monogenic* where a single gene determines inheritance, a first-degree relative has a 10 percent chance when the general population has a 1 percent chance, and the locus for the gene has been identified on several arms at C-13, C-5, C-15, and C-2. Huntington's disease (chorea) involves brain cells being killed in the caudate nucleus, which is involved in the coordination of movement and brain cells that involve cognitive function. The short arm of the C-4 is the (triplet/trinucleotide). *Nucleotides* are building blocks of DNA and RNA, three consecutive nucleotides form a codon triplet in the messenger RNA that codes for a specific amino acid, dynamic expansion mutation cytosine adenine-guanine (CAG) expansion disorder is Huntington's disease. CAG is related to the amino acid *glutamine*, the higher number of CAG triplets, the earlier the onset. Factors can be mutations, deletions, translocations, and arm rearrangements. In Huntington's disease, so much glutamine is added to protein that it becomes *toxic* to the nervous system.

Exons are portions of DNA that specify the portion of a sequence of a protein, introns are spaces between that do not code. Fragile X has the highest prevalence for mental retardation and involves *cytosine-guanine-guanine (CGG)* expansion and this interferes with protein transcription from the functional magnetic resonance imaging (FMRI) gene on the X chromosome.

Successive generations cause a greater phenotype (expression) at earlier ages. Repeats of cytosine-thymine-guanine (CTG) can cause *myotonic dystrophy*, which may cause cataracts in later life. Manic depression has been linked to C-10 and C-8, agoraphobia has been linked to C-3 locus, and panic disorder has been linked to C-2, C-1, and C-11. Scientific research continues to search for answers to try and help prevent and/or treat genetic defects.

In *biotechnology*, the *polyerase chain reaction (PCR)* process can make billions of gene copies within hours using a *thermocycler*. This process can be used in forensics, to detect diseases, to better understand cells and more. In *transformation*, the insulin protein hormone can be made by bacteria. A gene is put into *transvector plasmid* (small piece of DNA) and recombinant DNA is created. A plasmid is a small circular DNA fragment that can serve as a vector and is a key element in genetic engineering. Plasmids can give cells a selected advantage. A vector is a vehicle to incorporate genes into host chromosomes. Bacteria without plasmid (antibiotic resistant) will die. This is used for insulin and gene expression. Genetics play a huge role in people's lives and what is occurring at the *cellular* level within people is also highly critical.

Cells are the smallest unit in organisms that can carry on life. They have various functions including covering, lining, storage, movement, connection, defense, communication, reproduction, and more. Cells use energy to maintain homeostasis and reproduce. *Eukaryotic cells* are large and complex with a nucleus-contained DNA within chromosomes. *Prokaryotic cells* are small, they lack a nucleus, and their DNA is a single circular molecule that is not enclosed in a cell membrane. Fossils from billions of years ago reveal these types of cells, bacteria today are the only living *prokaryotes*.

Within the cell structures, both have a cell membrane and both contain cytoplasm, which is everything in the cell, except the nucleus in eukaryotes, and everything but DNA in prokaryotes. Both types of cells contain *ribosomes*, which are structures on which proteins are made. Cytoplasm contains specialized parts called *organelles*, which have specific functions. An organelle is a specialized subunit within a cell that is usually enclosed in its own lipid bilayer, a thin polar membrane. Many organelles are *membrane bound* in eukaryotic cells. There are compartments and this has its advantages and the compartments keep the organelles separate from the cytoplasm, the organelles are constantly growing, moving, reproducing, and appearing and disappearing. Organelles have very specific functions (i.e., muscle in people's leg contains greater number of energy producing organelles than a bone cell; striped, pulsating cells of the heart muscle are different from the box-like cells that make up growing layers of the skin; nerve cells for electrical signal, secreted hormones, sperm cells all become specialized at maturity). The evolution of cells into complex multicellular organisms was enabled via the ability to specialize for survival in complex environments.

Some other types of organelles are centrioles, which help organize *microtubules*, which are components of the cytoskeleton. Tubular polymers of tubulin are dynamic (alpha and beta tubulin) micro and *intermediate filaments* form the *cytoskeleton* (shape of cell). Intermediate filaments are *keratin* in skin and hair, *neurofilaments* of neural cells, and *lamin* for nuclear envelope. Microtubules make up the internal structure of *cilia* and *flagella* and are involved in mitosis and meiosis. The formation of *mitotic spindles* is a process where eukaryotic cells separate chromatids during cell division. Cilium is involved in cellular locomotion and flagella are protrusions that aid in locomotion from microtubules grouping called *basal bodies*. If protrusions are short and numerous, they are cilia; the longer and less numerous protrusions are called flagella. They are arranged in a 9+2 pattern and are found in sperm, female reproductive tract, and the respiratory area. *Endoplasmic reticulum* synthesizes carbohydrates and lipids. *Lyosomes* digest cellular macromolecules. *Mitochondria* provide energy for the cell via the breakdown of food. *Peroxisomes* detoxify alcohol, form bile acid, and use oxygen to break down fats. Chromosomes house the cellular DNA.

The assembly of proteins by ribosomes is an essential part of the *biosynthetic pathway*. Ribosomes are assemblies of eukaryotic cells (organelles that consist of RNA and protein). Ribosome is two chains of RNA, ribosomal RNA and more than fifty proteins. Ribosomes latches on to mRNA molecule and moves it along, capturing loaded tRNA, then joins their amino acids to form a new protein chain. There is a large subunit and a small subunit. A *polypeptide* is produced according to genetic code and the four phases are activation, initiation, elongation, and termination.

The *nucleus* contains the *hereditary info* and controls growth and reproduction and is bound in a double-cell layer called the *nuclear envelope*, which separates the nucleus from the cytoplasm. The nuclear envelope maintains the shape of the nucleus and regulates the flow of molecules in and out through *nuclear poles*, the nucleus synthesizes ribosomes and controls the synthesis of proteins in cytoplasm via mRNA. MRNA messenger and tRNA transfer help translate the protein-coding genes in mRNA into proteins.

The small subunit reads mRNA, large subunit joins amino acids from the *polypeptide chain*. The sequence of DNA-encoding protein may be copied many times into mRNA sequence chains, amino acids selected and carried to ribosome by tRNA. Once protein is produced, it can fold and produce a three-dimensional shape/structure.

Ribosomes are located in *cytosol/cytoplasm* and are free or they are *bound* to *endoplasmic reticulum*. Free ribosomes make proteins that function in the cytoplasm while bound ribosomes make proteins for the membrane or for export. Free and bound ribosomes are interchangeable and can also change numbers according to metabolic needs of the cell. Protein synthesis involves transcription and translation of the genetic code found in the DNA. The mRNA message is translated into amino acids. Amino acids are linked together by ribosomal RNA to form *polypeptide chains.*

Polypeptide chains undergo modifications before becoming functioning proteins. The proteins are very important *biological polymers* (large molecules composed of many smaller molecules linked together). The smaller molecules are called *monomers.* A large molecule is called a macromolecule and can have fifty monomers. *Polymers* shape the uniqueness of an organism. The DNA genetic code dictates amino acid identity and order. There are four types of biological macromolecules. *Carbohydrates* are composed of sugar for energy storage, *lipids* such as oil, fats, steroids store energy and cushion organs, *proteins* amino acid monomers involved in molecular transport and muscle movement, *nucleic acid*, which contain DNA and RNA instructions for protein synthesis (the transfer of gene information from one gene to the next). The loss of water creates bonds in assembly, which is called *dehydration synthesis*, and in *disassembly* water interaction causes bonds via *hydrolysis.*

Ribosomes from bacteria, archaea, and eukaryotes are the *three domains of life on earth.* They differ in size, shape, sequence, structure, and ratio of protein to RNA. The difference in structure allows antibiotics to kill bacteria by inhibiting their ribosomes, while leaving human ribosomes unaffected.

In cell reproduction, when cells reach a particular size, organelles help to prepare for cell division for the growth of multicellular organisms. *Cellular down regulation* is the reduction of the quantity of cellular components (i.e., RNA or protein in response to external variables), a *negative feedback mechanism* is used to reduce cells (i.e., sensitivity to hormones). *Cellular up regulation* involves a positive feedback mechanism and is the increase of quantity of cellular components due to a response to external variables. For example, there can be more sensitivity to hormones and molecules such as to *oxytocin* during pregnancy, which is released heavily during labor after discension of the cervix and uterus and after stimulation of the nipples for breast-feeding. The actions and sequences of events that occur at the cellular and genetic levels relay directly over into human reproduction.

The reproductive hormones released by the *pituitary gland* in the brain include *follicle-stimulating hormone (FSH)*, which is *follicle* in females and *spermatogenesis* in males. Another reproductive hormone released by the pituitary gland is *luteinizing hormone*, which is for the ovum in females and for testosterone in males. Finally *prolactin* is for female mammary glands. The *posterior pituitary gland* secretes oxytocin, which regulates the contraction of the uterus and the ducts of the mammary glands. The reproductive sex hormones are estrogen, progesterone, and testosterone. Estrogen and progesterone are produced and released by the ovaries and regulate the menstrual cycle, while testosterone promotes spermatogenesis in males and elicits the secondary sex characteristics.

Hormone function depends on the hormones solubility. Steroids are lipid soluble, while proteins (peptides) and amines are not lipid soluble. Steroids can diffuse across the target cell membrane and can bind to receptors in the nucleus, which activates specific genes in the DNA. This in turn makes proteins. Proteins and amines cannot enter cells by diffusion and they must bind to receptors on the cell membrane of the target cell. This stimulates the production of a second messenger called *cyclic adenosine monophosphate (cAMP)*. CAmp triggers enzymes, which lead to specific cellular changes.

The menstrual cycle has different phases. During the *follicular phase* (ten-day phase), hormones are received from the *anterior pituitary gland*. FSH stimulates follicles in the ovaries to grow, eventually one follicle takes the lead and dominates. The growing follicle releases estrogen, which stimulates and helps the uterine lining (endometrium) to thicken and also signals for the pituitary gland to release *lutenizing hormone (LH)*.

During the *luteal stage*, lutenizing hormone triggers ovulation, which is the release of the follicle from the ovary. The follicle burst and releases into the ovum, then next it moves into the fallopian tube oviduct for ovulation. It takes ten days to prepare for the implant of a fertilized cell. The ruptured follicle, now a fluid-filled sac condenses into the *corpus luteum* (yellow body). The corpus luteum continues to secrete estrogen and starts to produce progesterone. Progesterone stimulates the growth of the glands and blood vessels in the endometrium uterine wall. Without progesterone, the fertilized ovum cannot latch onto the uterus and develop into an embryo. At thirteen to fifteen days, if fertilization and implantation have not occurred, the corpus luteum shuts down and stops producing estrogen and progesterone.

During the flow phase (menstruation), the uterus reabsorbs tissue grown and sheds off the tissue (sloughing off) the excess. This is where the bleeding of menstruation comes from. However, if fertilized and pregnant, the *extraembryonic tissue* of the fetus releases *human chorionic gonadotropin (HCG)* to help maintain the uterine lining.

In the male reproductive system, FSH from the pituitary gland targets the *seminiferous tubules* to produce sperm. LH from the pituitary gland stimulates the *interstitial cells* to produce testosterone. Testosterone stimulates the testes to produce sperm cells. Cells in the testes undergo meiosis. The main tissue of the testes is the seminiferous tubules and this is where *spermatogonia* undergo meiosis. Spermatids mature in the *epididymus*. Interstitial cells, which are supporting tissues, produce testosterone and other androgens.

Sperm cells travel through the *vas deferens* and pick up fluids from the seminal vesicles, which provide *fructose* for energy. The prostate gland provides *alkaline fluid* that neutralizes the acidic fluids in the vagina.

Morphogenesis is when the sperm dissolves the *corona radiata cells* surrounding the egg and penetrate the *zona pellucida*, which is the area inside the *corona radiata*. The joining of the sperm and the egg produce the *zygote state*. In the zygote state, during week one or week two, there is rapid cell division, which is *cleavage* where the cells divide and form a solid ball called the *morula*. Cells multiply by twos. The morula becomes the *blastula* and produces a fluid-filled cavity called the *blastocoel* around week two or three, and the *blastocyst* moves onto the uterus (endometrium) around five to seven days after fertilization. Implantation into the uterine wall is made for nourishment.

Gastrula is when the cells migrate to the blastocoel and differentiate into three germ layers: the ectoderm, mesoderm, and the endoderm. The embryo will then begin to grow around the center axis/spinal cord, and the brain, spinal cord, heart, and gastrointestinal (GI) tract will form. The ectoderm outer layer develops into the skin, CNS, PNS, eyes, ears, and connective tissue. The endoderm of the inner cells develop into the mucus membrane, the lungs, intestines, the bladder, GI area, respiratory, and the access organs such as the pancreas, gall bladder, and liver. The mesoderm middle layer develops into the heart and circulatory system, and also the bones, muscles, kidneys, reproductive system, excretory organs, circulatory system, and reproductive system.

Also during week four to five, the placenta forms within this *embryonic period*. Chemicals are released by the embryo to stop the menstrual cycle and next *neurogenesis* will begin. *Organogenesis* is when the *neurula stage* begins and the notochord (the rod beneath the nerve cord) forms neural tube for the CNS. The fetal embryo develops amnion, chorion, allantois, and the yolk sac. The placenta and the umbilical cord are outgrowths of the membrane. The placenta is for nutrients and waste transfer and develops from the chorion and the uterine tissue. The umbilical cord connects the embryo to the placenta.

In embryo cardiac development, the heartbeat starts at around five to six weeks, and is detectable only by an *internal ultrasound*, but is not normally detectable until six to seven weeks. At around week six, the heart and brain are both active, the heart is pumping blood, and buds will become arms and legs. Once *organogenesis* begins, the brain separates into five areas.

Embryonic cardio physiology for *hypothesis one conductive synchronotrophy* poses that the embryonic heart starts to beat with the need for convective blood flow. However, evidence states that diffusion can provide oxygen, nutrients, remove metabolic waste, and create hormonal interaction. *Diffusion flux* proportional to the *minus gradient*, a higher concentration moves to a lower concentration region, called the *random walk*, occurring in thermal energy and microorganisms. *Hypothesis two* poses that in *prosynchrontrophy*, the heart starts to beat prior to the need for convective blood flow. The need for cardiac heartbeat is for cardiac growth, shaping, maturation, angiogenesis, and growth of vessels.

In reproduction, around 25 percent of embryos abort by the sixth week (i.e., six weeks after last menstrual period [LMP]). After six weeks into the process, around 8 percent of embryos abort (miscarriage). Around week eight is the fetus stage which is eight weeks after embryogenesis. The LMP occurs two weeks before *conception*. After eight weeks, around 2.5 percent of fetuses miscarriage.

A genetic *chromosomal abnormality* accounts for around 50 percent of all early losses. Maternal age and prior miscarriages are also important factors. *Induction* is where the tissue fate is determined and cells called *organizers* release a chemical called *morpohgen*, which moves to target tissues. *Homeotic genes* control the development of the embryo. Homeotic genes encode proteins that bind the DNA. *Differentiation* is the cells becoming more specialized. *Hox genes* control the position of the body parts. Genetic variability involves individual genetic differences and except for identical twins, no two people have identical alleles.

A *full-term pregnancy* is between thirty-seven to forty-two weeks, *postterm* is birth after forty-two weeks, and *prematurity (premature birth)* is childbirth before thirty-seven *gestational weeks*. Normally around 90 percent plus of babies that are born at or after twenty-eight weeks survive. *Retinopathy*, vision loss, blindness, and other conditions can potentially occur within premature births. *Teratogens (chemicals)* can cause harm within development if ingested by the mother. These chemicals can pass through the blood barrier to the developing child with alcohol and *fetal alcohol syndrome (FAS)*. The health of both the mother and unborn child within the development stage is highly critical to the development of all the biological systems and can help to increase the quality and quantity of the life span. When people maintain a healthy lifestyle, they increase the chances of genetic and biological processes going correctly, which improves the probability of having healthy children.

ᴄʜᴇ ᴄᴇɴᴛʀᴀʟ ɴᴇʀᴠᴏᴜꜱ ꜱʏꜱᴛᴇᴍ

Brain, Cranial Nerves, and Nervous System

The mysteries of the brain have been studied for thousands of years. The *Alcmaeon / Pythagorean school of Philosophy* from ancient Greece theorized that all sensory awareness is coordinated by the brain. As mentioned prior, sometimes it can take years for theories to be proven, and other times, it can take much, much longer.

People's genes provide the blueprint for their growth and development, and proteins made out of amino acids are the building blocks. The proteins are coded by the nucleotides (A, C, G) and T is the fourth nucleotide. Genetic sequences, CCG and CAG are repeated and some of these repeats are more rare and reserved. The reserved repeats can range across individuals on a continuum and may be linked to varying and potentially increased/decreased brain size and/or development. Like anything in the neurochemistry within the brain, an excess or depletion of a substance and/or of a function can potentially cause highly advanced development to occur or can lead to an impairment. If the absolute threshold for sequence repeats is eclipsed then there is the potential for brain disease.

The brain typically weighs around three pounds when at full-size. Being the male brain takes longer to develop than in females, the IQ range in males has a higher absolute threshold and it has been shown that there is about a 5:1 ratio in the number of male to female IQs that exceed the 130 level. But in turn, males also have more genetic brain issues on the opposite end of the spectrum such as within the *autism spectrum disorders (ASD)* category and also with males that have IQs which are lower than seventy. Females have a higher concentration of IQs in the center of the IQ bell curve.

Men tend to perform better in visual-spatial processing, math, precise control over the large muscle groups, and they tend to use the left hemisphere for reasoning, while women tend to use both hemispheres. This fundamental tendency variation creates a difference in the emotional and behavioral responses between the sexes. Women also tend to be better at recognizing nonverbal activity (i.e., detecting body language) and their senses are also tend to be more acute. Also the caudate nucleus is typically larger in women and the caudate nucleus is involved in language and comprehension amongst its other functions.

Brain size is related to the size of the head, but brain size has no direct bearing on intelligence. The brain grows tremendously from birth to age one in particular and by the age of four to six years old, 95 percent of the brain's mass development is achieved. There is however an early-life decline in the gray matter of the brain, which is called the *slope of adolescence*. This slope occurs when *synaptic pruning* is initiated to reinforce the synaptic connections, which are in use and to prune the idle circuits to maximize brain neural efficiency.

By the age of around sixty-five, the brain generally weighs around 2.6 lbs due to cell loss over the life course. The *frontal lobe* of the brain decreases by around 30 percent from ages fifty to eighty in many cases. The frontal lobe is the major area in the brain for our higher-level functioning. This is why we see examples of cognitive decline in some of our elderly population. In addition, sometimes brain cell loss occurs outside of the normal patterns.

An example of abnormal brain cell loss is in the brain of the known genius Steven Hawking who has *amyotrophic lateral sclerosis* (ALS), which is the death of the brain cells that control movement in progression over time. ALS is a degenerative disease of the motor neurons in the brain and in the spinal cord, which impairs muscle movement. The *bulbar type* impacts the cranial nerves, speech, and swallowing. If higher amounts of *glutamate* are left in the *extracellular space* due to reuptake issues, it can cause an *exitotoxin* increase. Cellular calcium channels can also be altered by glutamate and *aspartate* excesses. There are a number of different neurodegenerative brain diseases and disorders which can impact the brain.

Some other brain disorders include dementia, Alzheimer's disease (AD), Parkinson's disease, Huntington's disease, multiple sclerosis, and Lou Gehrig's disease. In multiple sclerosis (MS), there is myelin sheath damage, which impacts the conduction of signals between neurons. *Demylination* of the CNS is the hallmark of MS. Other issues are often optic neuritis, asymmetrical muscle weakness, and fatigue. MS can also cause immune system issues with inflammatory responses.

There are also some cases where a very high level of IQ and/or creativity ability is associated with the *liability* of having a mental illness at some point. Some famous people have suffered from mental illnesses, including Newton, Lincoln, Beethoven, Hemingway, van Gogh, and Dickens. Research into the genes associated with the neurodegenerative process is ongoing.

A very basic overview of some of the structures in the brain is as follows: the *corpus callosum* (which is typically larger in women) is a structural cross-channel brain structure that sends messages between the right and left hemispheres of the brain and is part of the *cerebral cortex*. If the cerebral cortex area of the brain is damaged, there can be some major issues such as cognitive decline and emotional issues. Each side of the brain receives tactile (kinesthetic) information from the opposite side of the body via the corpus callosum. The *language area* of the brain is typically on the left hemisphere of most people and includes the Wernicke's area (understanding of written and spoken language). Damage to the Wernicke's area can cause the loss of language reception, but there is typically the maintenance of speech production. The Broca's area is involved in speech production, damage to this area will likely result in the loss of speech production, but the maintenance of language reception.

Although damage to certain brain structures can potentially cause permanent deficits, in some brain injury scenarios, neural remapping and rerouting can potentially occur in the neural pathways and neural structures, and sometimes functions can be restored via new pathways by the neuronal connections, reaching the source area required to elicit a brain function. The adult brain can change and the mind can change the brain. Neuroplasticity is the ability of neurons to forge new connections and rewire, this activity can occur via the causal effect of the will, and the will and mental effort can create *physical force* that can alter the brain and brain chemistry by the power of *mental force*.

The power of *neuroplasticity* was first conceived long ago, when William James (1890) posed a theory of *brain malleability*, which was ignored for years. The brain is a changeable structure and there are brain *plasticity* pathways, where synapses can change due to learning, behavior, the environment, and neural processes, as well as from bodily injury. Neuroplasticity involves glial and vascular cells. Brain plasticity examples are found in learning (structural), *cortical remapping* as an injury response (functional plasticity) versus the old theory that the brain was *immutable* after the *critical period*. Innovation can be stalled when a majority overlooks those who are coming up with the answers and the solutions. In psychology and biology, the *critical period* is a period of heightened sensitivity to *exogenous stimuli*. There is *concurrence* that auditory, visual, and vestibular systems with disuse will result in *varying* future routing, but may be universal for emergent sensory systems. The *sensitive period* is the *extended* period of time that a structure can gain force with the proper stimuli. The brain can also self-regulate with instant recognition and self-correction with its adaptive capabilities and flexibility.

All of the sciences within the process of socialization have experienced the production of genius and innovation over time, and then have also experienced the corresponding rejection by others who are unable to conceive the genius and/or who want to suppress the innovation. Conflict and disagreement are part of socialization and they can inhibit the process of innovation. Unfortunately when someone comes out with an innovation of any kind, they are extending themselves within the socialization process and there are others with higher social roles and/ or a majority that will dictate the forward momentum of the innovation. Innovation can be considered *acting out* in some social circles and it can be a social risk. This is why many geniuses over time never received their proper credit during their lives. But fortunately there were enough brave pioneers to forge ahead in the study of the human brain.

There are two pathways to the brain which are the *blood-brain barrier (BBB)* and *cerebrospinal fluid (CSF)*. The brain capillaries have minute spaces between them and have tightly packed cell junctions. The two ways that molecules can gain access to the brain cell components and neurons are *lipid mediation* and *catalyzed active carrier transport*. In lipid transport, the movement is confined to small molecules and is proportional to lipid solubility. In the catalyzed transport system, there is receptor and mediating enzyme processes for nutrients (i.e., glucose, amino acids, and nucleotides). *Isolates* can incapacitate enzyme actions, which control some NTs, reducing dopamine and serotonin production. Isolates can also be destructive to the neural tissue and can also potentially instigate tumor generation.

CSF can also deliver nutrients and molecules to the brain. The *choroid plexus* is a capillary bed that secretes CSF. CSF circulates around the brain and the spinal cord and bathes the tissue with nutrients. The CSF also passes downward into the *subarachnoids space*, which circulates around the spinal cord. Reabsorption of the CSF is via lymph and blood capillary networks. Nutrients diffuse into the brain's structures. The *aqueduct of Sylvius* (which contains CSF and lies in the midbrain) can narrow if *neurotoxic* chemicals are introduced by the CSF, and this can lead to *hydrocephalus* (which is water on the brain and impacts neuronal communication). This can also cause *cell necrosis* (cell death) in brain structures. This type of damage can also potentially create the manifestation of a mental illness.

The *hypothalamus* in the brain has a high diffusion rate from the CSF, which can impact this vital component of the *neuroendocrine system*. Also *adenosine triphospate (ATP)*, cell energy stores, can be depleted by the continual firing of neuronal nerve cells to combat the *neurotoxins*. Damage to the brain's cellular structures can also release free radicals and this potentiates *oxidative stress*, neurodegeneration, impedance of enzyme reactions, and promotes DNA defects and mutations. The fewer predispositions and the healthier the lifestyle is that people lead, the better the chances are to maintain good health in the body and in the brain. There are many brain structures and chemicals that play a role in people's healthy living.

The brain is a very highly regulated biological superstructure regulated by various structures, brain chemicals (neurotransmitters and enzymes), and conductivity (electrical). Brain regulation involves *neural transmission* in the brain by both chemical and electrical impulses, which occur within it and the brain's corresponding periphery system, which include the spinal cord. Electrical impulses occur within the cells and chemical impulses occur between the cells. *Transduction* is when signals are converted to neural impulses beginning with the *thalamus* then onto other cortices in the brain. There are *excitatory NTs* that pass across the *synaptic gap* for firing and increase the likelihood of firing the next neuron and *inhibitory NTs*, which decrease firing. *Potassium (K)* and *sodium (Na)* are both integral in the depolarization of the neural cells, but they are not involved in the firing. *Receptors* shut down firing and release and *transporters* return chemicals back the original neurons. Brain activity can be monitored using a *positron emission tomography (PET)* scan device and also with an *electroencephalogram (EEG)* device for brain waves. *Sensory adaptation* occurs due to frequency, while *sensory habituation* occurs due to level of focus. *Sensation* can be thought of as *activation*, while *perception* as understanding the sensations. Amino acids also play a pivotal role in brain chemistry and activity including their interaction at neuronal receptor sites.

Neuron receptor site, N-methyl-D-aspartate (NMDA), is the predominant molecular device for controlling synaptic plasticity and memory function. Activation of the NMDA receptors results in the opening of the ion channel, which is voltage regulated. Calcium flux through the sites is thought to be critical in synaptic plasticity, which is a cellular mechanism for learning and memory. The NMDA site is *ligand-gated* and *voltage dependent* and requires coactivation by two ligands to include glutamate or aspartate along with a coagonist of either *D-serine or glycine*. D-serine removal can block excitatory neurotransmitters and D-serine can be released by neurons and *astrocytes* to regulate NMDA receptors. A positive change in the transmembrane potential will make it more likely that the ion channel in the NMDA receptor will open by expelling MG2+, which blocks the channel from the outside. This process is fundamental to the role of the receptor to memory and learning.

Depression treatment with *magnesium glycinate* and *magnesium taurinate* has been used in research and has been shown to produce rapid recovery. Na+, K+, and Ca2+ not only pass through the NMDA receptor channel, but they also modulate the activity. The Ca2+ and Na+ rush into the cell and the K+ rushes out of the cell, which increases the concentration of Ca2+ in the cell during *excitatory postsynaptic potential (EPSP)* activation. For *schizophrenia disorders*, receptor *antagonists* are a primary area of focus in brain research. Amino acids and their brain functions are also heavily involved in the sleep function. When people do not get the proper amount of sleep and/or the proper quality of sleep, this can produce a myriad of biological issues.

The *circadian rhythm* is part of the human biofeedback systems, which involves the conduction of both chemicals and electricity. There are different brain waves that occur throughout the day that can be measured with and EEG device. Issues with circadian rhythm can include *advanced sleep phase syndrome, irregular sleep-wake type*, and *non-twenty-four-hour sleep-wake type*, and they can potentially indicate *pathophysiology*. The circadian rhythm is impacted by internal chemical processes and also by nutrition, which is a vital component within a healthy sleep cycle. Within the sleep cycle, there is something called the *dawn phenomenon*, which typically occurs between 4:00 a.m.–6:30 a.m. in most people's circadian rhythm cycle.

In this part of the waking cycle, *dawn phenomenon*, cortisol, epinephrine and norepineprhine are secreted, raising blood sugar levels. *First-use glucose* is stored in the liver and plasma glucose and insulin starts to rise. The trigger for the dawn phenomenon is a nocturnal surge in growth hormone, which occurs less as people age normally, and typically early risers have a stronger growth hormone response. High carbohydrate intake can spike blood sugar levels, especially at breakfast time.

The *Somogyi effect* is a counter-regulatory response, and the system alarm for the release of stress hormones to get the blood sugar level (BSL) back to the homeostasis safety zone. Beta cells work on lowering BSL after meals. Basal insulin is secreted to lower BSL. Sixty percent of protein turns into carbohydrates over a seven-hour period, so part of protein is like a slow-release carbohydrate. Nutrition can heavily impact the sleep cycle, so if people are regulating their food intake properly, this can allow for the body to properly shut down at night and allow for an adequate amount of sleep. Sleep duration and quality can be measured by the chemical and electrical activities that occur within the brain. Brain waves indicate the various cycles of brain activity that occur within the sleep cycle.

Brain waves that are large (high amplitude) are slow (frequency). Slow-wave sleep is typically during deep sleep, namely stages three to four. *Beta waves* are low amplitude and high frequency. *Alpha waves* can create sensations called *hypnagogic hallucinations* and can also produce the *myoclonic jerk* (startle-like response). Stage 1 (five to ten minutes in cycle) is light sleep and easily awakened, eyes move slowly, and muscles slow down, it is the *theta wave*, which is high amplitude and low frequency. Stage 2 (five to twenty minutes in cycle), eye movement is stopping, is when the body temperature begins to drop in preparation for deep sleep. Stage 3 (five to thirty minutes in cycle) is when the extremely slow *delta waves*, which is light to deep sleep, are interspersed, which faster waves called theta waves (bed-wetting and sleepwalking are associated with this stage most often). Stage 4 (five to fifteen minutes) is the deepest of the sleep stages, prior to rapid eye movement (REM) sleep. No eye movement or muscle activity occurs during deep sleep. The brain is producing more delta waves than theta waves during this stage. (Bed-wetting and sleepwalking can occur during this stage and also night terrors).

Non-REM sleep is comprised of stages one to four and last from 90–120 plus minutes and the cycle repeats backwards prior to reach REM sleep (1, 2, 3, 4, 3, 2, 5 [REM]).

REM paradoxical *D-state* sleep (rapid eye movement) and a sharp back and forth motion, paralysis of the muscles to prevent the body from acting out in that can be intense during the cerebral stage. Occasional muscle twitches can be present. The first period of REM typically last ten minutes, and, each cycle, the time increases until the final cycle reaches around sixty minutes of REM sleep. A person can go through four to five cycles per night. *REM rebound* is when the body tries to compensate for deprivation of REM sleep in prior cycles.

Factors that can impact sleep can include stress, the environment, psychological issues, and/or neurological factors. *Hypnagogia* and *hypnopompia* are vivid dreamlike auditory, visual, or kinesthetic (tactile) sensations often accompanied by sleep paralysis and experienced when transitioning in or out of sleep. *Sleep paralysis* is temporary paralysis of the body shortly after waking up or falling asleep. When the brain wakes up from REM state, the body remains paralyzed, and this is sometimes accompanied by hypnagogic hallucinations. *Lucid dreaming* is aware of having the dream while having the dream, and having the ability to exert conscious control over the dream, these are of the most real and vivid dreams. There are two types of lucid dreaming the *dream-initiated lucid dream* (DILD) where the dreamer starts a normal dream and then becomes aware that he or she is dreaming and the *wake-initiated lucid dream* (WILD) where the dreamer goes from a normal waking state into a dream without any apparent lapse in consciousness. Nightmares that are recurrent should be examined as they can cause severe sleep disturbances and physiological issues for the long term. *Sleep-wake disorders* are often potential warning signs for medical or mental issues.

Insomnia (psychological interference) is an inability to fall asleep, stay asleep, or get enough sleep. Insomnia can impact over 60 percent of all people in the US at one time or another and over 5 percent–20 percent are impaired with *chronic insomnia. Acute* or *transient insomnia* are episodes, which last over a brief period of time. Chronic insomnia lasts one month or more, causes distress with activities of daily living (ADLs), is not a medical condition, can be comorbid with mania, depression, or anxiety disorders. For a primary diagnosis, insomnia cannot be related to another disorder. *Secondary insomnia* is traced back to another source such as a medical condition or an MI such as generalized anxiety disorder (GAD) or depression. Factors of insomnia are stress, anxiety, noise, light, circadian rhythm, or other biological reasons. A sleep journal can track the sleep disturbance patterns. To treat insomnia, behavioral and educational therapies are offered, and, if necessary, sleep medication (hypnotics) or herbal treatments (around 20 percent of all herbal treatments are for insomnia). The behavioral approach in psychology involves looking at patterns that occur before bedtime eating, exercise, etc., and the associations of sleeping and the bed itself (the bed and sleep were good). The educational aspect focuses on relaxation techniques. The prognosis is dependent on the individual as those who continue with unhealthy patterns have a very high propensity to relapse.

Hypersomnia can be primary or recurrent. They differ on frequency and regularity. *Primary hypersomnia* (idiopathic) is excessive daytime tiredness over a long period of time, were symptoms are present all or most of the time. *Recurring hypersomnia* can be one to many days over the course of a year, but there are periods in between without symptoms. Both conditions cause people to nap frequently and they are not refreshed after a nap. These are often confused with *narcolepsy*, but narcolepsy has a sudden onset and people with narcolepsy are refreshed after falling asleep. People with *Kleine-Levin syndrome* that has a 3:1 male to female ratio, may sleep for eighteen hours per day, can be irritable, and, in some cases, can make uninhibited sexual advances, they sometimes eat uncontrollably and gain weight (this condition is very rare). The population for hypersomnia is around

5 percent plus and around 5 percent–10 percent of all people who visit sleep centers are diagnosed with hyersomnia. The Diagnostic and Statistical Manual of Mental Disorders (DSM) criteria are:

1. At least one month.
2. Interferes with ADLs.
3. Is not related to nighttime sleep.
4. Not due to other MI or medical issues.
5. Three days at a time for at least two years.

The treatment can vary, and the condition may be an issue with the hypothalamus.

Sleep apnea (breathing issues) can impact around 10 percent plus of people in the US. The DSM-V categorizes apnea as those with apnea: *obstructive sleep apnea hypopnea*, *central sleep apnea*, or *sleep-related hypoventilation*.

Narcolepsy (passing out while awake) can impact thousands of people in the US. Narcolepsy involves uncontrollable sleep attacks. *Cataplexy* is a sudden loss of muscle tone. Narcolepsy is second on the sleep disorder list behind sleep apnea. Narcolepsy is an immediate entry into REM sleep. The hypothalamus has a cell communication issue caused by a gene mutation and some also believe that there is an immune system shutdown response.

Several genes factor in, but often there are environmental triggers. The onset is typically in late adolescence or early adulthood. The cataplexy condition (muscle tone loss) impacts around 75 percent of all people with narcolepsy. The sleep attacks can last minutes or move toward an hour, paralyzing the body during REM sleep. Some patients experience hallucinations, nightmares, and nighttime sleep issues. The population is around 1:1000 in America. To diagnose the condition, a *polysomnogram* can be administered overnight to monitor the vitals. There is also a *multiple sleep latency test* where onset to REM is measured. Narcolepsy is normally a chronic condition and there is no cure.

Sleepwalking and night terrors typically occur between age two to twelve and dissipate by adolescence. Adult night terrors typically occur from ages twenty to thirty. Around 1 percent–6 percent of children can be impacted by night terrors and around 1 percent of adults. These are some of the factors that impact the quality of sleep and general good health of people.

Sleep terror (night terrors) is repeated temporary arousal. The triggers can potentially be issues with CNS maturation, stress, sleep deprivation, physiological issues, and injuries. The average duration is fifteen minutes, and there is normally one episode per week. The age range is typically four to twelve, but they can occur at younger ages and in older ages including in adulthood. The population is up to 6 percent–7 percent with more males than females. The adult onset is normally between ages twenty to thirty and is often associated with an MI. Sleep terror involves abrupt arousal from extreme fear where attempts to comfort do not work, and the dreams are not recalled. *Nightmare disorder* has much less movement, with sleep terror people go back to sleep without ever having fully awakened. In nightmare disorder, there is recall and people wake up before the apex of the dream. The treatment for sleep terror is psychotherapy. Meds can include diazepam (Valium), which is a sleep-inducer sedative, which depresses the CNS. Normally sleep terrors decline with age. Also the amount of slow-wave sleep normally declines with age, and this is when the night terrors typically occur.

Nightmare disorder (dream anxiety disorder) is the occurrence of repeated dreams, which sleep feeds, which a person is threatened and frightened by, causing them to wake up. During the dream experience, there is a threat to one's life or safety. The fear normally increases during the dream, waking normally occurs prior to the dream climax. This is accompanied by anxiety, increased HR, and, if vivid, can be difficult to return to sleep. This cycle can cause irritability, anxiety, and depression. About half of the people who suffer from this condition may also have an MI and/or psychiatric disorder. These dreams can also be triggered by PTSD. The occasional or irregular nightmare is usually attributed to stress and/or anxiety.

Those most at risk for these dreams are highly creative people and highly sensitive people. The population in children is around 10 percent–50 percent. Around 3 percent of young adults have frequent nightmares and around 1 percent of adults have one or two nightmares per week. Women tend to have more than men. The DSM states that there must be repeated awakenings. When awake must be aware of surroundings, must cause distress in ADLs, and cannot have another root cause. Sleep terror differs because people are not fully awakened and don't remember the sleep terror episode or what caused the fear.

Sleepwalking aka *somnambulism* is repeating episodes of motor activity. Sleepwalking normally occurs in the first third of the night during the deepest sleep phase, sleepwalking can last from minutes to an hour, normally between five to fifteen minutes. There is normally no memory of the actions. There is a genetic factor with those having family members who have sleepwalking disorder, being ten times more likely to inherit the disorder. Physiological and psychological factors can trigger sleepwalking episodes. The DSM diagnosis is repeated incidents of motor activity where a person is unresponsive to communication and has a blank stare and dilated pupils. Sleepwalking is not recalled and there is no mental impairment upon waking. Sleepwalking is common from the ages of four to twelve, and normally peaks at around age twelve. As far as sleepwalking, around 10 percent–30 percent of all children experience a sleepwalking episode during their childhood. The population is around 1 percent–5 percent with more males than females, and, in adults, the population is around 1 percent. To diagnose, a *polysomnography* measures brain activity and physiological responses. In sleep terror, the difference is initial panic, but both have motor activity. Treatment can include hypnosis. Medications can include benzodiazepines (antianxiety), anxiolytics such as alprazolam (Xanax), or diazepam (Valium). The prognosis reflects that sleepwalking is typically done by around age fifteen with treatment. The major concern is injury. The sleep function is a strong indicator of brain function. The brain is a highly complex biological superstructure, and it contains many important mechanisms and components.

The *brain regions* are the *hindbrain*, which is the *rhombencephalon*; the *midbrain*, which is the *mesencephalon*; and the *forebrain*, which is the *prosencephalon*. Within these brain regions, there are many components, which each have a variety of brain functions.

The field of neuroscience research is ongoing and researchers continue to study, which brain functions are perpetuated by which modules of the brain. The *Brodmann areas* are the field of neurosciences brain *cytoarchitectonics* (mapping) of the functions of different brain areas, structure, and organization of the cells, and neuronal cell bodies that are associated with different brain functions.

The *cerebral cortex (cerebrum)* is one of the most important structures in the brain and it has eight different lobes and four lobes on each hemisphere: *frontal, parietal, temporal,* and *occipital*. The cerebral cortex is a thin layer of gray matter, which covers about two thirds of the brain, lying over or around most of the structures of the brain. It has folded bulges called *gyri*, which create deep fissures called *sulci* that add to its overall surface area. The cerebral cortex is the most highly developed part of the brain and it is responsible for people's cognitive elements, which include thinking, perceiving, judgment, humor, producing and understanding language, and more. It is the most recent structure to develop in the history of human brain evolution (higher functioning). The *dorsolateral prefrontal circuit* within the cerebral cortex is the last area of the brain to fully mature, and involves the most complex elements of EF such as adaptation, organization, and planning. The *orbitofrontal circuit* is involved in social impulse management. The cerebral cortex is the thinking and reasoning center. Some of the functions of the cerebral cortex are handled within certain brain regions (i.e., most people's language abilities are found on their left hemisphere). The *cerebral cortex* is divided into lobes.

The *parietal lobe* (somatosensory center) is involved in touch sensation from the rest of the body (the top of the sensory cortex receives signals from the lower body, the bottom of the strip receives impulses from the face and the head), the *frontal lobe* (EF) is involved in central and abstract emotion, the *occipital lobe* (vision), the *temporal lobe* is involved in memory, emotion, hearing, and language, and contains Broca's and Wernicke's language areas as well as many other important structures. The cerebral cortex and its units are the focal area for cognitive thinking, perception, and understanding. Damage to the cerebral cortex can cause major deficits up to and including death. There are some areas of the brain, which have been associated and have been connected to more specific functions.

Some of the areas that have been connected to motor movement and system relays include the thalamus, which is the relay center for motor signals to the cerebral cortex, is involved in both pain and attention, and it is an input center from the spinal cord via the CNS. The *fornix* is a C-shaped bundle for fiber that carries signals from the *hippocampus* to the thalamus. The *basal ganglia* is involved in motor procedure, body movement, action behavior, tic disorders, functions within a network which includes the striatum, and the substantia nigra. The cerebellum is a balance and coordination center, involves habitual muscle movement, specific motor function like throwing, the *motor cortex* is involved in voluntary movement but not specific movement. The *striatum* is a major input station for basal ganglia, thereby receiving information from the cerebral cortex. The striatum is divided into the caudate nucleus and the *putamen*. The striatum is known for planning and modulation of movement pathways, EF input, and working memory. The striatum area is activated by strong stimuli. The *ventral tegmental dopaminergic neurons* that innervate the striatum are associated with reward feeling. Huntington's disease (motor) is related to the striatium area. The substantia nigra is a very important brain area and hemoglobin is found in the dopaminergic neurons in the substantia nigra where it serves as an antioxidant. The substantia nigra releases dopamine, which is a key in motor function (lack of dopamine is correlated to Parkinson's disease) and *euphoria*. There are structures within the substantia nigra. The *pars compacta* is the input to the basal ganglia, which sends dopamine to the striatum. The *pars reticulata* is the output from the basal ganglia. The various brain structures communication via chemicals and electrical signals depending on the dynamics of the structures.

A *synapse* is a junction between neurons for the release and binding of NTs (neurotransmitter chemicals), presynaptic neuron axon terminal, a *synaptic cleft* is the space between neurons, a *dendrite* is the postsynaptic neuron, and with the NT lock and key system only certain NTs will fit into, certain receptors with specific shapes.

The *synaptic knob* is at the axonal end branch, which is adjacent to the synaptic cleft, when a nerve impulse reaches the knob, a NT is released from *vesicles* into the synapse, the NT diffuses across the gap and binds to receptors on the membrane of the adjacent neuron or muscle cell, this initiates the electrical charge in the membrane of the adjacent neuron leading to a nerve impulse in the cell. *Synaptic plasticity* is a special feature of brain cells that enables them to perform task to which they were initially not developed to conduct. *Spike-rate* and *spike-timing* are two characteristics that can strengthen or weaken *synaptic connections*. The threshold is the minimum amount of sensation to start a neural impulse, measured in *millivolts (mV)* the thresholds are inside and outside of the *neural membrane* and are referred to as the *sodium-potassium channel*.

Interneurons (INs) are neural impulses (action potentials) that travel along three types of paths: sensory, motor, and interneurons. INs are found in the CNS and there are roughly 2000–10000 INs for input and a similar number for output. Motor neurons in the brain fire and travel to the INs and then onto the sensory neurons for action. *Neural networks* are the neuronal network connections within the brain. Neurons are the building blocks of the CNS, communication between the neurons, and the signals are emitting from the axon of the neurons and into the receiving dendrites. *Excitatory neurons* amplify brain activity and account for about 80 percent of the neurons in the brain. *Inhibitory neurons* dampen brain activity and account for about 20 percent of the neurons in the brain. Gamma-aminobutyric acid (GABA) is the primary inhibitory NT in the brain. The brain communicates via different mechanisms and structures with the rest of the body.

The nervous system is a complex sensory system, which registers senses between brain, spinal cord, and the nerves. The nerves relay electrical impulses throughout the body via the nervous system. The motor cortex is a brain mechanism, which communicates on each side of the frontal lobes, which operate the opposite side of the body. The parietal region is part of the cerebral cortex; positioned at the back and top of the brain; involved in sensation, perception, and the integration of sensory input; involved in spatial relations in the visual field and also in touch, pressure, and temperature. The *motor homunculus* is involved with the cortex, muscle groups, hands, and face.

The myelin sheath is the white matter, which coats the neurons in the brain, is the electrical aspect in the electrochemical process of signal transmission, and increases signal conductivity, and can increase the speed of conduction via *salutatory conduction*. *Demyelination* can lead to MS. The *nodes of Ranvier* are the spaces (gaps) between the myelin sheath coating, which is on the neurons and which helps to speed impulses. Neurotransmitters send electrical and chemical signals and if the gaps are too large for electrical signals then the signals are converted to chemical signals, which are read by the synapses. Neurotransmitters are critical within healthy brain function.

Acetylcholine is *cholinergic* (choline), is an essential chemical that is concentrated in basal ganglia that acts between neurons and allows for signals to transfer between neurons, is involved in motor/muscle control, learning, memory, sleeping, and dreaming. A lack of acetylcholine is associated with Alzheimer's disease, which involves a loss of cells in the basal forebrain involved in sensory and motor control. *Amyloid plaque aggregation* and *tau neurofibrillary tangles* (causing microtubules to disintegrate) in the brain leading to neuroinflammation are also considerations for AD.

Dopamine is highly concentrated in the substantia nigra, midbrain, and hypothalamus. Dopamine is released by the substantia nigra within the dopamine pathway, is a modulator in drive, which involved in reward euphoria. If there is an excess of dopamine, this is associated with schizophrenia, and it may also play a role in manic activity. Dopamine is critical in movement and motor control, cognition, learning, and also mood, a lack of dopamine is associated with Parkinson's disease. There is progressive striatal and cortical dopamine receptor dysfunction in Huntington's disease, which is an *autosomal dominant neurodegenerative* disease, which can cause motor, psychiatric, and cognitive symptoms. There is also a loss of GABA neurons (inhibitory function) in the striatum. Endorphins are temporary elevators involved in reward and pain reduction, which are released during exercise.

GABA is the primary *action potential* inhibitory NT in the brain. GABA is for physiological and mental slowing. The GABA NT also controls the speed of nerve transmission, and it is involved in muscle tone and in the chloride flow in the neural network. *Monoamine oxidase* is the primary enzyme that breaks down the NT neurochemicals.

Somatostatin is a *neuropeptide* that inhibits thyroid-stimulating hormone (TSH) and is a growth hormone inhibitor. *Substance P* (neuropeptide) is a pain transmitter within the CNS and excitatory response to pain along with glutamate and lowers blood pressure (BP) for relaxation and also may play a role in mood disorders. Substance P also helps to stimulate the vomiting reflex from the medulla. The various mechanisms are crucial for the proper functioning and communication amongst the various brain structures.

The hypothalamus is another vital brain structure, and it is involved in autonomic processes like body chemistry such as libido; *lateral hypothalamus*, hunger, eating, and drinking regulation; the *ventromedial* is for satiety or fullness, insulin regulation, it also governs the body temperature and the hormone-producing endocrine system. The nervous and endocrine systems secrete hormones into the bloodstream for metabolism. The hypothalamus is also involved in *psychogenic functions* or mood functions such as emotions and the perceptions of feeling good or other. The hypothalamus sits below the thalamus. The hypothalamus is also a key component in the stress response.

In the *hypothalamic-pituitary-adrenal (HPA) axis,* cycle after activation by the *locus coeruleus,* which is the lowest part of the brain at brain stem and found in the pons, along with SNS activation of carbs, fats, and glucose for response energy. *Corticotropin-releasing factor (CRF)* is released by the hypothalamus, which stimulates the pituitary gland to initiate the heavily regulated stress response. There is an interaction with the amygdala, which is associated with fear and anxiety. The pituitary gland releases *adrenocorticotropic hormone* (ACTH), which in turn reaches the adrenal gland to release cortisol, corticosteroid hormone, a *glucocorticoid,* which increases the availability of carbs, fats, and glucose for the response. The glucocorticocoid has an inhibitory negative feedback loop effect on the hypothalamus to stop releasing corticotropin. If cortisol released within the stress activation process remains in the system for too long, it can begin to break down muscle, decrease the *inflammatory response,* suppress the immune system, and also create depression and psychosis on a neurological level.

Cortisol is a glucocorticoid released from the adrenal gland during stress response by the SNS after receiving the message from the pituitary gland in the brain via the ACTH. Cushing's disease is when the pituitary gland makes too much ACTH. Addison's disease is when the adrenal gland does not produce enough cortisol. *Hypopituitarism* is when the pituitary gland does not signal the adrenal gland to produce enough cortisol. Cortisol levels can be reduced via *parasympathetic action* or *opposing neuromodulator reactions* or releases such as in enjoyment or euphoria-provoking actions. Cortisol is involved in bones; the circulatory system; the immune system; metabolism of fats, carbohydrates, and proteins; the nervous system; and sympathetic stress response system within the HPA cycle. Normal levels taken at 8:00 a.m. in the morning range from 6–23 mg/dL, whereby the morning is when the levels of cortisol are typically the highest, and levels are typically lowest around midnight.

Oxytocin can be a neuromodulator in the brain to emit pleasure and/or offset stress hormones such as cortisol, and a lack of the oxytocin receptors (OXTR) is linked to maladaptive and aggressive behavior.

The pituitary gland is heavily involved in homeostasis, contains adrenocorticotropic, which is a modulator in the stress-response cycle, releases from the anterior pituitary gland after the hypothalamus releases CRF. When ACTH reaches the adrenal gland, cortisol is released within this stress-response cycle. Cushing's disease is when the pituitary gland makes too much ACTH. Corticotropin interaction with the hypothalamus is regulated by glucocorticoids (cortisol) in the *negative feedback loop.*

The adrenal gland is part of the endocrine system, sits on top of the kidneys, releases cortisol in the stress-response cycle, and can also release norepinephrine as hormone in this region versus as an

NT like in the brain. In the HPA stress cycle, persistent anxiety or withdrawal (depression), either real or imagined, can trigger the HPA stress cycle. The *Lazarus Appraisal Theory* postulates that we consider reaction and coping, which determines our responses.

The hypothalamic-pituitary-adrenal axis is activated via the locus coeruleus, which is the within the pons and is located at the lowest part of the brain, near the brain stem, and is the primary sensory connection structure, which also stimulates norepinephrine production in other areas of the brain. The LC controls the tempo of the brain for arousal and vigilance, and modulates the ANS and SNS for on and off instructions and communicates via *neural nerve circuits*. LC modulates the SNS arousal, which includes the release of carbs, fats, and glucose for response energy (energy is removed and/or depleted from other key areas of the body to prepare for action). The HPA axis and the locus coeruleus are linked within the limbic system, which is the emotional and memory-processing system. Interpretations are made in milliseconds within the limbic system.

The limbic system is located in the *rhinencephalon* area of the brain (a small donut-shaped network of neurons), which holds deep-rooted emotions including pain, anger, hunger, thirst, pleasure, and sex. The system contains the hippocampus, anterior thalamic nuclei, fornix, the amygdala, the mammillary bodies, gyrus, and septal areas, with connections to the locus coeruleus. The limbic system interacts with the HPA axis within milliseconds to transmit reaction information to stimuli either internal or external. The locus coeruleus transmits information to the hypothalamus. Some theories state that the limbic system may be larger in women, with a liability being depression and structural abnormalities of the limbic system are highly correlated with depression.

The locus coeruleus is located in the pons, the primary synthesis of the norepinephrine NT that is associated with fight or flight, occurs here, and interacts within the limbic system and HPA axis cycle. The pons/locus coeruleus is the lowest part of the brain located at the brain stem and is the primary sensory modulator and sensory connection. There are also connections to *endogenous opiates* such as dopamine, which is involved in pleasure and/or reward euphoria. Emotions can lead to stress and there are various factors that can impact people's responses.

There are personal and environmental factors that can trigger the HPA stress-response cycle. The influence can be brain system and function including genetic constructs (i.e., temperament, personality, and nurturing affect response), which can be positive adaptive reactions or maladaptive reactions. Emotions can be managed in advance by practicing emotion-focused coping. Within the HPA response cycle and interaction with the limbic system, we quickly appraise a secondary appraisal, which is our evaluation of our own resources available to cope with the problem or our perceived control, which may alter the *primary appraisal.*

Factors in the appraisal are cognitive such as memory, focus, judgment, outlook, temperament (i.e., anxious or calm); emotional symptoms such as moodiness, irritable, agitation, overwhelmed, isolation, and depression; physical symptoms such as bodily functions, regularity, function, etc.; and also behavioral symptoms, which include patterns such as eating, sleeping, relations, substance use, and habits. A stress marker in saliva is *amylase.* A *social stress test* such as the *Holmes-Rahe Social Readjustment Rating Scale (SRRS)* via LCUs (life changing events) can account for the number of life stressors.

Burnout can eventually lead to mental exhaustion. In the HPA cycle, another factor is *social defeat* whereby the association of losing a social confrontation or social confrontations within socialization and/or struggling within one's social role in a social *dyad* can create anxiety and fear. The thought of loss of access to social role position can heavily impact the cycle within the appraisal. If someone is distressed over time, this can potentially create GAD where there are higher metabolic rates and hyperactive brain circuits, with continuing and excessive excitation.

The *septo-hippocampal circuit* links the septum, amygdala, hippocampus, and fornix, and signals from hippocampus to thalamus. This circuit is involved in response regulation as well. GAD can lead to dysfunction in the *noradrenergic* (locus coeruleus) and *serotonergic* (rostral and caudal raphe nuclei) neurotransmission, and can disrupt the *innervation* to the *prefrontal cortex*, which can impact EF. There also can be decreased activity to the midbrain periaqueductal gray matter (PAG), which can result in defensive behavior and *posture freezing*, and also can create descending modulation of pain along the *spinothalamic tract* (spine origination area).

Overactivation within the stress response system can lead to transient and chronic illness, increased BP, hypertension, muscle decline, GI ulcers, reproductive issues, immunosuppression, premature aging, depression, and other psychological issues. *Sensitization* can also occur whereby someone is hyperresponsive to new stressors. The damage within the brain and nervous systems can create *maladaptive* adjustments and responses to stress. If the stress is prolonged, it can actually begin to change personality and alter the existing biochemistry (neurodegeneration). The worst types of stressors are prolonged, unexpected, and unmanageable. These types are the most damaging.

However some stress triggers can create a healthy bio response and *neurogenesis* neuroplasticity, and is this is why empirical experiences have become a newer focus within *psychotherapy*, based on this action potential. Some triggers are tied to *human drive*, and stress is a natural component within drive. People need to think about reducing their stress, and they need to develop adaptive ways to reduce their stress levels.

Exercise, breaks, creating more *predictability* in routine, discovery and planning of scenarios and responses, can help to protect versus the unexpected. There must also be a willingness to support the positive adaptive mechanisms for success. Maladaptive habits and addictions can lead to heightened hypersensitivity and can have a profound effect on one's mental and physical well-being. If there has been trauma involved or a trauma caused stress, a *critical incident stress debriefing (CISD)* could be highly beneficial. Eastern healing and meditation practices can be researched and also medications.

Medications could be looked at including *dexamethasone*, which is a glucocorticoid steroid for immune suppression, anxiolytic (minor tranquilizers) such as benzodiazepines such as alprazolam (Xanax), diazepam (Valium), and lorazepam (Ativan) at moderate dosages. The anxiolytics are good when concurrent with *selective serotonin reuptake inhibitor (SSRI)* to combat the early (first several weeks) anxiogenic impact of biofeedback via the serotonergic autoreceptors in raphe nuclei area. Tricyclic antidepressants (TCAs) and monoamine oxidase inhibitor (MAOIs) have greater S/Es. *Picamilon* is an over-the-counter (OTC) drug, which can cross the BBB and activate GABA receptors, which can produce an anxiolytic affect.

Seyle's General Adaptation Syndrome (GAS) considers stress and long-term chemical changes. A predictable biological pattern in people allows for *homeostasis* and *restoration*. There is a limited supply of energy to deal with stress. There are several stages within the GAS model. These are the following:

1. Alarm stage: The HPA axis and SNS produce instant energy. If the chemicals are not used in the response they can damage the system over time, HR, blood flow, etc.
2. Resistance stage: It involves the solution, repair and recovery, and reduction of adaptive energ. Without this recovery and with depletion to body stores, the cyclical overload can cause major damage to the biological systems. Hormones do remain in the ready state.
3. Exhaustion stage: Involves overload, maladaptive, creates dysfunction, and many areas are exposed, including the hippocampus within the HPA axis.

The *parasympathetic nervous system (PSNS)* is the organic bio system that normally counterbalances the SNS and it returns people to homeostasis.

Everyone has their own unique breaking point, a critical stress point which goes beyond their threshold area, and this is why people must not ignore the signs and symptoms that are impacting them. It is much easier to break down smaller concentrations of biological impairment than the heavy consolidations. There are also some other structures that play a strong role in bioorganic management.

The *medulla oblongata* is involved in autonomic functions and is the lower half of the brainstem connected to the cerebral cortex via the pons, is involved in life support functions and impacts cardiac, respiratory, vomiting, vasomotor centers (vasodilation and vasoconstrictor activity in blood vessels), heart rate, blood pressure, and is a relay connected to the reticular formation. There are nerves in this area, which react to the level of carbon dioxide in the bloodstream. If levels are too low the brain automatically adjusts breathing, sending a signal for the diaphragm to contract. There is also a backup system called the *hypoxic drive*, which simulates breathing when oxygen levels fall. If a person goes unconscious and regains consciousness, this restarts the respiratory drive.

The *reticular formation* is a series of netlike cells in midbrain, which are involved in somatic motor control (raphe nuclei within the reticular formation modulate the activity of the cerebral cortex), *neuronal circuits* connecting the brainstem (pons/locus coeruleus and medulla oblongata) to the cerebral cortex, neuronal network circuits of the RAS are modulated by complex interactions between NTs, the RAS contains choline (choline is the primary component of the neurotransmitter acetylcholine; a receptor or synapse using acetylcholine as its neurotransmitter is cholinergic). Choline is concentrated in areas such as the liver and the brain, acetylcholine acts in both the sympathetic and parasympathetic system, acetylcholine is released from *postganglionic sympathetic neurons*. The RAS also contains adrenergic components (adrenergic have to do with adrenaline/ epinephrine and noradrenaline/norepinephrine). Adrenergic pathways connect with the locus coeruleus (the nucleus in the pons area of the brain stem involved in physiological responses to stress and panic [HPA axis modulation], and is the principle site for the brain synthesis of the norepinephrine/noradrenaline NT), noradrenaline/norepinephrine can be released directly into the blood via the *adrenal medulla* (part of the adrenal gland, the adrenal gland doesn't release epinephrine/adrenaline or norepinephrine/noradrenaline as NTs, but rather as hormones, the amino acids, *tyrosine* and *phenylalanine*, are converted into the *catecholamines*—epinephrine, norepinephrine, and dopamine— high catecholamine levels in the blood are associated with stress, the HPA axis within the SNS), and too many activations can lead to *toxicity* in the CNS and nuclei in the brain stem. To note, a deficiency in the NT monoamine oxidase (role is degradation of the NTs) can also be responsible for higher levels of NTs in the bloodstream (pathways for RAS include facial nerves motor neurons, emotions from the limbic system/HPA axis stimulates the reticular-activating system (RAS aka the *extrathalamic control modulatory system*), this area is connected to the reticular formation and is responsible for arousal (somatic motor control relay), also relays through the spine via the CNS for balance and posture, pain modulation to the cerebral cortex from the spine, has projections to the thalamus, the dorsal hypothalamus and cerebral cortex, and its signal can reach the cerebrum. The RAS is also connected to the substantia nigra, which releases dopamine. Dopamine is an excitatory chemical. The RAS is also involved in the sleep-wake cycle where less neuronal firing occurs, and in the firing of neurons back into an attention state. *Habituation* is a process where the brain learns to ignore repetitive nonthreatening stimuli (i.e., things heard at night which can be filtered out in order for one to go into sleep cycle or repetitive stimuli from people). People with issues involving pain, alertness, and coordination may have damage to their reticular formation.

The pons is the relay center and nuclei for autonomic and sensory functions. The pons contain the locus coeruleus and is involved in arousal (HPA), autonomic functions, sleep, and is part of the lower brain stem (hindbrain), just above the spinal cord, is a major pathway for sensory information between the body (via spinal cord) and the higher functioning areas of the brain. The pons connect the cerebral cortex (thin layer of gray tissue that appears gray because its nerves lack the insulation of other parts of the brain which appear white; the folded bulges on cerebral cortex are called gyri, which create deep fissures called sulci which add to its capacity) with the medulla oblongata (hindbrain). The medulla oblongata controls autonomic functions, coordination of body movements, and signal relays. This area also controls facial expression. The pons is also involved in dreams, hearing, equilibrium, taste, touch and pain, motor eye movement, mastication, swallowing, and salivation. If the pons becomes demylineated, balance, walking, touch, speech, and swallowing are all impacted.

The amygdala is found at the end of the hippocampal arm, lower levels of MAO are associated with reduced volume in the amygdala, an area which is associated with emotional regulation, moral decision-making, *declarative-episodic bio-memory*, encoding for retrieval, charged (reactivated) via cues in neural nets, attention and emotional filter, facial recognition, response to defined stimuli, and works with *ventral hippocampus* (memory). Damage to the amygdala has heavy social impact and prevents new learning which is *anterograde*, people can remember the past, but nothing new. *Retrograde* amnesia is not remembering the past.

The *anterior cingulate cortex* (ACC) is involved in the EF areas of behavior regulation; rational cognitive functions such as reward anticipation, decision-making, empathy, and impulse control, motivation; is an autonomic activation center; has projections to the thalamus; is both an *effector* and can be a *cortical suppressor*; is involved in transient mood changes, modulation of emotional response, strategic control to frontolateral brain. The ACC has connections to the corpus callosum (relay bundle between hemispheres). The ACC also has Brodmann areas (24, 32, and 33) which are involved in autonomic functions (BP, HR and rational cognitive function, reward anticipation, decision-making, empathy, emotion). The ACC is also involved in the effort of early learning and problem solving, as well as measuring stimulus via conflict, error detection, attention, motivation, and modulation of emotional response.

The *dentate/cingulate gyrus* is involved in emotional impact and awareness while being part of the *hippocampal formation* and it is thought to contribute to new episodic memories, have a role in depression, define personality, cognitive style, patterns of behavior, and is one of the few areas to have high rates of *neurogenesis*. The limbic cortex is connected to the frontal, parietal, temporal lobes, and dendate gyrus, which is involved in behavior.

The *mesolimbic reward pathway* includes the *dopamine pathway* and the *serotonin pathway*. The serotonin pathway involves regulation of mood, cognition, memory, sleep function, and more. The dopamine pathway involves reward (motivation), pleasure (euphoria), motor function (Parkinson's disorder related to substantia nigra structure and the lack of dopamine), compulsion, and persecution.

Norepinephrine is from the locus coeruleus in pons, when well regulated, is a mood stabilizer, involved in arousal as well. In those with AD, there is a 70 percent loss of locus coeruleus cells that provide norepinephrine. Norepinephine is also an antiinflammatory agent around the neurons, glial cells, and blood vessels in the neocortex and the hippocampus.

Serotonin is a neurotransmitter, which regulates mood, impulses, and emotion. When well regulated, is a great mood stabilizer. Low levels of serotonin are associated with depression and also with *schizophrenic disorder* when in correlation with higher levels of dopamine. Serotonin is also associated with cardio, apetite, sleep, as well as memory and learning. Serotonin is also involved in muscle contraction and endocrine function.

The prefrontal cortex (higher-level EF) is involved in emotional regulation and inhibitory (impulse) control. The raphe nuclei, the medial portion of the reticular formation, sits below the substantia nigra, which is within the dopamine pathway, near the brain stem and is involved in the synthesis and release of serotonin, which plays a role in mood regulation, depression, and anxiety (within the serotonin pathway system) and is also associated with circadian rhythm (with transmission via the *dorsomedial hypothalamus* altering serotonin for sleep-wake cycles) and *pain sensation* (in pain sensation, they regulate the release of enkephalins, which inhibit pain sensation).

The septum is a membrane thought to be a part of the limbic system relay, at around three to six months old, an infant's membranes should normally fuse together to separate the left and right hemispheres of the brain. A cavity or void in this area can be associated with neuropsychiatric disorders such as bipolar disorder.

Memory is diffused bilaterally in the brain to several places and at the same time memory is localized. The caudate nucleus sits alongside the thalamus on both hemispheres and is innervated by dopamine neurons. The dopamine neurons originate from the ventral tegmental area (VTA) and the substantia nigra. The caudate nucleus is part of striatum, which is involved in the coordination of movement and brain cells that involve cognitive function. This system is heavily involved in learning and in implicit procedural memory. The hippocampus is located in the medial temporal lobe and is involved in the encoding of declarative memory (facts and events). The temporal cortex is involved in memory storage.

Hyperthymesia or *highly superior autobiographical memory (HSAM)* is when people can recall the vast majority of personal experiences in their lives. People with HSAM spend a lot of time thinking about the past and have an extraordinary ability to recall the past. Hyperthymestic people can auto recall events based on cues. The temporal lobe and the caudate nucleus are enlarged on the magnetic resonance imaging (MRI) of those with HSAM, and this is also linked to obsessive–compulsive disorder (OCD). There can be EF deficits with HSAM, which involves the *frontostriatal circuit.* The circuit plays a role in OCD, ASD, and attention-deficit/hyperactivity disorder (ADHD).

The caudate dysfunction in OCD involves transmission between the thalamus and the *orbitofrontal cortex,* which is highly involved in the higher level elements of EF. There is a glucose metabolic deficiency in the caudate. The caudate nucleus has also been related to the emotional response from visual beauty (neural correlates, which can include romantic love). Women tend to have larger caudate nucleus and women's senses are often more acute. The caudate nucleus is also involved in threshold control, which is the regulation of an excitatory reaction.

The hippocampus is involved in cognition, spatial memory, and *memory docking* formations. The *dorsal hippocampus* formation can realize neurogenesis of GC granules and excitability in dentate gyrus. The left hippocampus is involved in *recall* (bits and pieces) (i.e., what, when, why). The hippocampus is necessary for developing new memories and then relaying the STM to LTM. The mammillary bodies are inside the temporal lobe and are for learning and memory. There are also certain areas of the brain that are involved in brain maintenance and protection.

Glial cells provide nutrients for the neurons, there are around ten trillion nerve cells, 90 percent are glial, and the end of one axon can have 1000 terminals. The CSF provides nutrients and cushioning for the brain and spinal cord. The CSF is restored from the choroid plexus, located in the ventricles, which transport

CSF and ultimately protect the brain from trauma. The choriod plexus is a barrier between the blood and CSF, supplies CSF, and is located behind the pons and the medulla oblongata. The aqueduct of Sylvius is a canal with CSF that connects the third and fourth ventricles.

The third ventricle is located in the middle of the cerebral hemispheres, is between the left and right thalamus, protects the brain versus trauma, and is a pathway for CSF. The fourth ventricle forms the central canal of the spinal cord and is located behind the pons and medulla oblongata. It helps protect the brain from trauma.

The lateral ventricles protect the brain from trauma, are pathway for CSF, and are located within the cerebrum.

The *dura mater* is a tough fibrous sac that covers the brain, the outermost of three layers of *meninges*, responsible for keeping in the CSF. A *subdural hematoma* can result from head trauma, when there is a collection of blood between the *arachnoid* and the *dura*. The meningesare a membrane that surrounds the brain and spinal cord. When there is dysfunction in the brain, people's health can be heavily impacted.

Neural disorders involve a disease of the brain, spinal cord, or nervous system pathways, via a medical or psychological disorder. *Brain damage* can vary on the level of severity, depending on the area of the damage. With damage to the hippocampus, a person cannot form new memories; with damage to the Broca's area, a person cannot form speech; with damage to the Wernicke's area, people cannot understand language; damage to the frontal lobe can highly impact people's behavior and EF, hypothalamus, endocrine system issues (thyroid body temperature and TSH), adrenal, pancreas (insulin), sex glands, and HPA dysfunction.

Apoptosis is the gradual disintegration of nuclear components (axonal injury). ALS is associated with *chromatolyzed neuronal cells*, giving rise to the motor function impairment after elimination of EPSPs. Alzheimer's disease is also associated with neurodegeneration.

Nissl bodies are the site of protein synthesis in neuronal cell bodies, show changes under various physiological conditions and in pathological conditions where they may dissolve and disappear. Chromatoysis is used to distinguish the apoptotic process in neuronal cells where the Nissl substance disintegrates.

Nissl staining, use of agents like *thionin* and *aniline* to stain the *Nissl bodies*, which are *rough endoplastimic reticulum* (RER), and are at the site of protein synthesis in neurons. The cell body and dendrites of neurons can been seen.

Chronic traumatic encephalopathy (CTE) is neurodegeneration following repetitive concussive and subconcussive brain trauma. The aggregation and accumulation of *hyperphoshorylated tau* and *TAR DNA-binding protein 43 (TDP-43)* are involved. Tau proteins are abundant in the distal portions of axons on neurons of the central nervous system. They are proteins that interact with *tubulin* to modulate and stabilize axonal *microtubules* via *isoforms* and *phosphorylation*. When tau proteins are defective and can no longer stabilize microtubules, they can result in dementias and AD.

The brain also has twelve cranial nerves that are highly functioning specific. The *brain cranial nerves* are the *olfactory nerve (CN1),* which is for the sense of smell. The sense of smell is a *chemical* sense. The cranial nerve is for smell and can regenerate. The parts are of the organic system are the *bulb* and the *tract*. The tract fibers project from bulb to brain. Olfactory hair cells in nasal mucosa roots end in the bulb. *Chemoreceptors* are sensory receptors that transduce (detect) a chemical signal in the environment and turn it into an *action potential.*

Olfactory sensory neurons have *cilia* that protrude and interact with stimuli. The stimuli activate an action potential, which travels to the bony *cribriform plate* and then to the *glomeruli* within the *olfactory bulb*. The *olfactory cleft* is close to the brain, but the signal travels slowly, so it takes numerous molecules to trigger a response. Smell does not conduct through the thalamus or the midbrain, it conducts directly to the olfactory bulb and onto the cerebral cortex.

Humans have about twelve million olfactory receptors compared to about four billion in a bloodhound. Bloodhounds can smell the individual cells that have fallen from whatever they are searching for. The sense of smell is tied into the limbic system, which is involved in emotional response, and interacts with the amygdala and the hippocampus, which are also involved in memories. The strength of the emotional attachment tied to a particular scent can elicit a profound ability to recall the scent later from long-term memory. The association of smell, when tied with a strong emotion, is one of the most powerful memory recall triggers that humans possess.

To test the CN1, use a smell alcohol pad, coffee, tobacco, cloves, and while eyes are closed have people identify them. Colds can cause *parosmia*, which is the perversion of the sense of smell. Other issues with this organic system can be tumors, compression, lesions, and more.

The *optic nerve (CN2)* is for vision, visual acuity and fields, and does not regenerate. The parts are of the organic system are the tract, nerve, chiasm, and oculomotor nerve. The highly specialized parts are the rods and cones. Photoreceptors have pigments in receptor cells that absorb light energy and trigger action potentials.

Vertebrates have camera-type eyes that are capable of forming clear images. The eyeball has a lens, *sclera* (outer white), *choroid* (middle, dark brown, with blood vessels and pigment that absorbs stray light), a receptor-packed *retina*, and a transparent *cornea* covering the front of the eye. Choroid tissue extends from in front of the lens to form the iris. The *ciliary body* is an extension of the choroid layer. It functions with the suspensory ligament to attach and support the lens. The *aqueous humor* is a watery material between the cornea and the lens. The *vitreous humor* is a gelatinous material within the eye.

Focusing of the lens is called *accommodation*. Focusing in humans is done by changing the shape of the lens by the *ciliary muscles*. When distant objects are viewed, the ciliary muscles relax, while nearby objects cause the ciliary muscle to contract, reducing the tension of the suspensory ligaments and allowing the lens to assume a thicker shape. The cornea bends the light, but the lens finishes the focusing. With age, people's ability to focus their lens decreases. Glasses can correct this type of focusing ability. Nearsightedness occurs when the eye is too long and the plane of focus is behind the retina. Farsightedness occurs when the eye is too short and the plane of the focus is behind the retina. *Astigmatism* is an abnormality in the shape of the lens or the cornea, so that part of it does not focus properly.

Stereoscopic vision is the overlapping of each eye's visual field. Each eye sees the image from a slightly different angle and the brain creates a 3D image. This allows people to perceive depth of field. The rods and cones are the two types of photoreceptors. Rods cannot distinguish colors and do not provide sharp vision. They are more sensitive to dim light, are better at detecting motion than cones, and this is called *scotopic vision*. Rods are more abundant in the periphery of the retina. Rods have several hundred stacked membranous disks that contain the pigment, *rhodopsin*, there are around 120 million rod receptors in the eye normally, and they are 1000 times as sensitive as cones. Cones function in color vision. They produce sharp images, but they require bright light, and this is called *photopic vision*.

Cones are most dense in the back of the eye called the *fovea*. This area has the greatest visual acuity. There are seven million cones in the eye normally. They are concentrated in *macula* (yellow center of fovea in fovea centralis). There are three types of cones, and each responds to one color (red, green, or blue). This occurs because the visual pigment is slightly different for each color. The different combinations of red (64 percent of color concentration), green (32 percent of color concentration), and blue (2 percent of color concentration) produce other colors. For example, the brain interprets signals that come from the red and green cones as yellow. Red and green are concentrated in the fovea centralis.

The eye moves constantly so that light from the focused object doesn't fall on the fovea centralis. Red is not seen by the rods at night, so red lights don't spoil night vision. Rods and cones signal neurons called *bipolar cells*, which in turn signal ganglion cells. The processing of visual information occurs in the retina as well as the brain. In the dark, sodium gates are open and the cells are depolarized and release a neurotransmitter. Some bipolar cells are inhibited (hyperpolarized) by the neurotransmitter and other bipolar cells are stimulated (depolarized). When the light strikes *rhodopsin molecules*, their shape changes, causing sodium gates to close. As a result, the cells become polarized and the neurotransmitter becomes stimulated and bipolar cells that are inhibited by the neurotransmitter become stimulated, and the bipolar cells that are stimulated become inhibited.

Axons from the ganglion cells pass in front of the retina and then form the optic nerve, which join at the *optic chiasm*. The information is then transmitted to the thalamus and then onto the *primary visual cortex*. The information from the left part of the retina of each eye travels to the left primary visual cortex. Information from the right side of the retina travels to the right primary visual cortex. This produces visual *integration*.

There is a vision *critical period* and also a vision extended *sensitivity* period. The critical period is between three months to eight months for binocular vision, but visual sensitivity period extends out to at least age three. To test the C2 nerve, people can conduct the test by holding up fingers, and they can also use any other type of visual cue testing (i.e., the Snellen or E chart for acuity, and/or reading newsprint and determining far objects.

For *developmental vision* the progression should be as follows:

- Infant—should have a red reflex, be aware of light/dark, the random movement of the eye is due to retinal

development, *convergence* develops at two to three months, and hand-eye coordination appears
- Six months—can distinguish colors
- School-age—can begin to see refractive errors
- Amblyopia— reduced visual acuity in one eye
- Astigmatism—curve of the cornea prevents correct refraction
- Strabismus—eyes do not fix on the same point, muscle imbalance, 3 percent–5 percent pop.
- Diplopia—cross-eyes, double vision occurs with strabismus, muscular weakness; condition is correctable
- Myopia—light focuses in front of the retina (nearsighted)
- Hyperopia—light reflects beyond retina (farsighted)

Adults:
- Presbyopia—degenerative changes, loss of ability to accommodate to close object
- Cataracts—lens of the eye becomes opaque due to thickening and sclerosis, occur in 95 percent of those over sixty-five years old
- Macular degeneration—unable to distinguish fine print, see only gray in the center of the visual field
- Glaucoma—most common cause of blindness in those over forty, loss of peripheral vision, slow buildup of pressure, light sensitivity, light adaptation, optic nerve damage

Issues:
- Toddlers and school-age—rub eyes, squint, blink, headaches, and double vision
- Inspect:
- Eyelids/lashes—position, appearance, lid tags, fissures, ptosis
- Conjunctiva—color

- Sclera—color
- Cornea—opacity, light reflection
- Iris/pupil—shape, equality, color
- Lens—clarity, opacity
- Anterior chamber—depth
- Optic disc—yellowish-pink and is round or oval, clearly defined edges
- Fundus—orange
- Blood vessels—extend outward from optic disk

Test:
- Visual acuity—well-lit room, test both eyes at twenty feet away from chart
- 20/20 = normal with functional optic pathway
- 20/200 = legally blind, light, hand movement in front of face
- Pupils = distant dilate, near constrict
- Accommodation = convexity of lens to bring near objects in focus
- The six cardinal fields of eye gaze examine the CN nerves (III, IV, VI)

Eye Charting codes include:
- Right eye = OD
- Left eye = OS
- Both eyes = OU
- Sphere = Lens power measured in diopters, minus is *nearsighted* and plus is *far*
- Cylinder = Lens power for astigmatism via measure of meridians
- Axis = Is 1:180 of lens meridian, 90 is the vertical, and 180 is the horizontal
- Add = Magnifying on bottom of multifocal lenses to correct *presbyopia*

Some *visual effects* are *cognitive illusions,* which are unconscious inferences (ambiguous, distorting, paradox, and fiction). With an *ambiguous* perceptual switch, the interpretation of the parts make the whole consistent (i.e., the *necker cube* shows impossible line joining for depth) where the brain knows it is an impossible figure. The human brain scans from the left to right (naturally), within perceptual switching. The neural network has interchangeable stable states. *Figure ground distinction* is cognitive pattern matching where the overall figure versus pieces determines the mental interpretation, identifying figure from the background (i.e., the *Rubin vase* which involves edge assignment and shape perception), with competing stimuli (profiles or vase) and the optical illusion.

Distorting involves size, length, position, and curvature (i.e., the *café wall illusion* where the horizontal lines are straight, but *hue* to competing arrangements of vertical squares create an optical illusion, with the black and white contrast. *Paradox illusions* are aka the visually impossible, (i.e., the *Penrose stairs* continual descension in a clockwise direction. Other visual effects include the *Waterfall lithograph,* which is a two-dimensional illusion of depth and the *Penrose triangle,* which is also two dimensions. *Fictions* involve when an image is perceived even though not the stimulus and the brain fills in the gaps.

An *afterimage* is when people stare at the color green, then look at white surface, and the AI is red. If people stare at yellow, then look at a white surface, the AI is the color blue. The *autokinetic effect* involves the effect when a light is projected onto a dark wall, it is stared at, and then it will appear to move.

In color blindness, people cannot see red or green shades or blue or yellow shades which is *dichromatic,* while *monochromatic* can only see shades of gray.

The *contingent perceptual aftereffect* involves excessive stimulation and *competing stimuli* of a specific type (brightness, color, position, size, and movement) and leads to physiological imbalance. *Lateral inhibition* involves the receptive field of the retina, when light and dark cones compete with each other to become active, which inhibits adjacent receptors and causes *highlighted edges.*

The *motion aftereffect* involves looking at an object for a period of time that is moving in one direction. Then looking at a stationary object, the stationary object appears to move in the opposite direction. The nerves detect and activate during this effect. The *stroboscopic motion effect* is a cyclical, rotational, wagon-wheel effect, appearance of moving backwards (slow-motion effect), and is used with film and cartoons for motion The *motion parallax* is using perceptual cues such as distance, motion, depth perception, and proximity effect perception of depth and speed. Closer objects appear to move faster, while distant objects seem to move slower. *Relative speed* is when the speed between two objects is measured relative to fixed object.

The *phi phenomenon* is the continuous motion when viewing separate objects in rapid succession with lights going on and off which creates motion. *Vision persistence* is when the black frames on movies are not seen between frames, because the image lasts longer on the eye than shown.

In *visual perception*, proximity is when stimuli are perceived as belonging to a group if close. *Similarity* is when stimuli are perceived as belonging to a group based on appearance. *Continuity* is based on form perceived as belonging to group. *Closure* is the use of visual top-down processing and gap filling. *Constancy* (i.e., *shape constancy*) is the ability to maintain constant perception of an object, whereby movement doesn't change the shape. *Size* involves distance estimation and with familiarity, people can maintain knowledge of whether the distance is close or far. *Shape* entails effects with angles and illusions, and familiarity is the key. *Brightness* involves familiarity (i.e., people know a brick wall is normally red, but at night it is darkened, due to a spectrum wavelength change).

Depth cues can include the *visual cliff*, which involves spatial perception and is sometimes used to test infants around three months old. *Linear perspective* involves relative size cues. In studies for cultures that have never seen *linear perspective art*, relative size cues do not see these cues and also do not see some optical illusions, such as the *Müller-Lyer illusion*. Some visual stimuli are learned but many others are innate. *Interposition cue* is an effect where, if stimuli are blocking the view of other objects, they are perceived as closer. *Texture gradient* is the progression of fine detail to blurry appearance. *Shadowing* is when a light source can provide distance and depth cues. *Binocular cue* is when eye angles can create disparity when objects are closer and can cause convergence via eye-muscle coordination.

The *oculomotor nerve (CN3)* is for extraocular eye movement, lid elevation, pupil (papillary constriction), and lens shape. This is a somatic motor system (voluntary movement). To test, must use light and accommodation, in the six cardinal fields of gaze, the *superior rectus* moves the eyes up and outward, the *inferior rectus* moves the eyes down and outward, and the *inferior obliques* move the eyes up and in at forehead.

The *trochlear nerve (CN4)* involves downward and inward eye movement via the oblique muscles. To test the random oblique eye movement test, the six cardinal fields of gaze, the *superior oblique* moves the eyes down and inward toward nose.

The *trigeminal nerve (CN5)* is the largest cranial nerve and is involved in facial function, biting, and chewing. There are three branches on each side. The opthamalic (V1), maxillary (V2), and mandibular (V3) (mandibular has both motor and sensory neurons). The motor nerves form from the *basal plate* of the embryonic pons. The sensory nerves are from cranial neural crust and the *genesis* of bones, cartilage, nerves and connective tissues. Somatosensory (voluntary movement), sensation in cornea (eye), face and head (scalp), touch, pain, mucous membranes of mouth and nose, muscles for chewing, branchial motor chewing movements of the jaw is for mastication.

For facial pain, if normal, it is called *trigeminal neuralgia*; if more intense, the pain is called *atypical* facial pain. The pain is caused by the pounding of an artery on the nerve inside the brain. Seizure medications such as *carbamazepine, Trileptal*, and *gabapentin* can be used for serve pain or the muscle relaxant, *baclofen*, or antidepressants such as *amitripyline* or *Cymbalta*. Surgery can be used or a needle can be inserted into the nerve and radiofrequency can be used to destroy part of the nerve, which can cause numbness.

To test the CN5, the shape/dull and clench teeth test, and blinks upon touching of sclera, distinguish blunt and sharp stimuli.

The *abducens nerve (CN6)* is for lateral eye movement via *lateral rectus muscles* for refraction of eye to protect, movement of the eyes to the side. To test the CN6 for lateral eye movement, the six cardinal fields of gaze can be used, star pattern, H pattern, and for the CN6 nerve, the lateral rectus moves the eyes toward the outside.

The *facial nerve (CN7)* incorporates *neural pathways*. There are two distinct neural pathways that radiate (innervate) facial expression, each one originating from a different area of the brain. *Volitional facial movements* originate in the *cortical motor strip* (real-time voluntary control), these are less smooth with more dynamics, and are not symmetrical. *Involuntary emotional facial* actions activate in the subcortical areas and are synchronized, smooth, symmetrical, consistent, and reflex like anger, contempt, disgust, fear, happiness, sadness, and surprise are all smooth and ballistic.

The CN7 is also involved in special sensory taste in the anterior two-thirds of tongue (taste is a chemical sense), deep sensations from the face, *tympanic membrane* of ear (separates external from inner ear), senses pain and temperature from the ear area, branchial for facial expression, visceral motor for parasympathetic head glands, and labial speech. Taste is a combination of the sense of smell and taste, and therefore taste can be thrown off if one of the systems is impaired.

The five primary taste qualities are sweet, sour, salty, bitter, and umami. Taste receptor cells, *effector enzymes*, distinguish nutritious from noxious substances. Chemoreceptors for taste are on the taste buds, which sit on top of the tongue bumps called *papillae*. There are also buds on the soft palate, upper esophagus, and epiglottis. The higher the density of the buds is, the more intense the absorption. People can have anywhere from around 2000 to over 10000 taste buds. Those with higher levels are sometimes referred to as *super tasters*. Chemicals stimulate the *microvilli* (cells specialized for absorption) leading to depolarization of the receptors.

Gustation is involved with manipulation and discernment of the composition of food. The tongue is rich in *vasculature* allowing for fast transmission to the brain. There are two *chemoreceptor types* on the tongue, G protein-coupled receptors that bind to chemicals in food and create action potentials for sweet and bitter taste. Salty and sour flavors work via the ion channels directly. Neurons from the tongue travel to the medulla oblongata, then to the thalamus, and finally to the cerebral cortex.

To test CN7, have the person make a big smile, puff cheeks, raise eyebrows, close eyes, and use muscles to keep them closed.

The *vestibular cochlear (CN8)* nerve is for hearing and balance, and sound equilibrium (inner ear to the brain) via hair cells. *Cochlear* is hearing and *vestibular* is balance. *Internal auditory meatus* carry signals from skull to the inner ear, and there is one on each side of the skull. Relay of ear stimuli travels to midbrain, then thalamus, and onto the temporal lobe.

Sound waves vibrations are a series of compressed and uncompressed molecules of air. The pitch (frequency) of the sound depends on the number of waves (vibrations) per second. Bass is produced by few vibrations per second, while high-pitched (shrill) sounds are produced by thousands of vibrations per second.

Humans can generally hear a range of between 20–20,000 Hz vibrations per minute. Animals use *echolocation* and can hear from a range of between 100–1,400,000 Hz. The *amplitude* (height) of the wave is the amount of compression. Loud sounds elicit a greater level of amplitude resulting from more compression.

Mechanoreceptors are sensitive to mechanical stimuli such as pressure, sound waves, and gravity. Some are found in the skin, some in hair cells that contain cilia and the bending of the cilia causes depolarization. Mechanorecptors in the ear function in hearing, balance, and detecting motion.

The *pinna* directs sound to the *auditory canal*. The auditory canal contains hair, which functions to filter the air and modified sweat glands that produce earwax. The three small bones called *ossicles* transfers vibrations from the eardrum (tympanic membrane) to the inner ear. The ossicles amplify pressure twenty times. The ossicles are *malleus* (hammer), *incus* (anvil), and *stapes* (stirrup). Other areas in the middle ear are *round window, oval window* and *Eustachian tube*, which connect the pharynx and permits equalization for pressure.

In the inner ear lies the *cochlea*, which is a coiled structure resembling a snail. The cochlea contains three canals: the floor of the canal is the *basilar membrane*, which contains at least 24,000 hair cells. Movement of the hair cells triggers action potentials and results in the sensation of sound. The tectorial membrane protrudes into the canal just above the hair cells. The hair cells and the tectorial membrane are called the *organ of Corti*.

The functioning begins with the stirrup vibrating the oval window. Pressure in the fluid of the inner ear (vestibular and tympanic canals) causes the basilar membrane to move up and down with vibrations. The up-and-down motion of the hair cells pushes them up against the *tectorial membrane*, producing action potentials. Auditory information is carried via *transduction* from the cochlea to the midbrain, then to the thalamus, and finally onto the temporal lobe of the cerebral cortex.

The basilar membrane is narrow and rigid near the oval window, but widens toward inside of the cochlea. The narrow stiff position resonates (vibrates) at higher frequencies that the broad portion further inside. High frequencies like bells and whistles vibrate the narrow, rigid part of the basilar membrane, while bass sounds vibrate the membrane further inside. Louder sound causes greater movement of the basilar membrane and can cause permanent damage to the hair cells. The fibers going from left ear to the right hemisphere tend to produce a more powerful signal, which is called the *left-ear advantage*. Signals cross at the corpus callosum.

The *vestibule* can detect a tilting head or changes in velocity in one direction. It contains two small chambers called the *utricle* and the *saccule*. Within these chambers, hair cells have cilia that are embedded in a gelatinous material. The gelatinous material is also mixed with granules of *calcium carbonate*. When the head is tilted or when there is a change in velocity, the granules and gelatin move in response to the gravity or motion. Their movement bends the hair cells. When the cilia are bent in one direction, the frequency of the action potentials is increased. When bent in the opposite direction, the frequency decreases.

The *semicircular canals* are filled with a fluid that moves when the head is rotated. Because each canal is oriented at ninety degrees to each other, they are capable of detecting rotation in any direction. An ampulla is located at the base of each semicircular canal. The ampulla contains *cupula*, which are hair cells embedded in gelatinous material. When the head rotates; fluid in at least one canal moves past the capula, bending the hair cells and triggering action potentials.

Conduction deafness is an issue with a structural component. *Nerve or sensorineural deafness* is hair cell damage in the cochlea from loud noise. The cells do not regenerate. To test, a person can turn away and whisper to see if person can hear a whispered word, and also test for loud noises.

The glassopharyngeal is involved in taste in the posterior one-third of tongue, somatosensory, is sensitive to O2, CO2, PH, and temperature, have *general visceral afferent (GVA)* fibers, and pharynx muscles for swallowing. The CN9 elevates the larynx and pharynx via branhial motor (vocal folds for pitch and volume), which also protect the trachea (airway). Vocal folds produce phonation via vibration, *voicing*. If the glottis is open, this will produce a voiceless action or a faucalized voice (hollow or yawny). A closed or blocked glottis produces a harsh voice.

There is a sweet spot that can occur called a *modal voice*, which is at max vibration, with combination of airflow and glottal tension. Speech pathologists use a register to identify phonation and the modal voice is one of four which they use. Voice pitches can be considered (negative, weak, passive, etc.) in socialization. *Bilateral vocal fold paralysis* is the loss of function in the muscles in both the left and the right vocal cords. *Aphonia* is emotional distress impairing muscle coordination and the Broca's area in the brain is associated with speech. To test the CN9, check for swallowing and gag reflexes and tongue movement in all directions.

The *vagus nerve (CN10)* is involved in speech and language, sensory (external ear, pain and temp from the ear area), autonomic functions of viscera (state of body organs), CNS and motor neurons, and medulla oblongata pathway to effector organs and muscles. Efferent nerves come from CNS to muscles and glands. Afferent neurons via interneurons travel to CNS GVA fibers. To test the CN10, say, "ahhhhhh," swallowing and clear voice versus hoarse.

The *spinal accessory nerve (CN11)* is involved in speech and language, muscles in head and neck movement, skeletal muscles of the pharynx and larynx and sternocliedomastoid and trapezius muscles. To test the CN11, shrug shoulders, head resistance, and head turning.

The *hypoglossal nerve (CN12)* is involved in speech and language, skeletal muscles of the tongue except palatoglossal, swallowing, involuntary activity, voluntary via corticobulbar region in the spine, and movement in speech language (i.e., difficulty in making new voluntary sounds). To test, stick out the tongue, hold at midline, and move from side to side. The nervous system is the body's communication system.

The nervous system breaks out as follows:

Nervous system

CNS — Peripheral NS

Brain   Spine   Auto NS   Somatic NS

(gland and organs)   (voluntary muscle)

Sympathetic NS   PSNS (brake)

(stress mobilization system)   (counteracts sympathetic NS)

Neural networks are neuronal network connections within the brain. Neurons are found in the central nervous system (brain and spinal cord) and also in the PNS (ganglia). There are three groups of neurons: the sensory, motor, and effector neurons. Neurons are the building blocks of the CNS, and enable the communication system between the neurons. Communications between neurons are relayed via the signals, which are emitted from the axons of the neurons and received into the dendrites of other neurons. Axons are found in the CNS, especially in the white matter and in the peripheral system. A multipolar neuron possesses a single axon and many dendrites, which allows for the integration of a great deal of information to be received from other neurons. Multipolar neurons constitute the majority of neurons found in the brain and include motor neurons and interneurons.

Sensory neurons receive impulses via stimulation. Motor neurons transmit impulses outward from the brain or spinal cord to muscles or glands via motor fibers. The impulses of motor neurons are sent in order to produce a response (i.e., muscle contraction or secretion from a gland). Interneurons are links between sensory and motor neurons and are found in the brain and spinal cord. Pseudounipolar neurons are found in the PNS and contain an axon that has split into two branches: one branch runs to the periphery, and the other (central branch) to the spinal cord. Pseudounipolar neurons do not have dendrites and have receptors on skin, joints, muscles, and other parts of the body, which transmit to the dorsal root.

Neuron transmission is conducted by ionic gradients across the axonal membrane. The Na concentration is higher than K ions in extracellular fluid. Inside the axonal membrane and cytosol, the K level is higher in concentration.

The Na+K+ and ATPase pump pushes two K+ ions into cell for every three Na+ ions it pushes out of the cell and equals a net loss of the positive charge in the cell. Leaky protein channels can cause some K channels in plasma membrane to slowly diffuse K out of the cell.

Both Na+K+ and ATPase pump and the leaky K+ channel cause a *potential difference* between inside the cell and the outside interstitial fluid. The membrane potential is always negative inside the cell. The neuronal membrane is polarized. The charge in humans is -70 mV.

Action potential is the intensity that can excite a neuron. Neurons have a threshold, and there is an all-or-none response, and there are no partial responses. Depolarization occurs at the junction of the axon and the cell body, where a tiny gated sodium ion channel open up to allow Na to rush in. The charge goes from negative to positive inside the cell -70 mV to +35 mV.

Repolarization occurs once the Na ion channels close, the K channels open up, the K ions rush out and the electrical charge reverses again back to a negative inside charge. Although the charge returns to normal inside, the action potential ions are on the wrong side of the axonal membrane. This action potential is reestablished via the sodium-potassium pump. Three Nas are sent out for every two Ks brought in. There is a refractory period after each action potential. The cell threshold level is higher during the refractory period.

Neurotransmitters are electrical and chemical signals. If the gaps are too large for electrical signals, the signals are converted to chemical signals, which are read by the synapses. The space between neurons is called a synapse. An NT diffuses across the synaptic cleft and binds receptors on the dendrites of the next neuron. The NTs are located at the terminal end of an axon. Acetylcholine is the most important NT in the brain. It is released from the terminal end when $Ca2+$ moves in and is picked up almost immediately by the second neurons dendrites. Excess acetylcholine that is left in the synaptic cleft is broken down by acetylcholinesterase. Acetylcholine can also cause muscles to contract or inhibit postsynaptic potential. Acetylcholine is also released between neurons in the parasympathetic system. Norepinephrine is a peptide NT released within the CNS. GABA is secreted in the CNS and acts as an inhibitor.

Schwann cells wrap around axons and produce a substance called myelin sheath which is an insulator and a conductor. The nodes of Ranvier are the exposed area of the axon, which is not covered by the myelin sheath. Myelin sheath induces saltatory conduction, which increases the speed of the impulse.

The *nodes of Ranvier* are the spaces (gaps) between the myelin sheath, coating on the neurons that helps to speed impulses. The *parietal region* is located at the back and top of the brain, involved in sensation, perception, integration of sensory input, involved in spatial relations in the visual field, and also touch, pressure, and temperature. The thalamus is the relay center for motor signals to the cerebral cortex and involved in both pain and attention. It is an input center from the spinal cord via the CNS. The nervous system is a complex sensory system, which registers senses between brain, spinal cord, and nerves. The nerves are the conduits within the nervous system. The concentration of nerves varies over the body with high concentrations in the fingers, which are highly sensitive, and other areas. Nerves are electrical impulses that are in bundles, which run to various organs and tissues of the body. Because nutrients travel away from the nerve cell body along its processes, injury results in the disconnection of the peripheral portion of the process from the cell and nerve function is lost distal to the site of the injury. The spinal nerves are thirty-one pairs of nerves: eight cervical, twelve thoracic, five lumbar, five sacral, and one coccygeal. The spinal nerve is involved in general sense (touch, pressure, pain, heat, cold, etc.) from the neck, trunk, and extremities. The *pyramidal tract* involves important motor nerves on each side of the CNS that run from the sensorimotor areas of the cortex through the brain stem to motor neurons of the cranial nerve nuclei and the ventral root of the spinal cord. The *dorsal root ganglia* is a nodule on the dorsal root of the spine that contains cell bodies of nerve cells (neurons), carrying signals from sensory organs to integration centers.

Nerves that carry signals toward the CNS are *afferent* (travel from interneurons to CNS) and *efferent nerves* go from CNS to muscles and glands. The PNS is activated by impulses exiting the spinal cord to activate organs and muscles. The *dorsal root* is a sensory root, which combines with the ventral root to form the spinal nerve, general sensory and pain from muscles, tendons and joints. The *ventral root* (efferent motor root of spinal cord) is one of the two roots, the other being the dorsal root, which extends from the brain to the spinal cord. The dorsal root is sensory. This spinal nerve passes ventrally from the spinal cord and that consist of motor fibers. The ventral root joins with the dorsal root to form a mixed spinal nerve.

The PNS is all somatic voluntary muscle movements, autonomic involuntary functions, and the network of glands, muscles, nerves, and nerve bundles associated within the system. This system includes the skin, organs, blood vessels, etc.

The PSNS is part of the autonomic nervous system (ANS) involved in the restoration and conservation of energy, acts as countermeasure to the SNS, which is activated during HPA cycle, the PNS sends signals to slow autonomic functions, and increase the metabolic functions, which shuts down during HPA cycle, the metabolic system being digestion and allows calorie absorption for energy stores.

The SNS is a system that signals body to prepare for action, which is often called fight or flight. The HPA cycle is activated during this alert and the parasympathetic system is antagonist to restore system to homeostasis.

The *somatic nervous system* connects the brain and spinal cord to the *voluntary muscle system* which is part of the PNS, which also includes the ANS, which connects brain and spine to the *involuntary muscles and glands.*

GVA motor fibers (part of ANS) pain or reflex impulses from the viscera, glands, and blood vessels to the CNS. The visceral pathway is from sympathetic efferent pathway to the ventral root in the spinal column to the dorsal root ganglion where the cell body of the sympathetic visceral afferent nerve is located, then onto the *dorsal horn* of the spinal column where it is transmitted via a synapse to a neuron in the CNS.

A *motor fiber* is a nerve that carries impulses toward the muscles and glands.

A motor neuron is a neuron conducting impulses out from the brain or spinal cord. The *Skeletal nervous system* is bone in the skeleton, muscles attached via rods and hinges (SNS) parts that work together.

The *gate control theory* poses that there is pain priority in nerve passages, the gate opens with high pain and closes with lower levels of pain. Endorphins control lower levels of pain in pain response with their opiate characteristics. *C-fiber stimulation* involves nerve fibers, higher conduction velocity where pain the response is stronger, and responds to stronger intensity stimuli. *Polymodal* fibers can respond to various levels of stimuli (chemical, thermal, and mechanical). There are ranges of stimuli for integration, response, and ultimately return to homeostasis. The C-fiber *receptors* are nocireceptors responsible for the second burning pain.

C-fiber *warming* is involved in warmth sensation. C-fiber *ultra-slow histamine selective* is the itch sensation. C-fiber *tactile* involves sensual touch. *C-mechano- and metaboreceptors (muscles and joints)* are involved in burning and cramping in exercise. *C-vanilloid receptor (VR1, TRPV1)* are heat stimuli, ion channel opened for action potential inflammatory sensitization. *TRPV2* has higher threshold for heat.

Tranmembrane receptors are closed during resting conditions. When open, they allow Na and Ca influx to initiate action potential in fibers. *Transient receptor potentials (TRP)* are essential, damage to these can cause *naturopathic pain* when the threshold for pain is lowered.

The *skin nerves* are *free nerve endings* and they are for heat, light pressure, and pain. The *parietal brain region* has several functions including sensory (touch), temperature *indentation*, and pressure. Energy activation from stimuli occurs on nerve endings. *Pacinian corpuscles* are for firm pressure. *Meissner's corpuscles* are for onset and continuous light pressure. *Ruffini endings* are for continuous pressure. Skin receptors send action potential to the midbrain, then to the thalamus and onto the primary sensory cortex.

Digestive nerve regulators are *extrinsic* and *intrinsic*. Extrinsic nerves are outside nerves that come to digestive organs from the autonomic brain signal center. These nerves release acetylcholine and adrenaline. Acetylcholine causes the muscles of the digestive tract to squeeze and push with more force and also causes the stomach and pancreas to produce more digestive juice. Adrenaline relaxes the muscles of the stomach and intestine, and decreases the flow of blood to these organs. The *intrinsic nerves* make up a very dense network inside of the walls of the esophagus, stomach, small intestine, and colon. The intrinsic nerves are triggered to act when the walls of the hollow organs are stretched by food. These nerves release substances, control the release of juices, and control the movement of the process.

Neural disorders are the disease of the brain, spinal cord, or nervous system pathways, via a medical or psychological disorder. *Paresis* is partial paralysis and/or weakness in a muscle group, and if it occurs in the brain, it can cause seizures, impairment of brain functioning, and even death.

Parkinson's disease is a disease of the CNS, which can cause tremors, speech issues, and cognitive impairment. Damage to the cells that release dopamine (an NT associated with motion and coordination) is a major factor in this disease for which there is no cure for the progression.

Pain disorder is *somatoform* (physical), but not entirely understood, because psychological factors play a key role in the onset, severity, worsening, maintenance of pain. The *International Association for the Study of Pain (IASP)* classifies pain disorder as the real or probable tissue damage and perception of pain in part is a psychological response to a noxious stimuli. Pain is multidimensional. The CNS activity is simultaneous with cognitions and emotions. Acute pain is under six months, while chronic pain is over six months.

The four domains of interest in pain are the following:

1. Underlying organic, patterns, and set of causes
2. Experience of pain (severity, duration, and pattern)
3. Functional impairment and disability
4. Emotional distress (i.e., depression and anxiety correlations)

Causal contributions are measured for therapy priorities with a multimodal and multidiscipline approach. Common symptoms for pain disorder are negative distorted cognition, increase in pain and clinical intervention, insomnia and fatigue, depression and anxiety, social releases down, inactivity, passivity, and disability. The diagnosis involves ruling out medical issues, malingering, and factitious disorder. Must rule out somatization disorder, conversion disorder, mood, anxiety, and psychotic disorders.

Treatment can include acetaminophen, or nonsteroidal anti-inflammatory drugs (NSAIDs). Pscyhotherapy can be used for chronic pain. TCAs are effective for neuropathic pain (headache, facial, fibromyalgia, and arthritis).

The cycle is typically pain to depression to insomnia to fatigue, which is a *self-perpetuating* cycle. Cognitive behavioral therapy (CBT) is a therapy alternative that can restore self-efficacy, time limited, structured, goal-oriented, restructures ideas, and can identify or modify distorted thought patterns and/or sense of hopelessness. *Transcutaneous electrical nerve stimulation (TENS)* is a therapeutic option. *Surgical ablation* is the removal of part of a nerve pathway. Nerve blocks are for temporary control of pain, destruction of nerve tissue, for migraines, back, and more. In *complex regional pain syndrome (CRPS)*, 92 percent of patients experience a spread of pain and 35 percent say the pain spreads over the entire body.

Multifactorial disorder involves neurogenic inflammation. In *neurogenic inflammation*, there is local release from afferent neurons, which convert external stimuli to internal stimuli are activated by sensory input (vision, touch, hearing, etc.). They send projections into the CNS that convey info to the brain or spinal cord, activated by physical modalities (light, sound, temperature, etc.). Sensory receptors of the cell membrane convert the stimuli to electrical impulses (i.e., neurons containing mechanoreceptors are sensitive to tactile stimuli and olfactory receptors are sensitive to odors.

For *plasticity and neuroplasticity* in sensory disorders, *constraint-induced movement therapy (CIMT)* is designed to grow new neural pathways in paralysis and for stroke, which is CNS damage rehab.

A review of the sensory fiber types includes the fact that they can vary by axonal conduction velocity, myelination, fiber and size. C-fiber in somatosensory system, afferent inputs the signal from the periphery to the CNS. *Unmyelinated,* this causes slow conduction velocity (no more than two ms), and this is for deeper spreading out of stimuli. Damage and nerve regeneration involves the recovery of distal C-fiber, takes months, and may never regain complete function, or can cause abnormal function, or neuropathic pain. *Remak bundles* release trophic factors that promote regeneration of damaged axons.

There are three types of *second-order projection measures* in the spinothalamic tract. C-fibers synapse to second-order projection neurons. The three types are *wide dynamic range (WDR), high threshold,* and *low threshold. Second order neurons* ascend to the brain stem and the thalamus, within the spinothalamic tract (the main pathway associated with pain and temperature perception), the tract crosses the spinal cord laterally, which allows for identification of local injury.

The *beta* fiber is higher-conduction velocity and shallow and quick pain on a specific area and is the first pain. It is a response to weaker intensity of stimulus.

The cortex determines modality selection and range of stimulus. The brain then integrates the signals to maintain homeostasis.

The vanilloid receptor (VR), both C and beta, responds to elevated heat and chemical *capsaicin.* Capsaisin open ligand-gated ion channel causing an action potential to occur, (i.e., chili peppers are hot). This is essential to inflammatory sensitization to noxious thermal stimuli. VRL1 -52C+ and low pH are both transmembrane receptors that are closed during resting periods. Open Na and Ca rush in and initiate action potential across fibers, part of TRP. If damage to these heat receptors occurs, can result in neuropathic pain, by lowering the *heat pain* threshold.

Neuropathic pain syndrome can derive from lesions. In the CNS, lesions can lead to stroke, MS, and spinal injury. PNS would be toxic, metabolic, and inflammatory. Damage or lesion to C or beta can create abnormal sensitivity and pathological spontaneous activity. The presence of mRNA for voltage-gated Na channels lower the activation threshold, leading to hyperactivity. *Hyperalgesia* is increased neuronal response to noxious stimuli and increased pain.

For C-Fiber routing central sensitization of the dorsal horn occurs in spinal column, then glutamate releases, interacts with *postsynaptic NMDA*, then there is expression of voltage gates, nitric oxide migrates back to presynaptic membrane to enhance expression of voltage gates, resulting in *pain wind-up phenomenon*. *Wind-up* is associated with chronic pain and central sensitization at the minimum frequency of .33 Hz, FMRI is the heat pulse frequency. *Temporal summation of second pain (TSSP)* is connected to the brain center that regulates cognition, premotor activity, as well as the pain and sensory. *Allodynia* is a pain response to previously non-noxious stimuli. *Pathogenesis* is psoriasis, asthma, fibromyalgia, eczema, dystonia, chemical sensitivity, migraines, and more (sensitization to stimuli). Pain can lead to organic health dysfunction which can be physical and/or mental in nature. As with anything else, it is easier to treat pain with early intervention.

the Development Stages

A s discussed in the prior sections, there are many internal and external factors which can impact the process of human development. The critical period of development in psychology and biology is a period of heightened sensitivity to exogenous stimuli. It is common that many people will take for granted, both their general functions and abilities and then even more so their advanced abilities. In order for people to develop properly and to consolidate their development potential, there are numerous organic and environmental processes, which have to occur without error. The human being is the most complex thing that has ever existed. But there are times where the action potential of people is disrupted and/or distorted during development. The genetic and cellular components, which orchestrate human development, require a very precise series of events to transpire in order for normal human development and proper system functioning to occur. There are times where these functions and processes do not transpire in an error-free fashion, and this can result in organic dysfunction. External factors also are critical in the development stage. An organic dysfunction can manifest into a developmental disorder, disability, mental illness, or organic challenge, which can impact people's lives.

In the primary developmental stage, *feeding disorder* is a problematic disorder, which can manifest under the age of six. Feeding disorder is the failure for a person to consume enough food to maintain a *normal growth pattern* with a duration of one month or more, and/or loss of weight. This disorder does not involve *failure to thrive*, which has a medical or physiological explanation. Some factors of feeding disorder are a lack of nurturing. The failure of parent or guardian to read hunger and satiety (fullness) cues, parent MIs, and more.

Parental aggression, apathy, and/or a parent or guardian making the eating experience negative are also factors. A child's mental and physiological reactions to the external environment begin at birth. Unfortunately there are many people who do not understand the importance of choosing the appropriate style of human interaction during the early developmental phases. Other common associations with feeding disorder are with premature birth and developmental delays. Some other disorders can be CNS disease, sensory defects, muscle disorders such as *cerebral palsy* (CP), heart disease, and GI diseases such as Crohn's disease. In order to be considered a feeding disorder, a diagnosis of one of the other conditions must not be present.

The child's symptoms may mimic that of a starving child, where the child can be irritable, apathetic, and difficult to console. The younger the child with the disorder is, the higher the risk of their developmental delay. The prevalence in the population is around 1–3 percent of all infants and children. Normal children can potentially experience minor feeding issues at a rate of around 25–35 percent of the population. With premature births, the rate of feeding issues can be around 40–70 percent in prevalence. To qualify as feeding disorder, the condition must affect growth for a significant period of time and the child must be below the fifth percentile on the growth chart. The diagnosis is for the failure of a child to eat adequately for one or more months, impacting growth, not related to other condition, not from lack of available food or rumination disorder (constant regurgitation of food). This occurs before age six, and if another person/s feeds the child and there is an improvement, this also correlates to the condition. Under the proper treatment and direction, there is normally a 50 percent increase over a one-to-three-week period of food intake. For the training of the original parent, often a change of pace, position, location, and change of utensils is used. If feeding disorder is not treated, it can lead to permanent physical and mental damage.

Another type of feeding disorder is *avoidant/restrictive food intake disorder* (ARFID) that involves physiological and psychosocial issues, children and adolescents avoidance issues, and restriction in their eating. *Pica* is a disorder, which involves the craving people develop for non-food items such as dirt, ice, clay, glue, sand, chalk, beeswax, and hair; and this can potentially point to a nutritional deficiency. According to the DSM, the condition must persist for a month or more and be age relevant. There are some factors which can contribute to pica. One factor that has been recognized is that an iron deficiency can lead to people eating clay and the reason is unknown. Dopamine levels can also factor in if the levels are low.

The potential risk factors of *pica* are psychopathy, family disorganization, environmental deprivation, epilepsy, brain damage, mental retardation, pervasive developmental disorders, and more. Other things that may be eaten within the pica condition are paint, plaster, string, cloth, leaves, insects, cigarette butts, and more. Adolescents and adults are known to eat clay and soil. The age that pica is most common is between two to three years old, pica is inappropriate above the age of eighteen to twenty-four months. The population is around 25–33 percent of all young children. Nutrition is a critical element within human development and the level of nutrition can potentially impact many other organic systems including mental functions if there is a deficiency.

Mental deficiencies and learning disorders can result from genetic, organic and biological, and environmental factors. A *specified learning disorder* is a derivative of the consolidation of all disorders into a group and then adds *specifiers* for unique condition identification. For example within academia, reading, writing, arithmetic, and reasoning are all grouped together, then specifiers further break down the developmental issues.

Learning disorders can include speaking, listening, reading, writing, math ability, and other disorders. A learning disorder is where a child is two or more years below the standard age. The DSM states that the LD must include a cognitive deficit from brain dysfunction. Learning disorders are present in around 5–20 percent of school-aged children over varying periods of time. Learning disorders occur mostly in boys and can often be comorbid with ADHD. The factors are also often of a genetic nature. Factors can include the fetal environment, a low birth weight, sensory deprivation, and more.

The signs can include a child being sloppy, disorganized, having low attention, their independence in learning is lower. Also there can be social withdrawal and lower amounts of activities. Some other things that can accompany LDs are impulsivity, restlessness, distractibility, lower physical coordination, frustration, tolerance, lower self esteem, daydreaming frequently, and behavior and/or emotional changes.

Learning dysfunction can be in sensory-perceptual ability (vision, hearing, kinesthetic-touch), motor development; also in memory, attention, and language ability. The three most common LDs are reading, writing, and math. Within LDs, around 60–80 percent only have reading issues, often *dyslexia*. Common issues are identifying groups of letters, letter sounds, letter position, chaotic spelling, and word by word versus contextual issues.

Dysgraphia deals with the writing layout on the page, repetitions, omissions, and spelling errors. *Dyscalculia* (this term is eliminated in DSM-V) is *math disorder*, which is usually apparent by the age of eight or the second or third grade.

For dyscalculia, it can involve issues with reading and writing numbers, aligning numbers to calculate, performing calculations, and comprehending word problems. Some disorders can include Turner's and Fragile X for girls. There can also be associations over to reading and language issues. The symptoms are language, recognition/perceptual, mathematic, and attention. For the language within mathematics, it involves understanding math terms and concepts. For recognition, it involves identifying the signs, operations, and alignment of the numbers. Being able to count, memorize basic tables, and follow sequences are keys. For attention, copying numbers and ignoring signs are the keys.

The typical signs are issues with counting, memorization, operations (i.e., plus and minus), poor computational (simple arithmetic), slowness in calculation, number order errors, reading graphs, copying information, the concept of place value, alignment issues, word-problem issues, and symbol recognition. The DSM states that around 1 percent of children have *arithmetical dysfunction*, which is normally recognized by the second or third grade. Some children use memorization and calculation tricks to avoid detection, which can get them through to about the fourth or fifth grade (i.e., finger counting or repeated addition versus multiplication).

The *American Psychiatric Association (APA)* diagnosis requires: 1) psychological evaluation, and 2) the *Enright diagnostic test of mathematics*. There will be a search for other causes such as vision, hearing, mental limitations, and the fluency of language must also be ruled out as well. Children can be eligible for an *individualized education plan (IEP)*, which details specific accommodations to learning (plans can vary considerably), with a focus on basic problem-solving skills, math concepts, and ways to eliminate distractions and extraneous information. The use of concrete instruction is applied versus the abstract and theoretical approach. The *prognosis* is based on the following:

1. Type of difficulties
2. Resources available
3. Child determination level

There also can be nonverbal (NV) learning issues, with spatial and organization. The APA states that the LD must interfere with the academic achievement or ADLs in order to quality as an LD. IEPs can be developed for children with LDs.

For infants, the Bayley Scales of Infant Development can be used and there are also other tests for the older ages, which can include the *Woodcock-Johnson Scales of Independent Behavior*, and the *Vineland Adaptive Behavior Scale (VABS)*, which are frequently used. There is federal funding for testing and IEP programs, and education and skills training for ages three to twenty-one. When children are learning with LDs, they will learn at their own pace and with repetition. Learning disabilities can often be related to the dysfunction of various organic structures.

Developmental vision is a critical area within development. There is a vision critical period" and a period of extended "sensitivity". The *vision critical period* is between three to eight months for binocular vision, but *vision sensitivity* extends out to at least age three. Human vision is normally good by twelve months old. Babies like to look at faces and face-like objects, as well as symmetrical objects. Early vision is normally about twelve inches from the baby's face. An infant should have a red reflex and be aware of light and dark. The random movement of the eye is due to retinal development. Convergence develops at two to three months, hand-eye coordination appears at about six months and a child can also distinguish colors. At school-age, an eye specialist can begin to see any refractive errors. Some eye conditions include *Amblyopia*, which is reduced visual acuity in one eye, *astigmatism* is when the curve of the cornea prevents correct refraction, *strabismus* is when the eyes do not fix on the same point, and muscle imbalance, which is around 3 percent–5 percent of the population, *diplopia* is cross-eyes, and *double vision* occurs with strabismus muscular weakness, this condition is correctable. *Myopia* is when light focuses in front of the retina (nearsighted) and *hyperopia* is when light reflects beyond the retina (farsighted). Vision is a highly critical development area for many life functions. Language is another critical development area.

Within the child *language development* stages, a child by twelve months should normally be able to produce at least one word. It is unusual if a child is not speaking by eighteen months. If by the age of two years old, there is a lack of language production, one should seek an SLP.

SLP is conducted via the American Speech-Language-Hearing Association (ASHA). SLPs and audiologists all are involved in the identification and correction of disorders. Voice disorders can include pitch, volume, quality, resonance/duration, articulation/speech sounds, fluency (i.e., stuttering [forward disfluency]) and more.

Things to note are that girls are normally faster than boys at language acquisition and children with a *reserved* personality or disposition will sometimes wait and/or take longer periods of time to understand more information prior to speaking. Communication delays can include a child *grunting* and *pointing* as *commentary or understanding* and using NV actions. Verbal expression can lag in young children especially in boys. Some of the factors can be neurological, congenital anatomical, muscular condition, psychological, and brain nerve conditions.

Communication includes the use of words and gestures. The use of words, phrases, sentences in speaking, along with the ability to read and write, occur at *milestone dates* normally, although deviations are typical. Examples of deviations include *language delay*, which is the slow development of the spoken language and also *language disabilities and disorders*, which can have significant milestone dates deviation.

Developmental speech and language delays include *language* issues where meanings are interpreted from sounds and these delays are more *serious* than speech problems. Language entails identifying what words mean, how to make new words, how to put words together, and situational (context) combination use. *Language delay* is typically the correct sequence of words, but at a slower rate. Language delay affects around 5–10 percent of all children, primarily around the preschool-age. *Language disorder* can be receptive, which is difficulty understanding others, while *expressive* is difficulty sharing thoughts, ideas, and feelings. *Speech disorder* involves *articulation* issues, which is the production of letters and words, *voice* issues with *vocal folds*, other organic areas, and breathing to produce sound. *Fluency* issues are with rhythm, cadence, and can be voice (hoarse, nasal, etc.).

Language disorders can be *disfluencies* such as *stuttering* (child-onset fluency disorder) that can also come with *secondary behaviors* such as agitation, which makes the learning environment even more difficult. Fluency is the forward flow of speech while disfluency is the blockage of forward speech flow. Sometimes *interjections* are used by children between the ages of two to five such as um, like, and uh, which are considered normal for that age range.

With any speech and language issues, a hearing check is essential. The earlier an issue is diagnosed, the greater the progress can be. Identification and intervention is a key factor. Testing can identify whether child is a *late bloomer* or if there is a language issue. Factors can be genetics, environment (feral and deprived). *Gesturing* correlates strongly normally with a later bloomer versus a language disorder. NV communication can increase oral communication as language develops in stages.

The *first stage* is from birth and forward where there should be cooing and babbling. At two to three months, there should be circumstantial cries, which are responsive. By four months, a child should at least be *babbling* randomly, which even deaf babies do and this is an innate pre-wired *phoneme* exploration mechanism. By five to six months, babies should be babbling rhythmically. If the baby is not cooing or babbling then a specialist may have to be seen. At around six to eleven months, there is normally imitation babble with expression. The *second stage* is the *holophrase* or one-word stage, which normally occurs around age one. At twelve months, there normally are one to two words produced and babies normally recognize names, imitate familiar sounds, and understand simple instructions. If the first words are late or there are missing sounds, a specialist may have to be seen. The *third stage* is at around eighteen months or between one to two years old when a baby uses two-word sentences with vocabulary, animal sounds, uses words like *more*, understands *no*, waves good-bye, and this is the *telegraphic speech* or the two-word stage, where meaning is present, but this is not syntax. Children are only beginning to learn syntax at this age. An example of a typical sentence would be, "Marky hurted by head, so I throwed the truck at him." Babies will have about five to twenty words in their vocabulary, including names at this stage.

Misapplied syntax is called *overgeneralization*. Between two to three years old or twenty-four to thirty months is a *hyper-developmental age*, with body identification, the child says "me," V (verbal) and NV (nonverbal) combos are used. Children have around a 400–450-word vocabulary, use short sentences, do color matching, and use some plurals. Between three to four years old, children can tell a story, use four-to-five-word sentences, have a 1000-word vocabulary, say last name, name of street, and can do nursery rhymes. At four to five years old, the sentence length is at four to five words plus, there is use of past tense, 1500-word vocabulary, colors, shapes, and ask who and why. At five to six years old, the sentences are five to six plus words, there is a 2000-word vocabulary, spatial relations develop (on top, far), there is identification, and counting. If there are minimal consonants or vowels, a specialist may have to be seen. If there is pausing, sound combination errors, the reduction and/or deletion of difficult sounds with frequency and/or eating issues, a specialist may have to be seen.

The language *critical period* for tone, pitch, etc. states that first language acquisition must occur by the time the cerebral lateralization is complete in the brain at around puberty, and that language acquired after this period will be typically slower and less structural in most cases.

In *expressive language disorder*, there are two types which are *developmental* and *acquired*. Expressive language disorder involves difficulties with verbal and written expression, but language comprehension that is within normal limits, aka *specific language impairment* (SLI), memory issues are only for speech.

Phonological disorder is different and involves pronunciation issues. Issues with expressive language disorder can involve issues with putting sentences together, grammar, word use, communicating thoughts and needs, understanding is on par but cannot form *expressive complexity*. There is normally a lack of pronoun use (leave out "is"), substitution of *thing* or *stuff* for lost words. Language delays are experienced by around 10–15 percent of all children under the age of three and by around 3–7 percent of school-age children. Boys have around a 25–50 percent higher rate of occurrence than girls. Testing can involve NV testing, hearing evaluation, and more. The DSM criteria is low-speech level for age (expressive), must have age-level understanding (receptive), cannot be *mixed receptive/expressive*, issue most be more prevalent than other associated handicaps, and must acquire by high school.

Mixed receptive-expressive language disorder is difficulty both expressing and understanding language (receptive). The developmental cause is unknown and the acquired cause is damage to the brain. There are not *phonological* pronunciation issues as with phonological disorder. There are issues with constructing coherent sentences, using proper grammar, and with word recall. People are not able to communicate thoughts, needs, wants or do things with the same complexity as peers, and there is a smaller vocabulary. Receptive disorder is when a person has difficulty understanding incoming communication, doesn't follow directions, or has inappropriate response, and issues with (abstract nouns, complex sentences, and spatial terms).

The DSM states that people within the disorder can communicate, but at a lower level and have difficulty with ADLs. If a child does understand incoming language (receptive), then they would have expressive language disorder.

The population for the condition is around 5 percent of all preschool-age, and around 3 percent of all school-age children. The mixed is less common than the expressive. Around 40–60 percent of those with mixed also have phonological disorder (difficulty forming sounds). Reading disorder is an issue with around 50 percent of those with mixed. The child is also likely to have ADHD and/or ADD at around a 30–60 percent rate. Early intervention is the key.

Apraxia of speech (motor speech disorder) involves issues with sounds, syllables, and words, but is not due to muscle issues. The issues are with brain planning and coordination. And SLP is needed to evaluate speech issues. There are stages involved with apraxia of speech.

The Stages:- Baby, no cooing or babbling - The first words are late and/or missing sounds

- Minimal consonant or vowels
- Pausing and sound combo errors
- Reduction or deletion of difficult sounds with frequency
- (Sometimes) eating issues are associated

With the progression of apraxia, the disorder also involves working on expressive and spontaneous actions and reducing anxiety, and there is hypo- or hypersensitivity. There is testing done on the oral motor area (tongue, facial movement). The diadochokinetic rate (DDK) assesses the ability to produce series of rapid-alternating sounds, which are often called *tokens* such as "puh", "puh-tuh", "puh-tuh-kuh", which use the front of the lips, the middle tip of the tongue, and the soft palate (back of the mouth). Evaluation of the structures (lips, tongue, jaw, teeth, palate, and pharynx), breathing and *velopharangeal* function (mechanism responsible for directing the transmission of sound energy and air pressure in both the oral cavity and nasal cavity). When the valve does not close properly, the condition is called *velopharyngeal inadequacy* (VPI). VPI can be congenital or can be acquired later in life. Some causes of VPI can be structural like tissue deficiency, immobile soft palate, or *neurogenic* due to trauma, tumors, damage to cranial nerves (glassopharyngeal [CNIX9], vagus [CNX10], and accessory [CNXI11]) and damage to cerebellum. Also phoneme (basic unit of phonology) specific like *fricatives* (s and z), which are consonants produced by using *articulators*, and closing them together like the lip against the upper teeth or the back of the tongue against the soft palate; and *sibilant* use (tongue rolling while forcing air through narrow channel directing air over the edge of the teeth), *affricates* (ch and dj), which are consonant stops, as well as due to mechanical interference from enlarged tonsils, adenoids, and pharyngeal flap.

Conditions like *ataxia* (muscle coordination), *dysarthria* (motor speech disorder), and *stuttering* can impact the DDK rate. Treatment can include tactile touching of the facial areas, visual cues, auditory feedback, and multisensory feedback within a supportive environment

Speech sound disorder (formerly phonological disorder) is an inability to develop some or all of the sounds that are necessary for speech and articulation. The range on the continuum is from incomprehensible to slight mispronunciation. There are three categories. Structural can be tongue and roof of mouth, and must be corrected prior to language or speech therapy. Neurological is muscle or motor control issues in the brain and/or brain nerves (cranial nerves). Phonological, not otherwise specified (NOS), is due to an unknown cause.

The disorder is detected by age-equivalent consonants. There are three groups that have eight sounds each. The groups are the *early eight*, the *middle eight*, and the *late eight*. The early eight are emerging development between the ages of one to three years old and are m (mama), b (baby), y (you), n (no), w (we), d (daddy), p (pop), and h (hi). The middle eight are continued emerging development between ages three to six or seven years old and should occur with *consistent production*. The middle eight are t (two), ng (running), k-sound (cup), g (go), f (fish), v (van), ch (chew), and j (jump). The late eight should occur between ages five to seven or eight and are sh (sheep), s (see), th (think), th (that), r (red), z (zoo), l (like), and zh (measure).

The mastery of the late eight can extend out to and beyond age seven to eight years old. It is common to omit the endings, distort, and use sound substation for easier sound. The diagnosis at age four is still difficult to determine. The key is identifying slow development and more frequency in errors. People need to check hearing, reading comprehension, and check for language disorder. The DSM three criteria are age-equivalent comparison, causing ADLs issues, and not being due to another condition. At five years old, around 7–8 percent of children may experience SSD. There are more males than females in SSD prevalence. If the issue is a structural or neurological issue then substitutes are often employed, and the development may never to be 100 percent. Around 75 percent of the mild and moderate issues are resolved before age six.

Selective mutism is elective, can be social situational, is most common at school, and most often is diagnosed from preschool to the second grade. Selective mutism can also be associated with crying, clinging, but others may just bottle up or exhibit smiling, without talking. The onset often is under five years old and is frequently when school starts. The issues can impact school, social, and ADLs.

The diagnosis involves a duration of at least one month, must be a true *inhibition* versus a cognitive *deficit*, and there must be no psychological issues. The signs are anxiety, shyness, agoraphobia, and isolation. The prevalence is around 1 percent of the population. The treatment is positive behavior modeling to reduce anxiety. For example, people can use *stimulus fading* that is started by using a comfort person, then introducing a *new person*. Smaller groups are used to elicit a gradual change and prepare for the introduction into larger group. *Shaping* involves gestures, mouthing, and whispering to inspire. *Self-modeling* entails the child observing themselves doing the actions, which reinforces their self-confidence, and the *affect carryover* to a secondary target area. Role-play can boost their self-esteem and it can often find the root of the issue. *Picture exchange communication system (PECS)* can be used, which is picture exchange, NV can be used, unaided with body, and aided with props as well. Early intervention is the key.

For prevention, people can begin talking to their child with frequency right after their birth, respond to their coos and babbling, and, later, play simple games like *peekaboo* and *patty-cake*. When a child starts speaking, people should listen to child and they should allow five to ten seconds for their expressive communication. People should be sure to reward for their child's expression. People should never go negative on grammar errors, and they should instead model the correct grammar with positivity. The causes can be intrinsic, anxiety, OCD, depression, discomfort with the sound of their own voice (possibly amusia), and possibly language issues.

Stuttering which is now disfluency disorder is often hidden by children with the disorder by the rearranging of words in sentences, which is called circumlocution. Stuttering commonly involves repetition, prolongation, interjections (the word "um"). The diagnosis points to genetic factors, and the duration is at six months plus. The treatment is behavioral and the *rate of speech* (ROS) cadence is worked on. The learning environment should give people the time to express in order to reduce their stress/anxiety. The triggers can be grammar adaptation between age two to five, anxiety can cause muscle tensions and blockage. The onset is normally around two and a half years to four years old, and there are more males than females at a rate of three to four times higher.

Reading disorder involves issues with reading accuracy, speed, and comprehension, which are not at age level. The eye muscles must follow along, spatial orientation is needed for interpretation, visual memory is needed for meanings of letters and *sight words*, must have sequencing ability, sentence structure and grammar are required, must be able to categorize and analyze, must be able to use visual cues and pair with memory, must also be able to associate sounds to meanings and meanings must be retained for comprehension.

The causes can be genetic mutations, can be brain functioning, and around 90 percent of the children with reading disorder have other language deficits as well.

The signs are having issues with single-word identification, sound, sound order, rhyming, spelling, letter transposition, omitting and substituting words, poor reading comprehension, and slow-reading speed.

Other issues can be a delay in spoken language, confusion with directions (left or right hand), confusion with opposites (up and down), mathematics disorder, and disorder of written expression. The diagnosis must distinguish between slow learning and a lower level of intelligence. The factors are age, intelligence, educational opportunities, around 25–50 percent of children with reading disorder have ADHD, around 25 percent have CD CD. There is also a correlation to oppositional defiant disorder (ODD) and depression. Almost all have spelling issues and around eighty percent have language problems.

LDs are present in around 5–15 percent of the population, and around 80 percent of those with LDs have a reading disorder. Around 4 percent of school-age children have reading disorder. The *Individuals with Disabilities Education Act (IDEA)* (1990) ensures the children with LDs can have access to IEP, which is a customized instruction plan for children at a school designed for LDs with a cross-disciplinary educational approach. An IEP program is available through age twenty-one.

Programs such as *Project Read, Wilson Reading System*, and the *Herman Method* are often used. The basis is on sound/symbol phonics based, smallest visual components, multisensory (visual, auditory, kinesthetic), sees, feels, says, sound-symbol association, highly structured with remediation at level of single-letter sound, use of digraphs (pair of letters representing a single-speech sound), syllables, and then into words and sentences in a systematic fashion, repetitive drill and practice.

Famous people including two US presidents had LDs. The remediation received is crucial, to identify and correct the deficiency, and intensive reading education is required by age three to four in order to reach the full potential. There is a variation in results, which are depending on educational opportunities, the drive to overcome, intelligence, severity of the issues, and early intervention is important for the emotional and behavioral issues to come.

Disorder of writing expression (developmental expressive writing disorder) is when writing communication is substantially below the criteria of age, IQ, life experiences, educational background, and physical impairments. The impact is issues with physical reproduction of letters and words, organization of thoughts and ideas in written composition. Dysgraphia is the inability to form letters and numbers (may involve hand-eye delay coordination and focus/concentration issues). Other deficits are the inability to write words from dictation (visual STM) deficits and corresponding cognitive processing issues, and ability to organize thoughts and ideas in written compositions.

The associations can include attention delay, visual motor integration, and visual processing and expressive language. The symptoms are poor handwriting, letter formation, spelling, punctuation, grammar, cohesive sentences, and general academic and ADL issues.

For the diagnosis, it is estimated that around 3–5 percent of school-age students have the disorder. The disorder is normally diagnosed at around age eight due to the wide variance in the language-acquisition phase amongst developing children. The testing can include the Diagnostic Evaluation of Writing Skills (DEWS) and the Test of Early Written Language (TEWL). The disorder involves intensive remediation to potentially overcome.

Childhood disintegrative disorder (CDD) is the loss of language, motor, and social skills by the age of ten. The disorder is aka *Heller's syndrome*. With CDD, a child follows normal development and then declines. This condition is related to the *pervasive developmental disorders* such as the ASD. The disorders are genetically based with around 1 percent of the population having a PDD, with autism being the most serious.

Other PDDs include Rett's, where a child develops normally between five months and four years old, predominantly in girls. With this condition, the growth of the head stalls as well as normal brain and motor functions. CDD has more boys than girls and normally develops between age two and ten with two years of normal development. With the Asperger's, PDD, normally the language is okay, and with this condition, there are also more males than females. CDD is a prognosis which normally requires intensive long-term care.

With CDD, behavior changes normally precede function loss, and an EEG can pick up and register abnormal brain wave patterns. With autism, the skills that are gained are normally retained. Some of the issues with CDD are the loss of *receptive language skills*, which are understanding language of others, and *expressive language skills*, which is speaking and communicating (only 20 percent can) with CDD. This leads to social interaction issues and motor control (bowel and bladder) issues. Therapy can include psychotherapy, family education, and medication.

Motor development is another critical care of human development. It is impacted by the brain and neuron development more so than by reinforcement. The neurons become myelinated and connect in order to innervate the connections for motor ability. For example, babies normally roll over at around five and a half months, stand around eight or nine months, and walk at around fifteen months. In addition, reflex actions are checked to ensure normal progression. These are the following:

Babkin reflex—pressure for eight seconds on both of the palms (head flexion, head rotation, open mouth, or combo), should last up to twenty-six weeks.

Babinski reflex—toe moves up (hallux flexion), other toes fan, common in two and under (when the sole of the foot is stroked). If exists after age two, it could be a sign of nerve damage in nerve pathways (corticospinal tract, brain, and spinal cord), which runs down both sides of the spine.

Galant reflex—at five to six months, the skin on the back is stroked (there should be movement toward the touched side). If occurs past six months, there could be some pathology.

Glabellar reflex—tapping on the forehead (glabella, between nose and eyebrows), first taps elicit blinks, but if the blinking persists, could be sign of *Myerson's*, which is an abnormal sign of *frontal release*. Also a sign of future neurological illness (Parkinson's, dementia, etc.).

Palmar grasp reflex—palmar at five to six months, palm stroke (grip) or touch opposite side of hand for (reverse hand flare). If not, could be issues with frontal lobe.

Hemiplegia—total paralysis of arm, leg, trunk on the same side of the body.

Hemiparesis—weakness of one side of the body.

Infant sucking/rooting reflex—primitive survival reflex CNS (i.e., baby seeking a nipple), palate stimulation. This reflex wears off over time by frontal lobe inhibition.

Moro reflex—at four to five months, response to sudden loss of support, spread/flying arms (abduction) out, then bring arms inward (adduction), crying (when put down), and *unlearned fear in infants.*

Plantar reflex—downward response of hallux flexion in the foot (response to blunt instrument to sole of the foot).

Rooting reflex—cheek touch, turn head toward the side touched.

Startle reaction—reflectory to protect the back of the neck from whole body startle, eye blink.

Tonic neck reflex—one to four months, head turned to side (that side arm straightens) and opposite side arm bends. If goes past these months or holds reflex, could be issues with upper motor neurons (motor area of the cerebral cortex that carries information to V layer of motor cortex beta cells). This is the precursor to hand-eye coordination and preparatory for voluntary reaching. The *precentral gyrus* (most posterior in frontal lobe, pyramidal cells of the gyrus are also called upper motor neurons), fibers of the upper motor neurons project out of the precentral gyrus, ending in the brain stem where they decussate or cross with the lower medulla oblongata, the lateral corticospinal tract on each side of the spinal column, and the upper motor neurons descend to the level of the spinal nerve root. Upper motor neurons act along with lower motor neurons to innervate a fiber of the skeletal muscle. Nerve signals continue to muscles via the lower motor neurons. The NT, *glutamate,* transmits nerve impulses from the upper to the lower motor neurons where detected by glutamatergic receptors. *Glutamic acid* is one of twenty to twenty-two proteinogenic amino acids. Its codons are GAA and CAG. The role in LT potential is long-lasting enhancement in *signal transduction* between neurons. *Synaptic plasticity* is the ability of chemical synapses to change their strength (memories are encoded by synaptic strength [chemical strength]).

In Piaget's stage 1 sensorimotor model, he states that the *primary circular reaction* occurs at age one to four months (coordination of actions). *Secondary circular reactions* occur at age four to eight months (actions to trigger response). *Coordination of reactions* occurs at age eight to twelve months (intentional actions)—imitation, recognition, and shaking rattle for noise. And *tertiary circular reactions* occur at twelve to eighteen months (trial and error) sounds and actions for attention. When motor development is not appearing to run its natural course, there may be underlying reasons for the motor issues.

Cerebral palsy (neurological) involves balance, posture, and is a motor disorder that normally appears within the first few years of life. Issues can be with walking, writing, medical, seizure, and mental impairment. Babies can be *slow* to roll over, sit, crawl, smile, or walk. This can stem from developmental issues or damage to the motor function area of the brain. The frontal lobe of cerebrum coordinates muscle movements. The sensory cortex of parietal lobe is involved with positioning of the body parts and movement. The brain stem contains the motor and sensory pathways and the reflex pathway. The cerebellum is involved in motor coordination for walking, balance, posture, and coordination. CP is a highly complex disorder and the treatment can involve surgery, therapy, and medications.

Developmental coordination disorder (motor voluntary muscles) involves issues with subunit muscle, visual perception (eye muscle development), writing letters, drawing pictures, writing symbols, tying shoelaces, buttoning, and weak muscle tone. Around 6 percent of children between the ages of five to eleven have this disorder, and more males than females. Speech disorders are often closely linked to DCD. For the diagnosis, the IQ must exceed seventy, and the condition cannot be linked to muscular dystrophy (MD) or mental retardation. For success within remediation, the people with the disorder must attempt to avoid distress and require individualized training.

MD involves muscle weakness and muscle loss with an onset during childhood or as an adult. MD is a *genetic disorder* where the proteins, which protect muscle fibers from damage, can be passed or can mutate in the egg or developing embryo. The types of MD are *Duchenne*, which involves issues getting up/standing up, running, jumping, and large calf muscles; *Becker*, which is milder, slower progression, and onset is teen to adult; *myotonic* is the inability to relax muscles at will, face muscles often first; *limb-girdle* is hip-shoulder first, feet, and lifting issues; *congential* is from birth and is severe impairment; facioscapulohumeral (FSHD) is when the shoulder blades stick out like wings with arms raised, and has teen to early-adult onset; *oculopharyngeal* involves the drooping of eyelids, eyes, and throat are impacted, and the onset is typically during forty to fifties.

Rett PDD involves an impact on head growth and brain size which are decreased by as much as 30 percent, can be developmental failure, genetic mutation, a key protein that regulates brain development is affected. The onset is after five to six months of normal development and then hand movement is lost. At around thirty months, there is repetitive hand-wringing (hand-washing movements), and around 50–80 percent develop epilepsy.

This is an *X chromosome defect*, the *Y chromosome* determines the male's sex, a male born with Rett will not normally survive. The Y chromosome cannot compensate for a damaged X chromosome. The mutation has been associated with the long arm of chromosome *C-Xq28* and the protein is *MECP2*. The human genome project mapped the human chromosomes (1999). The development occurs at a rate of 99 percent occurrence while fetus is in the womb. The MECP2 protein controls the expression of other genes via interaction with methylated DNA.

Stage 1 early onset is at six to eighteen months, infant eye contact is decreased, toy play declines, head growth is slowed. Stage 2 is rapid deterioration, one to four years, and hand movement and language decline. Stage 3 is between two to ten years old, motor issues and seizures, may have increase in interest and decrease in irritability, most stay in this stage. Stage 4 is late deterioration, scoliosis, muscle rigidity, and decreased mobility.

The population for Rett disorder is 1 in 15,000 births.

The DSM states that normal development must occur before five to eighteen months, normal birth head size, followed by decline in growth, severe impairment of hand movement and language, hand movements will be clapping, wringing (wash), shaking of the chest or torso, unsteady, and stiff-legged with a wide gait.

Stereotypic movement disorder (SMD) involves head banging, nail biting, body rocking, playing with hair, thumb-sucking, hand flapping, nose picking, picking at self, self or object biting, self hitting, scratching, eye gouging, bruxism (teeth grinding), breath holding, sound-production issues, and more. The episodes cause harm or impair ADLs. The disorder is most prevalent in adolescent; increases with boredom, tension, and frustration. The intensity can range from slow to frenetic (wild/uncontrolled). The *differential diagnosis* applies and the disorder cannot be due to another disorder. Around 20 percent of infants and toddlers will have some type of stereotypic movement at one time or other, and it normally ends by age three or four. Examples can include body rocking or thumb-sucking. The onset is normally at five to eleven months. Around 60 percent of infants grind their teeth. These are called *passing phases* and are not SMD if they go away.

If the behaviors persist beyond the passing phase, children will often use mechanisms to try and control the actions such as putting their hands in their pockets and sometimes *physical restraint* is actually welcomed because it relieves their anxiety. Within the SMD population, around 25 percent are intellectually challenged (mentally retarded), and around 60 percent of those are of the profound level. There are high levels in the PDD spectrum. Boys are head bangers at a 3:1 ratio. The population is around 5 percent of all children.

Even children with normal intelligence and adequate caregiving can develop SMD. The DSM classifies the disorders as repeated, purposeful motor behavior with harm or ADL impact, not another disorder, not due to medicine or illness, and at least four weeks in duration. *Transient pediatric head banging* is not SMD (unless beyond the age four), nor self-stimulatory behavior. There is no specific treatment for SMD. The disorder normally peaks in adolescence, declines, and then disappears. The disorder cannot be prevented.

Attachment issues and disorders are typically related to early-life issues that derive from the age of three years old and under. Most neural pathways are closed off after age fourteen, but the EF can take anywhere from as early as age four to the mid-twenties to fully develop. A *radical attachment disorder* would be that of a *sociopath* where their only regret is getting caught (regret), which is an intellectual response. There is no remorse, lack of genuine interpersonal reciprocity, avoidance and inhibition, lack of empathy (cold), and emotional charge is undetected or unaddressed. This can manifest very early in the development stages. This is why the *nurturing* element is also a critical element in addition to the nature element. If people apply a permissive-submissive type of parenting approach with this type of child instead of monitoring and observing them, this can potentially release their negative core desires onto the people within their social rings and onto the collective of society.

Mary Ainsworth (a behavior expert) demonstrated the applications of the *psychology of behavior and attachment within development.* Mary Ainsworth posed that based on her studies that there are different types of attachment as follows:

Secure attachment (66 percent of participants) in *strange situation test.* There is trust and minimal distress, child confidently explores a novel environment, but distress occurs when the parent leaves and the child goes to parent when the parent returns.

Anxious-avoidant insecure attachment (21 percent) in strange situation test avoids caregiver, but explores environment; does not go to parents when they return, and this means that caregiver is likely disengaged and/or emotionally detached from the child.

Anxious-resistant insecure attachment (12 percent). The anxiety of exploration is derived from the mother or caregiver only tending to child on their terms. There is extreme stress when the parent leaves and the child resist comfort when the parent returns.

Stranger anxiety is a highly common element in children and typically should begin at around eight months, but can develop between six to twelve months, can reoccur later as well, but normally ends by the twenty-fourth month.

Reactive attachment disorder at two months infants normally follow their primary caregiver(s) with their eyes and show a smile response, and, at around five months, a baby normally reaches out toward their caregiver(s), normal infant bonding occurs by the eighth month of life with one or two primary caregivers. If this bond is not formed, there can potentially be severe physical and emotional consequences. The social problems can manifest and extend into childhood, adolescence, and adult life. The developmental issues can be both physical and mental.

Early-life bonding experiences lead to healthy attachments and healthy attachment capabilities. There are critical periods during which bonding experiences must be present for the brain systems responsible for attachment to development normally. These critical periods appear to be primarily in and around the first year of life, and they are related to the capacity of the infant and parents or caregiver to develop a positive interactive relationship. Positive social interaction is a requirement of health.

The factors that can impact attachment can include prenatal exposure to drugs or alcohol, separation from the primary caregiver, parent loss, neglect, trauma, abuse, chronic maternal depression, neurological issues, and also illness or pain, which is not remediated.

The early signs can include resisting contact, being unable to comfortably tolerate closeness with caregivers, seeming sleepy or slow; younger children can be withdrawn, passive, and have odd reactions. Some will have indiscriminate affection and may touch or cling to strangers, which may seem strange and can also be problematic due to the potential for stranger danger. When the cognitive systems are developing normally, the typical human instinct is to have *stranger anxiety*. The young children may also lack empathy for others. Other early issues can include learning delay, impulsive behavior and a lack of control, speech pattern issues, annoying and incessant chatter, a lack of eye contact, and dishonesty. Without intervention, there can be additional issues later such as poor conscience development, low self-esteem, inappropriate demands which may include throwing fits, poor peer relationships, destructive or cruel behavior, and physical aggression.

A state of anxiety is often what propels children with attachment issues to create chaos because chaos is typically what feels normal to children with attachment issues. The children become accustomed to the rush they feel within chaos. The rush they crave comes from dopamine, which is a neurotransmitter in the brain, which creates reward and euphoria.

Children will often display soothing behaviors such rocking, head banging, and biting, scratching, or cutting themselves. If a child is treated in a certain way, they will often model the behavior. Displays of aggression, impulse control, and a lack of empathy at younger ages can point to a child's inability to understand the impact of their behaviors and the emotions that correspond to their actions. If confronted with their behavior, a child may elicit a response. Regret is an intellectual response, while remorse is an emotional response. Most often, regret lies within having to talk about the situation and/or being caught doing something.

The DSM states that population for the disorder is around 1 percent and is higher by percentage in orphans. The DSM typifies attachment disorder as inappropriate social interactions before age five, inhibited or disinhibited interaction, cannot be a pervasive development disorder, unstable environment, and changing caregivers. Treatment and intervention are critical as a lack of intervention can lead to long-term prevalence. CBT can be used for older children and *play therapy* for younger children.

Within the interventions, the use of positive reinforcement is the key. While identifying the negative behavior and aligning on changing, the negative behavior is also critical. The use of positive reinforcement is the primary focus. Children with attachment disorder have a fear of intimacy, and their behaviors are their way of keeping emotional distance from others. A child needs to talk through their issues and feelings. CBT and/or play therapy are excellent tools and can be applied based on a child's age.

CBT helps a child understand the reasons for their behavior and the consequences of continuing the behavior versus choosing prosocial behaviors. Consequences must be chosen carefully as certain consequences can actually raise a child's anxiety level and fear causing further acting out. If a child fears that they will not be successful in avoiding their behavior issues, they may continue to act out. The techniques and the consequences should match a child's emotional age versus their actual age. Depending on the nature of the child's behavior, they may have to be supervised more frequently and/or constantly.

Some children may also regress and act out like a child of a much-younger age. Being the child is in a regressed emotional and mental state, the caregiver or mentor must not attempt to use logic and reasoning and/or try to argue complex points since the child will not comprehend the actions while in the regressed state. Any child can regress at a given point, but often a sign of abuse is the continual regression of a child and especially to a very young age. EF is a center of reasoning in the brain, which derives in part from the frontal cortex of the brain. In very young children and when children have regressed emotionally or are engaged in a chaotic state, EF and reasoning close off. This must be understood. The prefrontal cortex is flooded and the EF is blocked and/or is disengaged. In addition, as mentioned before, there is a wide continuum on when some people's EF has its genesis, and this can be delayed in many people into their late twenties. A child must be calmed down before they can possibly begin to try and understand a more complex and rational discussion.

Parents, caregivers, and/or mentors must be consistent, predictable, and repetitive. This is why the permissive-submissive parenting style does not work with children that have deficits within the area of behavior. These children need guidance, direction, and supervision. The goal is to teach a child or children how to control their anxiety, to not become hyperaroused and be prosocial within their social environment. When parents with the permissive-submissive style ignore behavioral issues, they are eroding the potential for character development, and they really believe that they are accomplishing something by pacifying the children when they see the guise of control that is elicited within the corresponding freezing of the behavior. But these maladaptive behaviors still exist at the core level, and they will normally manifest later outside of the reception of pacification. In addition children with behavioral issues and/or whom have displayed emotional regression continually, most often like to be informed of changes in their routine. Many of these children like to have some sense of control within their course. Preparing a child who has these issues ahead of time can help to avoid overwhelming the child and creating more anxiety.

Within CBT, children can be exposed to positive skills development (PSD). PSD can help children mentally review various behavior scenarios, reflect upon their own thoughts, consider the thoughts of others, and contemplate prosocial behavior alternatives, which will result in better outcomes. The children can be introduced to the understanding of benefits and costs. If a child can become adept at considering the costs and benefits associated with their behaviors, this can help them to choose outcomes, which will benefit them on multiple positive levels. Journaling is also another very powerful tool to help a child keep track of events and the emotions surrounding the events, which led to a particular feeling or behavior action.

Basic relaxation techniques such as deep breathing and focusing on the mechanics of breathing can also help a child begin to develop a foundation for reducing anxiety. Relaxing tense muscles is yet another method to help reduce the elements of arousal. Teaching a child to use positive self-talk will also help deter the negative thoughts that accompany anxiety and arousal. Also with self-talk, a child can be taught to understand how to reverse negative thoughts that are arising through *thought stopping*. When the negative thoughts are coming about, the child can use some sort of safe physical technique to snap out of the negative thought pattern and crossover to positive self-talk. Other things that can be taught can include having a child focus on a given object for a period of time to help filter out anxiety. There have been many studies posed and conducted over the course of time to try and determine the normal course of development.

In the highly critical area of *psychological development*, Sigmund Freud posed and relayed that the crucial stage in human development is the first five years. Freud posed that the first five years are crucial to the development of what will become the adult personality, the indentity must be controlled to satisfy social demands and the ego and superego balance the demands of the indentity for gratification into acceptable social channels. The individual must have their needs met within each developmental stage in order to move onto the next stage, but there can also be an issue where an individual is too well satisfied and becomes reluctant to leave the psychological benefit of a particular stage where there is overindulgence. The twin evil of pampering can lead to (overindulgence and fixation). Fixation is a person not moving past a psychosocial stage. Permissive-submissive parents contribute to this issue via their pampering. *Psychosexual libido* is the primary force the identity develops and without this, fixation can also occur. Aggression and libido are the two drivers of human motivation according to Freud.

Erick Erickson designed an eight-stage psychological development model and relayed that there is a positive outcome if all stages are resolved. Erickson stated that psychosocial ego identity is obtained via social interaction (socialization). Erickson posed that social competence leads to the appropriate social behavior and actions and that there is also the potential for conflict at each stage, and that ego quality and strength is essential to navigate through the life course. The human ego is fragile and in order for people to protect and maintain their ego, they will maneuver in a fashion within the process of socialization that attempts to avoid ego destruction.

Jean Piaget posed that even children play an active role in worldly social knowledge. Unfortunately even in modern society, people will still discount the relevance of children. Children incorporate their life experiences into their *schemata* via *assimilation,* and fitting new info into their schemata is called *accommodation. Mental operations* involve the progress of a child and their actions. The schema is a person's interpretation and integration process and that both knowing and understanding their experiences can modify their schema. Assimilation is encoding new information into the existing schema; however, most people subjectively incorporate new information into their existing mental set and schema. Many people become very narrow in their social views and develop a very rigid restrictive range along the social continuum within their social anchors. Accommodation is the process of altering one's existing schema with new information. Equilibrium is the balance of accommodation and assimilation within a person's schema, which dictates a person's well-round-edness, character, and personal growth potential.

> *Look at a situation from all angles and you will become more open.*

> —Dalia Lama

The models of these three psychological pioneers point to highly concrete and valid levels of progression within human development. The perpetual and cyclical problem within society is that few people either recognize or accept that Freud is 100 percent correct within his theory that the first five years of development are highly important and the most critical. There is so much biochemical and organic fusion that is occurring in this dynamic development stage that internal or external variances can cause dysfunction and/or lifelong issues for people.

It is common that people cannot conceive or they ignore how such a very young child can be equipped with such a powerful mind that is highly adaptive in nature. The personality and the temperament, which are the core elements of all human behavior, are genetic in delivery and they allow only a slight margin of error within the internal biological processes and the external nurturing process that will complete their development normally between the ages of around five to seven years old. It is also common that people mistake the control of the inner needs and desires by some people for their possession of a good and/or stable personality and temperament. There are children who are equipped to manipulate others at a highly accelerated point in their development. There are a myriad of other covariant cognitive elements that impact the expression and/or subsequent control of the personality and temperament.

This is why people can fool others quite easily within the process of socialization because there are those that are not in tune with how wide the behavioral continuum can be. As everyone possesses different core elements and cognitive abilities, trying to understand all of these variances is a science. And that science is called psychology. Psychology should be considered one of the most important of all of the sciences, but unfortunately, there are still many people in society who do not choose to validate its social eminence. Some people are so crass as to say such things about the social sciences and their depth as those are only theories. These people in society perpetuate the existing and cyclical social flaws, which inhibit human social evolution and the evolution of humanity. Each psychological pioneer (mentioned above in this chapter) outlined a series of *life stage models*, which have been combined (below) into age ranges for the purpose of a more consolidated look at the more specific stages of life.

The first combined group includes the following:

- Erickson stage 1 (birth/three to eighteen months) *trust versus mistrust*: leads to *hope and virtue*, and *safe and secure* versus *inconsistent and unpredictable*. (Erick Erickson stage 1/8)

- Piaget stage 1 (birth to two years old) *sensorimotor stage*: in this stage, there is coordination of senses for exploration; *developing object permanence*, which is mental representation of an object even when not seen by age one, and the reflexes of sucking and looking manifest during the sensorimotor stage. Primary circular reaction occurs at age one to four months (coordination of actions). Secondary circular reaction occurs at age four to eight months (actions to trigger response). Coordination of reaction occurs at age eight to twelve months (intentional actions)—imitation, recognition, and shaking rattle for noise. Tertiary circular reaction occurs at twelve to eighteen months (trial and error) sounds and actions for attention. Early representational thought occurs at eighteen to twenty-four months mental operations versus only action. (Jean Piaget stage 1/4)

- Freud stage 1 (birth to first year): if *fixated* at this stage, can cause dependency and aggression, oral personalities put things in their mouths when stress arises—children and beyond that continue to suck their thumbs. (Sigmund Freud stage 1/5)

In this first combined grouping, there are the initial elements of attachment, trust, safety, aggression, and the corresponding reactions that occur. Even at the very early stages of life and development, the level of care and attachment are being evaluated and the perceptive reactions to these factors are being adjusted to. The initial stages are highly critical within human development. It is amazing that the mind is so active and potentially vulnerable during these early-life stages. Unfortunately it is common that people do not understand the psychological component of child development that occurs alongside with the biological development. Early nurturing (environmental) mistakes can potentially become major issues if people do not adjust to the requirements of early-stage nurturing. Each development level is a progression of its antecedent level.

The combined stage 2 levels are the following:

- Erickson stage 2 (eighteen months to three years) *autonomy versus shame*: toddlers assert their will and confidence in ability, toilet training, sense of independence and more control versus self-doubt and inadequacy. Toddlers will use the word "no" a lot to exert their control, and is good to develop a healthy will; a healthy will and some control will help on a psychological level, biological level, and also with reactions/responses throughout life. (Erickson stage 2/8)
- Erickson stage 3 (three to five years) *initiative versus guilt* (leads to purpose): direct play and social assertion (play and imagination are essential). The word "why" is used a lot. Exploration will equal comfort. If discouraged, this

will create guilt and possibly inhibit future exploration. (Erickson stage 3/8)

- Piaget stage 2 (two to seven years old) preoperational stage: stage 2 Piaget, language is the most important cognitive development at this stage. Symbols are used for real-world objects, the ability to visualize objects and events mentally (i.e., playing house), typically occurs around age four to seven. Egocentrism can be in affect, although many do not have perspective yet. The *three mountain task* is a scene, children select picture of the scene they observed, and when children are asked to select what others had observed, they always select theirs. This task has a basis centered within the ego. *Law of conservation* for children under age five, very few are able understand that volume is conserved regardless of units. There are also still limitations in abstract thought and object relations. (Piaget stage 2/4)

- Freud stage 2 (one to three) *anal stage*: bladder and bowel competency, productive, or if fixated, can be *anal-expulsive*—wasteful, disorganized, impulsive, cruel, rebellious, and destructive or *anal-retentive*—rigid and obsessive can become an annoyance to others. Treatment during this stage is critical in development. This is one of the first stages of restrictions and performance. (Freud stage 2/5)

- Freud stage 3 (three to six) *phallic stage*: *phallic fixation*, fear of social inadequacy, Oedipus, Electra, or penis envy. Identification occurs within this period with same sex, whereby things like values, attitudes, and behaviors are internalized and adopted. (Freud 3/5)

In the *combined stage 2* level, there is the development of ego assertion, imagination within play, advanced exploration, and also the counteracting mechanism of restriction. A healthy balance can lead to a healthy will, and also the cognitive abilities are surfacing rapidly. It is common that many people suffer within their nurturing balance within this stage. Avoiding the twin evils of pampering and neglect are the key. The permissive-submissive parenting type has the potential to adversely impact children at this stage. On the neglect side these parents are not taking care of their children's behavior issues, they are instead pampering them. Many people do not realize that there are highly complex core and cognitive components, which are being impacted during this early stage, which can potentially manifest later at any time during a person's life. The individual impacts of each family unit can have the potential to affect the immediate social rings involved and also the collective society.

The combined stage 3 levels are the following:

- Erickson stage 4 (six to eleven years) *industry versus inferiority*: a formal education and its measurement of success by comparison (leads to competence), pride in accomplishments, more complex tasks, and vital to confidence. *Inferiority complex* can potentially lead to severe anxiety in later stages. (Erickson stage 4/8)
- Piaget stage 3 (seven to eleven years) *concrete operational*: mental operations, complex relationships, logical operational thought for objects, and concrete logic with abstract still being developed. *Inductive logic* from specific experience to a general principle (if there are minerals on Mars, then there will be minerals on Venus). *Deductive logic* is using a general principle to determine the outcome of a specific event (all dogs are mammals, all mammas have lungs; therefore, all dogs have lungs). *Reversibility* actions and associations can be reversed (order of relations). *Seriation* is the ability to sort objects and situations according to characteristics, for separation and differentiation, by area. Volume conservation, number conservation (a number stays the same if rearranged); if

this is not understood, skill not ready yet. (Piaget stage 3/4)

- Freud stage 4 (six to puberty/age twelve) *latent stage*: the *erogenous zone* sex feelings are inactive, development of ego and superego, is normally a calm *exploration phase* with peer interaction where social and communication skills are developed and self-confidence is built. Energy is placed into acquiring skills and knowledge, and most often the same sexes play with each other during this phase. (Freud stage 4/5)

In the combined stage 3 levels, the level of abstract thought is increasing, and there is an important identification which is critical between self-confidence and/or an *identity crisis*. People must continually use positive reinforcement with their children and be the support network that is required. Early-life assessments by children can potentially turn into lifelong issues. If the children are feeling inadequate as compared to other people, they can begin to become stressed, can act out, and become antisocial. Getting to the root problem is the key at this stage before the children become adolescents. Interventions of any kind during the stages of development are best served when they are done early. Many parenting opportunities, social modification opportunities, and character development opportunities are potentially lost to adolescence.

The combined stage 4 elements are the following:

- Erickson stage 5 (twelve to eighteen years) *identity versus role confusion*: adolescence (leads to fidelity), personal identity (finding self from within), determining role in society and social groups, or identity crisis later in life. (Erickson stage 5/8)
- Piaget stage 4 (twelve to adult) *formal operational stage* (adult reasoning): not all people reach the formal operational stage, having the logical ability to think

about and visualize abstract perspectives and concepts, *inferential reasoning* (about things and people that are not at hand and not having experience with), and then drawing conclusions, and deeper meanings of the outcomes of actions, which are important for long-term planning. *Metacognition* is thinking about the way one thinks and how others perceive them and then change the course, and also the use of the *trace thought process* to evaluate the effectiveness of how we solved a problem. *Complex situations* aptitude initiates around age thirteen to seventeen. The ability for the conduction of problem solving in a logical and methodical way that is capable of being organized and rapid normally manifest. Children can potentially have capabilities ahead of the age ranges listed in the models (logic, manipulation, and more). (Piaget stage 4/4)

• Freud stage 5 (puberty to death) *genital stage*: Freud's final stage in *psychosexual development* where a teenager overcomes latency, this is the *post-phallic stage*. The psycho gain is in the actual contact of the organs. This is a *balancing stage*. (Freud stage 5/5)

In the combined stage 4 levels, the elements of identity, social role, complex cognition, and sexuality are all being transformed and consolidated. Not all people reach the same levels of growth, development, and/or ability within or after this stage. In addition, some people can fail to reach the plateaus within all of these components, within select components, and some fail to develop these areas even through their adulthood. People have different genetics, core elements (personality and temperament), abilities, and social environmental factors, and this is the development level where the separation can really be seen between different individuals and groups. This is a stage where youth can begin to become more agitated and highly antisocial if they realize and perceive that there is separation occurring between them and other people. This is the final stage of childhood influence and the last opportunity for people to influence the youth prior to their adulthood.

The combined stage 5 level includes only Erickson stages 6–8, and they are the following:

- Erickson stage 6 (nineteen to thirty-five to forty years) *intimacy versus isolation* relations (fidelity or identity crisis): one must be satisfied with themselves to be fully prepared for intimacy and sharing of self with others. Balance in life is being created and future direction.
- Erickson stage 7 (thirty-five to forty to sixty-five years) *generativity versus stagnation*: evaluate and critique the life path and seize an opportunity to get back on track, may try to change identity to get to vision, evaluation of contribution or self-absorption, contributions in both family and society.
- Erickson stage 8 (sixty-five plus) *integrity versus despair*: satisfied with self and able to step away from stress and pressure, self-actualization through wisdom and coaching/sharing, a well-rounded person who is in touch with themselves is required to have peak experiences, being in touch means understanding oneself and the aspects of all other people.
- This stage involves the process of people taking everything that was learned in the initial stages of their lives and then incorporating what is learned within their adult socialization into the process of their adult decision-making.
- People have recurrent opportunities during their lives to self-correct and begin heading toward a healthy and successful life path, but if people take things for granted, procrastinate, and wait too long, they will learn the hard way that they cannot get back the opportunities and

the time that has been lost in their lives. People need to continue to grow in their lives, and then they need to help others grow in order to receive all of life's benefits.

These models of psychological development (above) are very concrete in outlining what is expected during the different developmental stages. Abraham Maslow designed a pyramidal model of the internal needs of people that they are experiencing during their developmental course (mentioned earlier), some of which are direct parallels.

The elements within the pyramid can be intermixed, but in order to be whole, a person must have built upon their basic needs and have added the other life qualities.

Maslow outlined the primary needs, which involve health, a support network, a healthy psyche, and then the higher life values, which can lead to *peak experiences* once self-actualization is reached. People also have desires, but desires are not primary needs. Desires however can create interference within people's life paths and they can interfere with the morals that are required to reach self-actualization. Kohlberg designed a life scenario judgment mode (mentioned earlier).

Just as in the developmental models and the hierarchy of needs model, if people do not develop on an individual level, also refuse to consider other people and other causes, they will normally have a limited positive impact on society where they conversely could have been a contributor to the collective good. And even if people are successful by other methods, the cognition that is realized upon that type of success versus the success outlined in the models will be of a completely different nature, and their thirst will never be fully quenched. This is why some people are never satisfied in life. Money and power cannot quench the soul. They can only fill a void in a short-term capacity while self-actualization eases the mind and soul creating inner peace in the long-term.

Regardless of the truths that have been presented over time, each person will ultimately develop their own form and system of motivation. The *drive-reduction theory* by Clark Hull states that inner tension and drive are to fulfill biological needs for homeostasis, which are primary needs and that the secondary needs are learned. If the secondary needs are desires, these can compete with the primary drives and then a person's system can become conflicted. Conflict is a part of life and most people can overcome conflict. But when there is conflict in children's lives, this makes their life course and their development much more challenging.

The *opponent-process theory* states that there is a baseline normal state in people and that when actions occur away from their baseline, people eventually will feel an opponent process to return to their baseline. Most people can resolve their inner conflict on their own. But it is common that people with behavioral issues require an outside intervention in order to return to their baseline state, especially children. A psychological response involves biofeedback and emotions that can dictate social outcomes. How people perceive and interpret social stimuli results in their emotions, which lead to their actions. People can learn how to minimize their stress and evaluate their mood which is the key in order to handle conflict. When people are not able to manage their stress this can be highly problematic. Stress causes a strain on people's adaptive capacity and threatens their well-being. Things like personality, mental construct, perceptions, physical health, strength, and more can all impact the stress response. Stressors can be internal or external, acute or chronic.

When a child or children are in turmoil during the developmental stages, the process of stress management becomes much more difficult, and this can lead to behaviors and behavior patterns, which can make it very challenging for their parents or caregivers to return them to their baseline level behavior and/or a range near it. When this type of activity occurs, family dynamics and social outcomes can be heavily impacted.